W9-BGL-515

WITHDRAWN

Social History of Africa

MAKING ETHNIC WAYS

Recent Titles in
Social History of Africa Series
Series Editors: Allen Isaacman and Jean Allman

Cotton, Colonialism, and Social History in Sub-Saharan Africa
Allen Isaacman and Richard Roberts, editors

In Pursuit of History: Fieldwork in Africa
Carolyn Keyes Adenaike and Jan Vansina, editors

Cotton Is the Mother of Poverty: Peasants, Work, and
Rural Struggle in Colonial Mozambique, 1938–1961
Allen Isaacman

Drink, Power, and Cultural Change: A Social History of
Alcohol in Ghana, c.1800 to Recent Times
Emmanuel Akyeampong

Gender, Ethnicity, and Social Change on the
Upper Slave Coast: A History of the Anlo-Ewe
Sandra E. Greene

Marriage in Maradi: Gender and Culture in a
Hausa Society in Niger, 1900–1989
Barbara M. Cooper

TANU Women: Gender and Culture in the
Making of Tanganyikan Nationalism, 1955–1965
Susan Geiger

Liberating the Family? Gender and British Slave Emancipation in
the Rural Western Cape, South Africa, 1823–1853
Pamela Scully

People Are Not the Same: Leprosy and Identity in Twentieth-Century Mali
Eric Silla

A Lion Amongst the Cattle: Reconstruction and
Resistance in the Northern Transvaal
Peter Delius

White Farms, Black Labour: Agrarian Transition in
Southern Africa, 1910–1950
Alan Jeeves and Jonathan Crush, editors

A Green Place, A Good Place: Agrarian Change, Gender, and
Social Identity in the Great Lakes Region to the 15th Century
David Lee Schoenbrun

MAKING ETHNIC WAYS

COMMUNITIES AND THEIR TRANSFORMATIONS IN TAITA, KENYA, 1800–1950

Bill Bravman

HEINEMANN
Portsmouth, NH

EAEP
Nairobi

JAMES CURREY
Oxford

Heinemann
A division of Reed Elsevier Inc.
361 Hanover Street
Portsmouth, NH 03801-3912
Offices and agents throughout the world

EAEP
PO Box 45314
Nairobi, Kenya

James Currey Ltd.
73 Botley Road
Oxford OX2 0BS
United Kingdom

ISBN 0-325-00105-7 (Heinemann cloth)
ISBN 0-325-00104-9 (Heinemann paper)
ISBN 0-85255-683-7 (James Currey cloth)
ISBN 0-85255-633-0 (James Currey paper)

British Library Cataloguing in Publication Data
Bravman, Bill
    Making ethnic ways : communities and their transformations in Taita, Kenya, 1800–1950.—(Social history of Africa)
    1. Taita (African people)—Kenya—Taita Hills—History 2. Taita Hills (Kenya)—Social life and customs 3. Taita Hills (Kenya)—Social conditions 4. Taita Hills (Kenya)—Politics and government
    I. Title
    967.6'2'00496395
    ISBN 0-85255-633-0 (Paper)
    ISBN 0-85255-683-7 (Cloth)

Library of Congress Cataloging-in-Publication Data
Bravman, Bill.
    Making ethnic ways : communities and their transformations in Taita, Kenya, 1800–1950 / Bill Bravman.
        p.   cm. — (Social history of Africa, ISSN 1099–8098)
    Includes bibliographical references and index.
    ISBN 0–325–00105–7 (alk. paper). — ISBN 0–325–00104–9 (pbk. : alk. paper)
    1. Taita (African people)—Ethnic identity. 2. Taita (African people)—History. 3. Taita (African people)—Religion. 4. Ethnicity—Kenya—Taita Hills. 5. Christianity and culture—Kenya—Taita Hills. 6. Community life—Kenya—Taita Hills. 7. Taita Hills (Kenya)—Social conditions. 8. Taita Hills (Kenya)—Ethnic relations. I. Title. II. Series.
    DT433.545.T3B73   1998
    305.8'0096762—dc21   98–12377

Cover photo: Mrisa, *Wutasi* follower, early 1930s. Margaret Murray Photo Collection, courtesy of Kenya National Archives and Documentation Service. #142/81.

Printed in the United States of America on acid-free paper.
01 00 99 98 BB 1 2 3 4 5 6 7 8 9

CONTENTS

Illustrations vii

Abbreviations ix

About Citations and an Orthographic Note xi

Acknowledgments xiii

Introduction 1

1   Settlements and Societies in the Taita Hills,
    to the Late Nineteenth Century 21

2   Community Under Stress: Sagalla, Environmental Crisis,
    and Missionary Imagination, 1883–1888 61

3   Early Colonialism and Taita's Local Communities, 1892–1910 80

4   Erosions of Lineage and Neighborhood in the Early Colonial Era 107

5   Becoming Taita: The Coalescence and Mobilization of
    an Ethnic Identity, 1900–1930 139

6   Being Taita, I: Progressivism, Education, and Changing
    Terms of *Kidaßida*, 1930–1950 183

7   Being Taita, II: The Cultural Politics of
    Socioeconomic Change, 1930–1950 206

8   Formal Power, Political Mobilization, and
    Struggles over Taita Identity, 1930–1952 229

Conclusion 252

Appendix A: Bura Church Baptism Rates Prior to World War I 257

Appendix B: Baptismal Records, Bura Mission, 1893–1917 257

Bibliography 259

Index 279

ILLUSTRATIONS

Maps and Diagram

Map 1. The Taita Hills 22

Map 2. Taita's wider regional setting 24

Diagram 1. Model of a low-zone based
nineteenth-century Taita neighborhood 33

Map 3. Chawia location and Taita Concessions, Ltd. 240

Photographs

1. Yale Peak, from elsewhere on Dabida, early 1930s 26

2. Sagalla's iron-sheet church, built in 1900 98

3. Market scene, 1920s Dabida 156

4. Jonathan Kituri, Werugha, early 1920s 168

5. Female students, late 1920s 170

6. A Christian progressive couple, early 1930s 186

7. An out-school at Mwakinyungu, Taita, in the early 1930s 194

8. Mbale School students, late 1920s 196

9. Mbale School show, 1928 197

10. Taita's Chiefs at a public meeting, 1933 232

ABBREVIATIONS

AAO	Assistant Agricultural Officer
AO	Agricultural Officer
CMS	Church Missionary Society
CMSA	Church Missionary Society Archives
CO	Colonial Office
DC	District Commissioner
DO	District Officer
FOCP	Foreign Office (Great Britain) Correspondence
IBEACo	Imperial British East Africa Company
HMSO	Her Majesty's Stationary Office
KASU	Kenya African Studies Union
KAU	Kenya Africa Union
KCA	Kikuyu Central Association
KLB	Kenya Literature Bureau
KLC	Kenya Land Commission
KNA	Kenya National Archives; Nairobi, Kenya
KUR	Kenya–Uganda Railroad
LNC	Local Native Council
NAD	Native Affairs Department
N/D	No date recorded on a cited source
PC	Provincial Commissioner
PRO	Public Records Office; London, England
PWD	Public Works Department
RH	Rhodes House Library; Oxford, England
SPCK	Society for the Promotion of Christian Knowledge
TCL	Taita Concessions, Limited
THA	Taita Hills Association
TTU	Taita Taveta Union

ABOUT CITATIONS AND AN ORTHOGRAPHIC NOTE

All dates given in citations are formatted as day/month/year.

Citations based on interview testimonies give a speaker's initials rather than full names. This protects the anonymity of individuals who agreed to discuss often delicate matters about the past with me. The citations do list locations and dates of interviews, and the bibliography gives the names of all those who were interviewed, without locations or dates. In rare cases when an interviewee's name is cited, the name appeared in another source. Citations of interviews with English officials and missionaries give their names, permission for this having been granted.

In this study, the symbol "ß" sometimes appears in words from the local languages of Taita and Sagalla. I do not know the technical terms to describe the sound that the symbol represents, but the experience of my ears tells me that it falls between "b" and "w"—softer–edged than the former, more b–like than the latter. My acquaintance with the symbol comes from Grace Harris, *Casting Out Anger: Religion among the Taita of Kenya.*

ACKNOWLEDGMENTS

In one way or another, many people and institutions helped shepherd this project through a dozen years of conception, research, writing, and revision. Official (but sincere!) thanks go to: Kenya's Office of the President, Kenyatta University, and the Taita district administration; the staffs of the Kenya National Archives, the British Institute in East Africa, the DANIDA library in Wundanyi (Taita), Bura (Taita) Catholic Church, the Public Records Office, Rhodes House Library, the CMS Archives, the Cambridge University Library, the Chevilly-la-Rue *Maison-Mère* of the Holy Ghost Fathers, the Stanford University library, and the Hoover Institute library, for help in the research; the U.S. Department of Education for a Fulbright grant; and the Graduate Research Board of the University of Maryland, for an award that funded follow-up research. A paper prepared under the auspices of a Zora Neale Hurston Fellowship from Northwestern University's Institute for the Advanced Study of the African Humanities helped nudge my revisions down the road, and its seminar's feedback on the paper pushed me along further. Collegial comments on papers given to the Maryland History Department Faculty Seminar and to its non-Western historians' Not-a-Party gatherings also helped considerably. Two of the book's maps and diagrams were prepared by Dana Kuan; the other two were made by the Cartography lab at University of Maryland, Baltimore County. The Kenya National Archives kindly permitted the reproduction of photographs from its collections.

Several people in Kenya contributed directly and centrally to the success of my research. I offer heartfelt thanks for their labors to Nathan Mnjama and his family, H. S. K. Mwaniki, Jacob and Sophie Mwakughu, Archie Mwambada and his family, Mrs. Ginorah Mganga and her son Jason, Juma Mwakitange and his family, Dishon Mghalu, Ben Mwakughu, Ms. Sumayya Mwashigadi, and the Mwandaba brothers.

Others who in some combination advised, helped, befriended, and supported me in Kenya include Zippy Sindiyo, Cory Kratz, Ivan Karp, Justin Willis, Paul Smoke, Muthoni Likimani, Judy Butterman, Paresh Jai and his family, Kostas and Sally Christ, Tom Wolf, Tabitha Kanogo, Dennis Doughty, Danyelle O'Hara, Salim and Cindy, Atwas, Kristin Shafer, Silas Mwashigadi, the Mshimbas, Kenya Archer, Cecilia and Ndoro, Paul, Mweu, Wellington, Daniel, Margaret, and Ophiro. Two gentlemen named Mwamburi made much else possible; one in spare moments from the DC's motorpool kept my decades-old truck running against long odds. The other was my landlord, gardening advisor, and occasional evening guest. Aftab 'Regge' Khan graciously (and often festively) housed me for most of my second round of research; the Sagalla Catholic Church just as warmly hosted the rest. I must express my appreciation in more blanket terms to dozens of others whose generosity and open hearts made working in Taita a privilege and a pleasure.

In England, I owe particular thanks to Martin Orrell, John Lonsdale, David Anderson, Cambridge University's East Africa seminar, SOAS's African history seminar, and the SOAS photography section. In the USA, the list includes Michael Salman, Muriel McClendon, Don Moore, Deb Amory, Lioba Moshi, Ann Biersteker, Jim Lance, Wunyabari Maloba, Karen Fung, Leo Caccia, the Stanford/Berkeley Joint Center for African Studies, Jackie Stewart, the Bisom-Rapps, Tamara and Ken Giles-Vernick, Francois Nsengiyumva, Luise White, Jean Hay, Robyn Muncy, Daryle Williams, James Rostron, Rob Wright, James Brooks, and Rebecca Allahyari. For more than can ever be expressed, I am perpetually and happily indebted to my sisters and parents. Sadly, four beloved contributors to my work and my life became ancestors before I could lay the book in their hands; many memories of Marie Perinbam, Archie Mwambada, Minnie Morrell and Sarah Bravman loom over these pages.

A number of scholars have offered encouragement and feedback for this project. Kennell Jackson and Richard Roberts supervised the dissertation; Alfred and Grace Harris helped me frame my initial research; Cory Kratz, Ivan Karp, Don Moore and Tom Spear commented on the Ph.D. thesis. Charles Ambler, Marie Perinbam, and Ira Berlin provided valuable feedback on much or all of the initial book manuscript, inching it towards its present form. Wendy Lynch has given it the most rigorous, searching, effective and continuous engagement of all. Her critiques and insights during the early writing of the book forced rethinkings that fundamentally revamped and greatly improved it; her readings of later drafts sharpened them up in myriad ways. In short, much of what is good in this study stems from a cooperative intellectual venture. For this—and for a great deal more—the book is dedicated to her.

Despite everyone's input, the usual caveat applies: mistakes, missteps, and other screw-ups in what follows below are my own responsibility.

INTRODUCTION

A Brief History of Initiation

The initiation of adolescent girls in the Taita Hills of Kenya went through re-markable changes over a fifty year period. In the 1890s, small communities in subsections of the Hills all held some version of initiation, but with consider-able performative variations, different valuations of its significance, even dif-ferent names for it.[1] Still, even with those localized differences, female initia-tion across Taita had certain similarities of formal structure and didactic purpose.

Adult teachers, mostly older women, took pubescent girls into a forest for two to eight days of instruction on the "secrets" of adult life.[2] They learned about sexuality and contraception, the dangers of men's seductions, and the rights and obligations of maturity and marriage. Initiation culminated with the entire local populace taking part in an all night celebration of dancing. Female initiates then went into seclusion in their parents' homes for anywhere from a few weeks to a year.[3] Across Taita, female initiation delineated the boundary between childhood and maturity; undergoing it was necessary to becoming socially adult. Only afterwards could a woman marry.[4]

In the early twentieth century, however, a handful of girls did something previously all but unimaginable: they declined to undergo initiation. The refusers came from Taita's nascent Anglican ranks, and usually—though not always—acted with the support—or at the insistence—of Christian parents.[5]

---

[1]   Most commonly it was called *Mwari* or *Kirindi*, though several other terms were used in parts of the Hills; interviews with Mrs. GM, Teri/Sagalla, 24/8/1988; MM, Mwanda/Mwanda, 15/9/1988; Mrs. SM, Ilole/Bura, 16/8/1988; MW, Ghazi/Mbololo, 5/7/1988; Mrs. SM, Mogho Mleche/Mbale, 4/11/1988. Some locales also initiated boys, though only a handful of them considered it as significant as female initiation.

[2]   Depending on the locale, instructors might have all been women, or a mix of men and women; interviews with Mrs. SM, Ilole/Bura, 16/8/1988; Mrs. SM, Mogho Mleche/Mbale, 4/11/1988; and Mrs. GM, Teri/Sagalla, 24/8/1988.

[3]   Interviews with Mrs. SM, Mwanda/Mwanda, 14/9/1988, JK, Ngerenyi/Chawia, 11/5/1988, Mrs. SM, Werugha/Werugha, 30/9/1988, Mrs. EK, Wongonyi/Mbololo, 7/7/1988, and NK, Mwatate/Chawia, 15/8/1988.

[4]   Interviews with JK, Ngerenyi/Chawia, 11/5/1988, Mrs. SM, Werugha/Werugha, 30/9/1988.

[5]   A few girls who refused initiation did so over objections from non–Christian parents and ex-tended families. One such case in 1910 led parents to disown the daughter who took shelter in a missionary's home and refused to leave. Church Mission Society (hereafter called CMS) Corre-spondence, G3 A5/O19, Miss Good's Annual Letter, 22/11/1910.

The religiously inspired demurrals were rare, for not only did uninitiated Christians face severely limited marriage prospects, they acquired an uncomfortably anomalous status as perpetual non–adults in the terms of their predominantly non–Christian societies.

The refusals also spurred denunciations from prominent non–Christians, who couched the criticisms in a language of overarching regional ethnicity. Rituals like female initiation, they said, were critical to conducting oneself properly *as a Taita*—itself a newly minted identity in this era, albeit one that embraced and reworked many social and cultural forms from the region's nineteenth–century local societies. By the 1920s, this ran through the language and teachings of female initiation: it now came to be seen as a crucial marker of Taita identity:

> [Initiation] was very important, without a doubt, very very important. . . . The Christian girls [who refused initiation] were scorned by the grandmothers and grandfathers . . . because they did not grab it. They thought those girls had no knowledge of Taita life, they are just outside. . . . I myself [was initiated] in those days, I became a Christian just recently.[6]

Interviewees explained that initiation in the 1920s taught them explicitly about Taita ways:

> *Mrs. MM:* You know, I cannot tell you many of the things we learned. They were secrets of women's life, secrets of *Kidaßida* [Taita ways].
>
> *BB:* Were you truly told, "these are Taita things," or did you just know that?
>
> *Mrs. MM:* We were told! We were told! These are things of *Kidaßida*. . . . The old women told us it is necessary to know these things to be completely Taita women.[7]

Only the firmest Anglicans refused female initiation early in the century; other early Christians felt caught in a dilemma. They took their new religion seriously, but both parents and daughters wanted to ensure the solidity of young women's social standing. Refusing initiation not only stigmatized girls; in parts of the Hills, they might be ostracized as not fully Taita. Many early Anglicans "backslid" long enough for daughters to be initiated, then later "recovered" their faith. But this equivocating left many parents and daughters uneasy about the moral choices they made.[8]

---

[6]   Interview with Mrs. SM, Werugha/Werugha, 30/9/1988; "just recently" meant the late 1950s. Also, interview with Mrs. SM, Mwanda/Mwanda, 14/9/1988.

[7]   Interview with Mrs. MM, Werugha/Werugha, 30/7/1993; also, Mrs. PM, Mwanda/Mwanda, 3/8/1993.

[8]   "Backsliding" could also make it difficult to be reinstated into the church; interviews with Mrs. MM, Lushangonyi/Mwanda, 21/9/1988; Mrs. GM, Teri/Sagalla, 24/8/1988; and NK, Mwatate/Chawia, 15/8/1988.

In the 1930s, Taita Anglicans, now a rapidly expanding group, developed a new way for their daughters to attain standing as Taita women. With the permission of church officials, they began to hold Christian female initiation ceremonies that in part copied (and in part unintentionally parodied) the non–Christian ones.[9] Christian initiations were, literally, tea parties, usually held in a school or church. Male and female church elders and the daughters' godparents conducted them, with European missionaries often attending, as well. The church elders did not teach about sexuality, concentrating instead on admonitions that the girls abstain from sex before marriage, respect parents, and respect the Church. The participants then enjoyed a few hours of Western–style, formal dancing. No seclusion followed the Christian gathering.[10] Most practitioners of Taita's indigenous religion thought Christian initiation laughable,[11] but accepted it as a lesser but analogous ritual, for it offered a way to keep Christians—now in virtually every extended lineal group in the Hills—within the pale of local society.[12] By the 1940s, Christian initiations were commonplace events.

Indigenous religionists thought Christian initiation reflected the Anglicans' lack of real knowledge of *Kidaßida* or "Taita ways," but Christians did not worry much about their derision. With a Christian initiation, a daughter could reasonably be called mature; the ritual gave her adequate acceptance as an adult in broader Taita society, and she could marry without difficulty. What mattered to Christians was that daughters underwent *some* sort of Taita initiation that marked the girls as having navigated the transition to adulthood in a culturally valorized fashion. If Christian initiation wasn't exactly a stellar example of *Kidaßida*, the pages below will show that by the 1940s, *Kidaßida* wasn't what it had once been, either.

Lines of Argument

The brief history of female initiation in Taita effectively synopsizes the major themes of this study. Most generally, I examine the emergence of a Taita ethnic identity in the early twentieth century, the historical and new resources from which people made it, and the continual remaking of it thereafter. To do so, the study analyzes how social groups in Taita formed and changed over a much longer period of time, and how the groups' social outlooks and beliefs coalesced, were contested, and changed, as well.

---

[9]   Interview with RM, Kaya/Chawia, 4/5/1988.

[10]   Interviews with Mrs. SM, Werugha/Werugha, 29/9/1988, RM, Kaya/Chawia, 4/5/1988, and JK, Ngerenyi/Chawia, 11/5/1988.

[11]   Interviews with RM, Kaya/Chawia, 4/5/1988; Mrs. SM, Mwanda/Mwanda, 14/9/1988; and Mrs. SM, Werugha/Werugha, 23/7/1993. According to RM, one result of replacing sex education with calls for abstinence was a rise in unwanted pregnancies among unmarried teenage Christians.

[12]   Interviews with Mrs. SM, Werugha/Werugha, 29/9/1988, and Mrs. JM, Sagassa/Werugha, 7/10/1988.

While cognizant of outside influences on Taita's societies, I argue that the social pressures that spurred contestations and change were shaped primarily *within* local social groups—sometimes through locally–rooted innovations by a segment of society, other times through the ways people like Taita's Anglicans tried to incorporate influences from without. Intragroup attempts to prompt particular changes, defend extant ways, or find compromises are described herein as cultural politics. Between 1800 and 1950, cultural politics in the region shifted their discursive focus from the content of localized social constructs—lineage and neighborhood—to the character of a transregional one: Taita ethnicity.

In brief overview, I argue that during the later seventeenth to mid–eighteenth centuries, different groups of migrants to various parts of Taita formed localized communities based on lineage (*kichuku*) and neighborhood (*izanga*). The various communities spoke different (though often related) dialects, and during the eighteenth and nineteenth centuries remained sociopolitically distinct from—and often hostile to—one another. Cultural political struggles over changes in nineteenth–century societies took place within each community, virtually never across localities. Still, intraregional migrations and interactions helped communities across the Hills gradually grow more socioculturally similar, fostering increasingly like structures of belief and social organization.

In the early twentieth century, some older men in local communities began to assert that all the people of the region shared a common, Taita, identity. In so doing, they also set out what they thought constituted Taitaness: adherence to properly Taita terms of conduct and belief. This shifted cultural politicking over social and cultural changes in Taita to what could/could not pass muster as *Kidaßida* ("Taita ways," or more loosely but evocatively, "A Taita way of doing things"). People embraced Taita ethnicity in subsequent decades, but its terms slid away from what the older men who initially invoked it had in mind. Those older men's ideas about how to be properly Taita were challenged from the very outset, and over time changed dramatically. By the late 1940s, the very concept of *Kidaßida* was losing its cultural–political clout.

Within this story, the study treats Taita ethnicity as a historically specific form of community building. This requires clarification, for if scholars of Africa now query "ethnicity" closely after long taking it for granted, "community" may well have replaced it as the term most prone to vague, under–considered usage. In recent historical writing, Africanists have variously, and usually with little explanation, applied "community" to groups that share some combination of territory, kinship, close relationships, color, shared experience of oppression, religious affiliation, and ethnicity.[13] The ubiquity of the term resides partly in its ready substitu-

---

[13]   Vivian Bickford–Smith, "Black Ethnicities, Communities, and Political Expression in Late Victorian Capetown," *Journal of African History* 36, 3 (1995); Jane Guyer, "Diversity at Different Levels: Farm and Community in Western Nigeria," in *Africa* 66, 1 (1996), and "Household and Community in African Studies," *African Studies Review* 24, 2–3 (1981); Patrick Harries, "'A Forgotten Corner of the Transvaal': Reconstructing the History of a Relocated Community through Oral Testimony and Song," in *Class, Community, and Conflict: South African Perspectives*, ed. Belinda Bozzoli (Johannesburg, 1987); Riva Krut, "The Making of a South African Jewish Community in Johannesburg, 1886–1914," in Bozzoli, *Class, Community and Conflict*; Charles Ambler, *Kenyan Communities in the Age of Imperialism: The Central Region in the Late Nineteenth Century* (New Haven and London, 1988).

tion for "group," and partly in its evocative power: community typically connotes not only some structural basis for a shared identity, but also group cohesion, harmony, and unity. In the latter regard, scholars sometimes treat "community" as a shorthand for a harmonious group effect.[14]

This study uses "community" with more analytic specificity, in hopes of dispelling some of the romanticizing haze that often envelops it. I posit, first, that a community is built largely upon people's efforts to develop and reproduce a domain of commonality, fellow–feeling, and shared beliefs and behaviors, *and* systems of controls and constraints over a group. Some members of a community set and/or maintain those controls and constraints, and may well benefit by them more than other community members. Second, community harmony and unity of purpose is not a natural state; shared outlooks, agendas, and assumptions in a community are deliberately or hegemonically fostered, reinforced in positive ways, and *en*forced by constraints and sanctions. Third, communities are composed and reproduced in contingent and historically specific circumstances. Despite the connotations of harmony and hegemonic claims of commonality that surround "community," communities may be riven by tensions, conflicts, authority struggles, competing visions, etc. As a result, communities' composition and reproduction—and their normative grounding—may well be contested and altered over time through cultural politicking.

Communities may form on any number of grounds, of course, and people may lay claim to several kinds of them at any given time, but some pervade people's lives more thoroughly and continuously than others. Such communities are usually rooted in close, ongoing everyday relationships and interactions; a succession of them became central to people's social identities in Taita. Those communities provided frameworks for rearing and socializing the young, channeled the productive and reproductive potential of adults, and supported and respected the old. They offered members material and social support, even as they set norms and terms of proper belief and behavior.

Despite these continuities, the forms of community in Taita changed over time in kind, scale, and ideological underpinning. Down through the nineteenth century, communities at their largest fit in compact subsections of Taita, and were grounded in notions of extended kinship and neighborliness. In the early 1900s, the emergent notion of Taita community reconfigured many aspects of local community ideology into a wider, and more generalized, ethnic commonality. Taita community coexisted with lineage and neighborhood communities, but as Taita ethnicity became more firmly established, it gradually attenuated the salience of more localized structures.

The book occasionally discusses communities in Taita as communities of belonging, because the sense of belonging they fostered in members—and the importance that community members attached to belonging—provided their

---

[14] See, for example, Paul Landau, "When Rain Falls: Rainmaking and Community in a Tswana Village, c.1870 to Recent Times," *International Journal of African Historical Studies* 26, 1 (1993). The article does not use community analytically, but has a section, and considerable subsequent discussion, on "Rainmaking and Harmony."

affective glue.[15] Belonging in a community not only granted access to needed resources,[16] it offered multiple, patently desirable forms of security and acceptance. Community belonging mediated the building of strong social ties. It afforded a person the material, psychological, and emotional support of knowing that a group shared in responsibility for one's well–being and saw that person as an integral part of the community's well–being. By belonging in a community, people ensured themselves access to peers they might befriend and rely upon, as well as older and younger people whom they could count on. Reciprocally, community belonging helped people understand what others expected of them and how they could fortify social ties by fulfilling those expectations. The young were enjoined to help meet the physical needs of their elders; the old were charged to see that the young had sufficient access to productive and social resources, and prospects for the future.

However, community belonging in Taita, as elsewhere, was not all warmth, reciprocity, and fellow–feeling. It carried with it deeply ingrained and at times intense pressures to conform to group norms of belief and behavior. Belonging also turned on acknowledging and respecting the authorities who upheld those norms. In what might be seen as the hegemonic character of communities, such pressures were often naturalized into what members of the community assumed or accepted as proper beliefs, or proper ways of doing things. Propriety, however, might be challenged, and the more coercive side of community belonging might surface as overt pressures to conform. The positive aspects of community belonging were not shams that hid a "true" coercive character, but along with social supports belonging carried expectations of adherence to the group's normative standards. The threat of sanctions reinforced expectations when socialization did not suffice.

Junctures of high tension can highlight how community norms reinforced inequalities of authority, standing and/or wealth. This study contends, however, that even in less stressful moments, norms and terms of "community" want unpacking—for the inequalities always existed, and, like other hegemonic orders, always needed reproducing and always stood somewhat at risk.[17] Tracing this out historically reveals that by the mid–nineteenth century, older men in Taita had established localized norms and terms of community that consolidated and naturalized their wealth and authority over women and younger men. Intracommunity tensions and potential challenges existed, but were mostly contained. Around the turn of the twentieth century, however, economic, political, and sociocultural changes enabled some women and young men to chal-

---

[15]   For a psychologically–based but similar view of belonging, George De Vos, "Ethnic Pluralism: Conflict and Accommodation," in *Ethnic Identity: Creation, Conflict, and Accommodation*, 3d ed., ed. De Vos and Lola Romanucci–Ross (Walnut Creek, 1995), 25–26.

[16]   On community as a provider of resources, H. W. O. Okoth–Ogondo, "Some Issues in the Study of Tenure Relations in African Agriculture," *Africa* 59, 1 (1989); and Sara Berry, "Social Institutions and Access to Resources," *Africa* 59, 1 (1989).

[17]   Jonathan Glassman's discussion of community, while not the main concern of this study, makes a number of similar points. See his *Feasts and Riot: Revelry, Rebellion, and Popular Consciousness on the Swahili Coast, 1856–1888* (Manchester, NH, 1995), 20–21.

lenge older men's predominance over local communities in powerful new ways. In response, many older men turned to the notion of Taita belonging, and made *Kidaßida* a vehicle for reasserting norms and terms of control. But the older men's initial version of "proper Taita ways" in the 1910s gradually lost ground to young men, women, and Christians. By the 1950s, a Christian senior elite was overturning *Kidaßida's* norm–setting force, and laying out terms for its own predominance—terms themselves that came in for challenges.

Some of the romantic mist surrounding community revisits old shibboleths about ethnicity. Each word has a whiff of nostalgic premodernity, but ethnicity in an African context often operates as a polite substitute for tribe and carries disparaging connotations. Like other kinds of communities, ethnic groups are often taken to have homogeneous outlooks; in line with this, a long tradition in Western social science treats ethnic groups as relatively free of internal conflicts over the terms of their social orders. More particularly, most Africanist literature on ethnicity either elides or ignores lines of tension within ethnic groups—a surprising truism, given all the attention scholars pay to conflicts *between* groups or classes.

Nevertheless, while Africanists have adeptly ferreted out the dynamics and significance of struggle on scales smaller (e.g., household, plantation, capitalist workplace) and larger (e.g., nation–state politics), intragroup tensions rarely draw notice in analyses of the origins and ideological reproduction of ethnic groups.[18] This study seeks to correct the oversight. The interplay between the fostering of community belonging and struggles over would–be shared terms of that community is often essential—even central—to understanding how an ethnic group takes shape and changes over time. It highlights several linked phenomena that this study analyzes: the ways ethnic ideologies can gain affective strength through their operation as ideologies of community belonging; how ethnic ideologies thereby endeavor to construct and naturalize creeds of unity and commonality; how inequalities of wealth and power nonetheless get built into the norms and terms of ethnic community; how predominant members of the group seek to perpetuate those terms; and how subordinate members of the group, while placing great stock in belonging within the community, may nevertheless challenge its received terms.

---

[18] A few topics provide exceptions. One is Kikuyu society in the era leading up to Mau Mau; see John Lonsdale, "The Moral Economy of Mau Mau: Wealth, Poverty and Civic Virtue in Kikuyu Political Thought" in *Unhappy Valley: Conflict in Kenya and Africa, Book Two: Violence and Ethnicity*, ed. Bruce Berman and Lonsdale (London, 1992); Tabitha Kanogo, *Squatters and the Roots of Mau Mau, 1905–63* (Nairobi, 1987); and Ngugi wa Thiong'o, *A Grain of Wheat* (Nairobi, 1967).

Some work on Zulu ethnicity also examines the ways intragroup tensions and struggles shaped the social order; Carolyn Hamilton and John Wright, "The Making of *AmaLala*: Ethnicity, Ideology, and Relations of Subordination in a Precolonial Context," *Southern African Historical Journal* 22 (1990); John Wright, "Notes on the Politics of Being Zulu, 1820–1920" (paper given at "Conference on Ethnicity, Society and Conflict in Natal," University of Natal/Pietermaritzburg, 1992); and Shula Marks, *The Ambiguities of Dependence in South Africa: Class, Nationalism and the State in Twentieth–Century Natal* (Baltimore 1986).

This brings us to cultural politics, a phrase with nearly as many meanings as card catalogue entries. One common use of it refers to the political dimensions of a cultural group; a second to the way different cultural groups act as political blocs within larger societies or states; and a third, to the politics of literary and artistic high culture.[19] My usage most resembles still another approach, Jordan and Weedon's querying "which cultural practices and products [a society] most value[s]," their attention to how "social inequality is legitimated through culture," and their conviction that cultural politics encompasses "the legitimation of social relations of inequality, and the struggle to transform them."[20] Some differences still remain: they focus primarily on how culture, cultural hegemony, and cultural struggle become inscribed in the intergroup power relations of highly heterogeneous societies and states;[21] my study inverts this and reduces its scale, asking instead how struggles and power dynamics shape cultural formation within a smaller, relatively homogeneous region.

By cultural politics, then, I refer to ways people in Taita struggled over the norms and terms of their communities.[22] The predominant seniors set those terms, tried to give them hegemonic authority, and defended them actively when necessary. Their subordinates often tried to alter those terms, seeking to reorder extant structures or trying to prompt change by using new resources or opportunities. This kind of politics may be overt and explicit, but may also remain unspoken subtexts of social struggles. In Taita, those with power at risk tended to make their cultural politics explicit: older men, and sometimes older women, laid out norms and terms of action and belief that they wanted their subordinates to follow. The subordinated, younger men and women with much to lose, often left the cultural politics of their challenges implicit, trying to minimize the overt conflict that their actions might provoke.

Taita ethnicity took shape in the early twentieth century at once as a community of belonging, and an arena within which intense cultural politicking over the terms of society took place. Through the idea of *Kidaßida*, older men tried to elide the growing distinction between the two, thereby fixing a set of meanings for the collective identity. In nineteenth-century

---

[19]   For example, Alan Sinfield, *Cultural Politics—Queer Reading* (Philadelphia 1994); Mary Darnovsky, Barbara Epstein, and Richard Flacks, eds., *Cultural Politics and Social Movements* (Philadelphia, 1995); Jerold Starr, ed., *Cultural Politics: Radical Movements in Modern History* (New York, 1985).

[20]   Glenn Jordan and Chris Weedon, *Cultural Politics: Class, Gender, and Race in the Postmodern World* (Cambridge, Mass., 1995), 5.

[21]   Ibid., 6.

[22]   Cultural politics differs from what I call domestic politics, social tensions, or struggles for gain conducted within a society's predominant rules. Cultural politics look to alter or uphold the rules. For example, Geertz has famously discussed how social tensions in Bali were expressed at cockfights. The highly elaborated, widely agreed–upon groundrules that framed the encounters mark this (in my idiom) as domestic politics; flaunting or circumventing those rules would cross over into cultural politics. Clifford Geertz, "Deep Play: Notes on a Balinese Cockfight," in *The Interpretation of Cultures* (New York, 1973), 437–40.

lineage and neighborhood communities, older men had been able to make community belonging on the one hand, and notions of propriety that supported their predominance on the other, virtually merge. As twentieth–century changes cut into their predominance, older men wanted *Kidaßida* and the idea of propriety to re–tie the fraying connections between community belonging and their everyday control over women and young men. Their efforts did not entirely succeed. Younger men, women, and young and old Christians of both sexes challenged many aspects of what early twentieth–century older men considered proper Taita ways. At the same time, however, people across the Hills were naturalizing Taita ethnic identity as deeply theirs. Slowly but surely, then, new terms of how to be Taita were conjoined to a deeply internalized perception of a continuous Taita identity.[23]

Situating the Argument

Ethnicity

Barth's introduction to *Ethnic Groups and Boundaries* has long towered over Africanist approaches to ethnicity.[24] He argues that ethnic identification proceeds from groups adapting to socioeconomic niches, then recognizing their distinctiveness from adjacent groups. Ethnicity, in this view, is inherently relational: it resides in a group's construction of a social boundary between "us" and "them." Barth's emphasis on the salience of intergroup difference has influenced most subsequent Africanist analyses. His attention to ethnicity's ascriptive, constructed character also made him the gravitational center of "instrumentalism." Instrumentalist arguments refuted "primordialist" explanations of ethnicity as an inherent human quality rooted either in biology or in social–historical, but ineffably fundamental, forces.[25]

Some studies have refined Barth's instrumentalist/relationalist approach in valuable ways: the essays in Spear and Waller's *Being Maasai* insightfully examine the connections between socioeconomic and ecological niches, the development and change of cultural forms, and the setting, negotiation, and

---

[23] This view of identity construction, while not explicitly following her approach, is in sympathy with Somers' call to see identities as narratively constituted and thereby avoid reifications of time, space, and relationality; Margaret Somers, "The Narrative Constitution of Identity: A Relational and Network Approach," *Theory and Society* 23 (1994); also Stuart Hall, "Ethnicity: Identity and Difference," *Radical America* 23, 4 (1989).

[24] Frederik Barth, introduction to *Ethnic Groups and Boundaries: The Social Organization of Cultural Difference*, ed. Barth (Boston, 1969).

[25] For a brief summary of the instrumentalist/primordialist distinction, see Thomas Spear, introduction to *Being Maasai: Ethnicity and Identity in East Africa*, ed. Thomas Spear and Richard Waller (Athens, Ohio, 1993), 15–17; for a fuller discussion, Richard Thompson, *Theories of Ethnicity: A Critical Appraisal* (New York, 1990). The most coherent sociobiological theory of ethnic primordialism is Pierre van den Berghe, *The Ethnic Phenomenon* (New York, 1981). For critiques of it, R. C. Lewontin, *Not in our Genes* (New York, 1984); and Bill Bravman, "Becoming Taita: A Social History, 1850–1950" (Ph.D. diss., Stanford University, 1992), 10–15.

crossing of ethnic boundaries.[26] Wilmsen and others have further explored how political power struggles inform relationalism.[27] But many works canonically treat Barth as axiomatic truth; one recent study begins with the dictum, "Any identity needs the presence of other comparable identities in order to define itself. Oromo identity has defined itself, and has been defined by others . . . in opposition to other comparable national identities."[28]

Unfortunately, followers of Barth's "boundaries" model have reproduced its analytical shortcomings along with its strengths. By locating the forces of ethnicization at the social borders of groups, it draws attention *towards* explaining intergroup distinctions, and *away from* the internal dynamics of how groups form and change. Each group tends to be treated as effectively homogeneous; when the forge of ethnic identity is a group's sense of difference from others, all its members are seen as melded together in shared contradistinction. This assumption of intragroup sameness bypasses processes of intragroup differentiation and struggle. It has become a staple of Barth–derived analyses: ethnic group formation boils down to people (who share language, a common economic orientation, and close daily interactions) developing distinguishing ethnyms and cultural forms to underline their difference from their neighbors. Since Barth's model provides no tools for locating and recognizing the salience of intragroup differences, studies using its blueprint tend to overlook a group's internal dynamics of differentiation, struggle, and negotiation.[29]

Yet power–laden differentiations within groups do exist, and may well fuel intragroup social processes that crystallize or reshape ethnic identity. This study argues that ethnic groups, and other sorts of communities, should not be assumed to be homogeneous; that an ethnic group's shared culture does not develop easily or quasi–naturally out of ecological or economic specialization; and that a group's differentiations and its internal struggles over the norms and terms of society figure vitally in how that group shapes and reshapes an ethnic identity. This is not to deny the significance of social boundary distinctions in the forging of ethnic identities. It treats such contradistinctions as part of how a sense of community belonging is constructed—and locates that aspect of community construction in an approach that accounts for both relational and internal processes of ethnic group formation.

A related view to Barth's treats African ethnicities as specifically colonial creations. The foremost work of this genre posits that Europeans spurred African ethnic group formation, either as a direct classifying imposition or through Afri-

---

[26]   Spear and Waller, *Being Maasai.*

[27]   Edwin Wilmsen and Patrick McAllister, eds., *The Politics of Difference: Ethnic Premises in a World of Power* (Chicago, 1996).

[28]   P. T. W. Baxter, Jan Hultin, and Alessandro Triulzi, eds., *Being and Becoming Oromo: Historical and Anthropological Inquiries* (Lawrenceville, NJ 1996).

[29]   Ibid. The closest this study comes to a discussion of internal Oromo dynamics is a statement in the introduction (p. 10), that the book's contributors "revel in the rich cultural and historical diversity of the Oromo."

can reifications of their own societies in response to colonial rule.[30] This "creation of tribalism" view occasionally renders Africans more passive in ethnic creation than the record might warrant, but moves beyond Barth to analyze how some elite Africans brokered ethnicity's spread for the sake of their own political authority and/or social standing, and examines ethnic ideology's popular reception.[31] However, this model of ethnicization raises new problems. It treats ethnic affiliations as powerful and deeply held, but does not consider whether or how they connect to prior histories of the now–ethnicized; precolonial societies and cultures get short shrift. Yet colonial era ethnicities were usually more than modern bricolage: earlier social formations and cultural beliefs and practices often carried forward, sometimes in altered form, and were invested with new meanings in ethnic societies.

Relatedly, the model precludes explanation of how some groups embraced ethnicity before colonialism. A sound observation underlies the attention to colonialism: Europeans who arrived with a view of African societies as inherently tribal often then facilitated the process of making them so.[32] Nevertheless, scholars have convincingly traced many African ethnic identities to long before Europeans appeared on the scene.[33] An overall approach to ethnicity must therefore make sense of its emergence in either period—for many African societies, including those in Taita, *did* generate or put new emphasis on ethnic identities in the colonial era,[34] and with good reason. Colonialism often gave rise to profound political, economic, social, and cultural changes that corroded established African social orders and enabled the fostering of new ones.[35] This was not a tidy, controllable process; Europeans and/or Africans by no means

---

[30] The best known of the former is Leroy Vail, ed., *The Creation of Tribalism in Southern Africa* (London, 1989); also, Edwin Wilmsen with Saul Dubow and John Sharp, "Introduction: Ethnicity, Identity and Nationalism in Southern Africa," *Journal of Southern African Studies* 20, 3 (1994). Examples of the latter include Martin Chanock, *Law, Custom and Social Order: The Colonial Experience in Zambia and Malawi* (Cambridge, 1985), and Wim van Binsbergen, "The Kazanga Festival: Ethnicity as Cultural Mediation and Transformation in Central Western Zambia," *African Studies* 53, 2 (1994).

[31] Vail, *Creation*, 11–15.

[32] See for instance Terence Ranger, "European Attitudes and African Realities: The Rise and Fall of the Matola Chiefs of South–East Tanzania," *Journal of African History* 20, 1 (1979).

[33] For eastern Africa alone, Spear and Waller, *Being Maasai*; Ronald Atkinson, *The Roots of Ethnicity: The Origins of the Acholi of Uganda before 1800* (Philadelphia, 1992); Justin Willis, "The Makings of a Tribe: Bondei Identities and Histories," *Journal of African History* 33 (1992); Pier Larson, "Desperately Seeking 'the Merina': Reading Ethnonyms and Their Semantic Fields in African Identity Histories" (paper presented to the African Studies Association annual meeting, Toronto, 1995); also, I. N. Kimambo, *Political History of the Pare of Tanzania* (Nairobi, 1969), and Steven Feierman, *Peasant Intellectuals: Anthropology and History in Tanzania* (Madison, 1990). Many 1960s to 1970s–era studies of precolonial Kenyan societies confidently treated them as ethnic; this might want reexamining, but in many cases that appellation would hold up; H. S. K. Mwaniki, *The Living History of Embu and Mbeere to 1906* (Nairobi, 1973); Gideon Were, *A History of the Abaluyia of Western Kenya c.1500–1930* (Nairobi, 1967); William Ochieng', *A Pre–Colonial History of the Gusii of Western Kenya, 1500–1914* (Nairobi, 1975).

[34] Ranger, "Matola Chiefs"; Vail, *Creation of Tribalism*; Chanock, *Law, Custom and Social Order.*

[35] A thoughtful, if mechanistic, political–economic argument along these lines is Prema Kurien, "Colonialism and Ethnogenesis: A Study of Kerala, India," *Theory and Society* 23 (1994). Appiah has usefully pointed out just how uneven the colonial process could be, and how limited its incursion might feel in certain times and places; Kwame Anthony Appiah, introduction to *In My Father's House: Africa in the Philosophy of Culture* (New York, 1992).

planned all the changes, and even deliberate reforms tended to have unintended, but far–reaching outcomes.[36] The flux often gave rise to social tensions within which ethnicizing claims flourished.

Finally, the "creation of tribalism" model posits a top–down view of ethnicity. Elites, whether white or African, impose it; everyone else receives and accepts it. This starts from a sound insight: elite attempts to instill and naturalize ethnic ideologies are interwoven with the elites' efforts to preserve and augment their authority. However, if we can agree with the Gramscian claim that hegemonies are never complete, sometimes at risk, and perpetually in need of reconstruction, then we can expect to find a more complex, struggle–filled process: elite attempts to naturalize their authority and prestige within the terms of an ethnic social order, non–elite challenges to those elite formulations, and elite responses and ripostes.[37]

Lonsdale has done an exemplary exploration of ethnic dynamics, explaining how the content of Kikuyu ethnicity was always disputed, but all the more so in the first half of the twentieth century, as a moral economy of self–mastery, patronage and clientship, and clients' opportunity was superseded by a harsher political economy. Kikuyu leaders espoused a unifying ideology of anti–colonial ethnic nationalism to paper over escalating rich/poor tensions and a moral coarsening of Kikuyu socioeconomic norms.[38] My approach resembles Lonsdale's in many respects, but parts company over the question of what actually constitutes "ethnicity." Lonsdale applies the term to precolonial regions where "linguistic, economic, and social similarity" overarched otherwise loosely linked local societies. Though "daily life took little heed of ethnicity," he posits that overall structural likeness nonetheless bound the little polities together.[39] Ambler, on the other hand, holds that in such regions "no settled and exclusive ethnic order defined social and economic relationships;" a larger "social order [was] in the making."[40]

This study leans towards Ambler's view. Sociocultural and linguistic similarities (or even commonalities) among communities, I argue, do not in themselves constitute ethnicity. The mobilization of those similarities—by some people, for some purposes, and as accepted by others in the communities, albeit conditionally—shapes ethnic identities. Precolonial mobilizations could certainly take place; Kikuyu ethnicity may well have been mobilized before colonialism. Too, Spear compellingly shows how Maasai ethnicity mobilized in the eighteenth century, and Atkinson demonstrates

---

[36]   For a good example of unexpected and unintended consequences unleashed by colonial policies, see Frederick Cooper, *From Slaves to Squatters: Plantation Labor and Agriculture in Zanzibar and Coastal Kenya, 1890–1925* (New Haven, 1980).

[37]   Shula Marks, in *Ambiguities of Dependence*, finds this sort of relationship in her discussion of changing popular responses to the Zulu kingship.

[38]   Lonsdale, "Moral Economy," 328–30. However, the only study I have found linking intragroup disputes to the creation of ethnicity discusses Australian Aborigines is Karl Neuenfeldt, "The Kyana Corroboree: Cultural Production of Indigenous Ethnogenesis," *Sociological Inquiry* 65, 1 (1995).

[39]   Lonsdale, "Moral Economy,"328–29.

[40]   Ambler, *Kenyan Communities*, 7.

that Acholi ethnicity has its roots in late–seventeenth–century political mobilization.[41]

I treat those ongoing mobilizations of similarity/commonality as a key indicator of ethnicity. I analyze how Hills communities became localized, then how and why they mobilized ethnically, fostering Taita identity as a new, overarching form of community. This argues for a relatively delimited definition of ethnicity, as against some scholars' juxtaposition of loose, precolonial (benign) ethnicity with twentieth–century (fractious) tribalism.[42] My view does not foreclose seeing ethnicity as a tool of colonial and independence era politics, nor deny the rigidifying effects of colonialism on ethnicity. But if ethnicity is sufficiently distinguished from not–ethnicity, the term gains the flexibility to delineate different kinds of ethnic mobilizations. "Tribalism" then describes how ethnicity may at times be mobilized as a system of heightened intragroup nepotisms and intergroup competition for power and resources, justified by essentialized claims about a group's common interests and other groups' difference. Even so antagonistic a version of ethnicity as this fits within the general ethnic phenomenon.

Some points here want reiterating for the sake of historiographical clarity: to locate the rise of Taita ethnicity in the colonial era is not to argue that ethnic identities in Africa are all colonial impositions. Looking to the ways similarities and commonalities are mobilized allows scholars to locate ethnic emergences whenever they happened. To trace an ethnogenesis to the colonial era is *not* to argue that all–powerful Europeans willed the group into existence and that Africans duly bought into it; nor to argue a variation on the theme, that African elites cynically tried to manipulate cultural symbols to draw subordinates into an ethnic false consciousness masking their continued subordination. Neither scenario captures the dynamics of ethnicity, and both verge on caricatures of lived social process.[43] They treat the power of elites as far more totalizing than is usually possible, and regard the subordinated as more guileless and malleable than recent scholarship and good sense suggest is prudent.[44]

I also argue that the historiographical division between ethnic instrumentalism and primordialism derives from a false distinction. Primordialism, in its non–biological form, turns on a combination of psychology and vague ahistoricality. Geertz, for instance, sees ethnicity as building on historical (i.e., instrumental) ties that nevertheless:

---

[41] Spear and Waller, *Being Maasai*, 9–14; Ronald Atkinson, "The Evolution of Ethnicity among the Acholi of Uganda: The Precolonial Phase," *Ethnohistory* 36, 1 (1989); also his *Roots of Ethnicity*.

[42] Lonsdale, "Moral Economy"; Robert Papstein, "From Ethnic Identity to Tribalism: The Upper Zambezi Region in Zambia, 1830–1981," in Vail, *Creation*; Carola Lentz, "'They Must Be Dagaba First and Any Other Thing Second': The Colonial and Post–Colonial Creation of Ethnic Identities in North–western Ghana," *African Studies* 53, 2 (1994).

[43] The second scenario may be appropriate for analyzing a caricature of a polity: see Anonymous, "Ethnicity and Pseudo–Ethnicity in the Ciskei," in Vail, *Creation*. Vail's summary argument has a mechanistic top–down quality, stating that African elites administered it and "ordinary people" accepted it, because they "had a real need for so–called 'traditional values' at a time of rapid social change." Vail, *Creation*, 11.

[44] James Scott, *Domination and the Arts of Resistance: Hidden Transcripts* (New Haven, 1990).

> are *seen* to have an ineffable, and at times overpowering coerciveness
> in and of themselves, . . . in great part by virtue of some unaccount-
> able import attributed to the very tie itself. . . . Some attachments *seem*
> to flow more from a sense of natural—*some* would say spiritual—af-
> finity than from social interaction (italics added).[45]

The italicized qualifiers fudge the question of whether primordial ties are inef-
fable or just appear that way; likewise, whether natural ethnic affinity really
exists or only the effect does. His claim thus combines finely honed observation with a flight from further explanation. In discussing how a sense of belonging was constructed in Taita ethnicity, this study seeks to explain deeply
felt ethnic ties as historical constructions.

To do so, my analysis borrows improvisationally from Judith Butler's explanation of how social constructions are discursively produced, constantly cited
and reiterated, and thereby materialized to the point of being rendered "real."
This process operates far below the level of explicit ideology, and below unspoken, hegemonic beliefs, as well. There is some risk that the terms of Butler's
project—how the body is seen to have its "sex"[46]—may not translate to mine,
since ethnicity lacks the body's materiality.[47] Yet ethnicity's non–materiality may,
in fact, make it easier to see how a construction becomes naturalized into reality through "reiteration of a norm or set of norms . . . [that] conceals or dis-
simulates the conventions of which it is a repetition."[48]

Again, for clarity's sake: this is not to suggest that ethnicity somehow lacked
reality, for it surely did become and remain real; the false distinction between
constructed and primordial ethnicity has here spawned a further spurious dichotomy. Taita ethnicity is a historical construction that over time became a
deeply felt—indeed, deeply assumed—part of people's individual and collective identities, to the point of being internalized or embodied as an aspect of
their basic "nature." The historicity does not diminish the reality. How did Taita
ethnicity become so profoundly naturalized? In large part by reconfiguring
people's already extant sense of, as well as need and desire for, belonging to a
community; De Vos's argument about the psychological importance of group
belonging, thus situated, proceeds from historical grounding that primordialist
theories lack.[49] The transference of that powerfully felt sense of community

---

[45]   Clifford Geertz, "The Integrative Revolution: Primordial Sentiments and Civil Politics in the
New States," in Geertz, *Interpretation*, 259–60. For other social versions of primordialism, Donald
Horowitz, *Ethnic Groups in Conflict* (Berkeley, 1985); and A. D. Smith, "The Supersession of Nation-
alism?" *International Journal of Comparative Sociology* 31, 1–2 (1990). For a critique of them, Jack
David Eller and Reed Coughlan, "The Poverty of Primordialism: Demystification of Ethnic Attach-
ments," *Ethnic and Racial Studies* 16, 2 (1993).

[46]   Judith Butler, *Bodies that Matter: On the Discursive Limits of "Sex"* (New York, 1993), 1–16.

[47]   Or does it? Metaphors of blood and assessments of physical features certainly locate ethnicity
in or on the body. Radovan Karadzic uses bodily metaphors to describe the Serbian nation, and
explains the killing or raping of non–Serbs as the "ethnic cleansing" of "alien bodies." Rob Nixon,
"Of Balkans and Bantustans," *Transition* 60 (1993).

[48]   Butler, *Bodies that Matter*, 12.

[49]   De Vos, "Ethnic Pluralism."

belonging to Taita ethnicity allowed people to locate their sense of mutuality and rootedness in it.

Community

"Community" often appears in Africanist titles, but nearly as often seems an afterthought in the texts.[50] It typically floats in the background of analyses, implying strong cultural bonds and/or tight social networks. Benedict Anderson's now classic *Imagined Communities* has cast relatively little shadow on Africanist discussions of community—perhaps because Anderson, too, gives less attention to community per se than to the imaginative process and one particular kind of community: the nation. Still, he usefully suggests that "all communities larger than primordial villages of face–to–face contact (and perhaps even these) are imagined."[51]

This recognition of community's constructedness invites an excavation: who imagines an agglomeration of people into a community at various junctures in its collective existence? How, and how do the means of doing so change? By what means and to what ends do people make associations of community? To what extent is the process hegemonic, and to what extent more explicit in its ideology (i.e., deliberately chosen or strategized)? To what extent are communities and their definitions imposed from without? These questions help to establish distinctions among several Africanist approaches to the subject.

Bozzoli combines Anderson's view of communities as elite creations that bridge (or blur) social divisions within a group, with a view, drawn from northern hemisphere labor histories, of communities as class–homogeneous enclaves, that shore up class consciousness but develop cultures that do not tidily mirror class ideologies.[52] Her analysis of communities formed by South African industrialization tilts towards the labor history approach, concentrating on how relatively (and increasingly) homogeneous urban groups of lower class and impoverished people fashioned communities to help cope with the segregation, dispossession, and dislocation heaped upon them.

Despite its many strengths, Bozzoli's analysis all but ignores the internal dynamics of those communities. It echoes a general labor history argument that privileged sectors of a community may take a lead in forming its collective culture and ideology without standing above and outside the community. But she gives no critical attention to that process, and so cannot query whether different blocs perhaps had varying agendas about their communities, or even saw the communities in rather different ways. Her approach also ignores the

---

[50]   For example, Jane Guyer, in "Diversity at Different Levels," uses the term to refer to a small town. In an earlier article, "Household and Community," her use of community appears to be a shorthand for problematizing "kinship," "lineage," and "association."

[51]   Benedict Anderson, *Imagined Communities: Reflections on the Origin and Spread of Nationalism* (London, 1983), 15.

[52]   Belinda Bozzoli, "Class Community and Ideology in the Evolution of South African Society," in Bozzoli, *Class, Community and Conflict.*

internal dynamics of how communities change, focusing only on brutal, external forces of change: state dispossessions and segregationist severing of interracial class ties.[53]

Ambler discusses community formation in the context of late–nineteenth-century East Africa. He defines a community as an "area—generally quite small—whose residents were sufficiently bound together by local social and political institutions . . . to permit unified action on a regular basis."[54] The ones he examines were drawn together for collective efforts to sustain life and well–being, collective defense, and collective security in times of hardship. His approach tracks tensions and negotiations that sprang from intracommunity differentiations, and thus follows community dynamics closely. In parts of the region, relationships—and consequently communities—were frequently recast by migrations of people seeking to break out of communities where solidified patterns of accumulation and power limited new opportunities for advancement.[55]

While Ambler's study usefully focuses in on the dynamics of community differentiation, it skips over important domains of interaction, for it examines intra-group relations almost entirely in terms of socioeconomics and political economy. It only passingly mentions community–fostering ideologies and the related cultural forms and practices that held people together (or failed to do so), were reworked over time, and faced severe stresses from wider economic and political changes of the era. This combination of emphases and elisions precludes analysis of cultural dynamics and cultural change. My analysis focuses on the interaction between political economy and cultural forms in Taita, for that interplay illuminates how the predominant in its communities socially and institutionally vested their position and tried to naturalize it. This is the social terrain upon which, in myriad small ways, young men, women, and Christians challenged and reworked the preeminence that older men sought to consolidate.

Willis's insightful work on the dynamics of community formation and change in later–nineteenth–century Bonde (Tanzania) is firmly rooted in an analysis of kinship relations.[56] It is a very flexible version of kinship, for social and ritual organization allowed an individual to claim kin ties with numerous groups: some nested within others, some similarly scaled but distinct in territory and/or personnel. Willis recognizes kinship as a power–laden ideology, discussing how a community's dominant elder men saw people as human and social resources, and reciprocally offered them security and social opportunities.[57] People's ability and willingness to shift kin (and thus community) allegiances became the main motor of community change. Senior men needed to maintain followings to retain their community power; individuals' ability to

[53]   Ibid., 34–36.

[54]   Ambler, *Kenyan Communities*, n. 5.

[55]   Ibid., 20–25, 43–48.

[56]   Justin Willis, "History, Identity, and Ritual in Bonde: The Making of Community in North–Eastern Tanzania, 1850–1916" (Ms., 1995); also Willis, "The Nature of a Mission Community: The Universities' Mission to Central Africa in Bonde," *Past and Present* 140 (1993).

[57]   Willis, *Making*, Introduction.

shift kin networks encouraged senior men not to exploit or mistreat juniors. People could also turn to alternative cosmologies, setting up allegiances that might challenge the extant community order.

My approach in many ways overlaps with Willis's. However, his explanation of community simultaneously reifies and over–generalizes kinship. His use of kinship ideology to explain community relationships, ranging from the lowest levels to that of Bonde's overall state,[58] neglects how little binding power it had at some levels. Rulers' references to kinship provided metaphorical justifications for power or actions, but the Bonde state mostly did not operate as a kin group writ large, and from Willis's evidence was not predominantly seen as one.[59] More widely, while a language of kinship may have pervaded community discourse in Bonde, it had less salience in settings like South African townships.

Any number of ideologies can provide the basis from which people build and maintain community. This study of Taita shows how kinship ideology operated alongside several other group–forming ideologies to construct community belonging and apportion power. In the early twentieth century, behaviors and beliefs, along with attempts to control them, became as central to discussions of community membership as kinship. Young, male labor migrants outside the Hills built bonds of Taita mutuality upon metaphors of "understanding," not kinship. By the 1940s, much Taita struggle turned precisely on whether descent or behavior defined community belonging. In short, this study situates kinship within a wider analysis of how group belonging is constructed, and how groups may be composed and reshaped over time.

Research Methods

The research for this book combines oral and written sources. I gathered the Taita oral material by conducting 144 individual interviews in people's homes during 1987–88, and a further twenty–four in 1993.[60] All of the interviewees were older men and women, with birthdays spread out over a roughly forty-year span. I guaranteed all interviewees anonymity when explaining what sorts of questions I would ask, a promise reflected in the book's somewhat circuitous citations of interviews.[61] In most interviews, a local man or woman ac-

---

58 Ibid., 6.

59 Here, the distinction Larson draws between different kinds of "belonging" is telling. Polity belonging and community belonging in Bonde certainly overlapped in their deployment of kinship ideology when the Bonde state existed. See Larson, "Desperately," 22–23.

60 Some interviews were repeat visits; 112 interviews were with men, 56 with women.

61 Interviews are cited in the text by the interviewee's initials, interview locale, and interview date. The last names of interviewees are listed in the bibliography, along with a separate breakdown of interview locales. I am preparing interview copies that hide the interviewees' identity, for deposit in the United States and Kenya. Meanwhile, interviewees who asked for taped or written copies of their interviews have them. I also interviewed three former colonial officers and a former missionary in England; all four were willing to have their names cited directly.

companied me to translate, if necessary, and to act as a cultural broker between interviewees and me.[62] Virtually all interviews were done either in KiSwahili, in which case the interviewee and I directly conversed, or with the translation between a local language—KiDabida or KiSagala—and KiSwahili.[63]

Structurally, interviews moved between my questions on particular topics and more open–ended invitations for interviewees to tell stories about their personal histories, their relationships with others, and their recent ancestors' lives. I focused interviews on relationships in familial, neighborhood, work, and social settings, with attention to intergenerational and intragenerational dynamics. I situated those concerns in questions about life stages, labor, education, religion and ritual, marriage, herding, politics, land, and wealth. Though most people were reticent about certain topics (e.g., initiation, Christian lapses), and few brought up social tensions without prompting, many proved surprisingly willing to discuss the difficulties and nuances of social relationships when asked about them.

I rarely asked for broad generalizations about Taita traditions or Taita history. Interviewees often made summary statements about both anyway, but the generalizations were usually situated in personal circumstances. Besides giving the summary claims firmer grounding, this provided me with a better footing for pursuing the claims. When tied to personal remembrances, different interviewees' broad statements about traditions and ways had the benefit— to me—of often contradicting one another. I did not try to decide whether one or another version told the "correct" story, but came to regard the tensions between tellings and experiences as indicators of social contestations. No doubt many interviewees circumscribed aspects of what they told me; some surely exaggerated, embellished, or misled about some things (or I mis–heard or mis– translated). These caveats most pertain to the time people had the vaguest memories of, the years before Taita's devastating 1880s famines; I use oral data for that time sparingly and cautiously.

Inevitably, too, everyone's personal narratives were grounded in their personal perspectives on what changes happened in the past hundred years, which ones were important and worthy, and what the changes meant. My research and analytic methodology embraces those differences of perspective. Though many people in Taita can locate their stories as part of the book's stew, the overall narrative does not reflect any one local perspective; it instead shows how I make sense of the collision of many perspectives. As I traced the fault lines of propriety through over 160 sets of personal remembrances, Taita's patterns of tension and negotiation emerged vividly to me, along with its changes in social identity.

Written sources include official documents in Kenya and England, missionary documents and personal papers, church records, old research reports, dissertations

[62]   Three people did this work for me in most of Taita: a man in his early seventies, a woman in her mid–fifties, and a man in his early thirties. Usually only one sat in at any given interview.

[63]   I offered to do the interview in whichever language the interviewee preferred. Roughly two thirds picked KiSwahili or soon switched to it. Many of those who chose a local language nonetheless understood at least some KiSwahili, and occasionally corrected the intermediary's translations. Two interviewees requested that we speak English.

and theses, published European memoirs and travelogues, and a few secondary works. Official records provided a large reservoir of European–generated information, observation and opinion; this data lays out much of the larger political–economic framework within which local issues played out. It also provides a translucent window into local Taita conflicts: officials recognized some local tensions, but rarely saw them the way local people did. Officials were sometimes more perceptive than postcolonial scholars might care to acknowledge, but other times they sorely misunderstood the issues they reported.

Mission records, too, have flashes of insight into local social tensions, but betray a tremendous capacity for misinterpretation at other junctures. They comment frequently on Christian/non–Christian relations, seeing them through the twin lenses of their evangelical endeavor and a strong bias about the superiority of Western civilization. Both mission and official sources provide an effective avenue into consideration of how Europeans understood themselves in Taita, and how they and Africans mis/understood each other.

Chapter by Chapter

Chapter 1 discusses the rise of localized communities in the Taita Hills since the 1600s, emphasizing the nineteenth century. It shows how the complex, multidirectional patterns of in–migration gave rise to clear (and sometimes hostile) distinctions between groups in different parts of the Hills. By the early nineteenth century, older men held predominant economic power, social authority, and religious position in local communities of belonging, over wives, adult sons, and daughters–in–law. It analyzes the extent and limits of similarities and interconnections between communities, and the wider ties to ancestral areas that local communities in Taita maintained.

Chapter 2 turns to a close examination of local community in one part of Taita, Sagalla, during the 1880s, a decade of dual stresses. A devastating famine and the first steady European missionary presence in the area at once rendered ties of community more apparent, and threatened to undermine them. The crises also underlined the shallowness of that era's Taita–wide networks of interconnection. Despite the strains on it, Sagalla community was rebuilt on local terms in the latter half of the decade. Chapter 3 moves into the 1890s, the decade of forcible colonial conquest, and early, predatory colonial rule. The weak colonial state did not yet significantly undermine local communities and their authority structures, but the first colonial-era threat to prior terms of community began to take shape, in the form of nascent Christian communities.

Chapter 4 focuses on how economic and political changes in the early twentieth century began to undermine local terms of community—particularly older men's ability to maintain their control over younger men. As colonial rule regularized, new political/administrative units and new Native Authority figures with new powers threatened older men's political predominance. At the same time, migrant labor and an emerging money economy threatened not only the older men's control over wealth, but their control over the very terms of wealth.

Chapter 5 introduces the older men's clamor of assertions about the existence of a Taita identity, and, as a corollary of it, Taita ways: *Kidaßida*. It situates those assertions in the context of colonial officials' receptiveness to ethnic categories, in colonial institutions that older men used to further their claims, and in the ways older men reconfigured ideas about local community belonging into a vision of Taita belonging. Older men's versions of Taita ways reclaimed their political and economic preeminence in the face of new challenges from Christians, young men, and young women. The chapter concludes with discussions of why people accepted the notion of a Taita ethnicity, but also how they challenged older men's terms of proper Taita ways from the very outset.

Chapters 6 and 7 track the ways that challengers gradually altered older generations' terms of proper Taita ways from the 1920s to the 1940s, even as they earnestly sought to maintain their sense of belonging in the community. These chapters look at a complex articulation of the migrant labor economy, the rise of cash–crop vegetable farming in the Hills, and the ways those economic changes played into extended household tensions over what counted as proper Taita work and wealth, and, between generations and genders, proper Taita *control* over work and wealth. The chapters also examine the continued spread of Christianity, the rapid growth of mission education, and the ways an ideological nexus of progressivism took shape as a counterweight to Taita ways. The combination of challenges by the young and the Christian, together with gradual generational turnover, slowly but definitely reworked what could pass as proper Taita ways. Even as Taita identity became fixed as a category of belonging, its content changed.

Chapter 8 analyzes how debates over Taita ways related to formal political issues. It looks at how popular distrust of colonial chiefs led many people in the Hills to support older men's views that chiefly authority lacked social legitimacy—and how, even with generational turnover, this view held constant. It then turns to the ways older men allied themselves with young political activists in the 1930s and 1940s, in a kind of politics that targeted the chiefs, the progressive Christian elite, and colonial officials. The lodestar issues behind these social tensions were European land seizures and colonial land–use rules for farming in the Hills. The politics were expressed, however, in a highly ethnicized idiom, for young activists seized upon old–style *Kidaßida* symbols to both cement their ties with older men, and to paint their opponents as either enemies of Taita or insufficiently Taita. The activists, however, used *Kidaßida* symbols and Taita identity to build a political coalition, not to inculcate everyday norms of social dominance. The power of older men to fashion the latter version of Taita identity had irrevocably declined.

1

Settlements and Societies in the Taita Hills, to the Late Nineteenth Century

Introduction

Geography is not exactly destiny in Taita, but it has powerfully influenced the history of the people who live there. The need to deal with Taita's physical distinctiveness—its many ecological zones, its complex topography, its apparently abundant but often unreliable rainfall, and its simultaneous isolation from/access to surrounding places and people—prompted the ancestors of Taita's modern inhabitants to fashion societies in particular ways. People in Taita lived amidst a giant labyrinth of steep slopes, multiple peaks, and crisscrossing ridges and valleys. From the 1600s to the 1800s, this encouraged localism and obstructed close connections across the Hills, yet to survive and prosper its inhabitants needed some wider networks of interaction. Some such ties linked subsections of Taita; others connected locales back to distant regions of ancestral origin.

Simultaneous separation and interaction became the warp and woof of life within the Hills, and also characterized Taita's place in the wider region. The latter is frequently summed up in geographical metaphor: many outside observers have called Taita an "island," and its inhabitants an "island people."[1] The metaphor, distinguishing between Taita and elsewhere, captures the Hills'

---

[1] Users of the metaphor include Joseph Thomson, "Through Masai Country to Victoria Nyanza," *Proceedings of the Royal Geographical Society* 6, 12 (1884): 692; J. Alfred Wray, *Kenya, Our Newest Colony: Reminiscences, 1882–1912* (London and Edinburgh, 1913), 15; Alfred and Grace Harris, introduction to "WaTaita Today," KNA, DC/TTA/4, bound typescript, 1955; and Andrew Nazarro, "Changing Use of the Resource Base among the Taita of Kenya" (Ph.D. diss., Michigan State University, 1974), 18.

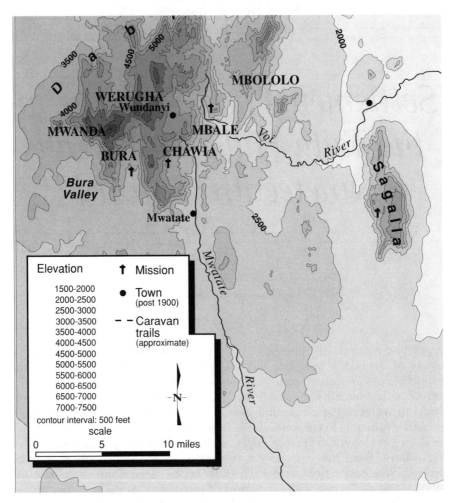

Map 1. The Taita Hills. Produced by UMBC Cartographic Laboratory.

prominence in the semi–arid plains of southeastern Kenya, for its heavily populated mountains rise abruptly from a flat, sparsely settled savannah. The next
densely settled areas lie at or beyond the horizon—in the mountains of what is
now northern Tanzania, or near the coast. Some writers elided the island metaphor from geography to sociology, suggesting that Taita's people had a long
tradition of isolation, and thus an insular Taita identity. One scholar explains
that 1950s–era WaTaita saw themselves as "living . . . a life of humanity and
domestication," compared to outsiders living less full lives out among "the
dangers of the wild" in the savannah.[2] Local ideology boiled down oppositions

---

[2]   Grace Harris, *Casting Out Anger: Religion among the Taita of Kenya* (Cambridge, 1978), 5–6.

of domesticity/danger and superiority/inferiority into the Hills versus the plains.

While the island metaphor nicely sums up one aspect of modern Taita consciousness, projecting it far back in time gives misleading impressions of the longer history of both Taita and the wider region. Historical analysis of regional processes of separation and interaction leads to a very different picture of pre–twentieth–century life in Taita: it seems less of a solitary is-land, and more like part of an archipelago in a well–traveled sea. The three steep, topographically complex mountains of Taita, occupied piecemeal through multiple small migrations, led to the establishment of communities at some remove from (and often hostile to) each other. However, the societ-ies maintained migration and trade ties with distant ancestral areas, and established new trading and migration links with other societies across the savannah. Taita's societies did over time develop ways to interact peace-ably with one another, and gradually built up a repertoire of sociocultural commonalities and similarities. Before the twentieth century, though, *local* societies within Taita shaped communities, defined the terms and issues of social struggles, and formed the basis of social identities. Taita was thus neither isolated nor a social monolith.

Taita Geography

The Taita Hills consist of a massif complex with multiple peaks, plus two smaller mountains.[3] From 1,500-foot plains in the east, the Hills climb steeply to 7,241 feet at the summit of the tallest peak. The three Hills and interspersed plains cover about five hundred square miles,[4] dominated by the large massif of Dabida. Dabida is a hundred miles west–northwest of the coastal city of Mombasa. From the seventeenth to nineteenth centuries, Dabida's most impor-tant trade center was Barawa, at the mouth of the Bura Valley.[5] A major trade route from Mombasa to what is now northern Tanzania passed this way. The major trade route between Mombasa and the central Kenyan highlands passed along the eastern side of Dabida.

Seven miles east of Barawa, and astride both old trade routes, stands Sagalla Mountain. Thirty miles southeast from Barawa and eighteen miles south of Sagalla is the smallest and least populated of the Hills, Kasigau. From Kasigau, Tanzania's Usambara mountains rise in the remote southern sky. From all Taita, the Pare mountains stretch across the west–to–south

---

[3]   For an overview map, see the Survey of Kenya, Series Y503, Sheet SA–37–14.

[4]   M. G. Power, "English Local Government in Taita District, Kenya," *Journal of African Adminis-tration* 6, 1 (1954).

[5]   Bura was a popular resting point for caravans; interviews with CA, Ilole/Bura, 17/8/1988; and Mrs. SM, Mwanda/Mwanda, 14/9/1988. See also the missionary Johannes Rebmann's account of resupplying his caravan at Bura in 1848; J. L. Krapf, *Travels, Researches, and Missionary Labours dur-ing an Eighteen Years' Residence in Eastern Africa* (1860; reprint, New York, 1968), 231.

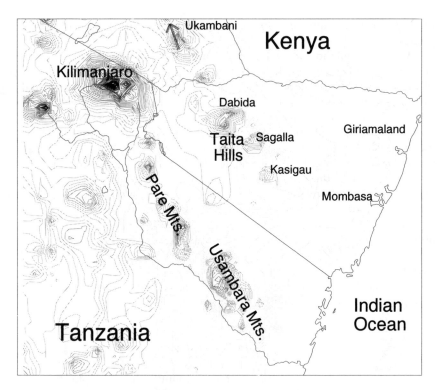

Map 2.   Taita's wider regional setting. Produced by Dana Kuan.
Source: Australia National University (CRES) and ESRI, Inc.

horizon. West of Dabida, Kilimanjaro looms in the distance.[6] The plains between the Taita Hills and those other highlands supported only scattered
human settlement in past centuries. Farther north and northwest the plains
become more hospitable: by the eighteenth century, Kamba settlers there
built up a major trade route that skirted Taita.[7] Maa speakers often roamed
the plains to the immediate west and south. In the distant east, on the coastal
hinterland, lay Giriama country.

The area's history from 1600 to 1900 was shaped by migrations and interactions with people in these nearby and middle–distant areas. The resulting
webs of ties gave modern WaTaita decidedly heterogeneous origins and far–

[6]   Kasigau is seventy–five miles from Shambaa. At their nearest points, Dabida and the Pare Mountains are about forty miles apart. Again at the nearest points, Dabida and Kilimanjaro are separated by fifty miles.

[7]   Kennell Jackson, "Dimensions of Kamba Pre–Colonial History," in *Kenya Before 1900*, ed. B. A.
Ogot (Nairobi, 1976), 183–214. Also interview with GM, Tausa/Mbololo, 31/5/1988, who mentions
that small bands of Kamba traders often settled temporarily at Ndii, on the plains at the northern
tip of Dabida, in the nineteenth century.

flung networks of kinship claims. People's responses to catastrophes such as drought or war involved reliance upon those extensive regional ties, and connected Taita into regional production, trade, warfare, and labor networks in the nineteenth and twentieth centuries.[8] Wide regional ties also, paradoxically, undergirded community localization in subsections of the Taita Hills, and the fractious, sometimes violent relations between those subsections before 1900.

People coming to Taita soon found out that its environment presented many challenges. Many new migrants and outsiders at first thought the Hills a place of natural abundance:

> How splendid the whole landscape, with its rich variety of mountain, hill, and dale, covered by the most luxurious vegetation! I could have fancied myself on the Jura mountains, near Basel, . . . so beautiful was the country, so delightful the climate. Our way was across the bed of a mountain stream, over hill and dale, through plantations of Indian corn and beans, . . . then along fields of sugar–cane and banana, till we descended into the [Bura] valley, with its rich pasturelands.[9]

However, those who lingered learned what Taita's inhabitants knew all too well, that droughts frequently occurred. Such experiences made their prose more terse: "Taita is not a land with water gushing out of the hills in every direction and a land of plenty; it is but a land of famine and death."[10] People had to adapt their farming, herding, and drought survival strategies to the enormous differentiations of microclimate that occurred within Taita. Broadly, the Hills divide into three ecological zones. The low zone rises from the 1,500-foot plains to roughly 2,500 feet. Slightly sloped or rolling country that reaches the foot of the Hills, the low zone is fed by only a few streams, has little permanent water, and receives sporadic rainfall even in wet seasons. Only the rainiest part of a typical year supports much cultivation there. However, the low zone abounds in good grazing land.

Next is the middle zone, ranging between 2,500 feet and 4,000 feet. Here the hills ascend steeply, cut by many ridges and valleys. Climates vary considerably within this zone, ranging from well–watered sections to arid stretches that merge into the low zone. The bulk of farming in Taita took place in the middle zone before the twentieth century. It is usually well fed by streams, swamps, rain, and irrigation works, though all can dry up in a prolonged drought.[11] The upper zone stretches from 4,000 feet to the mountain tops. The

---

[8] Feierman shows how situating the history of an area in different geographical contexts alters one's perspective on it. One can alternately see Shambaa history as that of a ruling elite protecting and exploiting its populace, and as the partial subordination of Shambaa into the Zanzibari political–economic orbit. See Feierman, *Intellectuals*, 106.

On the heterogeneity of Taita origins, see Peter Bostock, *The Peoples of Kenya: The Taita* (London, 1950), 4–8; E. Hollis Merritt, "A History of the Taita of Kenya to 1900" (Ph.D. diss., Indiana University, 1975), 47–74; A. H. J. Prins, *The Coastal Tribes of the Northeastern Bantu* (London, 1952), 102–103.

[9] Johannes Rebmann, on an 1848 visit to Taita, quoted in Krapf, *Travels*, 232.

[10] Wray to Lang, 29/3/1884, CMS Correspondence, G3/A5/01.

[11] On irrigation works, see Joseph Thomson, *Through Masai–land*, 3d ed. (London, 1968), 43; and C. W. Hobley, "Upon a Visit to Tsavo and the Taita Highlands," *Geographical Journal* 5, 6 (1895), 550.

Photo 1. Yale Peak, from elsewhere on Dabida, early 1930s. Margaret Murray Photo Collection, courtesy of Kenya National Archives and Documentation Service. #138/81.

upper zone is often cool and wet: rain, springs, and foggy mist make it a catchment area for the Hills. Some parts of the upper zone have been maintained as forest, some are barren and rocky, and still others have long been farmed. Irrigation works that have snaked down the Hills since the nineteenth century have their origins in the upper zone.[12]

Dabida, the main massif, has several peaks, each descending into large ridge/valley drainage systems. Small ridges and valleys are laced inside the larger ones. The large ridge/valley systems of different peaks interdigitate, adding to the labyrinthine effect. Cultivation is oriented around drainages; before the twentieth century the most valued fields abutted swamps in the middle and lower zones. The combination of altitude zones, ridges and valleys, plus differing rainfall tendencies, water access, vegetation, and soils all contributed to Taita's plethora of microclimates. As a broad generalization, people long used the richest, best watered fields for sugar cane and bananas. Other wet or dry fields might sustain a variety of crops, depending on altitude, season, and historical epoch. Most herding took place in the plains, though households up in the Hills often kept a few milk cows nearby.

Middle and upper zone planting precedes the November–December short rains (*sumesu*); planting in lower fields takes place around the long rains (*kwari*), which fall from March to May.[13] If rains fail, low zone crops are likely to wither, and middle and upper zone ones can quickly be imperiled. Before the twentieth century, if two successive rains failed virtually all Taita faced famine—and devastating droughts and famines have punctuated the history of the Hills. Consequently, that history is also marked by efforts to develop social and spiritual means to avert and/or cope with famine.[14] People shaped landholding patterns and social institutions to minimize a drought's impact or respond to a famine's ravages. They also fostered some interconnections beyond (and to some degree across) the Hills.

Patterns of Settlement

The ways that migrants came to settle Taita's terrain encouraged localization of communities and social identity down through the nineteenth century.[15] Although commonalities, similarities, and bridges did develop between communities, they did not give rise to a Taita–wide sense of community. Shared Taita–

---

[12]   The best sources on Taita geography are Alfred Harris, "The Social Organization of the WaTaita" (Ph.D. diss., Cambridge University, 1958); and Nazarro, "Changing Use." On climatic zones, A. Harris, "Organization," chap. 1. On irrigation, Patrick Fleuret, "The Social Organization of Water Control in the Taita Hills, Kenya," in *American Ethnologist* 13 (1985): 108–16.

[13]   For more detail on the agricultural cycle, A. Harris, "Organization," chap. 3.

[14]   For a thorough study of how drought, famine, and disease affected the history of east/central Kenya in the nineteenth century, see Ambler, *Kenyan Communities*, especially 95–100, 115–52.

[15]   This argument demurs from that of Merritt, "History of the Taita," 79, 125–26; his study assumes that Taita should have become politically and socially centralized along the lines of Pare, Kilimanjaro, and Usambara, and explains that environmental crises arrested an otherwise likely process.

ness would not become a meaningful form of identity or action until the twentieth century, when the local grounds of society, economy, and polity began to shift under the weight of colonial–era changes.

Immigration and Emigration

The history of migration to Taita by the ancestors of its present inhabitants is difficult to chart with precision. Settlers came in several waves and ongoing trickles, across a long span of time, and from a variety of different directions. Taita settlement effectively has multiple sub–histories; any one remembrance of immigration addresses only a single aspect of it. I call these stories remembrances, for "tradition" implies a formalism of narrative structure and transmission not found in Taita. Relatively few WaTaita can list many generations of ancestors and offer tales of the distant past. It is not guarded, empowering knowledge; no designated experts preserve migration stories or deep genealogies.[16] Nor have I found origin stories purporting to speak for all Taita. Since people in Taita did not regard themselves as "one people" until the twentieth century, this comes as no surprise.

Taita's first known inhabitants date to the first millennium A.D. Two non–Bantu language–speaking people are thought to have lived in the Hills then. Nobody in modern Taita claims to know the origins of the first group, hunter–gatherers that modern WaTaita refer to as "Dorobo."[17] The second group of early inhabitants probably migrated from the Ethiopian highlands to Taita by perhaps the ninth century A.D. They are said to have built the first permanent dwellings there, and to have been agro–pastoralists. They purportedly displaced their hunter–gathering predecessors, by some combination of killing them, driving them off, and gradually absorbing them.[18]

---

[16] On Taita's lack of "professional" oral historians or formal oral traditions, see Merritt, "History of the Taita," 20–22. Since Taita has no formal traditions, remembrances form the bulk of oral evidence. These include recollections by interviewees about themselves, their parents, in–laws, and grandparents; and stories told to interviewees by parents and grandparents. Remembrances, no less than traditions, need cautious handling by scholars. See Bill Bravman, "Using Old Photographs in Interviews: Some Cautionary Notes about Silences in Fieldwork," *History in Africa* 17 (1990); Corinne Kratz, "Conversations and Lives" (paper given at a conference on "Words and Voices: Critical Practices of Orality in Africa and African Studies," Bellagio, Italy, 1997).

[17] "Dorobo" derives from the Maa *Il torrobo* (roughly, "poor person"). Maasai use it as an ethnym for Maa–speaking hunter–gatherers in western Kenya. The term also derisively implies short physical stature. Merritt reports that WaTaita treat "Dorobo" as a general term for "aboriginals." See Merritt, "History of the Taita," 28, 30–31.

[18] Merritt, "History of the Taita," 28–32, 35–46; Thomas Spear, *Kenya's Past: An Introduction to Historical Method in Africa* (Harlow, England, 1981), 53; he views the large number of Southern Cushitic loan words in KiDabida as evidence of Ethiopian origins for this early group. Also, A. G. Hollis, "The Origins of the People of Taveta," *The Taveta Chronicle* 20 (1900), Church Missionary Society Archives (hereafter called CMSA), G3 A5/015(b); July 1900); Bostock, *Taita*, 4–5; Prins, "Coastal," 103; J. A. Wray, *An Elementary Introduction to the Taita Language, Eastern Equatorial Africa* (London, 1894), 99; and Krapf, *Travels*, 399. There is also archeological evidence of early Bantu language speakers in the area, but they had left or been driven from the area before the arrival of Bantu speakers whose descendants remain in the Hills. See Robert Soper, ed., *Taita–Taveta District Socio–Cultural Profile* (Government of Kenya and Institute of African Studies/University of Nairobi, 1986), 29–31.

The Bantu language ancestors of the present population first began to enter the Hills during the mid–sixteenth century.[19] Most studies agree that these migrants came in many waves, from many directions, over a long period of time.[20] The multiwave, multidirectional pattern of immigration localized societies in the Hills from the outset. The first of the sixteenth–century immigrants are thought to have lived in southeast Somalia or northeast Kenya; a few modern WaTaita refer to that area by its legendary name, Shungwaya.[21] Migrants made their way down the coast over several generations until, according to remembrance, a man named Mwanda decided to move his and his sons' families from the coastal hills near Mombasa to the mountains dimly distant in the western sky. Most eventually came to Dabida, settling in an area now known as Mwanda.[22] Shortly afterwards, another Bantu language–speaking group arrived, again a lineage–based group, led by a man named Munya. This group, the Wanya, also had its origins in the migration down the coast, but now hailed from a different part of the littoral. According to most tellings, they followed the Voi River to the Hills.[23]

At Dabida, Munya's people tried to settle near Mwanda's. In short order, a feud developed. Eventually, Munya's son, Walo, moved the Wanya to a part of Dabida now known as Mgange. Further migrants, with origins in the Juba River area of southern Somalia, also arrived sometime in that era, making their way to the Mbale region of Dabida.[24] A fourth group of Bantu language migrants reached the Hills in the late seventeenth century, from a different direction. A man named Ngasu brought his people down the Athi River from Ukambani, where they settled peaceably among the people of both Mwanda and Mgange. These people are said to have brought iron smelting skills with them.[25]

---

[19] James Mwakio, "The Origins of Wataita, Their Culture, and Their Political Evolution between the Early Sixteenth Century and 1963" (Master's thesis, University of Nairobi, 1978), chap. 2; Merritt, "History of the Taita," 45–50.

[20] They accord, too, with my limited research on the subject. One hundred seven of my interview respondents claimed knowledge of their origins in 1988–1989; a further twenty–one did so in 1993. While many claimed to come from the coast near Kilifi, many others cited Giriama and Duruma. Also commonly named were Pare, Usambara, Kilimanjaro, Ukambani and Maasai country.

The main studies are Merritt, "History of the Taita"; Bostock, *Peoples of Kenya*; Nazaro, "Changing Use"; Mwakio, "Origins of Wataita"; A. H. J. Prins, "An Outline of the Descent System of the Teita, a Northeastern Bantu Tribe," in *Africa* 20 (1950); and Prins, "Coastal." Only Mwakio argues that the main migration to Taita came from one area. His treatment of oral and linguistic evidence, however, is highly selective. See Mwakio, "Origins of Wataita," chap. 2.

[21] Seven interviewees claimed Shungwaya origins. For credulous and cautionary views about the existence of Shungwaya, see Neville Chittick, "The Coast before the Arrival of the Portuguese," in *Zamani: A Survey of East African History*, 2d ed., ed. B. A. Ogot (Nairobi, 1974), 107; and Spear, *Past*, 57. Spear also postulates that other settlers must have preceded the Bantu–language migrants to Taita, and influenced their language. See Spear, *Past*, 55–56.

[22] Merritt, "History of the Taita," 50–52, 280.

[23] Ibid., 53–54 ; Mwakio charts a different route for the Wanya, saying that they came to Taita via the Usambara mountains. Mwakio, "Origins of Wataita," chap. 2.

[24] Merritt, "History of the Taita," 53–5, 281, 284.

[25] Ibid., 54–55, 135–36; though archeological evidence shows that iron had been made in Taita over a millennium earlier, the technology was lost to the area for a long time.

Except for Ngasu's people, the migrant groups in Dabida by the late 1600s had settled at some remove from each other, and relations between the initial settlements were strained. The groups had distantly related origins and similar languages, but had lived apart in the more recent past; here, they tended more to suspicion and feuding than to cooperation. Spurred by perceived weakness of others or by ecological crises, groups in different sections of Dabida often raided one another:

> In those early days, fighting was about ruthlessness! . . . No, they were not wars for land, it was to grab cattle. People would go from here [Chawia location] and take cattle in Mgange, or in Kishamba. Or if they were weak in Mbololo, they could go there. . . . If they lost their cattle to drought, they used the last of their strength to grab more. That is how the people of long ago lived here.[26]

During famines, too, groups might raid each other to meet their needs, or to take advantage of the weak.[27] Intra–Hills raids remained frequent occurrences for centuries thereafter.[28]

Immigrants came more frequently in the 1700s. They arrived from virtually every direction: Usambara, Pare, Ukambani, Kilimanjaro, the southern Mount Kenya area, parts of the coast, the lower reaches of the Tana River, and pastoral societies in the nearby plains.[29] Now, too, ancestors of Sagalla's modern inhabitants arrived, largely from the coast north of Mombasa.[30] Despite the proclivity of Taita's societies to hold one another at arm's length, and despite the propensity they soon developed for raiding areas across the plains, immigrants were welcomed by the Hills' inhabitants. By the mid–nineteenth century, warriors from Dabida had a formidable reputation, yet were also known to "receive strangers among them and treat them very civilly."[31] The two proclivities came together in the practice of kidnapping outsiders to fortify a local society. Raiders sometimes seized women and children, then incorporated them into the raiders' lin-

---

[26] Interview with SM, Wusi/Chawia, 29/7/1993.

[27] Several interviewees commented on early insecurity within Dabida due to raiding from one part to another; interviews with GM, Tausa/Mbololo, 31/5/1988; and EM, Wundanyi/ Werugha, 11/7/1988. Nineteenth–century missionaries also observed a good deal of raiding.

[28] "Long ago, you could not go from Sagalla towards Dabida with your cattle if you wanted to keep them! And if you went too close to Kasigau, you would lose them, that's that." Interview with JN, Teri/Sagalla, 23/8/1988.

[29] For, respectively, Usambara, Kamba, Pare, and Giriama origins, interviews with Mrs. MK, Nyolo/Bura, 15/8/1988; EM, Shigaro/Werugha, 13/4/1988; SM, Kidaya/Chawia, 10/5/1988; and Mrs. MN, Teri/Sagalla, 25/8/1988. Many in Taita claim that Mwanda's population garnered strong Maasai influences by absorbing Maa–speaking captives into local lineages, but Mwanda inhabitants see it as a very limited phenomenon. Interview with Mrs. SM, Mwanda/ Mwanda, 14/9/1988. On other places of ancestral origin for Taita's inhabitants, see Merritt, "History of the Taita," 60.

[30] In seventeen interviews across Sagalla in 1988 and 1993, every person claimed origins in Giriamaland. This homogeneity contrasts markedly with Dabida.

[31] Charles New, *Life, Wanderings, and Labours in Eastern Africa*, 3d ed., (London, 1971), 336.

eage.[32] Young female captives were most prized, for a captor could marry her without paying bridewealth, or receive bridewealth for her if she married another:

> Those who grabbed my [great–great] grandfather [in a raid on Pare] made him into their child, because the minute you were grabbed and brought here, the one who took him made him his child completely. . . . He'll bring him up and marry him a wife, then give him the farms (as inheritance). . . . That's how my father was born [well off], because my [great–great] grandfather was brought in that way and . . . started to get those blessings.[33]

New immigrants thus fortified lineage numbers; voluntary ones might also broker trade,[34] or bring new skills or crops.[35] The resulting mixture of immigrants led one historian to call the Hills "a melting pot of different peoples and cultures."[36]

Too, throughout these centuries many people left Taita. Drought and famine figured prominently in departures, as did conflicts within or between groups in the Hills.[37] Most emigrants went to Kilimanjaro, Usambara, and Pare.[38] Between immigration and emigration, the post–1600 histories of Dabida, Kasigau, and the hill societies of today's northern Tanzania became thoroughly intertwined.[39] Sagalla and Giriama also maintained close ties of

---

[32] A ritually sanctified goatskin bracelet identified the captive as incorporated and, (if male), an inheritor. Interview with NN, Wumari/Chawia, 15/8/1988. C. E. Gissing, a British Vice–Consul in 1880s East Africa, noted that female captives became wives, not slaves. Gissing, "A Journey from Mombasa to Mounts Ndara and Kasigau," *Proceedings of the Royal Geographical Society* 6, 10 (1884): 557–58. Nineteenth-century Europeans called Sagalla 'Ndara.'

[33] Interview with NN, Wumari/Chawia, 15/8/1988.

[34] Trade may have been especially salient for migrants from Ukambani in the late eighteenth century, when trade with Taita and the coast was expanding. Interview with GM, Tausa/Mbololo, 31/5/1988.

[35] Merritt emphasizes these latter two roles, "History of the Taita," 63.

[36] Spear, *Past*, 56.

[37] Merritt, "History of the Taita," 68–70, 74; and I. N. Kimambo, *Pare*, 31–37.

[38] On emigrants to Kilimanjaro, Charles Dundas, *Kilimanjaro and Its People* (1924; reprint, London, 1968), 43–45; Derek Nurse, "The Taita–Chaga Connection: Linguistic Evidence" (Institute of African Studies Paper 93, University of Nairobi, 1978). For migrations to Usambara from Kasigau, H. W. Woodward, "Kitaita or Kisighau as Spoken on the Shambala Hills above Bwiti," *Zeitschrift fur Kolonial Sprachen* 4, 2 (1913–1914): 91–92; Feierman adds that "the overwhelming majority" of Usambara's early descent groups came from Taita. See Steven Feierman, *The Shambaa Kingdom* (Madison, 1974), 72, 74 n. Much of Pare's ancestry also traces to Taita. See Kimambo, *Pare*, 13.

[39] For instance, oral accounts in Pare, Shambaa, and Kilimanjaro all trace settlement and initial sociopolitical organization to lineage–based groups, as in Taita. Feierman describes Shambaa society as rooted in lineages, with lineage practices in many respects similar to those in Taita. Feierman, *Shambaa*, 31–37, and chap. 3.

See, too, Feierman's description of how medical practitioners in Shambaa augmented their training by going to other regions like Taita; Feierman, *Intellectuals*, 102. Kimambo also discusses how a local chief in Pare sought to augment his power by importing witch–finding medicines from Taita that would enhance his authority. See Kimambo, *Pare*, 149–50.

language and culture into the twentieth century.[40] Frequent small–scale movements of people continually reshaped and reinforced these interconnections, making eighteenth– and nineteenth–century Taita, despite its physical remove and internal social fractiousness, very much a part of overlapping regional systems.[41]

Geography, Resources, and the Development of Social Units

Fashioning Local Linkages

By the nineteenth century, lineage–based settlement of Taita had led to the firm establishment of patrilineage as the pillar of local societies' organization, land utilization, economic activity, authority relations, and cosmological order. In Shambaa, one lineage had by then imposed its political authority over Usambara (if in a contested, and in some locales, sporadic and secondhand way). One lineage also tried to extend its domination over Pare.[42] In Taita, no lineage ever tried to carve out political dominance over the Hills. Instead, a lineage controlled resources within a subsection of the Hills, the crucial resources being land, livestock, and people. Lineages did, however, build ties beyond their own numbers: to cope with the vagaries of terrain, climate, and weather, they developed connections to other groups, both within and beyond their own subsection of the Hills.

The terrain all but required a lineage to spread out its landholdings. Different seasons made some fields and grazing lands more viable for use, others less so. Generally, the most important variations were vertical.[43] A lineage needed land in different microclimates in order to produce food throughout the year. For instance, low zone, dry fields were planted January to March, in preparation for the long rains; those fields could not reliably sustain crops during the short–rains growing season.[44] Without diversification, people were vulnerable to deprivation. Diversification also provided the first line of defense against drought, for rains sometimes fell in one zone even when they went missing in another.

---

[40]   Interviews with Mrs. MN, Kizumanzi/Sagalla, 24/8/1988; and LM, Teri/Sagalla, 23/8/1988; when a ferocious drought struck Sagalla in the 1880s, nearly all its inhabitants fled to Giriamaland.

[41]   It was also at the fringe of other regional systems. For instance, Zanzibar's destabilizing impact on Shambaa increased Dabida cattle and captive raids on Shambaa, though Taita had little direct involvement with the Zanzibari slaving economy.

[42]   Feierman, *Shambaa*, and *Intellectuals*; Willis, *Bonde*; Kimambo, *Pare*.

[43]   There are, of course, qualifiers to this. Critical, too, are soil types and distinctions between a wet and dry field in the same zone. Interviews with JK, Kaya/Chawia, 3/5/1988; and MT, Kishamba/Chawia, 9/6/1988. Alfred Harris also notes geological differentiation along a southeast–to–northwest axis, with quartzite in the northerly section making human habitation more difficult. See A. Harris, "Organization," chap. 1.

[44]   Interview with Mrs. MM, Teri/Chawia, 22/7/1988. Also, A. Harris, "Organization," chap. 3.

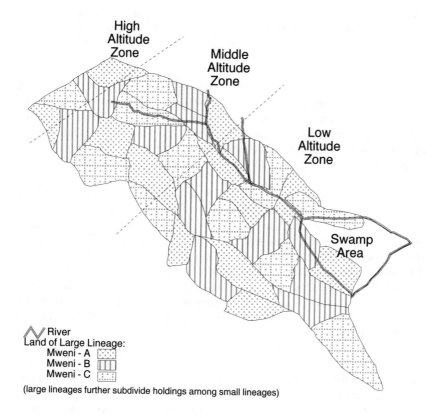

Diagram 1. Model of a low-zone based nineteenth-century Taita neighborhood. Produced by Dana Kuan.

Source: Author.

From early on, lineages built up landholdings with these concerns in mind. The resulting system dotted a lineage's fields up and down a ridge/valley drainage.[45] Its diversified holdings were interwoven with another one to three lineages' lands, forming a unit called a neighborhood (*izanga*).[46] Lineage elders oversaw the landholdings, ensuring that land in different climate zones was distributed widely enough among its members to give all an adequate means of subsistence:

---

[45] This pattern of landholding was universally commented upon. Interviewees, when asked the location of their own, their fathers', or their husbands' fields, named several areas with considerable variation in altitude, soil quality, and/or source of water.

[46] This, too, is common knowledge in Taita; on *izanga*, interviews with OK, Shigaro/Werugha, 6/4/1988; and KM, Tausa/Mbololo, 2/6/1988.

The elders were there to ensure that everyone got a portion—every-one. If you missed [land] what would you eat? . . . And if you didn't have a cow, you must be given one by your father . . . or an uncle, so your children could be given milk.[47]

Interviews indicate that individual property rights existed by no later than the mid–nineteenth century, though circumscribed by lineage controls.[48] Male members of a lineage commonly rented or sold land within a neighborhood, in exchange for other fields, animals, and/or *chofi* (sugar cane beer). Women had no formal land disposal rights, but often arranged informal, short–term land exchanges; they did more farming than men and often knew better the specifics of household needs and plot boundaries.[49]

Lineage livestock fostered still wider networks of interconnection. Most livestock were grazed below the Hills, in the surrounding plains. Most of that plains pasturage lay beyond the boundaries of any neighborhood: all treated it as an open resource, not subject to exclusive lineage rights. Still, for convenience and security, lineages tended to keep their plains livestock more or less directly below the neighborhood in which they lived. A lowland herd usually contained animals either from one lineage or from lineages in one neighborhood.[50] Teenage and adult men came down from the Hills, in four-day shifts, to graze them.[51] Women also went down to the plains to bring the herders food and carry milk back.[52]

Grazing needs and the desire for safe travel encouraged highlands–based lineages to foster relations with lineages based in adjacent lower reaches. Sometimes interlineage bonds were contained within one neighborhood; then, exchanges of land or livestock among the lineages helped knit the neighborhood together. Sometimes, though, connections crossed neighborhood boundaries. In those cases, the ties took a few different forms. A common one was livestock exchanges between lineages in vertically adjacent neighborhoods. This spread out a lineage's holdings, and, hence, its vulnerabilities to livestock raids and disease. Interconnections based in livestock exchanges had the collateral benefit of making raids between the allied parties unlikely.[53] Another form of tie was blood brotherhood (*mtero*), which cemented individual bonds between people not linked by lineage or neighborhood. Alliances and blood brotherhoods gave people some assurance of

---

[47]   Interview with OK, Shigaro/Werugha, 29/4/1988.

[48]   Interviews with PN, Ngerenyi/Chawia, 9/5/1988; EK, Ndome/Mbololo, 22/6/1988; and MM, Mwanda/Mwanda, 12/9/1988.

[49]   Among women, this, too, was common knowledge. Interviews with Mrs. DM, Shigaro/Werugha, 30/5/1988; and Mrs. FM, Lushangonyi/Mwanda, 21/9/1988.

[50]   Interviews with KM, Tausa/Mbololo, 2/6/1988; EK, Ndome/Mbololo, 20/6/1988; and SM, Mrugua/Bura, 19/8/1988; and WM, Choke/Mbale, 11/11/1988.

[51]   Interviews with SM, Ndome/Mbololo, 28/6/1988; SM, Kishamba/Sagalla, 23/8/1988.

[52]   Interviews with PM, Wundanyi/Werugha, 25/4/1988; and MM, Nyolo/Bura, 15/8/1988.

[53]   Alliances between vertically adjacent neighborhoods might survive a prolonged drought, but people from other neighborhoods would likely conduct raids.

personal safety in a region where movement outside one's neighborhood was fraught with danger.

Local Networks and Control over Persons

A lineage's leaders also sought to increase its size and control its members. For both purposes, leaders tried to maintain close control over women and young men. Attempts to control people, unlike land and livestock, did not foster wider webs of interconnection; instead, ties binding people to their lineages and locales were emphasized. Marriage, for instance, leaned heavily towards lineage endogamy. The ideology behind this emphasized maintaining control over people and their labor power, which were scarcer resources than land. This applied most crucially to women, who carried the lineage's potential for natural increase.[54] The main exceptions to lineage endogamy were marriages meant to reinforce ties between lineages in the same neighborhood.[55] Lineages became multilayered social units as their size grew. Though it is not clear exactly when and how, perhaps by no later than the early nineteenth century a distinction between the "large lineage" (*kichuku kibaha*) and the "small lineage" (*kichuku kitini*) existed among many societies on Dabida.[56] Perhaps the large lineage/small lineage distinction was made among some migratory groups to Taita as far back as the 1600s, but one interviewee confidently said no:

> Very long ago, our ancestors did not have these *vichuku vibaha* and *vichuku vitini*. No! They were just small groups, our ancestors. They . . . stuck close to each other, because they were afraid of strangers. When they raised enough people . . . and grabbed people and had enough cows, then they could have many doors [i.e., small lineage segments]. Many doors! But when they reached Taita, they were just few–few.[57]

By no later than the mid–nineteenth century, large and small lineage were virtually universal social units. A large lineage had its reference point in an ancestor credited with the lineage's settlement in that part of the Hills, or at least in an ancestor of minimally five generations back.[58] The large lineage defined the outer limit on claims to a common descent line, and on claims to landholding:

---

[54] "You marry within the . . . lineage to keep together with others in your lineage, . . . to keep wealth together within your lineage." Interview with MM, Ilole/Bura, 17/8/1988.

[55] A. Harris, "Organization," chap. 6.

[56] SM, Tausa/Mbololo, 3/6/1988 and JM, Wundanyi/Werugha, 15/7/1988 named nine and ten generations (respectively) of descent in their large lineages, and claim small lineages went back as far.

[57] Interview with OK, Shigaro/Werugha, 2/8/1993. *Vichuku vibaha* and *vichuku vitini* are the plural forms of large lineage and small lineage.

[58] Large lineages in the colonial period had roughly 500–700 members. See A. Harris, "Organization," chap. 6. In the nineteenth century, with population densities lower and more land available, they may have been smaller.

members of a large lineage had access rights to a portion of its land. The large lineage also formed the main large unit of religious practice.[59]

A small lineage, a segment of a large lineage, comprised four generations of descent from a common ancestor. The small lineage defined, among other things, the group over whom its oldest living men—its elders—in principle had direct authority. In practice, an older man's authority was also shaped by a host of factors like wealth, patronage, and ritual position.[60] A powerful elder's influence reached into the large lineage and the neighborhood; a weak elder might have trouble holding sway over small lineage members and resources. The small lineage also had extensive practical control over property: it apportioned its lands among its members, subject to occasional interventions from large lineages in times of crisis or large lineage–wide inequities adjudged gross and wrong. Finally, the small lineage marked the effective boundary of an inheritance group. Small lineages were strictly exogamous.

The Interplay of Similarity and Distinction

The consolidation of similar lineage structures across nineteenth–century Taita was one of several sociocultural similarities and commonalities that took shape across the region. They pose a puzzle: did several immigrant groups bring similar social and cultural forms with them, abetting the growth of Taita–wide similarities? Did social and cultural forms from one or a few groups come to predominate, and if so, how? Unfortunately, there is little evidence to apply to these questions. Did groups in the Hills develop similar social and cultural forms in response to similar conditions of life? Evidence suggests so, but does not obviate the likelihood that some migrants' social and cultural forms would flower and spread—for if Taita could hardly support all immigrants' prior practices, neither did it empty their heads of all prior ways and outlooks. Did intra–Taita migration play a role? Probably, for it happened a great deal, and increasing similarities within the region would logically follow from it.[61] Again, however, evidence for the inference is scant.

It *is* clear, though, that while broadly similar social structures spread across the Hills up to and through the 1800s, the structures emphasized local distinctiveness and local autonomy. The localism of the structures may have abetted their adoption, for they did not threaten to usurp the autonomy of Taita's local societies. Broad similarities and commonalities allowed people to recognize

---

[59] Many people made the point about nineteenth–century land access, including OK, Shigaro/Werugha, 29/4/1988; and Mrs. HM, Ndome/Mbololo, 21/6/1988. For which group rituals were performed by large lineage, and which by neighborhood in the late colonial period, see G. Harris, *Casting*, 122–36.

[60] Alfred Harris describes *kichuku kitini* at length in "Organization," chap. 6.

[61] Intraregional migrations were small–scale and quite common. When people moved within Taita, they severed ties in their old area, in favor of new ties in their new area. In some cases old lineage ties were lost to memory, but in many others people knew what lineages their ancestors left. Interviews with SK, Wundanyi/Werugha, 15/4/1988; Mrs. RM, Chawia/Chawia, 16/6/1988; Mrs. WM, Werugha/Werugha, 30/7/1993.

many words and ways of other societies in the Hills, facilitating some interconnections. However, the only meaningful large groups in the Hills remained the ones drawing upon kinship and neighborhood ideologies.

Elders' Authority in Local Societies

Localized Formal Authority

Authority within large and small lineages lay in the hands of male lineage elders, who continually reinforced it over women and younger men through control over lineages' material resources, and through domination of jural and religious institutions. Old age did not automatically bestow elderhood status. It also required accumulation of livestock and land, political–economic network building, and the achievement of high standing within the lineage–based religion (roughly similar across Taita), *Wutasi*.[62] Hubris or excessive pride purportedly hurt a man's ability to advance in ritual standing, in turn limiting his stature as an elder.[63]

Elders had jural and ritual responsibilities, not tight bureaucratic control over people.[64] Elders controlled the land and livestock of their small lineage, and, through that control over property, exercised authority over a lineage's women (who needed access to the resources), and young men (who needed the support of their elders to marry, set up their own households, and climb the ladder towards elderhood themselves).[65]

Authority brought reciprocal responsibilities. A father acknowledged sons' labors by providing them bridewealth livestock. An older man could also expect to provide fields to junior households in his small lineage: young couples typically began to have plots "cut" for them when they married, and received further ones over time. Women could not own land or livestock, but had fairly extensive usage rights to men's property. Still, an elder's ownership or disposal rights over his small lineage property did not cease until his death.[66] Adult sons might acquire some land and a few head of livestock independently, but even those might come under the *de facto* control of fathers until the senior men died.[67]

Younger men who resisted their seniors' authority might have property that would normally be passed to them reduced or withheld. By definition,

---

[62] Interviews with OM, Wundanyi/Werugha, 5/5/1988; CA, Ilole/Bura, 17/8/1988; and GM, Kishamba/Chawia, 24/9/1988. Also see Mwakio, "Origins of Wataita," chap. 3; and G. Harris, *Casting*, 66–71, 74–76.

[63] Interview with Mrs. SM, Mwanda/Mwanda, 14/9/1988; several others commented obliquely on this. See also Mwakio, "Origins of Wataita," chap. 3; A. and G. Harris, "Wataita Today," 39–40.

[64] This was common knowledge in Taita; it was discussed at some length in an interview with SM, Teri/Sagalla, 24/8/1988.

[65] Interview with AK, Shigaro/Werugha, 25/4/1988.

[66] On transmission of lineage property from older to younger men, interviews with Mrs. AM, Ndome/Mbololo, 20/6/1988; Mrs. GM, Shigaro/Werugha, 15/7/1988; and PN, Ngerenyi/Chawia, 9/5/1988; dozens of less detailed discussions could be cited.

[67] A. Harris describes inheritance in "Organization," chap. 7; also, interviews with SS, Tausa/Mbololo, 3/6/1988; and RM, Mlondo/Werugha, 27/9/1988.

threats to property ownership rights did not pertain to women, but women's use rights could have become vulnerable in various ways. A wife thought troublesome could see another of her husband's wives given better fields to farm.[68] Too, senior men could pressure women to conform by making their access to lineage networks of social support difficult. For example, communal labor to clear a woman's main fields for a season might come slowly.[69] Furthermore, women who often crossed the older men in their lineage jeopardized their sons' or husbands' inheritance possibilities.

Elders' formal authority came into play during small or large lineage disputes, and, for influential elders, neighborhood–wide cases.[70] After spokesmen for the accused, accusing, or disputing parties presented their arguments to the gathered elders, the elders discussed the matter for as long as several days, then gave their judgment.[71] The sanction power behind the verdict lay partly in the weight of their collective seniority, and partly in medicines and rituals they could use to curse the recalcitrant or perpetrators of heinous crimes.[72]

Localized Religious Outlooks

Religious organization, doctrines, and rituals also turned on lineage and neighborhood, reinforcing other localizations of social life across Taita. Similarities of religious belief did spread through the Hills. Indeed, enough commonality existed for *Wutasi* (from the verb *kutasa* [to pray/offer libation]) to gain wide acceptance as the name for religion in the Hills. Nevertheless, said one interviewee, "Each lineage . . . had their own shrine center; ours was for ours, and theirs for theirs. . . . They were not for mixing."[73] As late as 1950:

> [n]o ritual united all Taita as participants, nor was there one in which all communities or lineages were represented. No ritual was supposed to benefit the entire country in a specific way. [Ritual experts and shrines] were distributed throughout Taita by virtue of their attachment to lineages and neighbourhoods.[74]

Local distinctiveness also ran through many *Wutasi* forms. For instance, while all Taita's local societies conducted initiation into adulthood, there was no common term for it: Sagalla society called it *Kirindi*, while on most of Dabida it was known as *Mwari*. *Kirindi* rituals, fairly uniform in Sagalla, operated differ-

---

[68]   Interview with Mrs. PH, Mwanda/Mwanda, 3/8/1993.

[69]   Ibid.

[70]   The specific group of elders who convened in a given case depended on the lineages of the disputants.

[71]   This jural process was described in detail by OM, Wundanyi/Werugha, 25/3/1988 and 5/5/1988.

[72]   For a description of elders' juridical oaths and medicines, see G. Harris, *Casting*, 38–40.

[73]   Interview with MM, Mruru/Bura, 15/8/1988.

[74]   G. Harris, *Casting*, 122.

ently than those of *Mwari*. *Mwari* itself divided into a panoply of different practices on different parts of Dabida.[75]

Wutasi, like religions elsewhere, offered ways to address life's vagaries.[76] It provided explanations and technologies for coping with illness, intergenerational conflict, interpersonal strife, and drought. But it also helped older men manage their lineages and neighborhoods: in small lineages, it reinforced and justified elder men's control over women and young men, and parents' control over children. It made the large lineage the main unit of shared spiritual and ritual responsibility, within which elders exercised authority through their specialized knowledge of how to diagnose problems, prescribe solutions, and proactively ensure a lineage's well–being. Several *Wutasi* rituals also sought to ensure the peace, safety, and prosperity of neighborhoods, thereby strengthening neighborhood solidarity as against outside threats.

Wutasi focused on relationships between living persons and *Mlungu* (the creator and maintainer of the universe), and on those between the living and the spirits of their deceased large lineage ancestors (*ßaramu*). *Mlungu* and *ßaramu* were seen as able to intervene in the patent world to cause drought, famine, and illness, if angered by an individual's evil or by moral decay in a lineage or neighborhood. Too, one's actions or emotions made impressions on *ßaramu*, who were sensitive to dissension. *ßaramu* could bring misfortune to people who disrupted the peace of their lineage by fighting or "holding anger for each other in their hearts."[77] *Wutasi* then provided means for divining problems, along with rituals of remedy.[78] The ritual would appease the *ßaramu*, and so rid the living of their misfortune.

---

[75] For instance, on Sagalla and some parts of Dabida, girls' and boys' initiations were mandatory and equally important. In other parts of Dabida, both were mandatory, but female initiation was far more socially significant. In still other parts of Dabida, boys' initiation was optional. Interviews with DM, Teri/Sagalla, 10/7/1993; Mrs. GM, Teri/Sagalla, 24/8/1988; MM, Mwanda/Mwanda, 15/9/1988; Mrs. SM, Ilole/Bura, 16/8/1988; MW, Ghazi/Mbololo, 5/7/1988; Mrs. SM, Mogho Mleche/Mbale, 4/11/1988. Many other factors varied among local societies: the length of time devoted to initiation rituals, the particulars of the rituals, the arrangements for seclusion of initiates afterwards, the length of seclusions, whether both men and women were to be secluded. On and around Dabida, where the broadest tapestry of variations could be found, the basic social unit that bound the variations was the neighborhood.

[76] The point has been discussed by many scholars. Okot p'Bitek puts it directly: "Most of the religious activities in African religions seem to be part of the ways and means of dealing with existing or threatening dangers." See his *African Religions in Western Scholarship* (Nairobi, 1971).

More recently, Kirby has described this as the "problem–solving" aspect of African religions. Van Beek and Blakely regard it as part of religion's "instrumental nature." See Jon Kirby, "Cultural Change and Religious Conversion in West Africa," in *Religion in Africa: Experience and Expression*, ed. Thomas Blakely, Walter van Beek, and Dennis Thomson (London and Portsmouth, NH, 1994), 62–63; and Walter van Beek and Thomas Blakely, introduction to *Religion in Africa*, 10–13.

[77] Interview with PM, Ilole/Bura, 16/8/1988.

[78] For an overview of *Wutasi* in 1950, see G. Harris, *Casting*, 26–37. That much of its cosmology was in place by the 1860s is illustrated repeatedly in the accounts of European missionaries trying to evangelize Taita. The missionaries held local beliefs in contempt, but the rituals and outlook they described, nonetheless, inspire confidence that *Wutasi*'s cosmology had considerable continuity. The main missionary sources are the Church Missionary Society's Correspondence files relating to Taita; the personal diaries of J. Alfred Wray, the first missionary residing in Taita; the *Bulletins de la Congregation* of the French *Spiritans* (Holy Ghost Fathers); Krapf, *Travels*; and New, *Life, Wanderings*.

The main belief was that we live by the blessings and love of those who died. . . . In the same way, lack of children, lack of wealth, bad life, and being unsuccessful was because of an ancestor's anger. . . . The *Mlaghuli* [Diviner] . . . found the cause of your problem: which ancestor was angry, and what you could have done to bring the anger, and told you the problem will require this and this and this and this. . . . You go to do what? To do a sort of appeasement [to the ancestor], then you get rid of your problem.[79]

Wutasi rituals and cosmology informed many everyday activities, forging a close link between worldly behavior and cosmological order. Many *Wutasi* rituals, even as they maintained the peace of a lineage and/or neighborhood, regulated everyday behavior.[80] For example, each neighborhood ritually maintained a powerful defender medicine, *Fighi*, that guarded against outside dangers. People were enjoined not to dress or act like an outsider in the vicinity of a *Fighi*, lest it take them for one.[81] Too, when a neighborhood held rainmaking or crop furtherance rituals, not only was everyone's participation in the ritual necessary; people were admonished that when they upset the social peace, it angered ancestors and could cause environmental disasters.[82]

In these and other ways, *Wutasi* reinforced the lineage authority of older men. Often, divinations (done by elderly male ritual specialists) found that a younger person had angered a deceased ancestor by wrong behavior or angry emotions towards an older relative. The ritual to set this right enjoined the person who stirred up ancestral anger to alter their outlook or actions.[83] Conversely, parents' anger at a son who resisted their authority could cause misfortune in a lineage, necessitating a ritual in which the son would ease the ancestral anger, and offer a present to a living parent. At the worst, a recalcitrant son could be cursed.[84] Women's standing within *Wutasi* was subordinated to elder men's in ways that paralleled their overall subordination. Analogous to their usage rights in land and animals, women joined in prayers, and par-

---

[79]   Interview with JM, Kishamba/Chawia, 24/9/1988.

[80]   Interviews with GM, Kishamba/Chawia, 12/8/1988; and CA, Ilole/Bura, 17/8/1988; Mrs. EK, Wongonyi/Mbololo, 7/7/1988; and Mrs. SM, Werugha/Werugha, 30/9/1988.

[81]   G. Harris, *Casting*, 9, 125, and interviews with MC, Ndome/Mbololo, 20/6/1988; and MM, Ilole/Bura, 17/8/1988.

[82]   G. Harris, *Casting*, 127–36.

[83]   For instance, OK, Shigaro/Werugha, 22/8/1993, described how his great–great grandfather fell sick "for many years," until it was diagnosed that one of his sons "held a bitterness to that old man," and the appropriate ritual appeasements were performed. He later recovered. This example speaks to the three senses of religion's instrumentalism asserted by van Beek and Blakely: *Wutasi* here diagnosed tensions within society, and, through religious performance, addressed them. However, this was not a steady–state, structural/functional system; such a ritual did not resolve underlying generational and/or gender tensions. Rather, it supported an asymmetry of power that was subject to periodic challenges.

[84]   Interview with MM, Nyolo/Bura, 15/8/1988. The idea that a son could be cursed for resisting parental authority did not disappear with the rise of the colonial economy: The father of FM, Kidaya/Chawia, 12/5/1988, threatened to curse him, allegedly for not remitting a large enough portion of his migrant labor wages.

ticipated in most *Wutasi* rituals.[85] Women's participation was often a necessary component of small lineage, large lineage, or neighborhood rites.[86]

Despite that participation, knowledge of rituals and medicines, acquisition of personal shrines, and attainment of ritual offices—all ways of accounting someone influential—were closed to women and young men. Older men kept specialized knowledge of *Wutasi* close to the chest by explaining that others were incapable of understanding or using it:

> A woman could not be an elder. Women could not pray [*kutasa*] with proper beer! . . . How could they have the knowledge of elders? Could they control [powerful medicines]? No.[87]

> The old men of the past, the power they had was in their knowledge. They said that their expertise in medicines, . . . in rainmaking, were because they had gotten the wisdom that comes with age—you could only get the wisdom when you were old.[88]

Through *Wutasi*, elders developed ways to render their authority over women and young men self-evidently proper. Challenges to older men's authority could be defined as wrongful behavior that upset the natural order and wreaked havoc on society. This is not to say that older men cynically manipulated religious symbols and cosmological ideas for their self–aggrandizement; they, too, thought the system natural, even as they worked it to reproduce their power.

Community Belonging

The Construction of Community

If a community can be described as a group within which people foster ongoing relationships, share terms of reference, and derive a common social identity, then lineage and neighborhood surely were communities for people in nineteenth–century Taita. Furthermore, the dense, mutually reinforcing networks of lineage and neighborhood made them the people's main communities.[89] They were knit together by claims of kinship, land and livestock exchange, commitments to mutual support, intermarriage, shared rights and responsibilities to property, and religious bonds that bound individuals' well–being to the groups' well–being. In times of trouble, they were the group of first recourse:

---

[85] Interview with Mrs. WM, Mrugua/Bura, 19/8/1988.

[86] Women took part in blood brotherhood pacts (*mtero*) between men; they also had prescribed roles in rituals at lineage shrines, and in most neighborhood rites. See G. Harris, *Casting*, 64.

[87] When women did (*ku*)*tasa*, they made libations with unfermented sugar cane juice. Interview with BM, Njawuli/Mwanda, 3/8/1993.

[88] Interview with JM, Kishamba/Chawia, 24/9/1988.

[89] Smaller groups, such as work groups and warrior groups, were subsets of lineage and neighborhood.

> Long ago, people clung to their *kichuku*. . . . When you were in trouble, you turned to someone of [SM's large lineage], they were the first to arrive, . . . then others in the neighborhood will come to know.[90]

However, community in lineage and neighborhood societies did not exist simply as kinship grids, relations of exchange, and religious institutions. The continuous seeking, fostering, and/or enforcing of enduring affective ties metamorphosed people's structural connections into a collective consciousness of community. Hegemonic bonds like "kinship" or *Wutasi* fleshed out lineage and neighborhood structures as *felt* communities—communities in which people invested deep attachments of belonging. People's sense of belonging grew most immediately from their daily networks of interdependence and cooperation, which fostered a need of and commitment to the corporate body. People in the group came to feel that in dealing with the world's demands and vagaries, their futures would and should be intertwined. Across the Hills, lineage writ large and small provided the bedrock unit of community. It situated mutual commitment and interreliance in stories of shared ancestry, valorizing the kin group as one of longstanding unity. In myriad ways, kinship claims continually socialized people into group commitment and reliance. *Wutasi* added spiritual weight to the ties, while its invoking of ancestral spirits bound community past to community present.

Neighborhood as a community of belonging also drew on daily interaction and cooperation. Neighborhood ideology did not weave quite as dense a fabric of belonging; appeals to its shared history of commitments and reliance required a bit more generalizing. It found expression in the belief that within (but not beyond) neighborhoods, people reliably "understood" each other. Though not exactly kin, neighbors were kindred:

> In those days, neighbors knew each other like [they knew] their own lineage. . . . They helped each other like a lineage. They understood each other like a lineage.[91]

Neighbors' mutual understanding valorized, and was reinforced by, several practices: interlineage marriages; multiple, overlapping cattle loans and temporary land exchanges; neighborhood–wide rituals of group well–being; and the organizing of neighborhood warrior groups for collective defense.

Through lineage and neighborhood communities, Taita's nineteenth–century inhabitants built networks of support, made claims on resources, and garnered security for old age. They sought high standing in a community; men hoped to exercise a senior elder's considerable authority over it. But one did

---

90   Interview with SM, Wusi/Chawia, 29/7/1993.
91   Interview with JM, Wundanyi/Werugha, 11/5/1988.

not automatically gain influence, so belonging in a community also involved jockeying to scale its hierarchies of wealth, power, and status.[92]

The Teeth of Community and Cultural Politics

Individuals could not simply choose whether to belong to Taita's nineteenth–century communities: virtually everyone in the Hills was either born into one or quickly incorporated. Nor did community belonging only derive from and foster supportive relationships. Communities enforced norms and terms of belonging, pressing members to conform to particular outlooks and actions. Those norms and terms, expressed as proper beliefs, practices, and behavior towards others, were predominantly set by, upheld by, and beneficial to older men, often at the expense of younger men and all women. Breaking with norms of community could jeopardize one's prospects within it, or, more direly, threaten rights—such as inheritance—that normally followed from community belonging:

> One man in our *kichuku*, [X], was always giving trouble. . . . He made sorcery, that one! . . . He was told [by his elders] to keep off the people. . . . [X] lived there, [NM points to far in the distance], at the end of our lands. . . . His father left him nothing.[93]

Nevertheless, some people challenged received ways, triggering ongoing, mostly low–level social struggles. Those struggles, often between generations and genders over norms and terms of community, shaped the terrain of cultural politics.

Cultural politics (i.e., attempts to change, circumvent, or maintain received social norms and hierarchies), rendered visible community tensions over social order and ties of belonging—for lineage and neighborhood communities in Taita did not function as smoothly self–regulating systems. Structures of domination and challenges to them ran through local societies.[94] The challenges overtly or implicitly concerned who held what kinds of power, and how the norms and terms of society supported the powerful. Cultural politics addressed not only formal structures of authority, but also the power to ascribe meanings to actions, and therein to shape terms of community belonging and/or exclusion.

---

[92] Larson usefully distinguishes between "community belonging" and "polity belonging," which is mobilized "through a different set of legitimating referents." Nevertheless, the above implicitly argues that the two may overlap considerably. See Larson, "Desperately Seeking," 22–24; and Bill Bravman, "The Politics of Meaning in Taita, Kenya: Local Societies in the Nineteenth Century" (paper presented at the African Studies Association annual conference, Toronto, November 1994).

[93] Interview with NM, Wundanyi/Wundanyi, 28/7/1993.

[94] Several Africanists have examined how hegemonic orders arose and were challenged in nineteenth–century East Africa. My analysis is particularly influenced by two: Feierman, *Intellectuals*; and Jonathon Glassman, *Feasts and Riot: Revelry, Rebellion, and Popular Consciousness on the Swahili Coast, 1856–1888* (Portsmouth, NH, 1995).

The Terrain of Cultural Politics

The main grounds of cultural politics in Taita's nineteenth–century communities were tensions between older and younger men over the control of resources; between older and younger adults over how much day–to–day control the former exercised over the latter; and between elders and younger men over the accumulation of social authority. Lineage and neighborhood ideologies emphasized elements meant to obscure those tensions: intergenerational mutual support, long–term mutual dependence, and cosmological intradependence. Still, in struggles over rights and responsibilities, and through efforts to retain or refashion networks, the terms of lineage and neighborhood belonging were cast, affirmed, and challenged.

Lineage Political Economy and Control of Livestock

Older and younger men often struggled over the main resource of the local political economy: livestock. Older men's power relied heavily on control over livestock. Through its accumulation and exchange, older men built networks of patronage, clientship, and mutual commitment. Complex, often crosscutting animal loans, swaps, and sales established alliances and delineated influence.[95]

> Those who were poor used to herd for rich people, and get goats that way. When [the poor one] herds he's given a goat and progresses a bit. . . . Rich people continued increasing their cows, helping and being helped by the poorer ones. And the ones the rich man helped [would] stand with him.[96]

Men worked livestock networks for long–term relationships, not short–term profit. Loans were not settled quickly, usually not even in the lifetime of those who made the arrangement.[97] Older men built up influence through animal wealth channeled into such networks. A well–networked older man could maintain a dignified low profile in discussions and disputes, while his supporters represented his interests. This sort of influence was crucial, along with ritual position, for becoming an elder and then one of high standing.

Older men's control over animals kept younger men in check, but also kept capital pooled for livestock deals. Younger men received some animals upon marrying and could acquire more, but their seniors retained the vast majority of livestock. Too, whoever nominally owned individual animals, virtually all livestock remained in the older men's herds. Older men's control of livestock kept sons (and grandsons) dependent and working for them, ensuring that a son would not surpass his father's wealth while the father lived:

---

[95] Interviews with JM, Josa/Chawia, 9/4/1988; and GM, Kishamba/Chawia, 12/8/1988.

[96] Interview with AM, Shigaro/Werugha, 2/5/1988.

[97] Interview with LM, Mrugua/Bura, 18/8/1988; see also A. Harris, "Organization," chaps. 7–9.

[A son] depended entirely on the elder, eats from the elder, and is taken care of by the elder. . . . And since he has nothing, the elder must always be on top. . . . In the days of our grandfathers . . . the youth might try, but the child could never defeat his father. [If the young man managed to get a cow on his own,] he would be waiting for it to give birth, while his father has 20, 30, 50 cows! No, in those days the child would never exceed the elder.[98]

Older men tried to naturalize their effective power through axioms of small lineage propriety: fathers took care of their sons' livestock needs, and sons *should* not surpass their living fathers' wealth.[99] These axioms also supported the fathers' *de facto* power over sons' labor, and the labor of the sons' wives and children. But axioms of proper ways did not quash all dissent: many young men chafed at paternal control of livestock.

Young men did most of the work to maintain and build old men's herds in mid–nineteenth–century Taita, starting in their youth. When a young man married, his seniors provided him bridewealth cattle, usually from herds he tended. Single young men thus knew that certain livestock were "for them."[100] Married sons gradually had more animals designated for them, but only when an older man died did young men gain effective control of them.[101] Until then, younger men could not use "their" animals to establish independent networks of alliance, patronage, and clientship. A father, however, might make a deal using livestock already designated for a son.[102] If younger men did not appreciate having livestock kept from them, they could do little about it. A younger man who resisted paternal control or did not live up to his herding obligations endangered his inheritance.

Still, young men tried to circumvent aspects of the system. Herds grew mainly through natural increase and raiding, and while old men maintained close control over animals already in their herds, young men claimed some control over raided ones. Neighborhood–based warrior groups of young men conducted livestock raids across and beyond Taita. Participants divided up raid booty, and in turn were enjoined by their lineage seniors to place the animals in lineage herds. Despite all the above caveats, young men tended to regard those animals as "their" part of a lineage herd, and indeed they often became bridewealth livestock:

---

[98]   Interview with AK, Shigaro/Werugha, 25/4/1988.

[99]   This nineteenth–century ideology was commonplace among male informants. Interviews with JM, Wusi/Chawia, 5/4/1988; and MM, Ilole/Bura, 17/8/1988. On the construction of such cultural forms, see Pierre Bourdieu, *Outline of a Theory of Practice* (Cambridge, 1977). Particularly germane is his mention of "the ideological use many societies make of the lineage model . . . [to create a] universe of theoretical relationships within which individuals or groups define the real space of . . . *practical* relationships in terms of their conjunctural interests" (p. 19).

[100]   This was a commonplace understanding among older men interviewed.

[101]   Interviews with SS, Tausa/Mbololo, 3/6/1988; and RM, Mlondo/Werugha, 27/9/1988.

[102]   In principle, fathers were enjoined not to do so, but it still happened. Interviews with MT, Kishamba/Chawia, 9/6/1988; SM, Ndome/Mbololo, 28/6/1988; and JM, Wundanyi/Werugha, 15/7/1988.

MM: When they went to take cattle in those days, the days of [his great–grandfather], they were just going for their wives, you see? Those cattle, they were divided among the warriors.

BB: The young men kept them themselves?

MM: They were kept with their fathers' cattle, but they were for marrying. . . . They could not be used for anything else.[103]

If an older man used raided cattle in a non–marriage exchange, his sense of prerogative might well conflict with young men's expectations. Sons, with much to lose, rarely confronted seniors directly over such matters, but had ways to make their feelings known: "if you were angry that your father traded your cattle . . . you tell a brother; the brother, he tells his cousin; now that cousin tells your uncle, and your *mzee* (old man) will hear from him."[104] Too, as will be seen below, younger men began to develop another channel for livestock accumulation in the late nineteenth century.

Authority over Junior Households

Older men and women exerted considerable authority over their children even after the children married. When a young couple first married, the husband learned the duties and responsibilities of married life from his father, who also allocated the newlywed a few fields. The wife began her integration into the husband's small lineage by undertaking work for her husband and her parents–in–law.[105] This typically included cooking and household chores for the in–laws, and working in their fields along with her husband's fields. A young husband continued to tend lineage herds and helped in his father's fields, as well as attending to his own. The couple only set up their own household after a wife had her first child.

Young couples quickly tied into lineage and neighborhood mutual support networks: women in a lineage and neighborhood helped each other with child care, farming, and chores, and tended to the needs of those too old to work much for themselves.[106] Men's groups took care of herding and seasonal farm labor, mostly on a small lineage basis; neighborhood or large lineage groups organized martial bands to defend resources or territory, or to conduct raids.

But networks of mutuality distributed obligations unevenly: parents in effect compelled young couples to do extra work for them. Older men's resource control and older women's high standing in support networks backed up the disparity, which found expression in axioms that the young should respect and support their seniors.[107] Most extra work entailed chores and farming, and fell

---

[103] Interview with MM, Kishamba/Chawia, 8/6/1988.

[104] Interview with BM, Njawuli/Mwanda, 3/8/1993.

[105] Interview with Mrs. PN, Mwanda/Mwanda, 3/8/1993.

[106] Interviews with Mrs. DM, Shigaro/Werugha, 30/5/1988; and Mrs. RM, Chawia/Chawia, 16/6/1988.

[107] For more on this, see Bill Bravman, "Practices and Discourses of Work, and Struggles over Terms of Community in Taita, Kenya, 1850–1950" (paper presented at Institute for the Advanced Study of the African Humanities, Northwestern University, April 1996).

largely upon daughters–in–law. Young couples readily took up some of this labor, but not always as much as parents wished. How much a young couple worked for the husbands' parents depended partly on circumstances: a senior household with only one wife and few adult sons would likely ask more of each son and daughter–in–law.[108] In part, too, it depended on spoken and unspoken negotiations between women of different generations—dealings in which older women held most of the trump cards.

Political and Social Authority

Intergenerational attempts to alter extant terms of authority, and to rework the usual property/authority relationship, also prompted cultural politicking. Normally, older men maneuvered in their local communities to attain and augment positions of elderhood. Prominence as an elder required seniority, a substantial network of supporters, ritual knowledge, and up to three personal religious shrines. The process of fulfilling these aims gave a man standing and respectability in a lineage and neighborhood, but the long undertaking was laden with pitfalls; few reached high levels of elderhood, and then only late in life. [109] From those heights, however, leading elders exercised considerable influence over the resources and younger people of their communities.

In the later nineteenth century, however, a few non–elders used their position as warrior–leaders to challenge aspects of elders' control over younger men. Each neighborhood had a warrior leader (*kishingila*; pl. *vishingila*), who emerged meritocratically from the young warrior ranks.[110] Being younger men, *vishingila* by definition were not elders, and had no formal political power in neighborhoods. They lacked the political–economic, religious, and jural authority of elders, and trying to garner elders' authority would have gotten them in trouble. However, some leading late century *vishingila* did begin to refashion their position.[111]

First, they parlayed their martial or strategic reputations into attempts to develop wider networks of influence. Two *vishingila* stood out on this score. One, Mwangeka, from Mwanda, was reputedly the most formidable warrior in Taita. In the 1870s, he built an unusual alliance with warriors in the vertically adjacent neighborhood of Bura, even as he developed trading ties with Muslim traders from the

---

[108] Interview with Mrs. SM, Mogho Mleche/Mbale, 4/11/1988, who explained that her mother married into such a circumstance.

[109] Interview with MM, Choke/Mbale, 11/11/1988; on the attainment of Bag, Stool, and Bell shrines as steps in becoming a senior elder, see G. Harris, *Casting*, 34–36.

[110] "The *Kishingila* would lead people from here to take cattle in Mgange [Dabida], now they would gang up and attack Mwakitau, or go take cattle from where? Pare!" Interview with RM, Wundanyi/Werugha, 29/7/1993.

[111] Information for this topic stems from unusually clear remembrances of two such *Vishingila*, who became extremely prominent regional figures slightly later, in the 1880s and 1890s. Many stories no doubt exaggerate their abilities and accomplishments, but interviewees in each of the two men's home neighborhoods stressed how they were different from other *Vishingila* before the era of their greatest fame.

East African coast.[112] The alliance undoubtedly required the approval of senior elders in the concerned neighborhoods. Still, young men under Mwangeka's leadership were the only groups from different Dabida neighborhoods to forge such an ongoing, though fragile, relationship. It created new political–economic network–building opportunities, and gave Mwangeka unique interneighborhood influence and standing far beyond the warrior–leader's usual role.[113] Whether Mwangeka could have fully transformed and consolidated these changes, and how they might have ramified through intergenerational authority relations, is unknown; he died during a military action in 1892.

Too, a few *vishingila*, including Mwangeka and Mghalu of Mbale, began keeping their own herds, culled from the booty of their raids.[114] Remembrances do not explain how they built up herds without incurring elders' wrath, or if they tried to establish patronage/clientship networks to rival those of elders. Nor is it clear whether *vishingila*'s herds mitigated against the older men's tight control of animals, or if *vishingila* were somehow coopted into the extant system.[115] Nevertheless, the emergence of *vishingila* as herd owners suggests that some younger men sought to alter the age at which they could develop independent herds and build wealth–based networks of influence.

Intercommunity Bonds and Their Limits

The Scope of Cultural Politics

Cultural politicking in nineteenth–century Taita took place almost entirely within lineages and neighborhoods. At that juncture no ongoing sense of community embraced all of Taita; broader notions of ethnicity did not come into play. This view demurs from Lonsdale's argument that "in all of what became Kenya, ethnicity was wider than politics." To Lonsdale, nineteenth-century ethnicity was based in linguistic, economic and social likenesses, creating loose collective identities of mutual recognition and intermittent support.[116] Taita's communities did not fit this model; the networks of interaction and consequent fellow–feeling Lonsdale ascribes to ethnicity barely operated. Some intra–Taita connections bridged distrust, but neither the connections nor regional likenesses generated a meaningfully shared identity. Intra–Taita connections broke down at the junctures Lonsdale considers crucial to ethnic networks: times of stress. When famine and drought struck, communities in Taita tended to hoard resources and raid each other:

---

[112] Interview with SM, Kikesuni/Mwanda, 14/9/1988.

[113] The alliance was based in upper Bura and lower Mwanda. Interviews with Mrs. SM, Lushangonyi/ Mwanda, 19/9/1988; BM, Mwanda/Mwanda, 3/8/1993; LM, Mrugua/Bura, 18/8/ 1988; and SM, Mrugua/Bura, 19/8/1988.

[114] Interviews with OK, Shigaro/Werugha, 2/8/1993; and RM, Wundanyi/Werugha, 29/7/1993.

[115] Typical of the ambiguous comments on this matter was that of OK, Shigaro/Werugha, 2/8/ 1993: "*Vishingila* had their own herds. . . . They were like elders, but they were younger."

[116] Lonsdale, "Moral Economy," 328–29.

RM: Famine brought many troubles in those days, many. . . . Your *kichuku?* They will share your hunger. And long ago, if you were starving but there is food in Mbale, the warriors went at night, they will try and take.

BB: There was no trade for food in the day? Only raiding?

RM: It was no good to go in the day! If they knew, "those ones are starving," they just stole your things! Pah! [claps his hands]. . . . If they thought you are weak from hunger, they came from Mbale. They will come at night to take your last goat.[117]

Communities built extra–Taita networks for crises, back to regions where they had ancestral ties.

LM: When there was famine in Sagalla, we got help from Giriama. That is where our people went.

BB: You could not go for help at Dabida?

LM: You could not. . . . You must go to the people who know you.[118]

Ethnicity existed in nineteenth–century Taita only if the term allowed for virtually no felt bonds of shared history, interest, or destiny. Regional cultural commonalities *might* have been mobilized into a broader sense of community, but were not. This analysis shares Charles Ambler's view that "an intense localism" shaped community outlooks at that juncture; despite close linguistic ties and "shared fundamental cultural assumptions," there was no established ethnic order.[119]

Local Migrations

Despite the local focus of communities and cultural politics, people in the Hills did develop intraregional ties. Intra–Taita migrations, however, though not uncommon and doubtless contributing to regional likeness, [120] did not foster intercommunity ties. Single small lineages or small lineage fragments undertook most pre–twentieth–century intra–Hills migrations, and surely helped

---

[117] Interview with RM, 29/7/1993. Lonsdale refers to wider ethnic networks as "strategies of trust between strangers," cemented by marriage and trade, as insurance against hard times. See Lonsdale, "Moral Economy," 329. Marriage in nineteenth–century Taita, however, rarely stretched beyond large lineage, and virtually never left the neighborhood. And, again, trade ties within Taita, when they crossed neighborhood boundaries, tended to be only with a neighborhood immediately and vertically adjacent.

[118] Interview with LM, Teri/Sagalla, 23/8/1988. This last point echoes (and extends) Lonsdale's argument that nineteenth–century East Africans' "world was anything but narrow." Lonsdale, "Moral Economy," 329.

[119] Ambler, *Kenyan Communities*, 4–7.

[120] Stories of multiple movements by small lineage or household in the distant past were very numerous. Interviews with SK, Wundanyi/Werugha, 15/4/1988; Mrs. RM, Chawia/Chawia, 16/6/1988; MM, Shigaro/Werugha, 21/7/1993; and Mrs. WM, Werugha/Werugha, 30/7/1993.

spread cultural and linguistic similarities across Taita. If a group moved permanently to a different Hills neighborhood, those remaining behind considered them to have severed relations. Conversely, new immigrants to a neighborhood were absorbed into one of its large lineages, and worked into that neighborhood's social networks.[121]

The Extent of Blood Brotherhood

Blood brotherhood (*mtero*) probably generated the most connections across neighborhood boundaries of suspicion. Blood brothers established relationships of trust and aid, making agreements of mutual interest and support where no kin or neighborly bonds existed. Most commonly, men made blood brotherhoods to facilitate travel across otherwise hostile territory:

> Between Shigaro and Kidaya things were very bad. But if you have a blood brother there, . . . you just went to his place. Nobody harmed you because you had a brother there. . . . If a man hurts you, what will he tell your brother? No, you could go and return safely.[122]

Blood brotherhoods often secured routes of complementarity, providing herding groups from highland neighborhoods passage through lower ones to the plains, and encouraging some crop/animal trade between vertically adjacent communities. The agreements did not hold perfectly; despite the assurances of the above speaker, warriors occasionally pillaged passersby with blood brothers in that neighborhood. Then, however, the oath enjoined the "host" brother to give aid or restitution.[123] Overall, blood brotherhoods reduced much of the risk involved in traversing Taita.

Blood brotherhoods also facilitated positive interactions in a region otherwise notable for local insularities. The ritual form of blood brotherhood oathing itself demonstrated people's ability to develop and disseminate aspects of a shared culture: by the mid–nineteenth century, the basic ritual operated similarly across the Hills.[124] Blood brotherhood's meaning became universally understood across Taita, and most people honored the oaths. Ties of blood brotherhood facilitated trade and the exchange of information and ideas across the Hills.

---

[121] Interviews with Mrs. RM, Chawia/Chawia, 6/6/1988; and JM, Wongonyi/Mbololo, 7/7/1988. There were exceptions, chiefly if a group from one neighborhood gained control of territory in another one through juro–political maneuver. For instance, when a man in Shigaro illegitimately impregnated the daughter of a blood brother from a different community, the woman's father claimed land as recompense. His small lineage displaced the impregnator's family on the land, yet maintained prior lineage ties. Interview with MM, Shigaro/Werugha, 21/7/1993.

[122] Interview with AM, Shigaro/Werugha, 22/7/1993.

[123] On the host's responsibility to protect his blood brother and the lethal power of the oath. Interview with SM, Wusi/Chawia, 29/7/1993.

[124] The oath takers slaughtered an animal, mixed their blood with the animal's, drank or daubed themselves with a portion of the mingled bloods, swore an oath, and ate the animal's cooked meat. Interviews with SM, Mwanda/Mwanda, 15/9/1988; HI, Sagassa/Werugha, 4/10/1988; SM, Ndome/Mbololo, 28/6/1988; and SM, Kishamba/Sagalla, 23/8/1988.

However, blood brotherhood was at once too general and too frail an institution to foster a Taita–wide identity. It forged interpersonal ties not only among people across Taita, but among people across any large expanse: it did not differentiate between outsiders from elsewhere in Taita, and outsiders from Pare, Ukambani, or Mombasa.[125] Blood brotherhoods were also highly individual relationships that added to the networks, support structures, prestige, and standing of a man. They did not imply systematically closer links between neighborhoods (or even between large lineages). Blood brotherhoods allowed a specified outsider and his immediate companions to bridge the usual suspicions between neighborhoods, because someone in the host community vouched for him. In an implicit expression of the limits on the relationship, even longtime blood brothers did not engage in interneighborhood marriage alliances.[126]

Blood brotherhood also proved fragile in times of stress. For all its promises of mutual support, blood brotherhoods broke down well before kinship or neighborly ties when drought or famine struck: "When famine came, *mtero* meant nothing!"[127] Refuge lay farther afield, in more distant regions with ancestral relatives. And though blood brothers in theory needed fear no harm in each other's communities, hardship often gave lie to the principle. In all, blood brotherhood offered fitful glimmers of a possible Taita community, but no more.

Rituals

Rituals also fostered interaction across the boundaries of nineteenth–century communities, especially female initiation and some dances.[128] Pubescent girls from one large lineage constituted an initiation group, guided by adult ritual specialists from the neighborhood and sometimes beyond.[129] Initiation culminated in an all–night public dance open to adults from outside the neighborhood. On those occasions, the parents of the initiates assured outsiders safe passage through the host neighborhood. Men and women from surrounding neighborhoods often crossed the usual divides to partake in the dancing, drinking, and general festivities.[130]

Some minor dances induced people to meet across neighborhood lines, as well. In Sagalla, for instance, each neighborhood regularly held nighttime social dances called *Gonda*, mainly attended by already–initiated ado-

---

[125] Mwangeka, for instance, had blood brothers in and around Mombasa: traders and medicine makers. Interview with Mrs. SM, Mwanda/Mwanda, 14/9/1988. Another interviewee, PM, Ilole/ Bura, 16/8/1988, described a blood brotherhood his grandfather had with a tobacco trader in Usambara.

[126] This, I was told, would have violated proper marriage practices. The stricture may have prevented marriage alliances linked to blood brotherhoods, or, on the other hand, may have just reflected the fragility of blood brotherhoods. Interview with BM, Mwanda/Mwanda, 3/8/1993.

[127] Interview with LM, Kizumanzi/Sagalla, 3/7/1993; also, NM, Wundanyi/Werugha, 28/7/1993.

[128] Interviews with Mrs. CM, Shigaro/Werugha, 26/7/1993; Mrs. MM, Werugha/Werugha, 30/7/ 1993; and BM, Mwanda/Mwanda, 3/8/1993.

[129] Interviews with Mrs. CM, Shigaro/Werugha, 26/7/1993; and JM, Wusi/Chawia, 22/7/1993.

[130] The open character of initiation dances was common knowledge among interviewees.

lescents and newly married adults. *Gonda* dances in Sagalla were always interneighborhood events, and occasionally drew people from the nearer neighborhoods of Dabida.[131] *Gonda* was also danced in parts of Dabida; in several, though not all, of those neighborhoods people from adjacent neighborhoods could attend.[132]

Initiation and dances, again, probably helped spread sociocultural similarities across nineteenth–century Taita. Some initiation experts traveled widely to train initiates, surely spreading standardized ritual forms and perhaps setting out similar ways for, say, girls across the region to think about womanhood and their relations to men. Initiation and dances also provided non–neighbors a meeting ground relatively free of immediate suspicions and imminent hostility. People exchanged news, rumors, and small talk, becoming less unknown to each other in the process. At *Gonda* dances, young men from different neighborhoods boasted to each other of their exploits and the talents of their *vishingila*, even as they heard tales of *vishingila* from other locales.[133] Older men sometimes used the settings to discuss issues, gather news of far–flung events, or visit a blood brother.[134]

However, the gatherings did not give rise to other interneighborhood bonds. A given year typically brought one or two opportunities to attend initiations in nearby neighborhoods, plus a few chances to go to another neighborhood's *Gonda*. Despite this intermixing at the moment when a new group of the young was eligible to marry, dances among marriageable adolescents did not break down neighborhood endogamy. No related venues for broader interaction developed; no other forms of mobilizing a larger community arose through the gatherings. Once a dance ended, people returned to their local communities and resumed localized lives.

Traders and Ritual Experts

Some ritual and medical specialists spread a like pool of knowledge and skills across nineteenth–century Taita. In addition to initiation specialists, experts with skills like scarification itinerated widely to etch decorative patterns on male and female faces; any one practitioner surely spread a repertoire of related markings wherever he went.[135] Like blood brothers, though, ritual experts and traders also came from beyond the Hills, mainly the coast, Pare, Usambara, and Kilimanjaro.

---

[131] Interview with KM, Kizumanzi/Sagalla, 14/7/1993.

[132] Two of several who described *Gonda* as an open dance were GN/Mgange Nyika/ Mwanda, 20/9/1988; and MM, Ilole/Bura, 17/8/1988. Dabida interviewees spoke far more of attending other neighborhoods' initiation dances than of going to their *Gonda* dances. Perhaps this was because *Gonda* in Dabida was largely for courting potential spouses. In Sagalla, *Gonda* mixed courtship with more general socializing among young adults.

[133] Interview with MN, Lushangonyi/Mwanda, 22/9/1988.

[134] Interviews with MT, Kishamba/Chawia, 9/6/1988; and RN, Wumingu/Werugha, 1/10/1988.

[135] Interviews with Mrs. MO, Shigaro/Werugha, 2/8/1993; CA Ilole/Bura, 17/8/1988; and MM, Nyolo/Bura, 15/8/1988.

Some neighborhoods in the Hills developed economic links through intraregional trade networks for goods like crops, animals, tobacco, and clay. Such trade developed most extensively between adjacent neighborhoods along a single drainage, following paths of vertical complementarity.[136] But local trade itineraries involved few people, and, being mediated by blood brotherhoods, were culturally part of that set of relationships. They did not foster other or wider interconnections.

Dabida, Sagalla, and Broader Community

A mosaic of distinctions, interconnections, similarities and commonalities ran through Taita's societies by the late nineteenth century. On Dabida, a fair degree of linguistic and cultural heterogeneity reinforced the localized structures upon which notions of community were built. Only in Dabida's local communities did people find and continually revitalize the grounds to "understand each other." Further distinctions divided Dabida from Sagalla: various dialects on Dabida, for instance, resembled each other far more than any resembled KiSagalla.

Sagalla also distinguished itself by a mountainwide sense of community that emerged in or before the nineteenth century. Sagalla, like Dabida, had its lineages and neighborhoods, but Sagalla's geography and history contributed to a shared Sagalla identity, as well. Sheer size, or rather, the relative lack of it, had a hand in this. Sagalla would fit tidily in a fifth of Dabida massif, and is no topographical maze. Most people there lived within its main watershed, a long highland valley. Sagalla had far fewer lineages and neighborhoods, all in close proximity; few natural divides separated groups. Sagalla's people also had far more homogeneous origins than did Dabida's societies: virtually every lineage in Sagalla claimed ancestry in Giriama.[137] Sagalla place–names reflect this, reproducing Giriama place–names all over the mountain—even "Sagalla" is widely called a derivative of the Giriama word for a place to sit/stay.[138] In addition, Sagalla's sociocultural forms had more thorough–going commonality than did sociocultural forms across Dabida.[139]

---

[136] For instance, Wongonyi, a neighborhood in upper Mbololo, forged much closer ties with the adjacent lowland, Ghazi, than in the bordering highland, Rong'e. Interviews with MN, Ghazi/Mbololo, 4/7/1988; DM, Wongonyi/Mbololo, 6/7/1988; and JM, Wongonyi/Mbololo, 7/7/1988.

[137] All seventeen people (from fourteen large lineages) interviewed in Sagalla traced their ancestry to Giriama.

[138] The first person I interviewed there explained this etymology, and eleven interviewees in five Sagalla neighborhoods repeated it. Interview with JN, Teri/Sagalla, 25/8/1988.

[139] While my research in Dabida found considerable variations in initiation, marriage, and divination, Sagalla showed far greater homogeneity. For instance, diviners in different parts of Dabida sacrificed different kinds of animals for readings of entrails; they also conducted the ritual slightly differently. Interviews with MN, Ghazi/Mbololo, 4/7/1988; PM, Ilole/Bura, 16/8/1988; and MM, Choke/Mbale, 11/11/1988.

Sagalla's nineteenth–century neighborhoods exuded far less hostility towards one another. Raids between Sagalla neighborhoods ended far earlier than analogous raids in Dabida:

> *DM:* The early ones, they used to steal from each other, but they stopped that long ago. (laughs)
> *Q:* They stopped with colonialism?
> *DM:* Oh, no, *long* ago. Before the Europeans. *Long* ago.[140]

Travel between Sagalla neighborhoods entailed little risk. Elders from different neighborhoods met often, and one interviewee claimed senior elders of all Sagalla gathered to discuss important issues.[141] While outsiders from nearby neighborhoods attended initiations and *Gonda* dances in Dabida, analogous events in Sagalla drew visitors from the whole mountain. Some suggest, as well, that couples occasionally married across neighborhood boundaries.[142] Significantly, too, warriors from all Sagalla often banded together to raid outside territories (including Dabida), and to defend against outside raiders (including from Dabida). One war medicine sufficed for the entire mountain in the nineteenth century, suggesting that Sagalla had one *kishingila*.[143]

People on Sagalla shared not only commonalities and interconnections, but a sense of common contradistinction to Dabida, the closest locale of threatening outsiders.[144] Overall, lineage and neighborhood communities in Sagalla did not preclude the forming of a widely agreed upon, common Sagalla community of belonging. As one interviewee said, "*Kichuku* was there, neighborhood was there, but all of them were Sagallas. . . . They knew they were together."[145]

Patterns of Change in the Nineteenth Century: Warriors and the Wealth of Lineages

For most of the nineteenth century, Taita had a quieter event history than many abutting regions. Unlike in Shambaa and Pare, a centralized state neither drew together nor spun apart. Ivory and slave trading between Zanzibar and the East African interior spawned intrigue, insurrection, and devastation south of

---

140 DM, Teri/Sagalla, 10/7/1993. Intra–Dabida raiding continued until colonial conquest.

141 Interview with SM, Teri/Sagalla, 12/7/1993.

142 Interview with KM, Kizumanzi/Sagalla, 14/7/1993.

143 Interviews with KM, Kizumanzi/Sagalla, 14/7/1993; and DM, Teri/Sagalla, 10/7/1993. A short relay of horn blasts let all Sagalla know within minutes that enemies approached.

144 Virtually everybody interviewed in Sagalla called nineteenth–century relations with Dabida bad. KM, Kizumanzi/Sagalla, 14/7/1993, added that Sagalla's people banded together to fend off Maasai and Dabida raiders.

145 Interview with JM, Teri/Sagalla, 23/7/1993.

Taita, but, remarkably and luckily, mostly passed Taita by.[146] To the east and north, Zanzibar–based traders gradually supplanted earlier Kamba networks of ivory hunters and long-distance traders in the interior of what is now Kenya.[147] Taita mostly stayed out of the struggle over that trade, with local people content to resupply and/or raid passing caravans of either origin.

While avoiding the wider region's epic traumas, lineages in Taita managed to increase their territory and livestock holdings, albeit with distinct booms and setbacks. As an overall arc, wealth in Taita grew during the early and middle decades of the century, with livestock and effective land holdings declining thereafter. On closer view, any given year might see lineages on one side of the Hills flourish while those on another side struggled. Outsiders' predations played little part in this—on that score local medicines of defense (*Fighi*) worked admirably. Droughts, famines, and epidemics were the culprits.[148]

Taita's population grew in the first three quarters of the century through natural increase and immigration from surrounding areas.[149] Immigrants usu-ally made their way to those neighborhoods in the Hills where they could make claims of common ancestry. Immigrants from, say, north Pare knew which parts of Taita would welcome them, for large lineages in the Hills maintained ties with their ancestral homelands. Raids brought captive immigrants; they, like voluntary immigrants, were incorporated as full members of extant lineages.

As lineages grew in size, new lineages hived off and cleared new lands for themselves. In this way, most of Taita's arable land came under claim by the mid–nineteenth century.[150] Several late century droughts and famines re–emp-tied some land, but once a large lineage claimed an area, it tried to maintain the claims even if the land fell into disuse. By midcentury one or another lin-eage laid claim to nearly all the exploitable land in the Hills. During the midcentury population peak, intra–Taita migrations slowed somewhat. Later, as lineages sought to rebuild thinned ranks and reoccupy abandoned land, movement loosened up.[151]

Raiding and Wealth in the Nineteenth Century

Taita's local societies mostly flourished in the first three quarters of the cen-tury. The boom appears to have been fueled by the expansion of neighborhood

---

[146] Feierman, *Shambaa*, chaps. 5, 6; Feierman, *Intellectuals*, chaps. 2–4; I. N. Kimambo, *Penetration and Protest in Tanzania: The Impact of the World Economy on the Pare, 1860–1960* (Athens, 1991), chaps. 2, 3; and Willis, *Making*, pt. 1–3.

[147] For an overview of the Zanzibari system, Abdul Sheriff, *Slaves, Spices and Ivory in Zanzibar* (Athens, OH: 1987). For the decline of the Kamba networks, see pp. 168–70.

[148] Merritt, "History of the Taita," describes the impact of drought in great depth.

[149] Some immigrants were fleeing the upheavals in the increasingly violent political economy. In-terviews with NM, Wundanyi/Werugha, 28/7/1993; and MM, Mwanda/Mwanda, 12/9/1988. Also, Kimambo, *Penetration*, chap. 3; and Feierman, *Shambaa*, chaps. 6, 7.

[150] Interviews with OK, Shigaro/Werugha, 2/8/1993; MM, Choke/Mbale, 11/11/1988; and GM, Kishamba/Chawia, 12/8/1988.

[151] Interviews with OK, Shigaro/Werugha, 2/8/1993; and GM, Kishamba/Chawia, 12/8/1988.

warrior bands' raiding beyond the Hills. A European passing through Taita in 1872 described how warriors from the Hills ventured far and wide to capture livestock, the "*ne plus ultra* of desirable things."[152] Evidence for this warrior-led expansion of the livestock economy also exists within local remembrances:

> Our grandfathers did not have many cows. They went out [of the Hills] to look for cows. . . . They went for fighting; yes, wars. Our grandfathers started wars. [By] the time of our fathers . . . the colonialists came, so the fathers stopped their wars. But our grandfathers went to Shambala to grab cattle. . . . Yes, the Shambala people were fought and all their cattle raided. And you will hear the same things from the upper sides [i.e., people living in the upper reaches of Taita].[153]

The ideology of animals–as–wealth dominated the local political economy well into the 1900s.[154] In the early colonial period, older men would seek to turn that ideology and its associated norms into pillars of Taita identity.

Remembrances today claim that Taita's nineteenth–century neighborhood warrior bands had no regional peers. Like claims, no doubt, are made elsewhere, but neighboring areas corroborate Taita's reputation. In Kilimanjaro, warriors and war medicines from Taita were feared as far back as the late 1700s.[155] Nineteenth–century Pare and Shambaa–based traditions tell a similar story. In mid–nineteenth–century Pare, warriors from Taita were greatly feared and thought to have magical powers.[156] As a result of that reputation, a Pare man named Mashombo who resided for a time among kin in Dabida, used warriors from that Dabida neighborhood as mercenaries to consolidate his dominion over a large section of Pare.[157] In Usambara, a challenger to the Shambaa throne imported Dabida warriors as mercenaries for his attack on the king.[158]

---

[152] New, *Life, Wanderings*, 334; later on in his journey, near Bura, New met a party of warriors returning from a raid on Shambaa "with a large booty of cattle and women" (p. 479).

[153] Interview with GM, Tausa/Mbololo, 31/5/1988. He was right, too, that people up the hill would tell similar stories: interviews with NM, Wundanyi/Werugha, 26/5/1988; and MM, Mwanda/Mwanda, 12/9/1988. The "time of fathers" for someone GM's age, [he was probably born between 1905 and 1910], would encompass the late nineteenth century and beginning of the twentieth. The "time of grandparents" describes a generalized past, but more recent and more specific than the "time of ancestors." An interviewee's "time of the grandparents" roughly covered stories s/he heard grandparents tell of their youth, stretching back into stories the grandparents told of *their* parents' youth. In GM's case, the middle decades of the nineteenth century would coincide with when his grandfathers raided beyond the Hills for livestock.

[154] The most important, most respectable form of wealth was animal wealth, with cattle taking precedence over sheep and goats. Next came land, and third, reflecting the cultural hegemony of older men, was a man's wives and children. Interviews with GM, Kishamba/Chawia, 27/6/1988; and SM, Teri/Sagalla, 24/8/1988. Also see A. Harris, "Organization," chaps. 7, 8.

[155] Kathleen Stahl, *History of the Chagga People of Kilimanjaro* (The Hague, 1964), 297–98. She relates how Kombo, chief of Kilema, met a medicine man from Taita, and subsequently sent his son Rongoma to study martial techniques and medicine in Taita. Rongoma returned six years later with a group of warriors from Taita, (which neighborhood is not specified), and quickly rose to power.

[156] Kimambo, *Pare*, 151–52. He dates the incursions of Taita's warriors in Pare to before 1861.

[157] Ibid., 152.

[158] Feierman, *Shambaa*, 149–64.

In 1862 the mercenaries sacked and burned the Shambaa capital; thereafter, the challenger, Semboja, used another band of mercenaries from Dabida against a different set of rivals.[159] Raiders also struck Ukambani, Duruma, Kilimanjaro, and Giriama.[160] At the coast, Charles New learned that "the roads had been closed" between Duruma (on the coastal hinterland) and the Taita Hills, because of raids from Taita. According to New's source, "they had attacked with success most of the surrounding peoples, while they themselves dwelt in their mountain fastness in complete security."[161] An English missionary on Sagalla in 1883 observed that its warriors raided Pare, Shambaa and Duruma.[162] Warriors from parts of Dabida also raided for Maasai cattle and women in the plains north and west of the Hills. Europeans, who thought the Maasai East Africa's most formidable warriors, found this particularly noteworthy.[163] Finally, warriors in the Hills didn't always travel far for raids: with trade caravans passing Taita en route to the coast or the interior, opportunities came to them.[164]

However, warriors from the Hills almost never raided areas where they had ancestral ties. Because immigrants came to Taita from so many different directions, people from varying lineages had different views of where *not* to raid. For example, most lineages around Mbale/Dabida traced some ancestry to Kilimanjaro, and thus would not attack it. They later began to cooperate with Maasai for the same reasons, reinforcing the ties with blood brotherhoods. By contrast, the lineages around Kidaya/Dabida garnered much of their cattle through raids on Maasai.[165] Conversely, peaceable links

---

[159] Feierman, *Shambaa*, 157–59, 161, 164. On the second round of mercenaries in Shambaa, see Merritt, p. 161.

The German explorer von der Decken reported in 1861 that Shambaa's people held Taita's warriors in awe, believing they had much better war medicine. Semboja already had experience with them, for they had been raiding Shambaa for decades. See Merritt, "History of the Taita," 160; New, *Life, Wanderings*, 334.

[160] "Our grandfathers just grabbed cows from the Duruma and the Giriama. . . . The WaDuruma were afraid of our warriors. . . . For our grandfathers the difficulty was to reach there and return, . . . [but] to fight against them, ah!, it was just like this, [JM sweeps one arm, as if brushing aside an obstacle]." Interview with JM, Teri/Chawia, 5/8/1988. Also, interviews with NM, Ndome/Mbololo, 22/6/1988; and KM, Werugha/Werugha, 3/10/1988.

[161] New, *Life, Wanderings*, 306. New forgot that Pare and Shambaa were also mountain complexes, not inherently less defensible than Taita. When drought and famine later decimated Taita, outside raiders did then attack it. See Wray, *Kenya*, 26–27, 46–47, 53–54.

[162] Wray to Lane, 4/8/1883, CMS Correspondence, G3 A5/01; and Binns to Lang, 31/8/1883.

[163] PN, Ngerenyi/Chawia, 9/5/1988, states, like GM (fn 154), that it was grandfathers who first became rich, but in this case by raiding Maasai. Warriors from Mbale/Dabida developed specific techniques for fighting Maasai. Interview with MM, Mbale/Mbale, 7/11/1988. New, *Life, Wanderings*, 306.

[164] Europeans in the later decades of the nineteenth century reconfirmed New's observation of raids on passing traders. See Gissing, "Journey," 555; also see Morris to Lang, 11/1/1888, CMS Correspondence, G3 A5/05(a).

[165] Interview with MM, Mbale/Mbale, 7/11/1988, for relations between people from Mbale and surrounding people.

with Mbale–area lineages did not prevent Maasai from raiding other parts of the Hills.[166]

The interweaving of alliance/enmity between neighborhoods in Taita and different outside groups both reflected and reinforced localization among Hills communities. Down through the 1880s, raids across Taita remained common:

> You know in the past people [in Taita] used to disturb each other very much, they fought a lot, to make gains. . . . My grandfather [from Bura] was a very powerful, bitter person, he used to like fighting people. He went and fought in Sagaigo [a sub–location of Ngerenyi/Chawia], he defeated them, so he got a place and built. . . . He stayed there, . . . and our fathers grew up there.[167]

In another case, during an 1884–87 famine, small groups of men and women from Sagalla went to Mbale, hoping to trade animals and craft goods for much-needed cereals. Instead, their would–be trade partners seized the goods and the women.[168] Later, Sagalla was subject to raids from Mbale warriors who hoped to pilfer Sagalla's weakened and numerically diminished populace.[169]

Taita and Long-Distance Trade in the Nineteenth Century

This tapestry of intra- and interregional alliances and enmities likewise defined patterns of long-distance trade. The possibility of trading with any one distant region varied by neighborhood in Taita, generally as an inverse of raiding relations. Again, ancestral claims played a crucial role in establishing with which areas a particular Taita neighborhood traded: some Dabida lineages ran a brisk livestock trade with purported kin in north Pare, even as other Taita neighborhoods raided there.[170] Trade with Kilimanjaro exceeded raids on it, in part because it was relatively well defended. Still, Taita's biggest exports there were mercenaries and war medicines.[171] Many lineages in Taita traded mainly with Ukambani or the coast. Ukambani supplied goats to much of Taita, and dealt cattle and sheep, as well.[172] Warriors from Taita rarely raided Ukambani (the distance was formidable), but sometimes attacked Kamba caravans passing along the eastern sides of Dabida and Sagalla.[173] Yet traders from Ukambani to

---

[166] Gissing observed that Maasai often raided lower Sagalla, and were much feared there. See Gissing, "Journey," 556; also interview with GM, Tausa/Mbololo, 31/5/1988.

[167] Interview with PN, Ngerenyi/Chawia, 9/5/1988.

[168] Wray to Lang, 21/4/1884, CMS Correspondence, G3/A5/01.

[169] Wray, Kenya, 30–31, 52–54; see also pp. 43–44.

[170] Interview with MM, Kishamba/Chawia, 8/6/1988.

[171] On the quality of defense in Kilimanjaro, see Merritt, "History of the Taita," 165.

[172] Interviews with GM, Tausa/Mbololo, 31/5/1988; and EK, Ndome/Mbololo, 22/6/1988. Wray also repeatedly saw Kamba goat traders in Sagalla; for instance, two groups came within two months of each other in 1893. See his diaries, CMSA, 13/5/1893 and 12/7/1893.

[173] Several Europeans condemned these raids on Kamba caravans, giving Taita a notorious reputation. See, for instance, Wray to Lane, 4/8/1883, CMS Correspondence G3 A5/01; Gissing, "Journey," 555; and New, Life, Wanderings, 333–34.

Taita could count on hospitality and good trade if they reached a neighbor-hood with kin connections or blood brothers.

Trade with the coast gained increasing importance throughout the century. Some traders from Taita had long made the arduous five-day journey: a missionary met traders from Taita near Mombasa in the 1840s.[174] However, most trade came in the form of increasingly frequent coastal caravans passing the Hills. The caravans stopped at established spots, paid a protection toll, and traded.[175] European travelers' accounts indicate that caravans called at Kasigau, Sagalla, and along the southern and eastern sides of Dabida.[176] After a difficult crossing from the coast, caravans obtained good water and stocked up on food and extra porters in exchange for cloth, wire, and beads.[177] More than with other long–distance relationships, coastal traders and men from Taita relied upon blood brotherhoods to facilitate trade.[178] After leaving one market point in the Hills, though, a caravan might come under attack from a different neighborhood's warriors. Safe passage for a trader in one part of Taita meant nothing elsewhere in the Hills:

> Now some Swahilis had been bringing cloth here, [Mwanda], and they would spend the night with Mwangeka [their bloodbrother] . . . and their cloth would be bought and they would go back. . . . Now one time [several warriors in Bura] saw three Swahilis who had brought clothes. They beat [the traders] and one ran away, but two died.[179]

Coastal caravans often sought human captives, but traders in the Hills only rarely supplied them.[180] Taita remained on the distant periphery of the Zanzibari system that absorbed people and resources from an enormous swath of East Africa. Still, some slave trading did go on, and trade–minded men in Taita did not always wait for the coastal slave traders to come to the Hills. In the later 1800s perhaps two *vishingila* brought captives to the coast to sell them. Mghalu certainly did, but was caught in the act by British officials. He thereafter only sold captives

---

[174] Krapf's journal, 11/8/1847, KNA, CA/5/0/172, 58. I am grateful to Justin Willis for this citation.

[175] Not everyone paid happily. New, on his first journey to the interior, complained that upon reaching Kasigau "some people came out to meet us, peremptorily demanding blackmail. Somebody who had preceded us always paid toll to be allowed to pass that way, and it was insisted that we must do the same." See New, *Life, Wanderings*, 318.

[176] Krapf, *Travels*, 231–32, 264. The missionary Rebmann noted that "Mohammedan traders" had well–established connections at Bura in 1848. For Sagalla, see Krapf, *Travels*, 287; for Kasigau, see New, *Life, Wanderings*, 319.

[177] This trade affected dress in the Hills. By midcentury, and perhaps before, many men wore European-made cotton fabric, slung over one shoulder. Women wrapped themselves more fully in cotton against severe cold. Women also wore bead garlands around their waists and necks. Men and women both wore brass wire bracelets on their arms. Interviews with JK, Shigaro/Werugha, 11/4/1988; Mrs. MT, Tausa/Mbololo, 2/6/1988; and Mrs. FM, Lushangonyi/Mwanda, 21/9/1988. See also Thomson, *Masai–land*, 48–50.

[178] Interview with Mrs. SM, Mwanda/Mwanda, 14/9/1988.

[179] Interview with Mrs. SM, Kikesuni/Mwanda, 14/9/1988.

[180] During severe famines, however, some people tried to pawn themselves or their children for food. See Wray's diaries, CMSA, 1898–99, for several incidences of this.

to caravans of coastal traders passing Taita.[181] Mghalu kept traveling to the coast, for he had important trade relationships and blood brotherhoods there. He was also deeply curious about the British, who increasingly ventured into the East African interior. Mghalu reportedly ordered his warriors not to attack whites they might encounter around Dabida, but to be friendly—and to gather as much information about them as possible.[182]

Conclusion

Overall, the era from roughly 1800 to 1880 saw Taita's neighborhoods and lineages expand their livestock wealth, despite setbacks at the hands of drought and disease. Neighborhood–based warrior groups spurred much of that growth through raids elsewhere in the Hills and on societies farther afield. By the later nineteenth century, *vishingila* were gaining more social standing and power—and perhaps even setting up networks among younger men independent of elders' networks. But *vishingila* still posed little challenge to elders' authority over lineages, and corporately, neighborhoods.

In most of Taita, the tides of separation and interaction still favored localized forms of community. Increasing wealth allowed lineages to grow over the course of the century, and fueled the effective filling of the Hills. Drought, famine, and disease cut into the population later in the century, but almost all of Taita's land remained claimed as the *de jure* territory of one or another lineage. The increasing power of *vishingila* and their occasional interneighborhood alliances suggest that extant tight distinctions between neighborhoods may have been on the verge of loosening; in Sagalla, the distinctions *had* loosened, if they ever were as tight in the first place. Elsewhere, however, lineage and neighborhood continued as the bedrock communities through which people built and maintained ties of belonging—until, in four decades around the turn of the twentieth century, new groups and forces challenged the sway of elders and the insularity of local communities.

---

[181] Interview with DM, Mbale/Mbale, 7/11/1988.
[182] Interview with DM, Mbale/Mbale, 7/11/1988.

2

Community Under Stress: Sagalla, Environmental Crisis, and Missionary Imagination, 1883–1888

Introduction

The turbulent decades around the turn of the twentieth century visited severe disruptions upon communities in the Taita Hills. The 1880s rung in the era by conjoining well–known hardships, drought and famine, with a novel stress: the arrival of European missionaries. Drought and famine wreaked a familiar havoc on lineage and neighborhood communities across Taita, and, as before, exacerbated tensions between them. The new mission on Sagalla compounded those difficulties in unprecedented ways: it sought to replace local religious and authority systems with ones centered on Christian beliefs and the church's worldly authority. Though virtually nobody in Sagalla believed in the outsiders' theocratic vision, one large lineage's defense of the mission greatly exacerbated intracommunity tensions. The mission's subsequent suzerainty over a rump Sagalla group at the height of the famine encouraged its lead missionary to try to impose a Church–based community on the whole of Sagalla's re–expanded populace a few years later.

It was an extraordinary intervention: missionaries sought to promote, then to force, profound changes in the terms of Sagalla community. Elders initially tried to incorporate the mission within Sagalla's extant social institutions and religious practices. As it became apparent that the mission wanted to overturn not only spiritual beliefs, but key aspects of everyday life and community authority, Sagalla fractured into neighborhoods of mission support and opposition. The devastation of drought and famine deepened local fissures, but by

61

late 1887 mission opponents, bolstered by the mission's inflammatory actions, prevailed in labeling the mission a grave danger to all Sagalla.

Local community reconsolidated around opposition to the missionaries: the mission's prior (and few continuing) supporters were punished and redisciplined within the predominant order, and the mission was expelled. It also did not become a flashpoint for cultural politics in Sagalla, for no local group championed mission's terms of social and cosmological order as against local ways. Europeans could disrupt the extant terms of community for a time, but in the 1880s elders had the wherewithal to reestablish their sociocultural hegemony quickly and thoroughly. Still, conflicts over the mission involved not only Sagalla's people versus outsiders, but also struggles within Sagalla. In ensuing decades, those struggles would proliferate and intensify, and they would indeed become infused with cultural–political meaning.

Early Encounters as Mutual Misapprehension

Any one neighborhood of Taita during the 1880s had established long–distance trading and crisis support networks, as well as long–distance raiding targets. European records of traders from Taita conducting business at the East African coast date to the mid–1800s, though far older ties certainly existed.[1] In the latter half of the century, however, most neighborhoods became increasingly involved in trade along the coast, as caravans moving between Mombasa and the farther interior incorporated parts of the Hills into their trade routes.

By the 1840s, some traders from Taita saw Europeans at the coast as potential trading partners, and encouraged them to establish ties with Taita neighborhoods. In 1847, for instance, five traders from "Kadiaro" (i.e., Kasigau[2]) approached two Europeans in Mombasa's hinterland, offered a sample of resin for trade, and provided information about Kasigau, four days' walk into the interior. The Europeans bristled at the assumption that they were traders, for they were in fact missionaries: Johannes Krapf and John Rebmann of the Church Missionary Society (hereafter CMS).[3] They and many later missionaries came to East Africa not to trade, but to bring Christian salvation to people they thought benighted and morally stunted.[4] The majority of missionaries, earnest

---

[1]   Krapf, 178–79; in 1847, traders from Kasigau stopped by Krapf and Rebmann's station at Rabai.

[2]   Krapf, 178–79; some sources take "Kadiaro" to mean Sagalla: see W. Anderson, *The Church in East Africa*, (Dodoma, Tanzania, 1977), chap. 1; C. P. Groves, *The Planting of Christianity in Africa*, 2 vols. (London, 1954), 2: chap. 4. But Krapf's description is clearly of Kasigau. Krapf, 225, 227–28. See also the map in New, *Life, Wanderings*, chap. 1.

[3]   The CMS, while remaining in the Church of England, bore more similarity to the dissenting London Missionary Society in theology and outlook. See Eugene Stock, *History of the Church Missionary Society*, 3 vols. (London, 1899), 1: 57–65. For a summary of doctrinal differences between the CMS and high church Anglicanism, see T. O. Beidelman, *Colonial Evangelism: A Socio–Historical Study of an East African Mission at the Grassroots*, (Bloomington, 1982), 49–50.

[4]   For more on nineteenth–century missionary attitudes, see Jean Comaroff and John Comaroff, *Of Revelation and Revolution: Christianity, Colonialism, and Consciousness in South Africa*, vol. 1 (Chicago, 1991), 86–97, 109–17.

and inner–directed men, felt aggrieved at being mistaken for people of base material interests.[5]

Yet missionaries across East Africa would continue to be taken for traders, even as they, in turn, developed and clung to their own misconceptions of Africans. These imaginings of respective others formed a two–way street of misconstruals: several consecutive Sagalla perceptions of missionaries in the 1880s, each to a greater or lesser degree, misapprehended them. Meanwhile, missionaries there imagined African individuals and Sagalla social order in a way that bore only a passing resemblance to its society. In truth, both did make some canny observations, and each side in its own way came to appreciate the larger politics of the encounter. Most of Sagalla's people realized within a few years that missionaries greatly disrupted their society, while the first missionary in Sagalla believed, rightly, that only forcible European predominance of the area could quickly improve his evangelical prospects.

Still, missionaries and Sagalla's inhabitants defined each other according to entrenched predispositions more than observations. The encounter in the 1880s did not garner understanding and sympathy for the other's perspective, either. Each side clung to its cultural frameworks when interpreting its opposite's actions and outlooks.[6] Thus, people in Sagalla saw missionaries as traders, interferers with *Wutasi* and local authority, and potential blockers or bringers of rain. They also knew, of course, that the missionaries wanted people to follow their God, but at that point only a handful of people took mission preaching seriously; for everyone else, the other categories took precedence. On his part, the first missionary to Sagalla arrived steeped in European beliefs of African societies as inherently tribal and authoritarian.[7] When Sagalla gave lie to his preconceptions, he did not try to learn its local terms, but fell back on a different European idea: that Sagalla existed in an anarchic state of nature. And though the missionary's supervisors questioned his conduct in Sagalla, their assessments of Sagalla's social order echoed his.

European Missionaries and Taita, to 1883

Background to the Sagalla Mission

Church Mission Society missionaries began having contact with Taita's societies in the 1840s. Rebmann, one of the first CMS missionaries at the East African

---

[5]   For sympathetic discussions of missionaries' inner–directedness and sense of calling, see Max Warren, *Social History and Christian Mission*, (London, 1967), 44–49. For a slightly more critical view, see Robert Strayer, *The Making of Mission Communities in East Africa: Anglicans and Africans in Colonial Kenya, 1875–1935* (Albany, NY, 1978), 7–8.

[6]   This approach to the ways prior "structures of culture" mediate intercultural contact draws upon Marshall Sahlins's, *Historical Metaphors and Mythical Realities: Structure in the Early History of the Sandwich Islands Kingdom* (Ann Arbor, Mich., 1981), and *Islands of History* (Chicago, 1985), chap. 1.

[7]   For the same assumptions operating elsewhere, see Ranger, "European Attitudes."

coast, visited Kasigau briefly in 1847, and traversed parts of Dabida in 1848. In both locales people took him for a merchant, and, indeed, he saw other long-distance traders there. People brought him trade goods and invited him to settle, but his preaching met with bemusement. Rebmann, for his part, described people there as childlike, despondent, "stupid and fearful," in the thrall of magic, and subject to manipulation by "lying Mohammedan traders." He described elders he met as "Chiefs," though his text gave no sign that they were introduced to him as such.[8] He did not remain long enough to unsettle his assumption.

In the early 1850s, Krapf, Rebmann's colleague, developed a "magnificent conception of an equatorial line of Missions stretching right across the continent"— with one in Taita as the first interior link of the chain.[9] The idea lay dormant until the mid–1870s, when Henry Stanley publicly charged British mission societies to continue the evangelizing of Buganda that he began by placing an African Christian in King Mutesa's court. Donations for the task soon swelled to £15,000, and a separate £10,000 was raised between 1873 and 1878 for the Special East Africa Fund.[10] In 1875, the CMS established Frere Town, a freed–slave settlement near Mombasa; soon it became the CMS base for expansion towards Buganda.[11] In 1876, Harry Binns alit at Frere Town, charged to establish a mission at Taita as "the first logical step" in a chain to the interior. Binns visited the Hills in 1880 and decided to put a station at Sagalla. It had the altitude and—so it seemed—water to keep a European healthy, plus a population of several thousand. But a scandal in Frere Town spurred Binns's rapid promotion to an administrative position that tied him to the coast.[12] His replacement for Sagalla, J. Alfred Wray, arrived in 1883.

During Wray's 1883–89 stint, the political context of evangelization all but invisibly shifted. In 1887, the Sultan of Zanzibar granted concessionary rights over a vast portion of East Africa, including the Taita Hills, to the British East Africa Association, which in 1888 became the Imperial British East Africa Company (hereafter IBEACo).[13] Before then, the sultan had "ruled" Taita in like

---

[8] Rebmann took one trip to Kasigau and a second to Dabida, where he traversed Chawia and the Bura Valley; for further analysis of Rebmann's visits to Taita, see Bravman, "Becoming," 116–21.

[9] Stock, *History of the Church Missionary Society*, 2: 129; also Krapf, 300–50.

[10] For Stanley's charge, the financial gifts and the CMS's first organizational effort to reach Buganda, see Stock, *History of the Church Missionary Society*, 3: chap. 74; also Roland Oliver, *The Missionary Factor in East Africa*, 2d ed. (London, 1964), 40, 41; for the East Africa Fund, see Strayer, *Mission Communities*,14.

[11] For a critical examination of early Frere Town, see A. J. Temu, *British Protestant Missions* (London, 1972), chaps. 1–2. Strayer, *Mission Communities*, chap. 2, is less unsympathetic. Joseph Harris, *Repatriates and Refugees in a Colonial Society: The Case of Kenya* (Washington, DC, 1987), chaps. 2–4, offers a positive assessment, especially of the Africans involved with it.

[12] For Binns's choice of Sagalla, see CMS, G3 A5/01; Binns to Hutchinson 29/12/80. Binns was compelled to stay at Frere Town as the station's secretary when his predecessor in that role was dismissed for brutality and disrespect towards its freed–slave converts. See Temu, *British Protestant Missions*, 16–19; Strayer, *Mission Communities*, 16–18; and J. Harris, *Repatriates and Refugees*, 24–25, 35–38.

[13] For the specifics of the concession, see P. L. McDermott, *British East Africa or IBEA: A History of the Formation and Work of the Imperial British East Africa Company* (London, 1893), 1–16; the full texts of the 1887 concession and 1888 supplement appear on pp. 263–75.

manner to the king of a tiny planet in *The Little Prince*, who commanded that the sun set in the evening and not before. Company authority, too, was at first sporadic and fragile, with little impact on the structure of communities; in the 1880s it also went largely ignored. The initial gesture of Company rule was a series of treaties that IBEACo officials made with three elders in different parts of the Hills, conveying sovereign rights over the Hills to the Company.[14] The elders either did not understand what they were signing, did not take it seriously, or were playing a different game—for none had the right to make such an agreement for even his own neighborhood. That the agreements gave the IBEACo authority over the entire region would have seemed, in local terms, a multiple absurdity. Company officials, however, considered the treaties binding, and mistook the signatories for "chiefs."

Dealings with the Company by one of the three elders, Mbogholi, capture the shallow pageantry and weak underpinnings of the initial arrangements. Mbogholi apparently signed the treaty as part of a long–term gamble that cooperating with Europeans would accrue power to him.[15] Though not a senior elder in his lower Bura Valley neighborhood, his immediate domain of influence flanked a main caravan route. A shrewd trader who dealt regularly with caravans, he was among the few elders in the Hills who spoke Swahili. He knew something, too, of Europeans' prejudices and predispositions, and played on them when IBEACo agents reached Bura in 1887. He was the first elder to present himself, and did so with unheard–of pomp and circumstance, arriving with a horn fanfare and a throne. He deliberately gave the impression of being a formidable figure, and after signing a treaty flew a Company flag from his homestead.[16]

Mbogholi hoped to translate Company backing into prestige and wealth that would enhance his standing. Instead, he aggravated more senior elders in lower Bura, who stood by the elders' protocol of not carrying on in an undignified manner before strangers. When the Europeans left, several elders expressed their displeasure at Mbogholi's brinkmanship, and in 1888 nearly swept him out of his own eldership. He managed to ride out the crisis, but his reputation never fully recovered among other elders. Politically, the treaty did nothing for the signatories in the short term: no local prestige accrued to Mbogholi

---

[14] One was Mbogholi of Barawa, in lower Bura; another was probably Mwagodi of Mlalenyi, (now called Msau, in Mbale location). See J. Alfred Wray, personal diary, Church Missionary Society Archives, Birmingham, Eng., 7/6/1893; also C. W. Hobley, *Kenya from Chartered Company to Crown Colony*, 2d ed. (1929; reprint, London, 1970), 62. I have found no clues to the third signer's name.

[15] Mbogholi befriended the CMS mission on Sagalla, and provided it a small plot in 1886 for itinerating at Bura. In the 1890s he also invited French Catholic missionaries to settle in his neighborhood. See CMS, G3 A5/05, Morris to Lang, 11/1/1888, and Wray to Lang 7/2/1888; La Congregation du St. Esprit, *Bulletin de la Congregation*, Tome Troisième, 1891–93, Maison Mere, Paris, 786–87.

[16] Information on Mbogholi's low ranking among elders and sham self–presentation to the Company comes from Merritt's interviews at Bura in 1970. See Merritt, "History of the Taita," 216–17. My 1988 fieldwork turned up only general remembrances of Mbogholi as an opportunist. Interview with Mrs. MM, Ilole/Bura, 16/8/1988.

or the IBEACo.[17] Lower Bura did, however, become a base of trade for the Company in Dabida, which benefited Mbogholi's lineage economically.[18]

In 1888, the IBEACo set up a small station at Ndii, on the plain just northeast of Dabida, along the caravan route to Ukambani, Gikuyuland, and Uganda. Ndii did nothing for local trade, and Company officials initially had little impact on local governance; lineage and neighborhood authority continued unabated.[19] Ndii operated mainly as a relay station along the route between the coast and the interior, and as a node of Company presence in the area. The latter role was underlined by a small contingent of Company soldiers (mostly coastal Africans). Around the Hills, the Company's presence appears to have been mainly intended to protect passing caravans from raiders. In the 1880s, Company soldiers did not fare well at this, for they barely slowed local raids on caravans and other regions.

Additionally, though IBEACo soldiers once came to Sagalla to support the mission in a local dispute, the Company did not project an aura of forceful authority in the Hills. Their one intervention in Sagalla in the 1880s inflamed local opinion, spurring Sagalla lineages into a subsequent violent confrontation with the mission that the Company did nothing to check. In communities during the 1880s, then, local terms of authority and social order, not those of the IBEACo, continued to predominate. Willingly or not, the first mission to Taita was constrained by that context.

The Start of Sagalla Mission

Wray, accompanied by Binns and a large caravan, first reached Sagalla in late January 1883.[20] Their efforts to negotiate for a suitable site for a station brought them into contact with several Sagalla elders at a number of locales. According to local remembrances, a long–distance trader who had met the missionaries in Mombasa brought them to his home neighborhood on the plains below the eastern slope of Sagalla. He, of course, like several others the missionaries met along the way, saw the missionaries as likely trading partners or at least magnets for trade.[21]

In local remembrances, the missionaries wanted to put the mission there, but local people objected; "they did not want to stay with this albino." These

---

[17]   CMS missionaries heard rumors of his demise in 1888 (Morris to Lang, 11/1/1888),which, despite his troubles, proved exaggerated. Mrs. MM, Ilole/Bura, 16/8/1988, also described him as getting into hot water, but surviving it.

[18]   Interviews with MM, Nyolo/Bura, 15/8/1988 and CA, Ilole/Bura, 17/8/1988. The treaty signing may not have been crucial to Mbogholi's prosperity; his economic fortune may have simply reflected increased traffic through an already well–established trading locale.

[19]   Of ten people interviewed, 20/6/1988–5/7/1988, in the parts of Mbololo location nearest Ndii, none recalled themselves, their parents, or their grandparents carrying on significant trade there.

[20]   One hundred eighty porters carried basic supplies and a disassembled 12' x 20' corrugated iron house. See CMS, G3 A5/01, 1883, Binns' Report on the Mission to Taita, n.d., (received in London 10/5/1883); also, Wray, Kenya, 10–11.

[21]   Interview with DM, Teri/Sagalla, 10/7/1993.

accounts say the neighborhood elders overruled the trader, ruling that Wray must look elsewhere. Missionary correspondence makes no mention of a desire to settle on the plain, but describes a week of seeking a site atop the mountain.[22] However, missionary and oral sources agree on a key point: an uplands elder named Mwakichucho facilitated the final site choice. Like their predecessors, Binns and Wray thought him a chief, setting themselves up for later disappointment. Mwakichucho was the most senior elder of his neighborhood, Teri, and among the most prominent on the mountain, as well as a diviner and maker of medicines. But he did not correspond to the missionaries' imagination of a chief. They expected him to have absolute authority, but this did not exist either in Teri:

> Mwakichucho was the one who made people meet. . . . If people hear so–and–so has come, [the elders] were the people who were saying, "people come here, we need to think about this thing. How is it going to be?" So [the elders] will come and talk, and then they will decide what they are going to do.[23]

or more broadly in Sagalla:

> [Here i]n Teri, the people of Mwakichucho's lineage followed their mzee, Mwakichucho, and at Mgange they followed their elders. . . . Mwakichucho was very much respected in Mgange, very much! It was a respect of elder to elder.
>
> Q: Did Mwakichucho control the other elders?
> A: No, each elder had his own lineage . . . each had his own respect.[24]

Wray would learn the limitations of local authority and community in Sagalla the hard way, and, constrained by his preconceptions, never fully grasped the system.

Even Mwakichucho's descendants are not quite sure why he invited the mission into his neighborhood. He was not a long–distance trader and had not previously courted a European presence; "it was just luck" that the missionaries had arrived in his vicinity, and perhaps his quick calculation of possible advantages that spurred him to support their presence and offer them a place on his lineage's land.[25] As on the plain, the missionary presence in Teri was not universally popular. Some elders feared that the stranger would upset the cosmological peace of the region, and a few wanted Wray speared immediately. But Mwakichucho's leverage won out; his lineage members and those in his

---

[22] Interview with LM, Kizumanzi/Sagalla, 21/7/1993; compare with Binns' Report.

[23] Interview, SM, Teri/Sagalla, 24/8/1988.

[24] For the European side, Binns' Report. For the quote, interview with DM, Teri/Sagalla, 10/7/1993; also, CN, Teri/Sagalla, 22/7/1993, and SM, Teri/Sagalla, 12/7/1993.

[25] Interview with JL. Teri/Sagalla, 23/7/1993. Elders and traders elsewhere in the Hills, hearing about the missionary camp at Sagalla, came to offer sites for a station, as well. See Binns' Report.

patronage networks effectively had to follow his lead on the issue. His prominence and his reputation as a medicine maker cowed many others. And, unbeknownst to the CMS, he ritually adopted Wray as a dependent, in like manner to how other outsiders were incorporated into Sagalla lineages. Mwakichucho, then, tried to define Wray as a new recruit to his lineage, thereby committing the lineage and neighborhood to defending him.[26]

In short order, it turned into a very difficult relationship for all concerned. Wray neither understood the local social order nor wished to belong to it, and regarded himself as nobody's dependent in Sagalla. His desire to preach and exemplify Christian ways made no concessions to local expectations about proper behavior. Within a few years, local people and Wray each saw the other as deeply problematic, and Mwakichucho's lineage became increasingly discomfited and divided by its position as Wray's defender. When drought and famine devastated Sagalla in the mid–1880s, local, *Wutasi*–based constructions of the situation linked the disaster to a cosmological crisis brought on by Wray.

Sagalla Community and the CMS Mission, 1883–1889

Mission Constructions of Sagalla, 1883–1884

According to his colleagues, Wray initially made a sincere effort to get along with Sagalla's people. By mid–1884, he had a working knowledge of KiSagalla; he "seemed to know everyone, and everyone knows him. . . . He has evidently gained their respect and good feeling."[27] But behind the placid picture painted by fellow missionaries, strains already showed. Wray felt that despite their initial friendliness, most people in Teri inhibited his work. Furthermore, his observations of daily life around Sagalla convinced him that its society was dangerously unruly, a veritable Hobbesian State of Nature where "every man does what is right in his own eyes."[28] This derived from his misunderstanding of elders' authority and the autonomy of Sagalla's neighborhoods, as well as from his dismay at local raiding within and beyond the Hills.

Wray decided that "chiefs" in Sagalla were chronically weak. In his view, they could not closely control the behavior of subordinates, nor constrain dissent and quarrels that sometimes turned violent (and in one case spilled over into Wray's compound).[29] Worse still, they could not, or would not,

---

[26] "Mwakichucho [ritually sacrificed] a cow . . . to make Wray his child." Interview with DM, 10/7/1993; also, CN, Teri/Sagalla, 22/7/1993.

[27] CMS, G3 A5/01, Handford to Lang, 4/5/1884.

[28] Wray liberally sprinkled variations on this phrase through his letters, diaries, and book; this quote comes from CMS, G3 A5/04(b) Wray to Lang, 10/11/1887. In 1872 Rev. Charles New, after a few days visiting Kasigau, used almost precisely the same words. See New, *Life, Wanderings*, 333. The missionary conception of African anarchy as the only alternative to chiefly order was apparently well–established. See also CMS, G3 A5/05, Bishop Parker to Lang, 28/12/1887, and Parker to Wray, 21/8/1888; and Thomas Hobbes, *Leviathan* (London, 1962), 103.

[29] CMS, G3 A5/04(b), Wray to Parker, 22/8/1887, and Wray to Downes–Shaw, 8/9/1887.

prevent subordinates from hectoring and driving away people who showed interest in Wray's preachings.[30] He never tempered complaints about Mwakichucho's lack of firm authority with suggestions that he understood the delimited character of that authority. He instead believed that Sagalla's chiefs lacked strong character and therefore provided feeble leadership, which led to chaos.

Wray did realize that no leader's influence had more than a very local reach, but made this grist for his argument that weak leaders let Sagalla's people slide into anarchic self–seeking. Early on, he had thought that Mwakichucho's support of the mission would give his evangelical efforts a wide geographical legitimacy, but it did not. Mwakichucho could call on his lineage and neighborhood to physically defend the European, but could not suppress the uneasiness many felt about him, nor deter people else-where in Sagalla from speaking against him, or even, as the years passed, waylaying him.

The attacks and the general prevalence of raiding also influenced Wray's views on Sagalla. His 1883–84 letters often described local raids of passing caravans and herds on the plains. He soon saw, too, that warriors from Sagalla often went "to Usambara and Pare to rob at night."[31] He added that raids to the east had generated great enmity along the coast towards people from Sagalla—they dared travel that way only in large, well–armed groups. Wray did not think raiding a misguided strategy for amassing wealth, for he did not recognize any broad strategy in it. To him, raiding simply be-spoke moral wretchedness, and indicated that Sagalla's people would rather prey on others than undertake productive, character-building work. His eminently Victorian view was that they needed to learn "to work by [their] own hands, and not eat by the labor of another."[32] Wray would later try to teach them moral lessons about work, and about the value of strong central authority, as well.

Despite Wray's misunderstandings of and dissatisfaction with Sagalla society, he relied almost entirely on local goodwill and support for his safety and well–being;[33] neither the Sultan of Zanzibar nor the IBEACo had any effective power there. Wray lived in Sagalla by community sufferance; Mwakichucho's lineage in particular made sure that Wray was given protection and civil treatment:

> [people in the area] wanted to play–play with Wray. Mwakichucho said, "I don't want this. You people here, you should not play–play about with this white man." So people [in Teri] got the word.[34]

---

[30] CMS, G3 A5/01, Wray to Lang, 27/1/1884; and G3 A5/04(b), Wray to Lang, 15/10/1887.

[31] CMS, G3 A5/04(b), Wray to Lang, 5/8/1888.

[32] Ibid.

[33] Temu points out that all missionaries operating beyond the limits of European expansion simi-larly relied on local societies for their safety. Temu, *British Protestant Missions*, 36, 38.

[34] Interview with SM, Teri/Sagalla, 24/8/1988. People in Sagalla later nicknamed Wray's son Mwakichucho—whether to honor the boy or to tweak the elder is unclear.

Community Tensions over Sagalla Mission

Within a year of his arrival, Wray put his support system to the test through interventions in local events that required Mwakichucho's supporters to defend him physically. In 1884, Wray seized a captive girl from a passing slave trader, who threatened to come up and take her back by force. The slave trader amassed warriors from four Sagalla neighborhoods to attack Wray, but warriors from Teri in turn gathered to confront them. The would–be assailants backed down, which Wray credited to God's hand, without mentioning his earthly defenders.[35] Warriors from Mwakichucho's neighborhood defended Wray several more times, until local confrontations with him came to a head in 1887.

Still, Mwakichucho's support for Wray could not prevent people in Sagalla from deciding that the white man was trouble. Firstly, they soon realized that Wray would not bring much new trade and wealth. Wray's presence offered no great economic or political advantage to Teri or Sagalla. He provided some material benefit through cloth, beads, and wire that he kept on hand to barter for some foods and services. He did not, however, facilitate any wider trade; on the contrary, his interference in the slave trade drew the wrath of coastal traders.[36]

Second, people found Wray's religious message baffling and unaffecting, an experience that echoed African responses to Krapf, Rebmann, and others.

> It is really astonishing with what little concern these people listen to the Gospel story. They don't seem to think it has anything to do with them. . . . They have no idea of sin, nor will ever have until the Holy Spirit teaches them. They do nothing but laugh at the idea of a resurrection.[37]

When Wray expressed this despair in 1884, people had already withdrawn some of the credibility originally granted him. This, too, stemmed from misconstrual: local misunderstanding of Wray's preachings, perhaps combined with less–than–clear translations of them, led people to believe at first that Christianity promised immortality: "when Wray preached, he said the word of God was, 'if you abide in me, you will not die, even everlasting.'" The belief that Christianity offered eternal life drew large crowds to Wray's services. Soon, of course, an elderly churchgoer died, people decided Wray was lying, and church attendance plummeted.[38]

Third, people in Sagalla began to see Wray as a problem because he refused to take part in local rituals and derided *Wutasi* beliefs. His dissent and non–participation caused a fundamental cosmological problem, for they were

---

[35] CMS, G3 A5/01, Wray to Lang, 23/5/1884.

[36] CMS, G3 A5/01, Handford to Lang, 4/5/1884. In Wray, *Kenya*, 26, he writes that he was told, "White man, . . . we are not getting the profit out of you we had hoped for."

[37] CMS, G3 A5/01, Wray to Lang, 7/1/1884.

[38] Interview with DN, Teri/Sagalla, 10/7/1993.

seen as inviting ancestral wrath to descend upon the living. Wray, like many missionaries of his time, saw African indigenous religions not only as wrong, but as a series of pointless actions devoid of real content. Describing a gathering to divine the causes of a serious drought and coordinate rain restoring strategies, he wrote:

> During the night a horn is blown, and voices are heard, at such a place we will assemble. They then put on their best cloths, and every man is furnished with a long stick, which is supposed to impart the possessor great wisdom. They meet in an open place, . . . then the talk begins. One man makes a long speech. Presently . . . two of them get up and go out from the rest. They stand face to face. One makes a long speech at the top of his voice. When that is done they . . . return to the rest of the people, then a few will come out and sit by themselves and have a long talk, then that group will sub–divide itself and so on. This will go on for days and days.[39]

Yet if Wray had no interest in or respect for *Wutasi*, many in Sagalla were curious about Christianity. Despite the fall–off after people realized it did not offer immortality, some maintained an active interest in it, discussing Christian beliefs with Wray and sometimes going to church services.[40] They did not, however, think Christianity and *Wutasi* incompatible. On the contrary, they often combined prayers learned from Wray with *Wutasi* forms and practices:

> When Wray first came, . . . the people used to mix Christian things and *Wutasi* things together. . . .
>
> *Q:* Was it the Christians who were mixing?
>
> *A:* Christians were not there yet! Those old men and women of long ago were not Christians, . . . but they liked to mix, even *Watasi* when I was a child were mixing like that.[41]

Behind this lay a view that Christian rituals and prayers might provide alternative answers to cosmological concerns; if the new forms proved effective, some in Sagalla would willingly add them to their repertoire. Nearly all Sagalla's people, however, were troubled by Wray's lack of like ascriptivism.

Wray firmly believed that to accommodate Teri by participating in local rituals "would be breaking God's law by leaving him and following the Gods of [Sagalla]."[42] Taking this further and distressing people all across Sagalla as word of it traveled, he publicly insisted that *Wutasi* rituals and medicines, whether for war, rainmaking, or protection from wild animals, would not work.

---

[39] CMS, G3 A5/01, Wray to Lang, 29/3/1884; see also Wray to Lang 31/3/1884.

[40] People's interest did provoke intraneighborhood controversy: the curious were liable to be teased or scolded by others. See CMS, G3 A5/01, Wray to Lang, 27/1/1884, 31/3/1884, 8/5/1884.

[41] Interview with Mrs. NM, Kizumanzi/Sagalla, 24/8/1988.

[42] CMS, G3 A5/01, Wray to Lang, 8/5/1884.

He invited people to use medicines on him or his compound, and was pleased to learn that attempts were indeed made. He thought the medicines' failure would make people lose faith in them; then, he believed, they would turn to Christianity.[43]

The results were rather different. When *Wutasi* rituals and prayers proved ineffective, people decided that Wray was obstructing the rituals' desired outcome. They had expected him, like any other immigrant, to take part in group rituals of well–being for his adopted lineage and neighborhood. His refusals to do so, topped off by his denunciations of *Wutasi*, were widely viewed as profoundly disruptive of community *sere* (peace), which the ancestors would punish by visiting misfortune on the living. Thus, Wray's attempts to discredit *Wutasi* sowed suspicions about him, not doubts about it. Those suspicions came into sharp focus in 1884 and spread throughout the region when a severe drought overtook the whole of Taita. Throughout the Hills, rumor cast blame for the calamity upon Sagalla's missionary.[44]

Drought and Localism, 1884–1888

Taita's drought and famine of the mid–1880s is the oldest one about which many particular remembrances remain, and the first one described by outsiders.[45] When confronted with the disaster, communities turned to rituals of appeasement and local social networks as first lines of defense; as the situation grew desperate, communities across the Hills temporarily abandoned their neighborhoods in the hope of relief in the distant regions where they maintained claims and ties of ancestry. Intra–Taita response tended heavily towards intercommunity raiding.

Did the responses to this drought resemble prior ones? Wray's presence and widespread blaming of him for the drought may have made it less likely than usual that Sagalla's people would find help nearby. Perhaps, too, the drought of 1884–85 was unusually severe, crushing intraregional support structures that in previous crises worked well. On the other hand, had intraregional cooperation in most famines been the norm, one would hope to find remembrances and invokings of it; my inquiries turned up none. Additionally, widespread resort to regions of ancestral origin suggests that farther–flung networks were regarded as the main haven from local calamity. Appeals to ancestral regions—even across long distances—called upon notions of community bound up in kinship ideology. Prolonged hardship in the Hills mobilized no corre-

---

[43]   CMS, G3 A5/01, Wray to Lang, 31/3/1884, 15/4/1884, 8/5/1884, 6/8/1884; also Wray, *Kenya*, 48.

[44]   Sagalla grumblings that Wray brought on drought and famine broke out into the open in March 1884. By April, people in Dabida blamed the missionary, too; rumor there had it that the Europeans had driven him out of his own country for causing droughts. CMS, G3 A5/01, Wray to Lang, 31/3/1884, 21/4/1884.

[45]   Some people recall the existence of a famine a generation earlier, apparently in the late 1850s or early 1860s, but none had detailed remembrances of it. The main outside observations were made by Wray in his letters to the CMS, and in *Kenya*, 35–39, 45–57.

sponding ideology of support across neighborhood boundaries. Too, distant locales were more likely to be free of environmental crisis. If unique in some regards, local responses to the 1884–85 drought nonetheless seem rooted in prior ways of coping.

The Crisis in Sagalla and Wray's Community

When the short rains failed throughout the Taita Hills in late 1883, people across the region sought explanations for it. Each neighborhood conducted its own rainmaking ritual, the first requirement of which was that the ritual be performed properly. Widespread failure of the rains implied that the problem did not lie in ritual performance, but in the anger of *Mlungu* (God) at disruptions in the *sere* of one or more communities.[46] The most likely disruption was sorcery. In early 1884, some people around Sagalla grumbled that Wray not only refused to take part in rituals, but conducted sorcery that obstructed rain. As the March–to–May rainy season of 1884 approached, elders in Sagalla tried to heal the breach in community peace by getting Wray to take token part in Teri's rainmaking. Prominent elders repeatedly asked him to donate an animal to be sacrificed for the ritual. Wray consistently refused.[47] The rains failed, and accusations that he used his unfamiliar paraphernalia to make sorcery came out into the open and spread to Dabida.[48]

By mid–1884, famine gripped all the Taita Hills, but had hit Sagalla earliest, and, possibly, hardest. The famine generated many names, but in Dabida was often called *Njala ya Wasagha* (Famine of the WaSagalla).[49] As the plains became parched, Sagalla's people moved themselves and their livestock up the mountain, nearer to the remaining food supplies. The move also protected livestock from increasing predations by warriors from elsewhere in the Hills.[50] Sagalla community fractured when other neighborhoods, blaming Mwakichucho's people for harboring Wray, sought to plunder and punish Teri. When the slave trader convinced warriors from four Sagalla neighborhoods to attack the mission compound in May 1884, they were motivated in large part by anger at Wray's purported rain obstruction.[51]

---

[46] On rainmaking rituals, the importance of ritual form, and rain obstructions, see G. Harris, *Casting*, 29, 127–32.

[47] For example, CMS, G3 A5/01, Handford to Lang, 6/8/1884. Wray *did* sympathize with (and share in) the plight of Sagalla's people. Even as he criticized *Wutasi* rainmaking, he promised to entreat the Christian God for rain. Under the circumstances, however, that gave little comfort.

[48] Wray's bell raised considerable suspicion, perhaps because of the existence of a Bell shrine in *Wutasi*. People also distrusted the sound of Wray's rifle, his magnifying glass, his harmonium, and a book. See CMS, G3 A5/01, Wray to Lang, 15/4/1884, and 21/4/1884.

[49] Merritt, "History of the Taita," 100–112.

[50] Interviews indicate that during the 1884–85 drought, raids between neighborhoods in Dabida were common, as well; for example, interviews with OK, Shigaro/Werugha, 3/8/1993, and GM, Kishamba/Chawia, 12/8/1988.

[51] CMS, G3 A5/01, Wray to Lang, 19/4/1884.

Sagalla's people, regardless of neighborhood, had no recourse to Dabida during the crisis. Those who attempted to call upon blood brotherhood ties there had a rude comeuppance:

> In the days of that [1884–85] famine, some of the people said, "I have eaten *mtero* with so–and–so at Bura [Dabida], I have eaten *mtero* with so–and–so at Mwakinyungu [Dabida], now let me go to see them." Ai! If he came back alive, it was only good luck. [Laughs] [52]

In early 1884, when food was still reportedly available in Dabida, a few groups from Sagalla took goods there to trade. Instead, their goods were seized and the women among them taken captive.[53] The extent of the breakdown in relations was marked by the fact that, according to Wray, old debts were used to justify the seizures. If debts existed, then most likely *mtero* ties linked the parties. Claiming those debts as justifications for seizures suggested a termination of blood brotherhood.

By May, the utter failure of the 1884 long rains made food in Sagalla very scarce—Mwakichucho himself sometimes passed two or three days without a bite. Once famine took hold, disease followed: early that month, smallpox broke out in Teri. Other neighborhoods quickly turned from threatening to isolating Teri. The epidemic was the last straw of disaster, and the last nail in Wray's reputation. Shortly thereafter thousands abandoned Sagalla, making for ancestral regions in Giriama country at the coast. A large but uncounted number died during the arduous hundred-mile trek across parched terrain.[54] Similar emigrations emanated from Dabida: people left for Pare, Usambara, Kilimanjaro, and parts of the coast.[55] Sagalla's was the most extreme exodus, though: only about two hundred people from Mwakichucho's lineage remained. Even other Teri lineages departed.

Those who stayed, recently vilified by the rest of Sagalla for defending Wray, now relied on him completely. They had run out of food, goods, and networks, and saw him as their only hope for survival. Wray called them "my two hundred Friendlies," and kept them and himself alive on food supplied by occasional CMS caravans from the coast.[56] The Friendlies, in return, attended Wray's services and sent their children to a school he established. Wray states that they told him, "Our children will be your children, and we will be your big children. You shall be our chief, our king, our father, or whatever you choose

---

[52] Interview with Mrs. NM, Kizumanzi/Sagalla, 24/8/1988.

[53] CMS, G3 A5/01, Wray to Lang, 21/4/1884.

[54] People took the epidemic as further proof against Wray's supposed promise that his followers would not die. Interview with CN, Teri/Sagalla, 22/7/1993. All eight 1993 interviewees described the trek to the coast, as did five of eight in 1988; see also, Wray, *Kenya*, 52.

[55] Sixteen people in Dabida described emigrations because of this famine, among them MT, Kishamba/ Chawia, 9/6/1988; FW, Mgange Nyika/Mwanda, 20/9/1988; AM, Mogho Mleche/ Mbale, 4/11/1988.

[56] Wray, *Kenya*, 52. The record of Wray's correspondence lapses from mid–1884 to mid–1885, so reconstruction of this period turns largely on interpreting information in his book.

to call yourself." Whether someone spoke such exact words, let alone truly saw the relationship with Wray in this manner, is doubtful.[57] That they were utterly dependent on Wray's pipeline of food and needed to maintain his favor is certain: his carefully rationed supplies kept them alive.

In late 1884 and 1885, warrior bands from Dabida raided Sagalla several times, hoping to seize the remaining livestock of Mwakichucho's lineage. The Friendlies managed, with some difficulty, to fight off these attacks.[58] The CMS urged Wray to abandon Sagalla, for it was difficult to get caravans through to him. Not surprisingly, the two hundred in Sagalla were anxious that he stay, and he never considered leaving, for desperate circumstances had turned things his way. The famine and depopulation allowed him to replace Sagalla's "State of Nature" with his own orderly authority—he spoke of Sagalla as his "little kingdom"—and he would not abandon it.[59] Still, it was no light decision: food caravans *did* cease for a time, and starvation and death overcame some of the Friendlies. Wray suffered a two-month bout of malaria, compounded by malnutrition and exhaustion. When the long rains actually fell in early 1885, he finally left for the coast, and, in his weakened condition, nearly joined the legions who had recently died en route.[60]

The Resurgence of Sagalla Community, and the Downfall of Wray's, 1886–1888

Wray returned to Sagalla in September 1886. Mwakichucho's lineage still formed the bulk of Sagalla's population, and Wray's vision for Sagalla's future drew on his 1884 experience with them. He would preside as benevolent priest/king over an orderly theocracy; he would ensure the social peace, tame the people's violent, anarchic passions, and bring them to Christ. His first reunion encouraged those ideas:

> They would soon return to their old ways if I were not here to check them. . . . I [get] them to sit down and settle matters quietly. . . . I am very hopeful of them, they seem to do everything I want them. I have a great influence over them. I believe I could put my veto on anything that was wrong within a certain radius. Whatever [I tell them] is wrong they acknowledge it and wish to do right.[61]

However, once the drought had passed, members of Sagalla's other neighborhoods began to return from Giriama. The returnees quickly reestablished prior terms of community, giving short shrift to Wray's authority and vision of

---

[57] Wray, *Kenya*, 45; also 46, 48. Wray's book consistently collapses Sagalla's people into a single, quotable voice, which undermines the credibility of the quotes, but tells much about Wray's own consciousness. See Bravman, "Becoming," 109–114, 140–56.

[58] Ibid., 52–54.

[59] Ibid., 45.

[60] Ibid., 55–57.

[61] CMS, G3 A5/03, Wray to Lang, 9/1886.

society. To them, he was the reason they'd had to leave in the first place; that Mwakichucho's lineage had stood by him now counted more as a detriment to that elder's position than as an advantage to Wray. They saw Wray as no less a social and cosmological problem than before, and despite his imaginings of grandeur, he remained outside the renewed social order of Sagalla. He had no position of strength within a lineage, no ritual standing, no seniority; he had certain kinds of spiritual and material power, but nothing like overriding power. Over the next year, as Sagalla's lineage and neighborhood communities rebuilt themselves, Wray's vision of community was swept aside—a circumstance that he did not bear well. Eventually, he tried to shore up his declining authority with a show of European force, but that only concentrated local wrath upon him and further diminished Mwakichucho's reputation.[62]

As the returnees came back to Sagalla in late 1886 and early 1887, they chided Mwakichucho's people for giving Wray such a strong hand in the affairs of Teri. Wray tried to keep his small group loyal, and argued to the CMS:

> [This place] is ours by right. Of course I know that according to English law it could not be, but by their own laws and customs the right is ours. With them, if a man picks up a stranger he calls him his slave forever, so I argue that I have picked up a whole village, and they can't deny it.[63]

Most returnees did not bother to deny Wray's claims; they instead refused to cooperate with his interpositions, and set about reopening fields, restocking herds, and reviving neighborhood and lineage networks. Through cajoling, harassment and social sanctions, they whittled away the resolve of Wray's supporters among Mwakichucho's lineage. Wray had reopened a school and church in 1886, with both at first well attended. A year later, however, school attendance was nil, and churchgoing quickly approached the same level.[64] Now that the drought had passed, young people had their usual farming, herding, and housework tasks; in fact, since fields had gone fallow, paths had overgrown, and dwellings had crumbled, labor needs were that much greater. In addition, local bullying of the Friendlies drove down Wray's numbers.[65]

---

[62] In contrast to the detailed attention Wray's book gave the 1884–85 drought, it makes no mention of the difficulties of 1886–87. Bravman, "Becoming," 142–58, provides more detail on the latter crisis.

[63] CMS, G3 A5/04(b), Wray to Bishop Parker, 22/8/1887. Parker, aghast at Wray's position, penciled three exclamation points into the margin. Wray also here grossly (and deliberately?) misread how captives were incorporated into lineages. Strikingly, Wray for the next year referred to returnees as "outsiders," and himself, by contrast, as an insider (e.g., CMS, G3 A5/04(b), Wray's letters to Downes–Shaw, 8/9/1887, and to Lang, 15/10/1887). This positioning helped him justify (to himself, at least), his attempts to reorder Sagalla society.

[64] CMS, G3 A5/04(b), Wray to Downes–Shaw, 8/9/1887.

[65] On the former point, interviews with SM, Kishamba/Sagalla, 23/8/1988; Mrs. GM, Teri/Sagalla, 24/8/1988; and Mrs. NM, Kizumanzi/Sagalla, 24/8/1988. For an example of the latter, see CMS, G3 A5/04(b), Wray to Lang, 15/10/1887.

Not all the drift came from returnees' pressures on the Friendlies. Some parents resented Wray's presumptiveness. Some in Mwakichucho's lineage admitted that they had accepted his authority during the famine because they'd had no choice. Now they could choose, and would not follow his rules; furthermore, several told him, they had never meant to give up their own ways.[66]

As local forms of community reasserted themselves, Wray grew more insistent. He began visiting homesteads to hunt up children for school. Parents in response hid them from him, and a conclave of Teri elders decided that the school and church were to be boycotted. They also rejected Wray's assertion that he be allowed to arbitrate local disputes. As tensions escalated in mid–1887, Wray first reiterated his authority claim and vision of community for there:

> If I were to start a new station . . . I would build apart [from any village] . . . whoever came to live with me would be under my control. The day he refused to be controlled by me he would simply leave my village; thus order would be preserved. I ought to preserve order in *this* village, [i.e., the mission site amidst Mwakichucho's lineage], for it is ours by right.
>
> Yesterday I called all the men together and . . . said, "Whoever wished to have rows let him go elsewhere and not bring them here. Many people have come here lately and built their houses without asking anybody. . . . Now in future anyone who wishes to come here must first ask *my* permission, and I will make him swear that he will *1st* bring no war here, 2 that he will sow no discord, *3rd* that he will conform to the useages of the village.[67]

Then, using IBEACo troops, he tried to impose them forcibly:

> How can [the state of affairs here] be remedied? The only way I can suggest is to make ourselves Masters of the village in lieu of all the goods they have eaten belonging to us. Besides this, they are all in debt to myself, debts contracted during the famine. . . . If I could get a dozen decent people to come up . . . here I should perhaps strike a

---

[66] CMS, G3 A5/04(b), Wray to Downes–Shaw, 8/9/1887; and Wray to Lang, 15/10/1887.

[67] CMS, G3 A5/04(b), Wray to Bishop Parker, 22/8/1887; my italics. People at the meeting told Wray that a few other elders, not present, had to be consulted on this. They never got back to him.

The Comaroffs hold that missionaries' authoritarian dreams in Africa reflected their yearning for a world "in which technical progress . . . did not cause the massive social upheaval it had sown . . . in the north of England; in which the countryside was not disfigured, nor its free yeomanry dispossessed. . . . They sought, in other words, a modern industrial capitalist world without its contradictions." Jean Comaroff and John Comaroff, "Colonization of Consciousness in South Africa," *Economy and Society* 18, 2 (1989): 270.

Strayer argues persuasively that missionaries' doubts about capitalism drove them towards older models: "Insofar as they looked to the Western tradition for desirable cultural patterns for Africa, it was in the Middle Ages rather than the modern era that they sought inspiration." This "nostalgic medievalism" emphasized "the wholesomeness of rural communities, the religious integration of life, and the centrality of the church in the social order. . . . Africa presented a chance to build anew in a more congenial, essentially pre–modern environment." Strayer, *Mission Communities*, 90; see 87–96.

little terror into them. Unless something of this sort is done, I don't see how we can make any progress here.

Mr. Holmwood [an IBEACo officer on tour with a detachment of soldiers] could do it, and he being so near, I have taken upon myself to write to him. . . . [He] would have to . . . take two or three of the ringleaders to Zanzibar to chop sticks. . . . We might then bring them to their senses. . . . They owe their lives, their wives, and their little ones to the Society.[68]

Before Wray's horrified supervisors could prevent it, an IBEACo column scaled Sagalla. The company's European officer made a show of force and threatened to jail anyone who obstructed others from going to school or services.[69] As IBEACo rule was then only months old, the officer probably appreciated the opportunity to display the Company's teeth. The teeth, however, did not intimidate for long. Five weeks later, in October 1887, a group of warriors from a nearby neighborhood tried to drive Wray and a new companion missionary off a cliff. The last handful of Friendlies and armed servants from Wray's household rescued them, but a Sagalla bystander was inadvertently shot and killed in the process. Waves of warriors from throughout Sagalla then swarmed to Teri. After a day of siege on Wray's compound, elders from across Sagalla called off the warriors and gathered to discuss the killing. Their meetings took several days, during which they made Wray feed them lavishly. The stiff fine they imposed mattered less than the outcome that everyone acknowledged: the missionary's attempt to impose his authority, and his version of community, had collapsed.[70]

Nearly all of Wray's prior supporters were now alienated. The school stood empty, as did the church. The few who went no longer wanted to try the Christian prayers; instead, they went to mock the European ritual.[71] Wray hung on in Sagalla until 1890, when he finally acceded to two years of CMS requests that he take his overdue furlough.[72] Those in Mwakichucho's lineage who sup-

---

[68] CMS, G3 A5/04(b), Wray to Downes–Shaw, 8/9/1887; his supervisors strongly rebutted his claims, but too late.

[69] For Wray's account of Holmwood's visit, see CMS, G3 A5/04(b), Wray to Downes–Shaw, 20/9/1887. For the CMS supervisors' attempts to stop Holmwood's intervention and their dismay afterwards, see Downes–Shaw to Wray, 16/9/1887; Downes–Shaw to Lang, 27/9/1887; and Downes–Shaw to Wray, 27/9/1887; Wray defended his actions to Lang, 15/10/1887.

[70] Curiously, my 1988 and 1993 interviews at Sagalla turned up no remembrances of this incident, though people spoke of general tensions between their ancestors and Wray. Merritt, researching in 1970–71, also notes that "so vaguely remembered is this period of CMS work . . . that informants could contribute nothing of any significance." Merritt, "History of the Taita," 234, n. 40. The CMS letters describing this crisis are G3 A5/04(b), Wray to Lang, 10/11/1887; and G3 A5/05, Wray to Lang, 9/12/1887; and Morris to Lang, 8/12/1887.

[71] CMS, G3 A5/05, Morris to Lang, 11/1/1888; and Wray to Lang, 7/2/1888.

[72] CMS, G3 A5/05(b), Price to Lang, 4/7/1888; G3 A5/06: Price to Lang, 28/12/1888; Price to Pruen, 25/3/1889; Pruen to Lang, 29/7/1889; and Smith to Lang, 22/10/1889.

The Bishop of East Africa believed Wray unable to work with Sagalla's "native authorities." Yet the Bishop, too, saw Sagalla as a state of nature with an authority structure so weak that "it is difficult to define exactly what [it] consists of." He differed with Wray not over their vision of the Sagalla society, but over how to operate in such a place. See CMS, G3 A5/05, Bishop Parker to Lang, 28/12/1887; and Parker to Wray, 21/1/1888.

ported Wray before 1887 were stigmatized or worse for it. Mwakichucho himself lost a great deal of influence and prestige. Kibwangi, *Kishingila* of Sagalla and young brother of Mwakichucho, lost his position for having been too friendly with the European. In the post–famine flurry of herd–rebuilding raids, loss of this position probably cut into the wealth of Mwakichucho's lineage.[73]

In the late 1880s, Sagalla elders quickly and forcefully reestablished their own terms of community there. The CMS, effectively conceding that the crisis had crippled their efforts, closed Sagalla station. The rule of the IBEACo, exposed as ineffective, declined for a time to virtual non–existence. Sagalla's people still had the autonomy to imagine and deal with the missionary as they saw fit, which allowed them to pointedly reject Wray's attempts to refashion the social order. Too, the mission had not persuaded anyone in Sagalla to challenge the social order in any enduring way. In this regard, the wrangles of the 1880s brought on by the mission remained outside Sagalla cultural politics (i.e., they did not become a basis for intrasociety struggles to alter norms and terms of society in Sagalla).

However, IBEACo military force in the early 1890s would dramatically alter how people in society thereafter understood the missionaries and Europeans in general. In the aftermath of conquest, Christianity would make more headway among some in Sagalla. The converts and the culture of the mission would then begin to challenge local terms of community, as well.

---

[73] On the decline of Mwakichucho's prestige, interview with Mrs. NM, Kizumanzi/Sagalla, 24/8/1888; for this and Kibwangi's loss of position, see G3 A5/05(c), Morris to Lang, 10/8/1888.

3

Early Colonialism and Taita's Local Communities, 1892–1910

Introduction

In the 1890s, outsiders achieved a loose overrule of all Taita. Britain did not exert day–to–day control of local communities, but nonetheless imposed a new layer of authority above lineages and neighborhoods. The Europeans' sporadic suzerainty did not eliminate extant kin–and–locale–based power structures, but the outsiders did not use local authorities to exercise dominion, either. Instead, colonial military force provided the Europeans' ways and means.

Elders responded to that imposed presence differently in different locales. Some tried to counter force with force; others dealt directly and hospitably with the new authorities, hoping that the evident goodwill of a neighborhood would encourage overstretched colonial officials to leave it alone. Still others sought an intermediary who understood the unpredictable, dangerous new rulers, and could represent the community to them. The latter two approaches provided avenues by which missionaries were allowed, even welcomed, into communities across Taita. In the context of the colonial incursion, the missions attracted greater and more consistent local interest. The CMS soon gained its first converts, people who, unlike Wray's supporters of the 1880s, took Anglicanism's beliefs and social vision seriously.

Missionaries posed no political threat to Taita's established order by 1910, but the Anglican converts became a social one. They were shaping an alternative community, one centered not on kinship and locality, but on church belonging and spiritual fellowship. That Christian community crossed lineage and neighborhood boundaries, even as it challenged the cosmological bases of local social orders. As a result, the rise of a Christian community in Taita gave rise to new cultural politics over the terms of society in the Hills—a politics fraught with overt confrontations.

Imperial Force and Localized Responses in Taita, 1892–1900

The Extension of Colonial Force

If the IBEACo lacked the reach and reputation to protect a missionary in 1880s Taita, it soon thereafter projected coercive force far more effectively in defense of its trading interests. The Company cared little about expanding its trade with societies in the Hills—for it put only a slight effort into profiting from the region—but a great deal about traders crossing the region. Local societies' caravan raiding in the 1880s had led a British official to describe Taita as an area of "hill robbers, sitting on their mountains like hawks, or barons of old, watching for any weak party coming near their homes."[1] In 1892, to stop the raiding, the IBEACo began to put force behind its paper suzerainty. As befitted the localism of Taita's societies, their responses to European force were neither uniform nor coordinated. Elders in a few communities urged warriors to arms against Company soldiers. Elders of other neighborhoods chose to avoid armed confrontation, and still others cooperated with the British authorities, hoping for new opportunities from the relationship.

The 1892 incident that precipitated forcible Company intervention began when warriors from Mwanda (in Dabida's eastern highlands) raided the caravan of a cloth trader named Mohammed bin Ali, shortly after the caravan left its overnight campsite near lower Bura.[2] The raiders dressed in Maasai clothing, hoping to hide their identity from their victims. In an unusual innovation prompted by Mwangeka,[3] *kishingila* of Mwanda, his warriors had planned to coordinate the raid with some upper Bura warriors, as part of the interneighborhood warrior cooperation he'd fostered between his section of Mwanda and Bura in recent years. Several Bura elders disliked this cooperation, for it blurred the social boundary between their own fighting forces and a

---

[1] C.E. Gissing, quoted in CMS, G3 A5/05, Morris to Lang, 11/1/1888; Gissing expresses similar sentiments in "A Journey."

[2] Public Record Office (hereafter PRO), Foreign Office 84/2552 195, Nelson to Mombasa Administrator, 5/5/1892.

[3] Mwangeka was an ornery youth who grew into an outstanding fighter and raid leader. He was said to possess medicines that repelled bullets or arrows. See Merritt, "History of the Taita," 241–44. He is remembered today as a *Kishingila* of legendary proportions. A female descendent said one of his medicines froze Maasai in their tracks, so he and his warriors could kill them easily. Interview with Mrs. SM, Weni Mwalenjo/Mwanda, 14/9/1988. Nor was his reputation confined to Mwanda: in Mbale, on the other side of Dabida, people remember him as a daunting warrior and almost superhuman physical presence: "His body was like Goliath." Interview with MM, Mbale/Mbale, 7/11/1988.

Mwangeka's coastal trade ties reputedly included trade in war medicines with a coastal Swahili blood brother. Interview with Mrs. SM, Kikesuni/Mwanda, 14/9/1988.

rival area's; the ease with which both sides now breached the alliance under-lined its fragility.[4] Mwanda warriors decided at the last minute to fight alone, then kept all the purloined goods for themselves and their lineages.[5]

Mohammed bin Ali survived the raid, and reported it to the IBEACo in Mombasa, which sent Captain Robert Nelson and a column of Company sol-diers to punish the raiders. Mohammed bin Ali had not been fooled into think-ing the raiders were Maasai, but did claim they were from Bura.[6] Bura's dis-gruntled elders, however, readily pointed fingers towards Mwanda and Mwangeka.[7] These elders, displeased enough by the ongoing cooperation be-tween rival neighborhood warrior groups, also resented the attack on Mohammed bin Ali, their coastal trading partner.[8] Nelson led his column up the Bura valley to the Bura–Mwanda border. There a detachment of Mwangeka's men set upon the soldiers with bows and arrows. The soldiers opened fire, killing fifteen in short order, then burned several villages and seized all the goats and sheep they could manage.[9]

As Nelson's soldiers prepared to camp for the night at the homestead of a sympathetic Bura elder, Mwangeka and his warriors launched a surprise head–on assault. After the first fracas, his brother Mashika had warned Mwangeka not to attack, but Mwangeka reportedly called the soldiery "only women, Swahili women, what can they do to me?"[10] The warriors by every account fought fiercely and determinedly, but within half an hour rifles overwhelmed arrows, spears, and medicines. Mwangeka and an uncounted "large number" of warriors lay dead, as against one death and twelve wounded for the Com-pany soldiers.[11]

Word of the decisive defeat of Mwangeka swept across Taita, and dramati-cally altered local societies' regard for the Europeans. Elders were stunned that the outsiders had broached the mountain fastness and, apparently immune to a neighborhood's best protective medicines, slain the man widely regarded as

---

[4]   Interviews with PM, Ilole/Bura, 16/8/1988; MM, Nyolo/Bura, 17/8/1988; and Mrs. SM, Kikesuni/Mwanda, 14/9/1988.

[5]   Interview with Mrs. SM, Kikesuni/Mwanda, 14/9/1988; also Merritt, "History of the Taita," 238–39; PRO, Foreign Office 84/2552 195, Nelson to Mombasa Administrator, 5/5/1892.

[6]   PRO, Foreign Office 84/2552 195, Berkeley to the Secretary, 22/5/1892.

[7]   Merritt, "History of the Taita," 241–43.

[8]   Interview with PM, Ilole/Bura, 16/8/1988.

[9]   PRO, Foreign Office 84/2552 195, Nelson to Mombasa Administrator, 5/5/1892.

[10]   A quote for the annals of famous last words. Interview with Mrs. SM, Kikesuni/Mwanda, 14/9/1988. It was substantively confirmed by Mrs. SM, Weni Mwalenjo/Mwanda, 14/9/1988.

[11]   PRO, Foreign Office 84/2552 195, Nelson to Mombasa Administrator, 5/5/1892. One interviewee said Mwangeka was defeated because local rivals learned the secret of his medicine and sold it to the soldiers. Interview with MM, Njawuli/Mwanda, 12/9/1988. Another claimed that Swahili trad-ers, having been attacked by Mwanda warriors, complained to Mwangeka's Swahili blood brother at the coast. The blood brother then counteracted the medicine he had given Mwangeka, leaving him vulnerable to his attackers. Interview with Mrs. SM, Kikesuni/Mwanda, 14/9/1988. Wray surveyed the battle scene a few years later, talked with an acquaintance there, and felt that had Mwangeka's warriors attacked before Nelson's troops reached the clearing where they were set-ting up camp, the fight would have turned out differently. Wray's diaries, CMSA, 9/6/1893.

the area's greatest warrior. Never again did a neighborhood warrior group try a direct assault on Company troops.[12] A few years later, the IBEACo stationed a larger column of soldiers at Ndii under the British official there. The Company presence did not alter elders' authority over lineages and neighborhoods in the 1890s. For that matter, Company rule rarely affected local societies' day–to–day affairs. Even raiding did not stop immediately, continuing sporadically down to the end of the century. The official and his soldiers, however, became a noted and feared presence, a force that could rain down disaster on a neighborhood. In 1895, the East African Protectorate (EAP) replaced the IBEACo, but for people in Taita the changeover made little immediate difference.[13] In both guises the Europeans remained distant authorities who nonetheless had to be appeased, kept in the dark, or held at arm's length.

Predatory Colonialism, 1893–1900

A favorite justifying chestnut of Britain's imperial proponents distinctly resembled Wray's "state of nature" argument about Sagalla. *Pax Britannica*, they said, would bring peace and security to benighted people who otherwise lived in dangerous, disorderly, chaotic conditions.[14] People in Taita during the 1890s experienced the new colonial order rather differently: as arbitrary and summary expropriation combined with the potential for ruinous attacks. An 1898 punitive expedition reveals this erratic, predatory character at its extreme: two soldiers from Ndii climbed up Dabida, approached a man milking his cow, threatened to conscript him for forced labor, then tried to steal the cow. The irate man killed one soldier, but was in turn killed by the other, who then fled back to Ndii. The dead soldier's rifle was taken to Mwaidoma, the *kishingila* of the area. The European officer at Ndii went to Mwaidoma's, seized the rifle, and executed him on the spot. When Mwaidoma's people then chased the European off, he sent for two companies of the 1st Baluchi regiment. The troops killed eighty in the neighborhood, burned homes and food supplies, and seized over sixty head of livestock for good measure.[15]

The new colonial government only infrequently resorted to such terrorizing shows of force, for a soldier could normally go into the Hills with his rifle, invent a pretext, and lead a cow away with impunity. People in 1890s Taita

---

[12] Three more colonial sorties struck Taita: one in 1895, in Mwanda; a second, in 1896, on the plains near Ndii; and a third in 1898, on the Bura/Mwanda border again. On the first, see Wray's diaries, CMSA, 2–4/11/1895; on the latter two, see Merritt, "History of the Taita," 254–61.

[13] As Lonsdale and Berman point out, the initial British staff of the East African Protectorate was mostly old IBEACo employees. See John Lonsdale and Bruce Berman, "Coping with the Contradictions: The Development of the Colonial State in Kenya, 1895–1914," *Journal of African History* 20, 4 (1979): 495.

[14] For instance, C.W. Hobley, an IBEACo employee who later became a senior colonial official, wrote in 1896 that Company sorties and punitive raids suppressed intertribal raiding, proved to already–allied tribes that the EAP could guarantee the law and order it promised and redress wrongs, and made it safe for small parties to travel freely. See Hobley to Commissioner, 22/9/1896, in *Kenya: Select Historical Documents 1884–1923*, G. H. Mungeam (Nairobi, 1978), 122.

[15] Merritt, "History of the Taita," 256–61.

quickly learned that fighting off a plundering soldier might spur a response that escalated an individual's sufferings into mass tragedy. Thus, the initial *Pax Britannica* effectively gave soldiers in British uniforms license to prey on people who feared the consequences of self–defense. Soldiers could usually get away with beating a man up, tying him to a tree, and demanding livestock as ransom for releasing him.[16] Soldiers with orders from Ndii to levy a fine of goats in Sagalla might help themselves to extra goats along the way, selling them en route at Voi, (a new town on the plains just east of Dabida), to supplement their meager salaries.[17]

One might expect people in Taita to respond to these predations with resistances great and small. Such acts did take place, and some neighborhoods remained hostile to European rule throughout the 1890s. But local societies' responses to early colonialism varied far more than the historiography of African resistance in Taita (and elsewhere) often suggests.[18] The long prior history of intra–Taita rivalries and enmities, as well as some neighborhoods' previous trade and/or friendly relations with Europeans, produced wide–ranging responses to even these provocations. In some areas, subtle and not–so–subtle postures of resistance shaped people's dealings with the colonial order. In others, elders sought direct, cooperative relations with colonial officials, hoping thereby to keep colonial soldiers out of their neighborhoods. In one neighborhood, an elder hoped his close state connections would give him a local leg up on the other elders. In another, elders turned to an outside intermediary to help them understand and deal with the new state.

Tacit and overt resistance to the incursions of Europeans in the 1890s stemmed mostly from neighborhoods high up Dabida, particularly Mwanda and Mgange. These neighborhoods had not previously been unusually insular or confrontational; Mwangeka himself had trade ties at the coast. But disdain for outsiders did run high, as Mwangeka's comments about the

---

[16] The victim described this incident to Wray. See Wray's diary, CMSA, 13/12/1895. Dozens of like accounts crop up in his diaries, and he presumably heard only a small proportion of them.

[17] Wray's diary, CMSA, 20/12/1895. These cases illustrate a widespread problem of early colonial rule: order–minded Company officials could not control their field staff on a day–to–day basis. In 1898 Wray reported daily complaints about the soldiers, adding in 1899 that soldiers profited more from Taita than did the state—a claim that, even if not literally true, is evocative enough to make its point. See Wray's diaries, CMSA, 25/10/1898 and 7/11/1899.

[18] H. A. Mwanzi, "African Initiatives and Resistance in East Africa, 1880–1914," in *Africa Under Colonial Domination, 1880–1935*, ed. A. A. Boahen, vol. 7 of UNESCO *General History of Africa* (Berkeley and Los Angeles, 1985), 156–57. Mwanzi's vision of united Taita resistance is greatly at odds with the evidence and analysis presented here. For a recent championing of resistance scholarship, James Scott, *Domination and the Arts of Resistance: Hidden Transcripts* (New Haven, 1990).

Several recent studies critique the assumptions of resistance scholarship: Jonathan Glassman, *Feasts and Riot: Revelry, Rebellion, and Popular Consciousness on the Swahili Coast, 1856–1888* (Portsmouth, 1995), 8–17; Frederick Cooper, "Conflict and Connection: Rethinking Colonial African History," in *American Historical Review* 99, 5 (1994); Sherry Ortner, "Resistance and the Problem of Ethnographic Refusal," *Comparative Studies in Society and History* 37, 1, 1995; and Michael Brown, "On Resisting Resistance," in *American Anthropologist* 98, 4 (1996). For a reconsideration of resistance in Taita in the 1890s, Bill Bravman, "Contextualizing Resistance to Colonial Conquest in Taita, Kenya: Some Assembly Required," paper given at African Studies Association annual conference, San Francisco, 1996.

Swahili soldiers showed.[19] Despite local experience of the 1892 column that shattered Mwangeka's forces and plundered lower Mwanda, the 1898 confrontation between the farmer and soldier that escalated to a mob attack of an EAP officer and a punitive expedition took place in Mwanda. Long after the 1890s, the area's people remained largely aloof towards Europeans and their local allies. Many in Mwanda, for instance, blamed people from upper Bura, the area just below, for Mwangeka's defeat. Pointing to Bura people's friendliness with the whites and Swahilis, they claimed that Bura warriors had discovered the secret of Mwangeka's medicine and passed it to the EAP soldiers. Relations between people from Bura and Mwanda, often cooperative before 1892, soured and remained poor well into the twentieth century.[20] When Bura–based Catholic missionaries set up a Mwanda outstation in 1895, the icy local reception soon convinced them to abandon the effort.[21] As late as 1950, colonial officers thought Mwanda the most uncooperative and difficult part of Taita to govern.[22]

Community Strategies in
Response to Colonialism, 1893–1900

Other neighborhoods in the Hills, however, cooperated with Company and colonial authorities during the 1880s and 1890s—not because they were traitors, collaborators or dupes, but because elders in those areas thought it a sensible, prudent, and/or opportunistic way to deal with outsiders who sometimes posed little threat, but at other junctures seemed volatile and dangerous. Elders across Taita fully expected to maintain their authority over their lineages and neighborhoods, and did so through the 1890s. Those who steered their neighborhoods towards friendly ties with Europeans, however, proved far better at minimizing the presence and predations of Company/EAP soldiers. The areas most notable for their cooperation, Mbale and the lower Bura Valley, suffered notably few incidents of early colonial plunder.

---

[19] "He was a proud man, an arrogant man. Our ancestors, they all were that way, all of them. They did not fear any outsiders, [not] even the whites." Interview with GN, Mgange Nyika/Mwanda, 20/9/1988.

[20] Ill–feeling was compounded by Bura's hosting of some soldiers who, for months after the sortie, periodically raided Mwanda for animals and women. Interview with Mrs. SM, Mwanda/Mwanda, 14/9/1988.

[21] Interview with MM, Mwanda/Mwanda, 12/9/1988. He contradicts the reports of Father Mével of the Holy Ghost Fathers, who said he was well received in Mwanda in 1893, and that by 1895 the outstation "ha[d] been witness to a large movement of conversion." MM's account seems more credible: from 1895 to 1907 Mwanda disappears from the *Bulletins Generaux*. The 1907 report then states that the Fathers have decided to *start* a station in Mwanda. *Bulletins de la Congrégation*, Tomes Troisième, Quatrième, et Onzième, 1893, 1896, 1907–08.

[22] A district officer said of Mwanda at midcentury, "Presumably the persistent cold winds that sweep though this location are partly responsible for the ungracious demeanour of many of the people," adding that a "small clique of bloody–minded" people were responsible for the state's problems in the area. Kenya National Archives (hereafter KNA), DAO/TTA/1/1/159, Agricultural Safari Diaries, 15/8/1951.

Mbale by the early 1890s counted Mghalu among the ranks of its elders. Even in his former role as *kishingila*, Mghalu had ordered his warriors to befriend Europeans, so as to better assess them. As an elder, he counseled a similarly friendly stance. This did not spring from fear, for Mghalu had courage to spare, but from his strategic sense. Through frequent trading at the coast and the intelligence he gathered, Mghalu had a fair sense of the Europeans' technologies and techniques, and thought it the better part of valor to avoid armed clashes with them. After Mwangeka's defeat by IBEACo soldiers, Mbale's other, more senior elders took his advice to heart. Mghalu spoke for Mbale's elders in dealings with European officers at Ndii, (always comporting himself with great dignity and an air of authority). The Europeans, in turn, considered him their most reliable contact in that part of the Hills.[23]

In lower Bura, Mbogholi pursued a similar strategy for somewhat different ends. A trade–minded man based near an important caravan route, he believed that official and trade ties with Europeans would enhance his neighborhood authority. He had thrust himself to the forefront when an IBEACo agent reached Dabida in the late 1880s, and forged associations with missionaries and colonial authorities in the 1890s, even inviting the Holy Ghost Fathers to settle on his lineage lands in 1892.[24] Like Mghalu, Mbogholi made himself the Europeans' main contact in his part of Taita, and minimized EAP soldiers' predations there. However, while Mghalu came to be highly respected, garnering seniority and a formidable reputation among Mbale's denizens, Mbogholi's stature remained shaky. More senior elders in his neighborhood derided Mbogholi's transparent attempts to vault himself over them. The tactic worked to some degree with Europeans, but left him and his descendants unpopular and untrusted in lower Bura.

In Sagalla, yet another approach prevailed. Sagalla elders, shocked and impressed by the IBEACo's crushing of Mwangeka's warriors, wanted their own warriors to avoid confrontations with the new authorities.[25] Yet elders also wanted to curtail the Company/EAP soldiers' frequent predations of Sagalla. No Sagalla elder looked to establish direct colonial ties in the manner of Mbogholi or Mghalu. Mwakichucho, the Sagalla elder most experienced with Europeans, might have done so, but he apparently died between 1889 and 1893.[26] The elders instead decided that a European missionary could help them deal with the new authorities. This strategy's relationship to Mwangeka's defeat is

---

[23] Interview with MM, Mbale/Mbale, 7/11/1988. Popular memory has not charged Mghalu with collaboration or failure to resist; he is widely respected for his acute accumulation of ever-greater authority until his death in 1910.

[24] *Bulletin de la Congrégation*, Tome Troisième, 1893, 786–92. Once again, Mbogholi represented himself to the arriving Europeans as a mighty chief. Fr. Mével, "Rapport sur le pays et la mission du Taita," 1893, cited in Merritt, "History of the Taita," 216.

[25] When Wray visited Sagalla in early 1893, he said its elders feared an attack by Company soldiers. See Wray's diaries, CMSA, 5/2/1893.

[26] Local remembrance gives no precise year for Mwakichucho's death, but his name appeared often in Wray's writings before he left Sagalla in the former year, and was entirely absent from them after Wray returned.

clear: a few months before that battle, a gathering of Sagalla elders firmly re-jected a CMS offer to re-post a missionary there. After Mwangeka's defeat, however, Sagalla elders sent a delegation to the coast, to ask that one occupy the old station.[27]

Wray himself returned to Sagalla in 1893.[28] A gathering of twenty elders met with him to negotiate their mutual accommodation: he would respect their authority and not compel anyone to do anything. They in turn would not ob-struct his teaching and preaching.[29] Clearly, in the new context of the mid–1890s, local imaginings about Wray had changed significantly. Nobody consid-ered him either a valuable trading partner or a pressing political threat.[30] Many still saw him as a potential source of cosmological trouble, but a relatively small one compared to the social and cosmological (and physical) rupture in *sere* that Company officers and soldiers might bring.

Elders now regarded Wray as a potential buffer between Sagalla's commu-nities and their distant but dangerous new rulers. They hoped to use him as their advocate with the colonial authorities; as an effective spokesman to his fellow whites for Sagallans' needs and views; as someone who could explain to them the European authorities' thinking and intentions; and as a check, by his very presence, on the Company/EAP soldiers. These hopes and imaginings worked out far better than those of the 1880s, for Wray quickly embraced the new roles elders envisioned.

Up to 1910, Wray often mediated relations between Sagalla's people and the new colonial state. Among his more dramatic interventions, he helped pre-vent an uprising by Sagalla's young men and an imminent punitive expedition in 1895, by clearing up a false rumor that the government was about to forcibly repatriate all living women ever brought to Taita from outside areas.[31] He pre-vented another punitive sortie in 1901, by convincing European authorities that

---

[27] CMS, G3 A5/08, Tucker to Scott, 3/2/1892; and Wray's diaries, CMSA, 8/2/1893. Wray re-ported often in 1893 that people in Sagalla feared the Company, and that they thought his presence would improve their situation. See Wray's diaries, 2–5, 8/2/1893, and 4, 8–11/6/1893.

[28] He stayed for four months that year, and returned permanently in 1895, together with his new wife. CMS officials at the coast and in London debated long and hard before sending him back. See Bravman, "Becoming," 156–57, 175.

[29] Wray's diaries, CMSA, 20/4/1893. Both largely honored this agreement. In March 1896, Wray reported that now virtually nobody in Sagalla opposed his presence. CMS, G3 A5/012, Wray to Baylis, 24/3/1896.

[30] Wray noted this several times, including CMS, G3 A5/012(b), Wray to Baylis, 6/6/1896.

[31] Many of the women in question came to the Hills as child captives of raids. All had been incor-porated into local lineages, most were long since married, and some were grandmothers. Wray guessed over a thousand women would be removed from the Hills if the rumors were accurate. They were not; there *was* an order to return *some* women captured from Pare. Sagalla's elders, hearing the correct information via Wray, kept their warriors in check; twenty women were re-turned from Sagalla, with some compensation paid to the husbands. On the other hand, in a high-zone neighborhood of Dabida, warriors took up arms against the rumored seizure. A column of soldiers went to the neighborhood, shot two warriors, seized a few dozen women to send to Pare without inquiring whether they came from there, and stole several dozen goats while leaving. Wray's diaries, CMSA, 3–20/11/1895; and interview with Mrs. NM, Kizumanzi/Sagalla, 24/8/1988.

Sagalla warriors had been falsely accused of attacking a railway labor gang.[32] In 1905, acting on information from Sagalla elders, his intervention prevented dams from being built atop Sagalla for a European plantation on the plains; the dams would have submerged much of the mountain's most fertile land. Again at local elders' instigation, he helped correct a 1906 land concession that wrongly granted another European plantation a large block of actively farmed lowland.[33]

The missionary presence also afforded some recourse against soldiers' predations. Taita's people could not easily protest their actions directly, for a gauntlet of soldiers outside the European official's office obstructed access to him, often beating, robbing, and sending away would–be complainers.[34] Now Sagalla's people took complaints against soldiers to Wray, either after Sunday services or just after an incident.[35] Wray at first sent letters of complaint to Ndii, but when he learned that soldiers were intercepting them, he or his European assistant went directly to Ndii's officer–in–charge. Though European officers sometimes preferred to turn a blind eye, they often punished the transgressors.[36] Soldiers gradually took to picking less on people around Sagalla.

However, using a missionary intermediary also had consequences that Sagalla's elders had not counted on. Wray, while sympathetic to his version of Sagalla interests, also fundamentally supported the right of the colonial state to rule. Though this hardly affected community autonomy in the 1890s, state interventions began to reorder Sagalla society profoundly after the turn of the century. Then, Wray's mediation helped enmesh Sagalla within the new colonial order. In 1901, for instance, a Hut Tax was imposed to pull Taita more thoroughly into the colonial labor system and the money economy. Wray tried hard to have Sagalla excluded from the tax, but upon its final enactment told people they must pay it. In later years, he helped officials collect it and supervised public–works labor by tax defaulters.[37]

Thus, by using a missionary to buffer the demands of European officials and minimize confrontations with colonial soldiery, Sagalla elders inadvertently abetted and hastened their communities' incorporation within the expanding colonial system. By not interacting with colonial officials directly, they also left themselves more vulnerable than Mghalu or Mbogholi to having their authority bypassed as the new colonial order took shape. In

---

[32] Wray's diaries, CMSA, 2–6/5/1901.

[33] Wray's diaries, CMSA, 28–31/10/1905; 13, 30/12/1905; 1–5/1/1906; 10–11/2/1906, 3/4/1906.

[34] In one case, with the European officer away from Ndii, soldiers locked up a complainant from Dabida for several days and beat him severely. Wray's diaries, CMSA, 24/8/1898.

[35] In the mid–1890s, Wray recorded large numbers of such complaints in his diaries each year. For the meetings after Church, CMS, G3 A5/015, Kathleen Wray, June 1898.

[36] Wray's diaries, CMSA, 9–12/8/1898, 30/8/1898.

[37] Wray pleaded the case for excluding Sagalla in a private meeting with the commissioner of the Protectorate, but did not persuade him. See Wray's diaries, CMSA, 18, 22–24/11/1901, 5/1/1902. On tax collection and labor supervision, see his diaries, Feb.–June 1904.

short, their reliance on Wray smoothed Sagalla's subordination to colonial rule, and facilitated the subsequent weakening of their own standing. In the 1890s, this outcome was far from evident, for even as Sagalla avoided the violence and destruction going on elsewhere, its elders continued to hold sway over their communities. But in the 1900s, as colonial rule and its economy became firmly established, the bases of elders' authority would face severe new challenges.

Like Mghalu and Mbogholi, then, Sagalla elders' response in the 1890s to the colonial incursion emphasized strategic choices meant to preserve community autonomy. For all the variations in neighborhood responses, local elders everywhere assessed strengths and circumstances, weighed potential allies and opponents, and pushed for their interests with a state that in 1893, was only sporadically present, but violent, grasping, and baffling. In Mwanda, they believed that the whites could be driven out or held off. But while Mwangeka's warriors fought valiantly against the colonial incursion into their neighborhoods, they became neither a rallying cry nor a model for the whole of the Hills. Mghalu and Mbogholi minimized the outsiders' immediate impact by establishing positive, direct relationships with the Europeans—an approach that later enabled both to resituate their authority within the consolidating state. Sagalla elders, having decided against forcible resistance, hoped the missionary would help them weather this storm, and in the short run got what they sought.

Local Communities and Christian Community, 1893–1910

The Emergence of Christian Community at Sagalla

The CMS's renewed evangelical effort in Taita proved more successful than the first: missionaries in Sagalla began performing baptisms in 1900, and over the next few years two CMS stations opened on Dabida. By 1910, Dabida far surpassed Sagalla in garnering Christian adherents and inquirers.[38] On both mountains, a new kind of community based on Christianity started cutting across lineages and neighborhoods. Christian community posed a serious challenge to local communities, for its tenets disavowed some of their crucial norms and beliefs even as its membership cut across their social/spatial boundaries. Local and Christian versions of community proved more porous and accommodating in practice than in principle, but conflicts and tensions emerged nonetheless—tensions that had to be addressed, finessed, or obfuscated.

The new Christians did the most of this work, negotiating between the cultural politics of belonging within local communities and the cultural poli-

---

[38] Between 1900 and 1910, Sagalla averaged 8.6 baptisms per year. The station at Mbale averaged 15 per year by 1909. In that same year, a new station at Wusi (Dabida) reported 64 adherents preparing for baptism. See CMS, G3 A5/018, 1909 Annual Letter of J. A. Wray, 5/1/1910, and Annual Letter of John Maynard, 16/2/1910.

tics of their faith within the mission. Contrary to an old argument about early Christians in so–called stateless societies, most early converts in Taita had not been socially marginal.[39] *After* converting, though, many did struggle to avoid marginalization, for CMS Anglicanism forbade participation in "heathen" practices central to *Wutasi*—and thus crucial to belonging in lineage and neighborhood communities. For instance, converts were to abstain from *Wutasi* rituals of life transition (like initiation) or community well–being (like rainmaking or defense). Their participation, if revealed, could jeopardize their church standing. Yet demurral could draw local disapprobation and weaken converts' standing in their lineages and neighborhoods. For the next half century, Christians wrestled with ways to resolve such tensions without gravely alienating either side. In so doing, they continually renegotiated the terms of both local community and local Christianity.

As the above implies, CMS beliefs and practices represented not only a new religion, but an alien cultural framework—one not a little antagonistic to local ways. Nevertheless, Christianity and local ways did not operate as self–contained, hermetically sealed cultures that individuals simply chose between. Nor, for that matter, did the culture of Christianity straightforwardly overwhelm and replace local ways; a far more complex interaction developed. Local interpretations of Christianity were not—could not be—made by letting go of all prior interpretive frameworks. To a large degree, a process of analogizing mediated local people's understanding of the new faith. Some analogies were conscious and explicit, others deeply assumed, but all, inevitably, derived from received cultural categories.[40] Converts could recognize and perhaps jettison some prior outlooks relatively easily; others, however, were less amenable to quick unearthing or rapid reformation. This layering and more gradual reconfiguring of Christian and local outlooks remains embedded in people's later twentieth–century explanations of religious change:

> [A particular *Wutasi*–based ritual] was one way of treating evil–spirited people. . . . When they hear the drumming . . . then they dance and the evil spirits leave them. [But] the Christians believed that you can survive evil, you can also avoid the evil spirits, you can fight against them, just by believing in the Lord Jesus Christ, and he will save you from all these troubles.[41]

---

[39] L. H. Gann and Peter Duignan, in *Burden of Empire* (London, 1967), 276, called them "runaway slaves, exiles, or old women without relatives, . . . the *déracinés* of tribal society." Besides the conceptual problems with this formulation, my interviews and even a quick overview of baptismal patterns suggest that most early converts had "mainstream" standing in established lineages. Most pointedly, Mghalu had two sons educated by the missions. Both were baptized, and one succeeded to his father's substantial influence. Interview with MM, Mbale/Mbale, 7/11/1988.

[40] Sahlins, *Historical Metaphors*; on the inexactness of intercultural analogizing, see Roy Wagner, "Dif/ference and Its Disguises," in *On the Other: Dialogue and/or Dialectics: Mark Taylor's Paralectics*, ed. Robert Scharlemann (Lanham, 1991).

[41] Interview with JM, Wusi/Chawia, 5/4/1988.

Long ago, people feared . . . feared their ancestors would give them trouble. . . . Now we know it was not the ancestors bringing evil, it was the Devil. Yes, the Devil! He was hiding behind the ancestors! [switches to English] He was very strong, he made them like his puppets![42]

Missionaries' messages or cultural categories did, of course, have persuasive or coercive cultural power. Jean and John Comaroff have ably shown how missionaries worked to "seize control of the signs and practices of everyday life, [and] . . . enmesh local people in the underlying *forms* of the European system."[43] Some Christian underminings of everyday local forms certainly happened in Taita: in short order, for instance, the European week joined the four–day herding cycle as a basic calendar unit.[44] However, changes in Taita often derived less from direct European impositions than from intra–African struggles between Christians and *Wutasi* followers over the terms of local society. In those struggles, Christians sometimes did privilege European forms: the rectangular houses arranged in rows earned one predominantly Christian settlement the nickname *laini* (i.e., line).[45] But in other instances, Christians engaged local signs and practices not to replace them with European forms, but to rework them into parallel hybrids at once plausibly local and "safe" for Christians.[46] This affected not only everyday practices (like the forming of teetotaling Christian work groups), but key rituals like initiation. Cosmologically, too, the above quotations suggest that people often articulated their Christianity in locally–rooted cultural categories.

From the outset, then, people's understandings of Christianity in Sagalla and Dabida were mediated by local conceptual frameworks. Through ongoing engagement with Christian tenets and mission culture, local frameworks gradually changed; so, too, would Christianity in the Hills. This did not mean that Christians and *Wutasi* followers easily accommodated one another. But cultural common ground and affective ties allowed most to understand the value of flexibility and reconciliation in their struggles. *Wutasi* followers sought to maintain the centrality of local forms and practices, and in some ways succeeded up to 1950. Christians, however, gained social tolerance for many Christian forms and practices, and managed to alter some local forms and practices to meet their needs.

---

[42] Interview with AM, Shigaro/Werugha, 26/3/1988.

[43] Comaroff and Comaroff, "Colonization," 267; also their *Of Revelation*, 4–5, and chap. 6.

[44] Wray's diaries, CMSA, 10/4/1893. Colonial rule and the colonial calendar would add ordering power to the week.

[45] Interview with MT, Kishamba/Chawia, 9/6/1988; see also Comaroff and Comaroff, *Of Revelation*, 204–205.

[46] This view concurs with Landau's argument that "BaTswana have to be recognized as generating their own conflicts, and so their own history, within an evolving field of behaviors simultaneously beholden to colonial desires." Paul Landau, *The Realm of the Word: Language, Gender, and Christianity in a Southern African Kingdom* (Portsmouth, 1995), xii.

Mission Community and Sagalla Views of Christianity

The emergence of a Christian community required people to start taking the European religion seriously, inquire into its workings, and eventually avow allegiance to it, a process that began first on Sagalla. Colonial conquest could not in itself cause such changes, but it significantly altered the context of evangelism. After the 1882 defeat of Mwangeka, Sagalla elders made an essentially political decision to invite back the missionary they had driven away; they agreed, as part of the bargain, to not systematically prevent people from listening to his preaching and teaching. They did not guarantee, however, that people would turn out to listen.

Yet people did turn out. In 1884, Wray had thought a congregation of six cause for hopefulness, and in that decade fifty at church was an enormous crowd. In June 1896, nine months after Wray's permanent return to Sagalla, congregations often reached 300–400. This was no temporary bulge: in 1900, Sunday attendance ranged from 140 to 500, averaging 266.[47] The sustained turnouts suggest that people did not treat Christian services as a short–term novelty. Nor do the numbers derive purely from the church's role as a forum for venting complaints or uncertainties about colonial authorities: such matters usually concerned only a handful of people in a given week. Colonial conquest's key contribution to Christianity's new prominence was not the climate of order (or disorder) it brought, but that it convinced many people to take the Europeans' spiritual power seriously.

In the 1890s, it appears that many people in Sagalla concluded that the Europeans' deity was indeed powerful and should be ritually appeased— along with deceased ancestors addressed through *Wutasi*. After 1893, those Sagallans (and some from Dabida and Kasigau) wanted to better understand and propitiate the Christian God, so that He would bestow (or not withhold) bounty, especially rain. Obstruction of Wray's itinerating and preaching ceased entirely in Sagalla, and loosened up considerably in Dabida.[48] People did not rush to embrace Christian theology and abandon their own, but many more came to listen at church, and, by following the forms of Christian prayer as well as modifying *Wutasi* ritual forms, sought to placate the Christian deity.

There was no great difficulty about reconciling propitiation of the Christian God with continued belief in *Wutasi*. In contrast with the CMS view that only Christianity counted as proper belief, *Wutasi* followers took an inclusive, ascriptive approach to the divine world. Participation in *Wutasi* rituals of rainmaking, divination, protection, etc., did not preclude prayers by other means, as well. Strayer describes turn–of–the–century East African religions as "eclectic or pragmatic—almost experimental—in character."[49] This ascriptive outlook

---

[47] CMS Correspondence, G3 A5/01, Wray to Lang, 23/5/1884; G3 A5/012(b), Wray to Baylis, 6/6/1896. The 1900 attendance average comes from forty–three individually reported services; attendance fluctuated by agricultural season. See Wray's diaries, CMSA, 1900.

[48] Wray's diaries, CMSA, 20/4/1893, 10/6/1893; and CMS, G3 A5/01, Wray to Lang, 21/4/1884.

[49] Strayer, *Mission Communities*, 53.

continued into the 1950s, allowing non–Christians who so chose to take part in Christian and *Wutasi* rituals without fear of underlying contradiction.

The careful attention people on Sagalla gave to proper dress, forms, and postures of Christian prayer illustrates one aspect of how their understanding of the European religion drew on their extant cultural categories. In *Wutasi*, the success of a prayer, offering, or divination required correct performance: a ritual's participants followed its specific forms very carefully.[50] Likewise, attendance and prayer at the Sagalla church in the 1890s was very much a matter of form, albeit in a more deliberate sense than the phrase usually implies. In that regard, Wray correctly judged in 1896 that it had become "fashionable" to attend church on Sunday. Congregants paid close attention to the forms of prayer, kneeling in the prescribed manner and closing their eyes.[51] A regular churchgoer asked if she should remove a wire bracelet from her son's arm. Wray answered such questions again and again, with earnest entreaties about how outer trappings did not matter.[52] Another follower asked to attend Wray's daily English language prayers. No matter that she could not speak the language, she said; to be in the posture of prayer, covering her eyes, would be enough.[53]

A few soon moved beyond the focus on form; some churchgoers over time became well versed in mission beliefs, outlooks, and cultural values.[54] Points of resonance between elements of CMS Christianity and elements of *Wutasi* aided the familiarization.[55] For instance, *Wutasi* envisioned an interactive continuum between the patent and spiritual worlds: spiritual "agents conceptualized as person–like in varying degrees" could intervene in the patent world to cause misfortunes for living persons who committed moral offenses. *Wutasi* supplied means of divining the moral cause of disorder, and offered ritualized ways to ameliorate the wrong and placate the ancestral spirit.[56]

In principle this diverged from CMS Anglicanism's sharp natural/supernatural divide (i.e., Heaven, Hell, and earth do not overlap or blur into one another), and from Anglicanism's more distinct juxtaposition of the material and spiritual. In practice, though, there were powerful similarities. Wray and other CMS missionaries followed a low–church theology that saw the material

---

[50] For descriptions of rituals and the importance of performing them correctly, see G. Harris, *Casting*, chaps. 4–6.

[51] Wray's diaries, CMSA, 10/5/1896; Wray struggled long against local treatment of Christianity as a ritual form, exhorting people to experience Christianity internally, as an acceptance of Christ's message into their hearts.

[52] Wray's diaries, CMSA, 2/8/1896.

[53] Ibid., 13/10/1898.

[54] "The first ones, . . . Wray and [Maynard], they never got tired of explaining about God and Jesus. They continued and continued, and . . . now you see what they are saying." Interview with WM, Choke/Mbale, 11/11/1988.

[55] This runs against the grain of Robin Horton's argument that African societies turned to Christianity when local beliefs failed to explain the wider cosmological world modernization revealed to them. *Wutasi*'s cosmology proved far more durable and adaptable than Horton's framework allows—even among many who formally (and sincerely) became Christians. Robin Horton, "African Conversion," *Africa* 41 (1971), and "On the Rationality of Conversion," *Africa* 45, (1975).

[56] G. Harris, *Casting*, 26.

and spiritual worlds as deeply, even instrumentally intertwined—God caused particular good and evil things to happen in the patent world, and might respond to entreaties by the faithful about specific needs.[57]

This conjuncture of beliefs about supernatural intervention provided a key point of contact between *Wutasi* and Christianity around the turn of the century. It enabled a crucial parallel of functions between the faiths. Even as community rain-making rituals worked to ensure that spiritual agents would not obstruct rain, CMS missionaries offered a direct alternative: rain prayers to the Christian God. CMS Anglicanism even offered instrumental analogs to *Wutasi* totems. Wray encouraged people to ask God's intervention for specific needs, and many took him up on it. In 1901, a group of women facing a swollen river prayed at the near bank for God's protection before trying to cross it.[58] In 1905, a young man on a four–day trek across the savannah feared that he would be devoured by lions. Doubting the efficacy of his talismans and protection medicines, he appealed to the Christian God using Christian forms, and promised to convert if spared to live. Spared he was, and he duly offered himself as a catechism student.[59]

Wray had disparaged local forms of protection since the early 1880s. At first this produced a harsh response, but in the 1890s and 1900s, as Christianity offered direct alternatives to *Wutasi* for like concerns, it began to have the effect he desired. In 1906, bubonic plague broke out in the Hills; twenty years earlier, people would have blamed Wray for the epidemic, and his denunciations of *Wutasi* remedies would have only exacerbated matters. Now, however, forty women and men came to declare their desire to convert, hoping that the European God would protect His followers from illness.[60]

Christian Rainmaking

This changed outlook came across strikingly in local responses to an 1897–1900 drought and famine in Sagalla. Some *Wutasi* followers again blamed Wray for the crisis, but another approach emerged, as well, and spread beyond Sagalla. In January, 1899, the short rains season was ending with little rain having fallen. *Wutasi* rain prayers had not worked anywhere in the Hills; Wray had again refused to participate, although this time he made no derisive public statements about the local rituals. This time, too, some in Sagalla took a different tack: they decided to see whether the European God could unblock the rain. Eight Sagalla men came to Wray and asked him to intercede with God to bring rain for their crops. Wray spoke with them about Christianity, then had them kneel with him while he prayed for rain.[61]

---

[57] According to Strayer, many CMS and other Evangelical missionaries believed in the efficacy of prayers for Divine intervention. See Strayer, *Mission Communities*, 7.

[58] Wray's diaries, CMSA, 12/1/1901.

[59] Ibid., 28/8/1905.

[60] Ibid., 17/6/1906 to 28/10/1906. Of the forty, twenty–one were women, eleven were men, and eight were unspecified.

[61] Wray's diaries, CMSA, 3/1/1899.

Word spread rapidly around Sagalla, setting off a chain reaction. In the next sixteen days, fourteen groups of men and women came from all across Sagalla to have Wray lead them in rain prayers for their lineages or neighborhoods. When rain fell heavily on 19 January, Wray believed God had answered their prayers, and that Sunday admonished a packed church to offer Him thanks.[62] Hardships did not end there, for a locust swarm soon thereafter descended upon the new crops. But popular opinion blamed a local man's behavior, not Wray's, for the locusts.[63]

This assignment of blame, notable for not targeting Wray, also demonstrated that people had not abandoned *Wutasi*–based ideas about why disasters happen, i.e., that a person's wrongful thoughts or acts would anger spiritual agents who then caused misfortune. Local incorporation of Wray's rain prayers marked an alteration, not an abandonment, of extant cosmology. Rainmaking rituals anticipating the rainy season continued;[64] appeals to Wray for rain prayers became a contingency when the *Wutasi* ritual did not suffice. People in Sagalla thereby acknowledged the Christian God as a serious spiritual force in their cosmos: He could prevent rain, but then could be placated by the ritual appeals that Wray prescribed and led. As a general appeasement, most Sagallans also agreed to curtail certain practices that the missionary called sins against the Christian God, such as farming or hunting on Sundays.[65]

When the long rains failed in late 1899, people came for Wray's rain prayers from farther afield. In December, an elder from Kasigau, thirty kilometers away, came with a goat to ask for rain prayers. *Wutasi* rainmaking included an animal sacrifice, but in Dabida this called for a sheep,[66] so it is not clear whether the elder was offering a sacrifice or a gift. Wray had the man kneel and pray with him, then traded maize for the goat.[67] A few days later, three men came to Wray from the closest part of Dabida, Mlaleni, asking for rain prayers. They brought Wray fowls, which, once again, Wray would not accept as an offering in exchange for prayer. And once again he had the men join him on their knees while he led them in prayer. Rain fell in Mlaleni for the next two days, and the men returned to offer prayers of thanks.[68]

---

[62] Wray's diaries, CMSA, 3–19/1/1899; group sizes ranged between three and twenty-one.

[63] Wray's diaries, CMSA, 20/1/1899 to 2/2/1899.

[64] Interviews with Mrs. GM, Teri/Sagalla, 24/8/1988 and Mrs. NM, Kizumanzi/Sagalla, 24/8/1988. Grace Harris observed rain prayers still being performed on Dabida in the early 1950s. See G. Harris, *Casting*, 127.

[65] On people's observance of this stricture, see Wray's diaries, CMSA, 21/1/1899.

[66] G. Harris, *Casting*, 128–30. The elder's name was Mwangojilo.

[67] Mwangojilo became a frequent visitor of Wray's, for the weather treated Kasigau cruelly in the early twentieth century; he journeyed to Sagalla at least eleven times between 12/1899 and 12/1909 for rain prayers. Despite his regular contact and good relationship with Wray, Mwangojilo did not convert to Christianity. See Wray's diaries, CMSA: for 1899, 21/12; 1900, 7/5, 15/12; 1901, 4/6, 13/12; 1903, 24/7, 24/11, 31/12; 1904, 1/1, 6–7/4, 5–8/7; 1907, 31/12; 1908, 7–8/1, 22/3, 31/12; 1909, 26/4, 17/6, 17/12, 28/12.

[68] Wray's diaries, CMSA, 29–31/12/1899.

This continued for the rest of Wray's residency in Taita, into 1910.[69] In 1903, people came to Sagalla from the drought stricken upper reaches of Dabida, preferring Wray's rain prayers to those at the new CMS station near them, in Mbale, Dabida.[70] When one group from the plains came to Wray for rain prayers, he instead offered practical suggestions about irrigating from a nearby river. The supplicants, thoroughly familiar with irrigation, insisted on prayer.[71] They had come to Wray to right wrongs in their relationship with spiritual forces; new irrigation trenches could not redress a cosmological problem.

As with other rituals, people seeking Christian rain prayers took matters of agency and correct form seriously. Wray often told rain prayer supplicants they could offer their prayers directly to God.[72] Perhaps people did so, but if the rains were late, they wanted Wray to lead the prayers in the proper ritual manner. This mirrored *Wutasi* rainmaking: each neighborhood had a designated Rainmaker, and while participants in the ritual had to perform prayers correctly, he was nonetheless "very much the man 'doing the work' of rainmaking."[73] Many likewise saw Wray's ritual leadership as crucial to the effectiveness of getting down on their knees and appealing to the Europeans' God. Wray knew that few of his rainmaking supplicants heeded his preaching about inner conversion to Christian belief. Still, despite bouts of anger about it, he never recorded an instance of refusing a request for rain prayers.[74]

Cultural Politics and the Advent of Christian Community, 1895–1910

Though few in Sagalla gave credence to Anglicanism's beliefs and spiritual messages in the 1890s, a handful did begin to take the religion seriously enough to contemplate converting. Exactly what drew them more deeply into Christianity's tenets has not come down through written or oral sources, but in a decade that began with European conquest and stretched into periods of hardship and uncertainty, some people clearly found the mission's explanation of spiritual power compelling, and appreciated the spiritual and material supports it offered.[75] In the children's school and adult classes, this small group

---

[69] Wray left Kenya for good on 14/11/1910. See CMS, G3 A5/018, Wray to Baylis, 14/10/1910.

[70] Wray's diaries, CMSA, 18/7/1903 and 6/12/1903.

[71] Wray's diaries, CMSA, 30/11/1903. For the long prior history of irrigation, see Fleuret, "Organization of Water"; KNA, PC/Coast/2/11/66, Report by DC, AO, and Surveyor, 16/11/1936; and Thomson, *Masai–land*, 43.

[72] Wray showed the first people who came to him for rain prayers how they could do so themselves, and continued encouraging people to pray for rain on their own thereafter. See Wray's diaries, CMSA, 3/1/1899.

[73] G. Harris, *Casting*, 127.

[74] For his frustration at the rush of non–believers to church when the rains were late, see Wray's diaries, CMSA, 17–19/1/1905.

[75] Strayer similarly describes the late nineteenth century in interior East Africa as a time of "disintegration, change, and reformation," with missions as centers around which people could seek alternative institutions of reintegration. Strayer, *Mission Communities*, 52–53.

learned reading, writing, and the essentials of Anglican theology. In the process, they also became acquainted with the moral culture of the mission.

Though they did not fully take up the CMS version of Christianity, followers did acquire a richer understanding of and appreciation for its messages and mores. They also adopted many of its forms, some of which, like the mission style of dressing, were patently visible. More mundane adaptations, like saying grace before eating, stood out by their contradistinction to predominant local ways: "My mother . . . said Grace before eating, every time she ate. Grandmother said 'what is that?' 'It is Grace, . . . I thank God for food.' 'Huh.' They said this every day."[76]

Thus the mission followers brought Christianity into the realm of Sagalla's cultural politics, for they began pushing local ways long since habituated back into the realm of practices whose meanings would be struggled over. The CMS wanted its new followers to be models, standing apart from *Wutasi*'s heathen ways, which augured poorly for intracommunity peace. Most Christians, however, entered the fray cautiously: they willingly differentiated themselves from their local communities—but only up to a point. They were unwilling to think or act so differently as to risk severing local ties of belonging. Piecemeal, followers developed terms for their own, Christian, community, and engaged in a cultural politics that altered local society, yet kept most Christians within the pale of their residential communities.

By 1900, the CMS considered a few candidates ready for baptism. Given the above discussion, conversion (which to missionaries meant abandoning prior beliefs and wholeheartedly embracing Christian ones) is not an unproblematic term. Religious identification could not be isolated from cosmological notions and cultural categories, and despite converts' identification with Christianity, a consciousness rooted in local ways profoundly shaped their beliefs. In a social sense, though, "conversion" accurately reflected their willing choice to align themselves with Christian precepts and teachings. They knew they would be expected to refrain from *Wutasi* practices, which posed problems for their standing in their local communities. They chose neither casually nor hastily, for the training required of Sagalla's early converts took years. But some people did indeed undertake the change: in 1900 two men were baptized, followed by two women in early 1901, and eight women, four children, and a man late that year.[77]

In 1902 Wray gained ordination and began performing baptisms regularly.[78] Thereafter, many longtime churchgoers declared themselves: in 1904, on three different Sunday services, individuals stood to state their desire to become

---

[76] Interview with JM, Wundanyi/ Werugha, 18/7/1988.

[77] Wray's diaries, CMSA, 18/2/1900; 10/2/1901; 8/12/1901. The first two occasions had friendly crowds of about five hundred, drawn perhaps by the novelty and pomp of the ceremony. Over a thousand people came to the third set of baptisms, which coincided with the opening of a new, iron–sheet church.

[78] It took Wray decades to convince the CMS to ordain him. See Bravman, "Becoming," 107, 109–11, 157.

Photo 2. Sagalla's iron-sheet church, built in 1900. Author's photo, 1988.

Christians. In 1906, a total of thirty–two, in ten services, rose to "accept Christ."[79] Churchgoing became more than a curiosity, more than a venue for social grievances or rain prayers. Growing numbers of people now declared commitment to the Christian God, a dramatic act that set them somewhat apart from local society and to no small extent at odds with it. By late 1909, converts were still a fraction of Sagalla's populace, but a substantial one: eighty–six baptized Christians, twenty–four baptismal candidates, and fifty–two girls and forty–eight boys in mission school.[80]

Evangelical efforts by some early converts spurred much of the growth. By the end of 1900 one convert, Marko, was preaching and leading services throughout Sagalla.[81] The curious increasingly learned about Christianity from African itinerants to their neighborhoods: by 1909 six Sagalla men worked as paid CMS Agents, and the mission's four African teachers often did local preaching, as well. The CMS also employed a local woman evangelist, but mainly expected the wives of married Agents to "volunteer" time.[82] Sagalla Agents roamed from the foothills of Dabida to Kasigau, becoming the main spokesmen of the CMS creed.[83] Too, early Christians often tried to convert others in their household or lineage.[84] As a by–product of this, the merely curious often listened to local preachings rather than attend the main Sagalla church; by 1908, converts and serious followers composed the bulk of the Sagalla church's congregations.[85] Those converts, moreover, were clearly forming a new kind of community.

Christian community, tentative and tenuous in the early 1900s, was no less real for that. It forged commonalities, support structures, affective bonds, continuous interactions, and group identity on grounds other than those binding together lineage and neighborhood communities. Sagalla Christian community transgressed the geographical bases, and the ideologies of shared history and kinship, that lineages and neighborhoods called upon. While many Christians came from Mwakichucho's lineage or Teri, at least as many came from farther–flung neighborhoods.[86] Their root commonalities were church teachings and their affective fellowship of shared belief in its message. Socially, followers

---

[79] Wray's diaries, CMSA. The first instance was 12/6/1904, when two men did so. It happened twice more that year. The figures on 1906 represent a ten–month period, for Wray took another furlough that year. Curiously (or rather, incuriously), Wray wrote no comments about the phenomenon.

[80] CMS, G3 A5/018, Wray's Annual Letter, 5/1/1910.

[81] Wray's diaries, CMSA, 26/8/1900; 2,11/12/1900.

[82] The woman, baptized Mary Bahati, earned less than her male counterparts: 7/= per month, versus the men's scale of 12/= and 10/=. CMS, G3 A5/017, "Schedule of Native Workers," 9/1/1904.

[83] CMS, G3 A5/017, Wray's Annual Letter, 5/1/1910. For their itinerations, see, e.g., Wray's diaries, CMSA, 29/9/1904, 20/8/1906, 5/5/1908. Wray's diaries for the 1900s detail many cases of people converting after initially learning about Christianity from Agents.

[84] For example, Wray's diaries, CMSA, 7/3/1905, offer an account of a woman named Sarah trying to convert her mother.

[85] By 1908, the average Sunday service attendance fell to 109. Wray's diaries, CMSA, 1908.

[86] Interview with KM, Kizumanzi/Sagalla, 14/7/1993.

shared in preparing for baptism and confirmation, attended church with one another, and socialized together in ways that reinforced their commitments to church precepts. They also shared the experience of distinguishing themselves from others in their lineages and neighborhoods:

> When they entered the church they really had to hold to each other, they had only each other. . . . When their brothers . . . and their fathers . . . went to drink *chofi* [sugarcane beer], they . . . could not go with them, they just remained with each other. . . . If you stay together, you will hold to your faith. So those ones, they held to each other. These days . . . it is not so hard, everyone is helping. Then it was very hard, very![87]

Christians who lived near one another could offer some of the social support that lineage and neighborhood communities otherwise did. For example, men's lineage–based communal work groups drank beer provided by the household whose fields they had worked on that day. Convert men, however, were enjoined to not drink beer, and convert women were not to brew it. This practical and symbolic difficulty bespoke a more general problem: CMS demands, in principle, required converts to withdraw from certain forms of lineage mutuality. Some converts responded by forming up new work groups, based on their shared adherence to CMS precepts; both men's and women's versions of Christian work groups arose.[88]

Sagalla's converts, then, formed a community not only around what they shared, but around what, in principle, they rejected. The CMS expected Christians to remove themselves from *Wutasi* practices from the mundane (e.g., beer drinking, which was associated with *Wutasi* libations as well as drunkenness), to the profound (e.g., participation in rituals of lineage and neighborhood well–being). Christian community therein also pressured its members to uphold Christian standards. Not everyone subscribed to this aspect of Christian community, though, and it became an arena of intra–Christian cultural politics, pitting advocates of strictness and vigilance against backsliding, against those who allowed (or indulged in) slippage. The latter group practiced more flexibility in mediating between Christian demands and local ways, for the sake of maintaining lineage and neighborhood relationships. And maintaining those local community relationships was by no means easy for early converts.

Confrontations over Early Christianity

In the 1880s, Sagalla communities saw Christianity as an outsider's rupture of their cosmological peace. Nascent Christian community in the 1900s posed a different threat: converts' beliefs, actions, and associations challenged basic precepts of local societies from within. This entrance into Sagalla's cultural

---

[87] Interview with SM, Teri/Sagalla, 25/8/1988.
[88] Interview with DM, Teri/Sagalla, 10/7/1988.

politics soon cut deeply, for believing Christians had to partly disassociate themselves from the intertwined mores, rules, and cosmology that underpinned lineage and neighborhood as communities. Their faith could set them beyond the religious authority of elders, make them abstain from rituals of community well–being, prevent them from tending to ancestral shrines, limit their participation in networks of social support, even disrupt the proper running of households. *Wutasi* followers did not take these challenges lightly. They rarely severed individuals entirely from lineage or neighborhood belonging, but they often strongly pressured people either not to convert, or to fulfill their obligations to their neighborhoods, lineages, and households despite having converted.

Small lineages often applied the keenest pressure against conversion, especially women's conversions. For reasons not discussed in written records nor easily gleaned from remembrances nearly a century later, women made up the majority of the early Christian inquirers.[89] One general cause may have been the church's stand on alcohol. Women had to brew *chofi* (sugarcane beer) for husbands and fathers–in–law, who used it for *Wutasi* libations and for social drinking; women could not drink it. At least some women saw in Christianity a chance to refuse this task, and thereby to put a dent in their husbands' drinking.[90] One woman told Wray that as a Christian she would no longer brew beer for her often drunk, abusive husband. When she made good on her pledge, he burned her in the chest, but she remained in the church, and continued her refusal.[91]

Many Christian women continued to brew beer—and doing so partially mitigated the consequences of converting—but all women who wanted to convert when husbands or fathers had not done so nevertheless risked incurring men's disapproval or wrath:

> Only a woman with great strength and faith converted if the others in her [house] did not. Many women wanted to join [the Church], but they could not, because the fathers said no, the husbands said no. If the man objects, the woman must wait . . . unless she was very strong.[92]

Wray recorded several instances of husbands or fathers battling women over conversion. One irate husband promised to leave his wife, effectively expelling her from his lineage; she backed down.[93] Some non–Christian men also objected to the ways a wife's conversion affected the conduct of household life. When one Christian woman refused her husband's plan to have a *mganga* (local medical expert)

---

[89] Female interviewees mostly denied to me that women had any particular reason to flock to the early church, or that Christianity meant anything different to women than to men. Perhaps so, but I fear I did not find the best ways to ask about the subject, or that I was not the best person to pose those sorts of questions.

[90] Interviews with Mrs. GM, Shigaro/Werugha, 27/5/1988; Mrs. AM, Ndome/Mbololo, 20/6/1988; and Mrs. MN, Teri/Sagalla, 25/8/1988.

[91] Wray's diaries, CMSA, 4/12/1904, 19/1/1905.

[92] Interview with DM, Teri/Sagalla, 10/7/1993.

[93] Wray's diaries, CMSA, 22/8/1905.

treat their sick child, the husband promised to throw her out if the child died.[94] Female converts also faced pressures from women who saw conversions as threats to *their* social networks. Three kinswomen threatened and harassed one convert, eventually waylaying her and tearing down her house. They rebuilt it and paid a small fine, but neither the three, nor the elders of their lineage who set the punishment, expressed much remorse about the attack.[95]

Men and boys who converted faced pressures, as well. Christian and would–be Christian youths' school obligations conflicted with herding responsibilities that took them away for four days at a time. Adult men who did not drink beer forfeited participation in any number of minor and major rituals woven into the fabric of lineage and neighborhood life.[96] Other objections and pressures were not so specifically gendered. An early convert drew the anger of her son and daughter–in–law, who feared that her Christian death and burial would prevent them from performing *Wutasi* rites to placate her spirit—hurting *their* well–being.[97] More typically, though, older members of a lineage objected most to conversions. Fathers decried sons and daughters–in–law who abandoned local ways; elders blocked youths from converting by declaring them too young to be allowed to make such a decision.[98]

Many *Wutasi* followers, both male and female, responded to the coalescing of Christian community by stiffening public opposition to Christian preachings and ways. One woman replied to a 1909 sermon about her "future life" by declaring loudly that "she did not care one iota what happened to her."[99] *Wutasi* followers often refused Western treatments for injuries and illness, calling the missionary medicine nonsense.[100] Not only did most people reject Christianity, claims that it had brought misfortune to Taita still circulated widely. In 1909, a Christian woman said that many of her neighbors hated the converts, blaming them for the droughts and famines of the prior twenty–five years.[101]

---

[94]   Wray's diaries, CMSA, 19/3/1906.

[95]   The woman's daughter said "My mother was . . . one of the first Christians. She got a lot of problems. . . . The other women in her *kichuku* really fought her for it, they told her she was just lost." Interview with Mrs. GM, Teri/Sagalla, 24/8/1988.
      Several days after the incident followed the sort of coincidence that assuredly did not hurt Christianity's spiritual reputation: all three women fell sick. The woman whom they'd attacked attended them, and they recovered. Perhaps it is just a further coincidence, but the next month an unusually large number of women turned out to help build a new house on the mission grounds. Wray's diaries, CMSA, 3, 21–23/12/1896; 2,5,30/1/1897.

[96]   Interviews with SM, Teri/Sagalla, 24/8/1988; DM, Teri/Sagalla, 3/7/1993; and KM, Kizumanzi/Sagalla, 10/7/1993.

[97]   Wray's diaries, CMSA, 17/2/1901.

[98]   Wray's diaries, CMSA, 27/10/1904.

[99]   This echoed an ongoing skepticism in the Hills about Christian notions of afterlife and resurrection. See Wray's diaries, CMSA, 6/1/1909; also CMS, G3 A5/018, V. Verbi's Annual Letter, 12/1909.

[100] Wray's diaries, CMSA, 28/2/1904.

[101] Wray's diaries, CMSA, 11/1/1904 and 23/7/1909. Most people incorrectly remembered the time before missionaries arrived as an era of reliable rains. The tendency to idealize the climate of the distant past continues today. Despite the well–established record of several severe droughts and famines from the 1920s through the 1940s, most interviewees spoke of those years as bountiful.

Faced with these pressures, many early Christians in Sagalla sought ways to accommodate the demands of their lineages and neighborhoods, yet keep within the bounds of the Church. Their attempts to find a Christian middle way proved difficult. Some continued beer brewing and drinking, and some still took part in *Wutasi* rituals, in order to maintain their affective and material ties in local communities. Most Christians continued to participate in local practices to at least some degree. Strict Christians criticized slippages of this sort, but "lapses" rarely led to someone's removal from the church.

> Christians could not go to dances, they could not dance at *Mwari*, they could not [be at the rites for] *Fighi* [the neighborhood Defender medicine]. . . . But if you look in the shadows, they were there. The church elders were there, and the Christian children.[102]

For many converts, straddling between strict Christianity and local ways also reflected their ambivalence about the Christian exclusivism. A daughter of one of the early converts, though herself raised Christian, took part in *Mwari* (female initiation): her upbringing had left her feeling isolated from her peers, and she wanted to join them in this crucial life–event. Like the non–Christian majority, she also considered initiation crucial to being regarded as an adult woman. Her (Christian) mother supported the daughter's choice; after her husband's death, she, too, had returned to local dances and rituals. Still, both mother and daughter remained in the church, becoming stricter Christians in later years.[103] But in later years, too, Christians had more social fora of their own, and more people openly imbued their Christianity with local cultural forms—for instance, by developing a Christian version of initiation.

Through the first decade of the 1900s, Sagalla Christian converts' ambivalences dominated that community's cultural politics. In 1904, several Christian women admitted to partaking in dances and brewing beer, and warned other women that conversion made it difficult to get a husband. In 1905, a Christian woman advised another woman against baptism. A year later, a man publicly renounced his conversion, to "follow his fathers." But converts' gestures were usually smaller and less dramatic: they continued to use indigenous preventative medicines to ward off disease, or kept *Wutasi* paraphernalia in their homes.[104] Such practices continued for many decades, all across Taita.

The Spread of Christianity to Dabida, 1893–1910

Around the turn of the century, Christianity spread to Dabida. Here, too, far from being a refuge for the socially marginal, it attracted many from highly

---

[102] Interview with Mrs. NM, Kizumanzi/Sagalla, 24/8/1988.

[103] Interview, Mrs. GM, Teri/Sagalla, 24/8/1988.

[104] Wray's diaries, CMSA: 1904 for admissions—10/6/1904; 1905 advice—18/3/1905; 1906 renunciation—15/9/1906; preventative medicine—27–28/11/1908; paraphernalia—23/4/1906. There are many other examples.

respected lineages and even gave some of them additional social leverage: two prominent men considered missions useful devices for consolidating or augmenting their standing vis-à-vis fellow elders and the new colonial state. Though neither became Christian, both encouraged conversions, saw some of their children mission educated and baptized, and garnered chiefships for Christian sons in the colony's Native Administration.

One of the two was Mghalu, by the turn of the century a senior, prominent elder in Mbale. Missionary sources say Mghalu invited Sagalla's missionaries to build a station near his homestead in 1900. He told them that many had died in Mbale during the 1898–99 famine, while people in Sagalla fared much better. With a missionary in Mbale to pray for Mghalu's people, disaster might not recur.[105] There is surely some truth in this story, but its presentation of Mghalu—a former *kishingila* who dabbled in slave trading—as a quaint, unsophisticated but compassionate fellow is not part of it. Mghalu's strategy of friendliness to EAP officials while avoiding armed confrontations with colonial soldiers had served him well. A junior elder in the early 1890s, he had used his acumen, networks, and growing wealth to extend his authority beyond levels most Mbale elders previously held.[106] However, his rapid climb in political and economic strength stirred up dissatisfaction among some senior elders.

It was in that context that Mghalu traveled to Sagalla in 1900. Inviting the CMS to build a station at Mbale under his patronage helped him build an alliance with a block of Mbale elders—some of them his erstwhile opponents— who also saw potential value in a mission there.[107] As a check against some other senior opponents, Mghalu decided to align himself more fully with the increasingly entrenched European presence.[108] The mission would also provide him with broader networks of alliances: local raiding had declined since the early 1890s, but many people from distant neighborhoods traveling regularly to the mission still thought it wise to ensure their safe travel with blood brotherhoods. As new inquirers converged on the mission, so too did new blood brotherhood networks converge on Mghalu, augmenting his standing within and beyond Mbale.[109]

Mghalu offered the CMS a fine plot on his lineage's land, and a station began operating in 1900. John Maynard, who had worked with Wray since the late 1890s, headed the mission, and soon employed two other Europeans and a dozen African agents.[110] The level of staffing and the overt support of Mghalu

---

[105] W. Anderson, *Church in East Africa*, chap. 6.

[106] One interviewee described Mghalu as "a new man" who exercised the power of a colonial chief even before colonial rule; he also held that unlike colonial chiefs, the "office boys" of the DCs, Mghalu's precolonial power derived from his own social and political strength. Interview with MM, Mbale/Mbale, 7/11/1988.

[107] Interview with OK, Shigaro/Werugha, 2/8/1993; W. Anderson, "A History of the Church in Kenya, 1844 to Now," Occasional Research Papers: Christianity in Contemporary Africa, vol. 10 (Makerere University, 1973), 11–12.

[108] Interview with MM, Mbale/Mbale, 7/11/1988.

[109] Interviews with JM, Wusi/Chawia, 22/7/1993, and AM, Shigaro/Werugha, 2/5/1988.

[110] CMS, G3 A5/015, Bishop Peel to Baylis, 26/3/1901.

allowed Mbale mission to build up a core Christian community far more quickly than in Sagalla, though that community had similar difficulties and trials. Dabida's widely scattered Christians faced more cultural political struggles with *Wutasi* followers, and had more difficulty banding together in mutual support. Mghalu's neighborhood, however, became a Christian stronghold, and he emerged as by far the most powerful elder in the Hills. He also arranged for an orderly succession of power within the new colonial system: his mission edu-cated, Christian son, Thomas, became the first colonial Chief of (the much en-larged) Mbale location in 1908.[111]

The establishment of a mission in lower Bura had parallels with the event in Mbale, but also significant differences. Here, as in Mbale, an elder seeking to augment his authority propelled the process. That elder, Mbogholi, had pur-sued this tack since the 1880s. His contacts with Wray nearly destroyed his standing then, but in September 1892, only a few months after Mwangeka's defeat, he presented himself at the head of an impressive entourage to wel-come French Catholic missionaries from the Holy Ghost Fathers to his neigh-borhood. Mbogholi arranged for the Fathers to have rights to a large block of land near the mouth of the valley.[112]

The Fathers interacted with local people in a far less restrictive manner than the CMS missionaries. A priest itinerating in the upper reaches of the val-ley drank *chofi* with an elder in the name of learning local customs, not exclud-ing ritual libations in the manner of *Wutasi*.[113] The Fathers also took a far more liberal approach to baptisms (in 1898 they performed fifty–two; in 1902 they did 225),[114] and in turn, expected far less rectitude from the baptized. The first decade of the 1900s witnessed far less friction over Catholicism in Bura than Anglicanism generated elsewhere in the Hills, largely because the line between Catholicism and *Wutasi* often blurred to near nonexistence. Bura's Sunday ser-vices drew congregations in the hundreds, many of whom had been at local dances the night before and would drink *chofi* later that day.[115]

Mbogholi, however, could not capitalize as effectively as Mghalu on his ties to a mission. He retained a good name with the missionaries, but the ease of relations there made his mediation less necessary and less significant. He was EAP officials' main contact in the area, but several senior elders in the lower Bura valley still blocked his access to more senior standing.[116] Their con-tinued disdain gave him a reputation as an interloper trying to use European connections to attain what his conduct did not merit. Mbogholi, like Mghalu,

---

[111] On the appointment of Mwaiwasi/Thomas to the chiefship, see KNA, DC/TTA/3/1, Political Record Books 1910–12, "Chiefs and Headmen." Mghalu, while he lived, was understood to be the power behind his spokesperson son, an arrangement befitting a dignified elder.

[112] KNA, DC/TTA/3/8/97, and *Bulletin de la Congregation, Tome Troisième*, 1891–93, p. 786.

[113] *Bulletin de la Congregation, Tome Troisième*, 1891–93, letter of Father Mével, 2/2/1893.

[114] Bura Baptismal Records, Book 1 (Bura Catholic Church, Taita).

[115] Most interviewees around Bura acknowledged this unashamedly, including Mrs. MK, Nyolo/Bura, 16/8/1988; Mrs. SM, Ilole/Bura, 16/8/1988; and LM, Mrugua/Bura, 18/8/1988.

[116] Interview with BM, Njawuli/Mwanda, 3/8/1993.

had a mission-educated son named the first colonial chief of Bura. But the son, Mwanjila, did not fare as well as Thomas—partly because of his reportedly ineffectual character, and partly because, like Thomas, he inherited his father's reputation.[117]

Conclusion

In the last decades of the nineteenth century, local communities around Taita faced difficult decisions about how to respond to the incursions of European missionaries and officials. Different neighborhoods' responses led to different short–term outcomes, but by 1910 all would be swallowed up in a unified administration of the Hills and subject to itinerations by European and African Christian evangelists. Lineage and neighborhood communities withstood the initial phases of this transition, but the domestic incorporation of CMS Anglicanism initiated a new kind of cultural politics, one that in the long run might undercut their cosmological bases—and eventually their social bases. The consolidation of colonial rule in the early twentieth century threatened other facets of lineage and neighborhood as community, as well. Lineage elders, with most to lose from these changes, would have to find other ways to constitute their authority.

---

[117] The 1914 DC described Mwanjila in very unflattering terms: alcoholic, untrustworthy, and with little influence in his own community. See KNA, DC/TTA/3/3, Headmen–Character Reports, 1913–14; local remembrances of him are no kinder, e.g., interview with SM, Mrugua/Bura, 19/8/1988.

4

Erosions of Lineage and Neighborhood in the Early Colonial Era

Introduction

Colonial rule's consolidation after 1900 fueled changes that disrupted community ways across the Hills. As colonial administration stabilized and expanded, it gave rise to a new, overarching political structure that superseded and effectively devalued prior political authority. Christian beliefs represented a standing rebuke to local communities' cosmology and authority structures, as well as to many everyday practices. The Christian presence was consolidated by a slow but steady increase in its pool of converts, and given prominence and favor by colonial political authorities. Taxation, migrant labor, and the rapid growth of a cash–based economy affected several layers of the region's authority relations; gave rise to new means of accumulating wealth and new definitions of wealth; and facilitated new practices and discourses of work.

Some changes, such as sons' new efforts to control economic resources, built upon and accelerated processes that predated colonialism. Others, like the colonial imposition of its power through new territorial units of administration and new local authorities, were unprecedented. All, however, became arenas of struggle in communities across the Hills—between generations, between genders, and between religious affiliations. The struggles centered on whether and how people might modify extant practices and beliefs, how much they might do so, and what meanings to ascribe to the changes: if Christians did *not* put their daughters and sons through initiation, could a lineage accept that with equanimity? Could the uninitiated be considered fully adult by *Wutasi*–following neighbors pondering marriages?

This chapter argues that early colonial changes threatened Taita's local communities both as units of belonging and as instruments of older men's predominance. Christians might now pose fundamental threats to community well–being; colonial chiefs were quite nearly the antithesis of what gave a lineage

107

elder standing and power; wage labor began to undercut the material bases of how lineage seniors had long controlled sons and daughters–in–law. The colonial rulers' social categories, spatial units, and tools of administration paid little heed to lineage and neighborhood structures. But though early colonialism distinctly weakened lineage and neighborhood structures, it was not only younger men, women, and Christians who tried to seize colonial opportunities. Older men, too, reached for new possibilities, seeking to rebuild the material basis of their wealth and to remake their communities in ways that would reground their predominance.

Political Authority, Political Units, and the Consolidation of the New State

The Transition to Regularized Administration

Around the turn of the century, Britain's rule over the Taita Hills shed its sketchy, randomly predatory quality, to emerge as a more predictable, farther–reaching bureaucracy. It imposed itself more fully and continuously on the region, and in so doing affected local discourses and practices of community construction. Regularized colonial rule generated new spatial units of administration and new structures of political authority that overrode lineage and neighborhood boundaries and authority structures. The changes created new opportunities and new difficulties.

In 1895, Britain replaced the overextended, financially prostrate IBEACo with direct rule through the East Africa Protectorate. At first this changed little in how Africans and Europeans interacted; Company field staff often simply switched employers. An ex–Company agent initially "oversaw" the EAP's Taita outpost (Ndii) from over 100 miles further inland, rendering European power as distant and arbitrary in Taita as before. Through the 1890s, the EAP barely maintained control over the plains immediately surrounding Ndii station, let alone extending its effective purview to within the Hills.[1]

In 1900, however, colonial attention increased. After five different (and often indifferent) field officers vaguely oversaw Taita for six years, the EAP built a Taita headquarters at Mwatate, nearer and far more accessible to the Hills' main population. Six different officials ran the post from 1902 to 1910, but two accounted for over five of the years, giving Taita's colonial administration regularization and continuity.[2] In 1912 the headquarters moved again, to the rap-

---

[1]   Ogot argues that from 1895 to 1901, the Foreign Office cared more about completing the Kenya–Uganda railroad than about effective administration of the interior. See Bethwell Ogot, "Kenya Under the British, 1895–1963," in Ogot, ed., *Zamani*, 251. For a participant's view of the IBEACo's financial failure, see Hobley, *Kenya*, 68–72. On the EAP's administration of Taita, see G. H. Mungeam, *British Rule in Kenya, 1895–1912* (Oxford, 1966), 34.

[2]   KNA, DC/TTA/3/1, Political Record Books 1910–1912, List of District's Officers. The two who served long enough to get some feel for Taita were C. S. Reddie (3.5 years) and R. Weeks (2 years).

idly growing new town of Voi, on the plains just north of Sagalla and astride the rail line between the coast and Uganda. Voi was farther from the heart of the Hills than Mwatate, but the colonial administrative infrastructure by then reached into every locale.

By 1900, too, telegraph lines connected the colony's main offices to Taita. In 1895, a five–day, arduous trek separated Taita from the coast; now, a day's train ride easily moved people and goods, and information could travel faster still. Official oversight and policy direction became stronger and more constant at every level, routinizing the colonial staff's duties and curtailing its earlier roguishness. Colonial rule still relied heavily on hubris and mirrors in much of the interior, and Taita would remain, by its officers' accounting, thinly staffed into the 1930s.[3] Nevertheless, increased routinization of the state and the planting of its sociological and administrative categories compelled a reconceptualization of local spatial units and authority relations that rippled through the local societies.

Administrative Categories and Local Categories

The most fundamental change was perhaps all but invisible to the new administration that wrought it: British officials saw Taita as a single administrative unit. With their template of African societies as inherently tribal, they assumed that the closely settled Hills had long been socially unified, despite piecemeal official observations contradicting that view.[4] Colonial administrators therefore treated Taita as a "natural" sociogeographical entity, and its population as, naturally, a people. The EAP made its administrative "Taita" when establishing itself in 1895.[5] This new conceptualization of the Hills, together with a new authority figure for it, (the District Commissioner), gave a unitary "Taita" its first political reality.[6]

The colonial refashioning of Taita altered local community routines in numerous ways. For example, the EAP forcibly curtailed raids and armed con-

---

[3]   In 1933, the district commissioner wrote that Taita "maintained its unenviable reputation of being the most understaffed of any 'one man' district" in the colony. See KNA, DC/TTA/1/1, Taita Annual Report, 1933. In the 1930s, Taita was assigned an agricultural officer, and after World War II, a district officer worked under the district commissioner.

Even after World War II, Taita was considered a backwater post. One former official secured a promotion to district commissioner by agreeing to go to Taita and not transfer for five years. Interview with Peter Walters, 25/2/1988.

[4]   For instance, the district commissioner in 1910 described the district as effectively fifty or so pieces, each with a headman "of little or no authority." See KNA, DC/TTA/3/1, DC Weeks, 1910.

[5]   PRO, FOCP 6761 XLII, Hardinge to Salisbury, 6/7/1895, lays out the district structure; also KNA, DC/TTA/3/1, Political Record Books, 1910–1912. Officials in charge of Taita under the EAP bore the title of Collector. When the Colonial Office took over in 1905, it replaced that title with District Commissioner (DC).

[6]   This point resembles David Low and John Lonsdale's, that district administration "not only transmitted the external demands which prompted people to aggregate with their neighbours, but gave them, if often unintentionally, the political resources which helped them do so." See their "Introduction: Towards the New Order 1945–1963," in *History of East Africa*, vol. 3, ed. David Low and Alison Smith (Oxford, 1976), 25.

frontations within the Hills, and attacks on distant societies, by around 1900. This had multiple, crosscutting impacts on neighborhood and lineage structures: on the one hand, it foreclosed an important form of building up lineage herds (and older men's lineage–based wealth and authority):

> Our fathers, ehh . . . the colonialists had already come, so our fathers could not start any wars for animals. It was our grandfathers who went to Shambala to grab cattle from those people.[7]

Yet it also deprived *vishingila* of their means to challenge older men's stranglehold on wealth, and cost warrior groups their main reason for being. Then again, the decline of raiding and skirmishes greatly loosened up everyday movement in Taita: people could now traverse the Hills singly or in small groups—walking from upper Dabida to the DC's office or a new shop in Mwatate—with little fear for their safety.[8] 'Neighborhood' still demarcated an area where people held property and "really knew each other," but lost its spatial role in defining zones of protection or danger.

Colonial alterations in Taita's formal authority structure also had far–reaching effects on neighborhood and lineage. Most broadly, by 1910 an entirely new scale of overarching authority could impose itself on people in ways lineage elders never even attempted. The DC, often helped by African intermediaries, demanded cash from people on an annual basis; commandeered their labor on short notice; enforced other whites' land claims in and around the Hills; arrogated the right to judge serious criminal cases; and broke up neighborhood warrior groups—replacing them with a unitary African police that concentrated "legitimate" force beneath his authority.[9] In these and other ways, people across the Hills drew together in shared recognition of the district headquarters as a new political center for them all.

People throughout the Hills struggled to live with, benefit by, and set limits on this imposed authority—and, as colonial officers found, there were indeed limits. Officials could compel some actions through sheer force, but only for a relatively short time, and then in the teeth of increasing evasion and opposition.[10] In everyday interactions over administrative desires, a great deal of give–and–take

---

[7]   Interview with GM, Tausa/Mbololo, 31/5/1988.

[8]   "After the whites arrived here, you could walk where you wanted in Taita, without any problem." Interview with JK, Werugha/Werugha, 3/10/1988; also with OM, Wundanyi/Werugha, 5/5/1988.

[9]   Despite the regularization of district administration in this era, officials in the field were delegated a great deal of authority by their superior officers. See L. H. Gann and P. Duignan, *The Rulers of British Africa* (Stanford, 1978), 213–16.

[10]   The most extreme examples of compulsion in Taita took place around World War I, with the conscription of labor for railway construction and the infamous Carrier Corps. By 1917, large numbers of young men were evading Carrier Corps conscription, and district officials were trying to shield them from it. PRO, CO 533/152, 6/2/1915 and 18/2/1915; KNA, PC/Cst, 1/9/25, Taita Laborers; and PC/Cst/1/13/123, Taita Military Porters. Also, interviews with SM, Wundanyi/Werugha, 22/4/1988; and MM/Kishamba/Chawia, 8/6/1988.

transpired.[11] For instance, early DCs tried to turn young men from the Hills into the primary labor supply at nearby sisal plantations on fixed–term contracts. Taita's men, though, refused to "bind [themselves] for the stated time," were highly selective about what tasks they would undertake (for unskilled labor on the sisal plantations was regarded as bad, poorly paid work), and never worked the plantations in large numbers. However, so long as young men performed migrant labor *somewhere* (which their fathers pushed for, too), Taita's colonial officers felt they had pressed the matter as far as they could; attempts to direct where and when young men worked backfired, reducing the overall migrant labor supply.[12]

Still, in carving out standoffs with state authorities or seeking some sort of benefit from the government, people in the Hills had to engage it through its institutions, like the Taita–wide Native Authority figures and Native Law systems. There, they invoked and located themselves by the colonizers' categories and language about Africans, predicated on tribe, tribal custom, and tribal traditions. In other words, the European assumption of a single Taita gave weight to a set of conditions that altered consciousness in Taita: institutions, practices, and discourses of authority that defined Taita as a single administrative entity promoted new social categories, as well. These changes weakened the authority structure of lineages, and reduced the importance of neighborhoods as spatial units.

Two linked institutions (and concomitant discourses) particularly weakened lineage and neighborhood as *social* units: chiefship, and the areas over which chiefs presided, administrative "locations." Both dated to 1908, when the state named one chief each for the locations of Chawia, Bura, Mwanda, Mbale, and Sagalla. Before that year, administrators had seen the Hills as subdividing into approximately fifty "village" territories—a roughly accurate correspondence to the number of neighborhoods.[13] The new locations, which dwarfed the size of neighborhoods, became the main low–level units of an administration managed not by elders, but by the chief and his subordinate staff. Each location inevitably combined together neighborhoods previously aloof from one another. Lineage elders who took part in location–based "traditional" institutions (like Elders' Councils and Native Law courts) thus did so across prior lines of division.

Chiefs, Locations, and State Power vs.
Elders, Neighborhoods, and Respectability

In Taita, chiefs emerged from virtually nowhere to become the main day–to–day representatives of colonial authority. Those who wanted something from

---

[11] For a critique of the idea of the all–powerful colonial officer in the field, see Justin Willis, "'Men on the Spot' and Labor Policy in British East Africa: The Mombasa Water Supply, 1911–1917," *International Journal of African Historical Studies* 28, 1 (1995).

[12] KNA, PC/Cst/1/12/40, Taita Inward, letter of DC Reddie, 8/4/07; and letters of his successor, Traill, same file.

[13] KNA, DC/TTA/3/1, Political Record Books, 1910–12, Chiefs and Headmen; PC/Cst/1/12/51, Taita Inward, 1/1/1904; PC/Cst/1/1/115, Taita Inward, 26/3/1906.

the state (and those who had to answer for something to it) usually dealt first with the chiefs, generally on the chiefs' terms:

> Long ago, if . . . someone from [the next neighborhood over] stole my goats, what would I do? I asked for young men like you to grab them back! Maybe you killed the one who stole them! . . . When the whites arrived you could not do that, no. . . . You went to see the chief, he will send his soldiers to take the goats. Then the thief must be taken to jail in Voi.[14]

From the European end, DCs relied on chiefs to maintain day–to–day control over locations, and expected them to uphold colonial authority and rules. Completely bypassed by this new spatial regime of authority were elders and *vishingila*. The latter's role virtually disappeared after the turn of the century.

Chiefs occupied a peculiar position in the Hills. Because no analogous institution had existed in Taita's nineteenth–century communities, installing chiefs raised contradictions in European templates about African societies. The DC who appointed the first chiefs noted that Taita previously had only elders with limited authority. Yet later in the same report, he described the 1890s *kishingila* Mwangeka as "chief" of Mwanda.[15] That schizophrenic perspective of chiefs continued throughout the colonial period. Most DCs in colonial Taita understood that chiefs were not genuinely "traditional" figures. From the outset they considered chiefs adjuncts who would collect Hut Tax, guard forests, report on events and diseases in their areas, and generally act as executors of the DC's orders, whether to prevent *Wutasi* practitioners from drinking beer and holding dances near the missions, to seize young men to work as porters for the state, or to recruit labor for private employers.[16] Yet DCs also easily slipped into regarding chiefs as having a quasi–natural local legitimacy, for chiefship— even when fashioned from whole cloth—struck many British officials as an inherently African institution.

Some chiefs did command local respect, although not because of the office *per se*; most, however, found chiefly power more tenuous than officials acknowledged. Though chiefship compelled new practices and discourses, chiefs individually learned that commanding respect or attaining respectability was an uphill climb. Chiefs' difficulties had several root causes. First, the degree of authority they purportedly held had no precedent in the Hills, and many people considered their attempts to apply it impertinent.[17] Chiefly interventions in

---

[14] Interview with MM, Wundanyi/Werugha, 21/7/1993.

[15] KNA, DC/TTA/3/1, Political Record Books, 1910–1912 Chiefs and Headmen. The DC here cited, R. Weeks, worked in Taita for over two years before making the appointments.

[16] KNA, DC/TTA/3/1, Political Record Books, 1910–1912 Chiefs and Headmen; PC/Coast/1/12/28, Mombasa Outward, 25/2/1904; PC/Coast/1/1/128, Mombasa Outward 24/7/1908.

[17] As colonial officers and missionaries never tired of pointing out, lineage elders exerted little direct command over many everyday events. DCs soon picked up Wray's old lamentations about the weakness of elders: "The Wataita[,] . . . having no chiefs, . . . are thoroughly independent." See KNA, PC/Coast/1/1/115, Taita Inward, 26/3/1906.

everyday matters were often represented as meddling in affairs rightfully none of their business:

> The chiefs started when I was already a woman. . . . People were not happy with chiefs, they asked, "why do they bring us leaders who disturb us? . . . They bring words and words [i.e., difficulties] about everything. Now, why are they like that?"[18]

Furthermore, chiefs' authority derived neither from local consent nor local terms of authority; the colonial state imposed it on local societies. Ties to the DC personified a chief's authority ("The chief and the DC were just one blood, you could not say anything between them"[19]), while the chief's police and jail provided the lash of state power. Chiefs' power flew in the face of elders' ideology that authority came through age, experience, wealth, network building, and ritual position. Adding insult to injury, chiefs were generally far younger than elders, and most were Christians. Both factors made chiefly authority seem all the more presumptuous.[20]

Many elders actually agreed that Europeans should use young Christian intermediaries between local societies and the DC; the rub lay in how different groups envisioned the chiefs' role. Elders thought it helpful to have someone communicate regularly with the white rulers, but most senior elders considered the task inappropriate to do themselves; younger men who spoke KiSwahili and could make the trek to the DC's office fit the bill nicely.[21] Besides, a chief's work involved a great deal of public fussing and pronouncing and ordering–about, the sort of indignity unbecoming to self–respecting senior elders, who strove to wear their authority with humility and calm restraint. They had long left it to younger male kin or supporters to exercise opinions publicly; elders listened, then came to decisions in private discussions. So elders pictured younger men in the role of chiefs, but only as an extension of prior terms:

> Those who had age and wealth, they didn't want chiefhood. They said, "if the Europeans want to make someone run–run, we will give them this [young man]. If the Europeans want to kill him they will kill him." So the old men gave that job to the young.[22]

---

[18] Interview with Mrs. FM, Lushangonyi, Mwanda, 21/9/1988.

[19] Interview with RM, Kaya/Chawia, 4/5/1988.

[20] Interviews with JM, Wundanyi/Werugha, 17/4/1988; and with MM, Nyolo/Bura, 15/8/1988. The view continued into late colonialism. See A. and G. Harris, "WaTaita Today," 139. Two of the five original chiefs already professed Christianity when appointed. See KNA, DC/TTA/3/1, Political Record Books, 1910–1912 Chiefs and Headmen. By 1931 Taita had eight chiefs, all but two of them Christians. KNA, DC/TTA/1/1, Annual Report of 1931.

[21] Interviews with SM, Kidaya–Ngerenyi/Chawia, 25/4/1988; and with AM, Shigaro/Werugha, 2/5/1988.

[22] Interview with JM, Teri/Sagalla, 25/8/1988. See also A. and G. Harris, "WaTaita Today," 44–46.

Many elders considered themselves above the young chiefs' orders, still the true authority figures of their communities. This posed a delicate problem for chiefs, most of them junior lineage members who wanted to avoid damaging their standing and prospects within their lineages.[23] Chiefs also keenly understood that their power had no indigenous social basis, that it was not respectable power in elders' terms, and that disapproval of many chiefly exertions held sway not only among the gerontocracy, but across most of the population.

Under the circumstances, the early chiefs trod lightly when it came to elders' practices and prerogatives. They often failed to enforce measures directed at elders (e.g., restrictions on beer drinking or jural use of poisons),[24] setting a precedent that lasted through most of the colonial era. It cast them in an unflattering light among European officials, who regularly complained of Taita chiefs' "weak character."[25] The British expected these young, often Christian men to execute orders vigorously and enforce colonial edicts energetically. Colonial officers, like elders, considered chiefs mediators, but of a different kind: chiefs would explain the rules to their people as they enforced them, and their office's natural prestige would give the orders local legitimacy. Here, again, though Taita chiefs were a British creation, schizophrenic assumptions about chiefly legitimacy allowed officials to overlook the lack of local sanction behind chiefly power.

Still, the very existence of young Christian chiefs and territories, called locations, hurt the position of lineage elders, and challenged the sociopolitical importance of neighborhoods. Colonial governance, which was indeed reordering the social landscape, bypassed both prior institutions. That left elders in a difficult position: aspects of their authority were being usurped and little new authority was flowing to them, while great authority went to unready and unworthy youths. Most chiefs were virtual boys in elders' eyes:

> The old men of long ago, they just looked down on the chiefs as children. My grandfather said that Johana [Mwandango, first chief of Chawia location] was . . . a child who played [at being] a man! He called Johana "my child," . . . yes, it was sharp words, to remind him.[26]

Elders' views of course clashed sharply with what the state expected of its functionaries: an elder's low–key dignity, public restraint, and reliance on quiet consultation did not fit its job description for chiefs. Though careful around

---

[23] "[When] the elders in this neighborhood . . . continued with their work, when they met for their work, they couldn't be objected to by the chief or sub–chief. No, they would do the work [as] they liked." Interview with MM, Nyolo/Bura, 15/8/1988.

[24] See the DCs' complaints on this score, in the "Chiefs and Headmen" section of the Political Record Books for 1910–1930: KNA, DC/TTA/3/1; DC/TTA/3/3/2; and DC/TTA/3/3.

[25] One DC described the chiefs as having "little character and energy." A few years later, another called them willing to issue orders, but reluctant to make people carry them out. See KNA, DC/TTA/1/1, Annual Reports of 1926, 1929.

[26] Interview with NM, Wundanyi/Werugha, 28/7/1993.

elders and their concerns, most chiefs strove to realize the colonial version of their authority when dealing with non–elders.

Chiefs, Colonial Power, and the
Elders' Model of Proper Wealth

In one respect, however, chiefs did take elders as models of authority: both associated authority with personal wealth. Elders considered wealth accrual and wealth–based social network building necessary precedents of authority. Chiefs reproduced the association of wealth and authority, but reversed it: they used their office to enrich themselves, hoping it would secure them networks and stature thereafter. Chiefs almost invariably wanted to parlay wealth into respectability and elderhood once they retired: "When Johana got old . . . he wanted very much to be an elder. . . .He offered my grandfather loans of cows."[27] In amassing wealth as young men, chiefs hoped to elude elders' linking of wealth and authority to respected seniority.

Chiefs acquired wealth by using their authority to supplement their meager salaries. It was a quick climb: if the DC in 1904 could note that his chosen local headmen were "often as poor as the generality of the people," by the 1910s that no longer held true.[28] Colonial officers inadvertently abetted the enrichment, for they gave chiefs considerable purview and responsibility, while maintaining limited supervision of them and paying them a pittance: a chief's salary in the 1910s barely topped that of a platform sweeper at Voi railway station.[29] Chiefs' enrichment usually took the form of appropriating goods or labor, mainly from younger men and women. Extending the state practice of conscripting labor for public road building or official porterage, one chief used conscripts and jail convicts to farm his fields and haul stones for his new house.[30] Other chiefly expropriations included seizure of livestock, chickens, and food from people for real or invented infractions of colonial rules.[31] Most chiefs of the 1910s and 1920s could not easily parlay expropriated wealth into respectable elderhood, for their conduct aggravated many elders and generated widespread public resentment. But successful or not, chiefs' abilities to set up new channels of accumulation and (possibly) lasting influence threatened not only elders' political positions, but also their economic preeminence.

Two men exemplified the possibilities and pitfalls awaiting early chiefs, elders, and non–elders of the new locations. In 1908, Mghalu of Mbale and Mbogholi of lower Bura had aged enough to make chiefship unseemly for them,

---

[27] Ibid. Johana retired in 1931. KNA, DC/TTA/1/1, District Annual Report, 1930.

[28] KNA, PC/Coast/1/12/51, Taita Inward, 1/1/1904. Headmen, the predecessors of chiefs, had considerably less state authority.

[29] KNA, DC/TTA/1/1, Taita District Annual Report for 1920.

[30] Interviews with DM, Mbale/Mbale, 7/11/1988; JM, Kishamba/Chawia, 12/8/1988; and Mrs. MM, Ilole/Bura, 16/8/1988. Europeans seeing the fine fields or sturdy house praised the chief as an example to the community. KNA, DC/TTA/3/3/2, Political Record Books, 1920.

[31] Interviews with LM, Mrugua/Bura, 18/8/1988; and Mrs. VM, Sagasa/Werugha, 6/10/1988. Once again, many interviews could be cited.

but each placed a son among the five original chiefs. Mghalu's son Mwaiwasi, baptized Thomas soon after his appointment, was lightly regarded by Mbale elders in 1908. Mwaiwasi, having spent the previous few years in Mombasa, seemed to the elders "just a Swahili, he knows nothing."[32] That view changed in short order. When Mghalu died around 1911, Thomas inherited the lion's share of his wealth and social networks, and showed himself to have been an adroit student of his father's strategic sensibilities. He used his office to extend his wealth and networks throughout his career, while drawing praise from Europeans for his authoritative manner and "progressivism." He neutralized many potentially hostile elders by avoiding direct assaults on their prerogatives and using his inherited networks judiciously. Still, though partly operating within the elders' milieu, he greatly scaled back the political salience of lineage and neighborhood elderhood in Mbale. Finally, he generated fear among Mbale's weaker lineages for his propensity to coerce labor from them for his personal projects.[33] Mbale under Thomas was Taita's largest and most populous location, but he held a firm grip on it and thoroughly integrated it into the colonial sociopolitical order.

Meanwhile, in the lower Bura Valley, Mbogholi's son Mwanjila had a rather different experience as the first chief of the new Bura location. Just as Mghalu's prominence helped Thomas, Mbogholi's lack of wider respectability handicapped Mwanjila. Mwanjila did not stand to inherit influence the way Thomas had, and never enjoyed the local stature Thomas did. Like Thomas and most other early chiefs, Mwanjila used his office to enrich himself, but Mwanjila neither commanded the respect of elders nor neutralized them. Soon he also failed to inspire awe or fear in younger people. He became widely disliked, was rendered ineffective, and in 1920 resigned in thinly veiled disgrace.[34] Bura location in those years remained to no small extent an amalgam of neighborhoods where lineage elders effectively retained a great deal of influence.

Work, Wealth, and Small Lineages:
Taita and the Colonial Economy

Colonial changes in the intertwined realms of work and wealth profoundly affected lineage and neighborhood communities in the Hills. Older men in the later nineteenth century had exercised a near monopoly over livestock and farm-

---

[32] Interview with WM, Shigaro/Werugha, 18/4/1988. The suggestion that Mwaiwasi knew nothing referred more to his tender age than to his working in Mombasa.

[33] Interviews with DM, Mbale/Mbale, 7/11/1988; Mrs. AM, Choke/Mbale, 10/11/1988.

[34] Mwanjila's ineffectual character compounded his difficulties: the 1914 DC called him a drunkard, untrustworthy, prone to lying, and with little influence in the community. Still, when the British army summarily deposed him in World War I, the governor of Kenya protested. Mwanjila was reinstated after the war, only to be forced into resigning by the 1919–20 DC. See KNA, DC/TTA/ 3/3, Headmen—Character Reports, 1913–4; DC/TTA/3/3/2, War Diary, 21/9/1914; PC/Coast/ 1/1/266, District Annual Report for 1918; and DC/TTA/1/1, Annual Report, 1919–20. Also, interviews with MM, Nyolo/Bura, 15/8/1988; and MM, Nyolo/Bura, 17/8/1988.

land, the main forms of exchangeable wealth. Livestock was the more important of these for men's day–to–day exchanges,[35] and for building up a man's
social networks and religious position: various rituals required animal offer-
ings, including rituals for attaining high religious standing. The predominant
ideology of property and work in the later nineteenth century held that the
eldest men in a small lineage owned virtually all its resources. Wives and unmarried daughters had use–rights to property; sons' wives gained usage rights
through their husbands. Sons knew that senior men would gradually parcel
resources out to them, and that they would inherit larger blocs of fields and
livestock when their fathers died. Meanwhile, sons worked for their fathers
and could not surpass the fathers' wealth while the fathers lived. These everyday hegemonics were expressed in lineage axioms that rendered older men's
predominance natural: this was how local communities properly worked.[36]

Some *vishingila* had challenged these versions of wealth and work in
the late nineteenth century, but they came under far more extensive and
dramatic strains after 1900. Interlocking changes altered patterns of work
for young men and their wives, and opened up new intergenerational cultural politics over the nature and control of wealth. The changes had multiple, far–reaching effects on Taita. In the first decades of the century, small
lineage heads managed those effects well: they reconstituted sons' work in
ways that maintained seniors' control over wealth, used that wealth to fuel
new growth in livestock holdings, and intensified the work that daughters–
in–law did for small lineages. Their initial successes, however, were not
stable; younger men's and women's continued cultural politicking over work
and wealth would, by the 1930s, increase the autonomy of junior households and reduce the juniors' dependence on older men, thereby eroding
the old power structure of small lineages.

Making Money Matter: New Forms of
Work, New Forms of Wealth

Nineteenth–century Taita had no indigenous form of money. Some men involved
in long–distance trade made limited use of currencies circulating at the coast,
but those moneys meant little in the Hills. There, long-distance exchanges and
virtually all local trade either operated on barter terms or used animals as currency. People in the Hills generally sought ornamental goods, cloth, or wire
when working as caravan porters or trading their foodstuffs to passing caravans.[37]

Money made its way into wide use through one of colonialism's least at-
tractive institutions: taxation. The Hut Tax, instituted in the Hills in 1902, prod-

---

[35] Among women, land exchanges of fields to which they had use rights were most important.
Interviews with Mrs. NM, Kizumanzi/Sagalla, 24/8/1988; and Mrs. FM, Mogho Mleche/ Mbale,
2/11/1988; see also A. Harris, "Organization," 253–54.

[36] This view of elders' power derives from Bourdieu, *Outline*.

[37] Thomson, *Masai-land*, 40–55.

ded household heads into their first experience of needing money on an ongoing basis.[38] One purpose of the cash–based tax was to compel Africans to enter
the colonial capitalist economy, especially as labor, and it did indeed have that
effect in Taita.[39] However, using and engaging in commoditized labor, production, and consumption did not mean that communities in Taita quickly displaced the ways livestock worked as wealth for capitalist terms of wealth. If
colonial capitalism now impinged on Taita in various ways, older men initially
used it to reinvigorate locally–based notions of livestock–as–wealth. In so doing, they gave lie to the old scholarly dichotomy of traditionalism vs. modernization—for their actions show them not avoiding colonial capitalism, but trying to bend it to their purposes.[40] Livestock–as–wealth eventually lost its
ascendancy, but older men's reworkings and revitalizations of it continued into
the 1950s and beyond.

   How did all this spring from the 1902 edict that household heads in Taita
annually pay 2/= (two shillings) for each hut of their household? Though nominally a low amount, generating that money triggered a series of broad social
changes. Raising cash often strained the immediate resources of poorer small
lineages, and even among wealthier ones required involvement in markets that
exchanged money for goods or labor.[41] Few people in the region sold produce
or animals for cash at that juncture, so tax money came primarily from wage
labor.[42] Most such wage work was manual labor that called for young, strong
bodies.

   Older men therefore sent out their sons for wage work in significant
numbers within a few years of the start of the Hut Tax.[43] This began to
reconfigure how work bound people into their lineages. Women's and young
men's work for their seniors had been a fundamental part of lineage com-

---

[38]   From 1902 to 1906, the DC allowed a few people to pay taxes in goats, rather than cash. KNA,
PC/Coast/1/12/31, Taita Inward, 5/10/1905.

[39]   Officials also used land alienation to push Africans into the labor market. For a fuller discussion of these topics, Sharon Stichter, *Migrant Labour in Kenya: Capitalism and African Response* (Harlow,
1982).

[40]   Neither was this a case of coexisting modes of production. That model holds that capitalism
subordinated essentially unchanging *pre*–capitalist modes of production, wrongly seeing Taita's
economy as clinging to static vestiges of the past. People in the Hills participated in capitalist
production relations, using them to remake and reinvigorate *non*-capitalist economic forms. This
process held contradictions that gradually spurred further changes.
   On modes of production, see Aiden Foster–Carter, "The Modes of Production Controversy,"
New Left Review 107 (1978); Bernard Magubane, "The Evolution of Class Structure in Africa," in *The
Political Economy of Contemporary Africa*, ed. P. Gutkind and E. Wallerstein (Beverley Hills, 1976);
Stichter, *Migrant Labour in Kenya*.

[41]   A 1905 rate increase to 3/= compounded the strain. KNA, PC/Cst/1/12/31, Reddie Inward,
27/3/1905.

[42]   A (very small) food–for–cash trade supplied Voi and European–owned sisal plantations in the
nearby lowlands. Most of the trade involved lower zone farmers close to Voi or the plantations.
Interview with RM, Kaya/Chawia, 4/5/1988; and KNA, PC/Cst/1/12/51, Reddie Inward, 11/4/
1904; and PC/Cst/1/1/179, Quarterly Report, 5/1/1912.

[43]   "In the last two years the desire for labor has increased a great deal, and this will likely continue, if irregularly." KNA, PC/Cst/1/12/40; DC Reddie Inward, 8/4/1907.

munity in the later nineteenth century. Lineages reproduced themselves through that work; axiomatic knowledge that the young worked for seniors undergirded a community–building ideology of lineage as a bedrock support group. Older men and women had over time accumulated the power to effectively compel such work from their juniors, but community–building axioms justified it as a part of the natural (and reciprocal) order of things: a son, daughter, or daughter–in–law did certain sorts of work for the benefit of their seniors. Seniors, in turn, provided the young with material and spiritual supports, and meshed the young into networks of group support. Along with women's usage rights and the promise to young men of eventual resource control, a key community–building reciprocation was the promise that older men would give marrying sons bridewealth cattle from the small lineage's holdings.

With stints of migratory labor and the rapid dissemination of money in early–twentieth–century Taita, patterns of work and a lineage's means of amassing wealth changed. Older men's control over both became slightly attenuated, and had to be reconstructed for the new context. When young men had mainly herded, their labor and their contributions to the wealth of their lineage had been combined in one activity (i.e., herding–as–work had rendered young men's wealth–generating efforts inseparable from their elders' naturalized "rights" over lineage property). This idea is perhaps clearest when contrasted with raiding–as–work: in that realm, young men had constructed a notion of seized cattle as "theirs," even though the claim was rendered ambiguous by the livestock's placement in lineage herds under seniors' control.

With migrant labor, a distinction between sons' work and a lineage's wealth became evident. Wage work did not redound directly to lineage elders; instead, it put a highly fluid form of compensation, money, directly in a young man's hands, often at a locale far removed from parental oversight. Money's portability, small size, and easy transformability into goods and services allowed young men to make direct use of it relatively easily:

> With money temptation was there. . . . Youths in those days [around World War One] saw fancy clothes and they really wanted them! . . . Drink was there. . . . You could buy beer and drink until you cannot walk to the bushes to pass water, [laughter].[44]

Money, then, could potentially deprive parents of their direct control over the fruits of their sons' work. Parents in response tried to elide the distinction between a labor migrant's work and the small lineage's wealth, and to mask the difference between wage work and prior work.

Fathers claimed control over sons' wages as a continuation of prior patterns: fathers controlled sons' labor power, and sons worked to "earn" the bridewealth that a father gave. Older men represented migrant labor to sons as a continuation of work for bridewealth:

---

[44] Interview with OK, Shigaro/Werugha, 2/8/1993.

> We knew that to get bridewealth from our fathers we must go outside to work. . . . Long ago, the work of youths was herding cows . . . for the *kichuku*, but in our time it was the work of money.[45]

Just as young men in the nineteenth century had not controlled the fruits of their work, young men now should not expect to keep their wages from the colonial labor economy. Fathers regarded wage work as embedded in the same relationship that herding had been: fathers controlled a son's labor in the name of the lineage. Behind the elision of herding and wage labor lay an attempt to maintain a tight relationship between a son's work and the lineage's wealth. Early in the twentieth century, this became an explicit axiom: sons turn over their cash wages to their fathers. At first, the vast majority of them did:

> *Q:* What did you do with the money you made from your work?
> *A:* I gave it to my father.
> *Q:* All of it?
> *A:* Nearly all! At Voi . . . I made 4/= [a month], and gave 3/= to my parents. . . . Later, [in Mombasa], I rented a room and bought food, . . . but I still sent most of the money home.[46]

Fathers used their sons' wages to pay the Hut Tax, purchase a few consumables,[47] and do what sons' labor had done before: augment small lineage herds under the fathers' control.[48] Though no reliable figures exist for Taita's overall importation of animals, records clearly indicate a huge increase in money coming into the district during the early 1900s, and anecdotal evidence suggests that livestock trade grew with corresponding briskness from as early as before 1910 to the onset of world depression in 1930.[49] Though the evidence for

---

[45]   Interview with PN, Ngerenyi/Chawia, 9/5/1988.

[46]   Interview with MM, Lushangonyi/Mwanda, 22/9/1988. Similarly, NM, Ndome/Mbololo, 22/6/1988 and SK, Werugha/Werugha, 29/9/1988.

[47]   A survey of the seven small shops in the Hills in 1917 gives a good indication of the most popular items for cash purchase: blankets, various grades of cotton cloth, and cigarettes. KNA, PC/Cst/1/19/82.

[48]   Interviews with JK, Kaya/Chawia, 3/5/1988; FM, Kishamba/Chawia, 12/5/1988; KM, Tausa/Mbololo, 2/6/1988; SM, Wongonyi/Mbololo, 6/7/1988; PM, Ilole/Bura, 16/8/1988; JM, Teri/Sagalla, 25/8/1988; DM, Mlondo/Werugha, 28/9/1988.

[49]   Though oral evidence indicates that cash affected herd sizes well before World War I, Taita district officials first noted the far wider circulation of money and rapid growth in the livestock market during the war. Officials handled the remittances of many Africans doing war work and oversaw auctions of livestock seized from Tanganyika. See DC's Safari Reports from 1916, KNA, PC/Cst/1/22/32; in 1918 the DC wrote that the population had become "very rich just now, as the war brought a great deal of money to them." See KNA/PC, Cst/1/12/269. Also, interviews with JM, Wongonyi/Mbololo, 7/7/1988; and GM, Mgange Nyika/Mwanda, 20/9/1988.
   Another indicator of income, tax revenues, jumped from 31,794/= in 1914 to 55,650/= in 1918, partly through a rate hike to 5/=. In 1920, without another rate rise, tax revenue reached 81,192/=. KNA, DC/TTA/3/3/2.

broad generalizations is sketchy, it seems that sons' wages enabled many fathers to increase their livestock holdings fairly rapidly.[50]

Ideologically, fathers' efforts to establish axiomatic control of their sons' wages initially succeeded. Using sons' pay, older men replaced now–forbidden raiding with the purchase of animals to augment their herds from without. In return for the sons' money, fathers continued to supply bridewealth cattle. Despite the ideological success, however, fathers' control over sons' wages was slipping. Furthermore, in the minds of unmarried sons, cattle bought with wage remittances would ultimately be passed on to them—a view linked to late nineteenth–century youths' assertions that the livestock they captured in raids was *for* them.[51] Still, unmarried sons had little control over animals older men bought with their wages. They often knew which ones their wages had paid for, but the animals remained part of the father's herd, potentially subject to exchanges, and with the animals' offspring often accruing to the father.[52]

Migrant Labor, Money, and
Slippages in Small Lineage Ideology

Retrospect reveals that older men's early twentieth–century reinvigoration of livestock–as–wealth was its high–water mark, for sons' wage labor ushered in contradictions that later greatly weakened Taita's livestock–based political economy. Younger men's access to and handling of money reduced older men's axioms of economic domination from justifications of extant control to a gambit of claimed authority in the face of reduced control. That is, older men's control over sons increasingly depended on getting sons to accept that they *should* hand over their earnings. As gambits go, however, it proved a powerful and durable one, structured as it was into wage labor discourses and practices from the beginning.

Distinct patterns developed in the region's migrant labor system well before World War I. Parents sent adolescent boys for their first taste of wage work at the sisal plantations then being established in the lowlands around Taita. Too young for the grueling work of cutting sisal, boys loaded cut leaves onto carts or did other ancillary tasks. They worked for a month or two at a time, often living on the estates while working, though most could walk home and back on their days off. Typically, slightly older men from their neighborhood who also worked at the estate helped them get the jobs, and both parents and

---

[50] Interviews with SM, Wongonyi/Mbololo, 6/7/1988; and FM, Kishamba/Chawia, 12/5/1988. Herds shrank dramatically in the drought–and–disease-ridden late nineteenth century. No statistically reliable basis for comparing herd sizes and growth rates for mid–nineteenth and early twentieth–century Taita exists, but cash purchases certainly allowed for the most rapid increase in Taita's herds since *at least* the late 1860s, when raids on Shambaa and Pare reached their peak.

[51] Interviews with JM, Wongonyi/Mbololo, 7/7/1988; MW, Lushangonyi/Mwanda, 23/9/1988; RN, Wumingu/Werugha, 1/10/1988; and JK, Werugha/Werugha, 3/10/1988.

[52] Interviews with AK, Shigaro/Werugha, 25/4/1988; and MW, Ghazi/Mbololo, 5/7/1988; also A. Harris, "Organization," chap. 7.

plantation managers counted on them to keep an eye on the youths.[53] Parents also groomed these adolescent boys into the practice of giving over virtually all their earnings:

> When I was a boy . . . all that money, . . . all of it went to my father. Without question. Without a doubt. . . . I could not say, "this is my money," I gave it to father; not, "I will keep this part and give him that part." No.[54]

Adolescents' wages on plantations before 1920 hovered around 4/= a month (roughly a half to a third of adult wages), plus food and housing.[55] However, most of Taita's adult men steered clear of the plantations, for the main work, sisal cutting, was difficult, dangerous, and poorly paid.[56] The few local adults at the plantations usually did skilled jobs like running machinery.[57] Most local men sought less onerous, better paying work further afield, and the plantations soon resorted to recruiting adult labor from hundreds of miles away.

Young adult men, both married and single, had several options for wage labor outside the Hills. The arrival of the Kenya–Uganda Railway (KUR) brought many employment opportunities. Some tasks on trains, like fireman's work, took men from Taita far up and down the line. But many KUR jobs kept men local, largely at the growing town of Voi. Railway jobs based there included cargo handling, repairing track and bridges, loading water for the steam engines, maintaining the station and other physical structures, and construction gang work. Wages before 1920 ranged roughly from

---

[53] Twenty–three of the 101 men interviewed in 1988 worked on sisal plantations as youths, as did four men interviewed in 1993. Their testimonies on work, contact with home, and the roles of older men all substantially agree.

[54] Interview with RM, Wundanyi/Werugha, 29/7/1993.

[55] Interviews with SK, Wundanyi/Werugha, 15/4/1988; SM, Tausa/Mbololo, 3/6/1988; and PM, Ilole/Bura, 16/8/1988. Boys' wages on the plantations dipped as low as 2/= per month. JM, Wundanyi/ Werugha, 11/5/1988.

[56] Sisal is a tough, succulent plant with leaves up to six feet tall, used to make rope and twine. Sisal cutters used a long, sharp knife, and the leaf has spiny edges tapering to a sharp thorn on the end. Working with the tools and the leaves caused cuts and abrasions, which often festered. Government Labour Inspectors visiting plantations around Taita in the 1930s reported seventy cases of men with "ulcers" [festering sores] at one plantation alone. Inspectors found the plantation conditions deplorable and work rules awful. Taita's sisal plantations also had a bad reputation with workers: men recruited from western Kenya deserted in high numbers before arriving, for countrymen they met en route warned them about the conditions. See Labour and Medical Officers' Inspection Reports on Taita Concessions Ltd., KNA, PC/Cst/2/16/6; also C. Guillebaud, *An Economic Survey of the Sisal Industry of Tanganyika* (Welwyn, Eng., 1958), chap. 4.

[57] Mainly, they ran tractors and sisal processing machinery (decorticators, crushing rollers, and brushing machines). Others worked as maintenance mechanics or supplies clerks. Typical interviewees included PM, Wundanyi/ Werugha, 23/4/1988, a foreman who oversaw the operation of an estate's decorticators—seven of its eight machines being run by men from Taita; also PM, Ilole/Bura, 16/8/1988, who worked first as a clerk, then as a field supervisor.

For an overview of sisal processing, see S. G. Barker, *Sisal: A Note on the Attributes of the Fibre and Their Industrial Significance* (London, 1933).

8/= to 12/=.[58] Some young men liked railway work because its close proximity to the Hills kept them near their lineages and homes. Parents and wives approved of KUR work for the same reasons:

> My wife and mother were bringing up the children, . . . and mother told me not to work further along the railway, Nairobi or Mombasa. So I stayed here [working for the KUR]. My mother told me don't . . . work at distant places, if you work at distant places we will have problems with the children, . . . we will have problems with food.[59]

From early on, however, many young men ventured farther from the Hills for the promise of better wages, and for the experience of life in a major city like Mombasa. Work in distant towns also put them farther from the reach of their lineages, allowing more slippage between axioms of parental control and the way lives might be lived.

Mombasa became a magnet for young migrant men from the Hills. Once there they gravitated towards certain kinds of jobs. Many found work in a niche for which their upbringing had prepared them well: tending herds for the city's dairies.[60] Early in the century, the herders grazed cows near the edge of town. Later, dairy workers cut silage and brought it to stall–fed cows. Other dairy jobs included milking and distribution work. Dairy work typically paid at least what adults earned cutting sisal, a minimum of 12/= per month plus food and perhaps housing, to do more agreeable labor under better conditions:

> Aahh!! You cannot even compare the harsh life of Voi [sisal] Estate to . . . the dairy in Mombasa. The Indian [in Mombasa] . . . kept us in his own compound, in a place much better than the filthy estate rooms. . . . We ate together with the Indian from one plate. . . . He liked me because I did my work well, and looked after his cows well, and never gave him problems. . . . I kept to that Indian for nine years, until he moved to Zanzibar.[61]

Mombasa's Public Works Department (PWD) also employed many men from Taita. PWD workers from the Hills mostly did manual labor on city infrastructure. The work made more physical demands than some other jobs, but paid comparatively well, usually at least 2/= better than unskilled labor at private businesses.[62] A third major source of work by the 1910s was casual (day–

---

[58]   Interviews with WM, Shigaro/Werugha, 18/4/=1988; GM, Tausa/Mbololo, 31/5/1988; SM, Tausa/Mbololo, 3/6/1988; and Mrs. SM, Werugha/Werugha, 30/9/1988.

[59]   Interview with GM, Tausa/Mbololo, 3/6/1988.

[60]   Of the 101 Taita men interviewed, fourteen worked at some point for dairies in Mombasa. Most dairy owners for whom they worked were Indians; whether Indians owned most of the dairies, or whether men from Taita just tended to work more for Indian dairymen than for others, is not clear from my findings. Interviews with EM, Shigaro/Werugha; SM, Kidaya–Ngerenyi/Werugha; and MM, Kishamba/Chawia.

[61]   Interview with SM, Wundanyi/Werugha, 15/4/1988.

[62]   PWD work and wage sources include PM, Wundanyi/Werugha, 23/4/1988; JK, Kaya/Chawia, 3/5/1988; and BM, Wusi/Chawia, 5/5/1988.

to–day) labor at Mombasa harbor. Known as *kibarua* labor, it didn't tie workers to long–term contracts.[63] On the other hand, no contracts meant work was not necessarily available on any given day; *kibarua* work lacked the stability of contract labor.[64] Most men from Taita doing *kibarua* labor worked as stevedores at Kilindini harbor. *Kibarua* workers got paid by the day or, occasionally, per load. In the 1910s, *kibarua* stevedore labor typically paid 1/50 a day.[65] Other kinds of *kibarua* work were available, as well:

> Digging pit toilets you could ask 2/= [a day], . . . because it was very tiring, it took three days. Or you could work for a mason. The masons came to [Mwembe Tayari] market to take workers, who just waited there. . . . He just points out, "You, come," and . . . he might keep you for a month. But it was still casual work, he paid you at the end of the day, the next day the same, like that.[66]

If work was plentiful, *kibarua* laborers could earn far more money than monthly workers, often 30/= per month and more in the 1910s: "You could get a monthly job, it paid about 20/=, but we didn't like those monthly jobs, *kibarua* paid better."[67]

Mission–educated young men from the Hills also did migrant labor: skilled or clerical work either around the Hills or farther away. Many of the educated at first stayed close to home, teaching school. Education was mission run, so taking up teaching meant working for a missionary society. Teachers had high status among local Christians and, increasingly, among *Wutasi* followers, but the work paid less well than some other jobs for which their education qualified them.[68] Teaching thus required some combination of commitment to education, desire or pressure to work close to home, and feelings of Christian mis-

---

[63] Networks of casual labor from Taita burgeoned during and after World War I. For an overview of Mombasa's port labor situation, see Frederick Cooper, *On the African Waterfront: Urban Disorder and the Transformation of Work in Colonial Mombasa* (New Haven, 1987). However, Cooper mistakenly groups workers from Taita with those from farther inland who tended towards monthly contract work (*Waterfront*, 28). Given the Hills' proximity to the coast, *kibarua* workers from Taita could and did, contrary to Cooper's assertion, return seasonally to Taita for domestic agricultural work. Interviews with EM, Shigaro/Werugha, 13/4/1988; JK, Ngerenyi/ Chawia, 11/5/1988; FM, Kidaya/ Chawia, 12/5/1988; and Mrs. SM, Mwanda/Mwanda, 14/9/1988.

[64] "When work slowed and *kibarua* jobs were hard to get, we were sorry for not taking permanent jobs. You could find twenty people waiting ahead of you for *kibarua* work." Interview with JK, Werugha/ Werugha, 3/10/1988. Officials disliked this instability; the state saw *kibarua* work as an economic problem of "undisciplined" labor, and considered casual laborers, living relatively uncontrolled in Mombasa, a social problem. Cooper, *Waterfront*, chap. 2.

[65] Interviews with FM, Kidaya/Chawia, 12/5/1988; MM, Nyolo/Bura, 17/8/1988; and JM, Wundanyi/Werugha, 11/5/1988.

[66] Interview with FM, Kidaya–Ngerenyi/Chawia, 12/5/1988.

[67] Interview with FM, Kidaya–Ngerenyi/Chawia, 12/5/1988. *Kibarua* workers provided their own food and housing, but most former *kibarua* workers with whom I spoke still figured that they came out well ahead in the comparison.

[68] Interviews with JM, Wusi/Chawia, 5/4/1988; AM, Shigaro/Werugha, 2/5/1988; and Mrs. GM, Shigaro/Werugha, 27/5/1988. Missions could not compete with private sector or government salaries. See J. Harris, *Repatriates and Refugees*, chaps. 3–5.

sion. It was also one of the only skilled jobs available to, and respectable for, women. By the 1910s, most educated men sought more lucrative work, and a fair number of male teachers eventually moved on for the same reason, leaving teaching increasingly to educated women.[69]

Below the Hills, nearby concerns took in some of the educated. Sisal plantations around Mwatate, Voi, and Taveta hired them as storekeepers, clerical workers, and (for those with vocational training) masons, driver/mechanics, and carpenters. The railroad hired educated young men in similar capacities, and the DC employed some as clerks, court translators, and the like.[70] But many educated men from Taita, like their uneducated counterparts, followed the promise of better salaries to Mombasa. Quite a few found work at its post office, but Taita's educated workers dispersed more widely through the urban job market than did its uneducated laborers.[71]

No matter what sort of work Taita's young labor migrants did, parents admonished them to remember that they had binding ties at home. To a large extent, those ties were rooted in older men's control over resources: small lineage heads controlled what sons stood to gain as bridewealth, marriage property, and inheritance.[72] Migrant sons who failed to live up to their fathers' expectations for maintaining ties risked seeing their inheritance cut back in favor of a "better" son.[73] Yet more than sanctions prompted youths to maintain ties. Doing so reinforced ongoing, affinitive bonds of community: keeping up good relations within the lineage and neighborhood reproduced deeply felt networks of belonging and social support.

Young men doing migrant labor outside the Hills had two main obligations. First, they were to send or carry their wages back to their fathers.[74] All understood that migrants had expenses away from home, and there was little supervision of how much young men spent on themselves, but they were expected to remit most of their pay for the wealth of the small lineage.[75] Remit-

---

[69] JM, Wusi/Chawia, 5/4/1988, left teaching for Native Administration; also, JM, Shigaro/Werugha, 20/4/1988, for the Agriculture Department; AK, Shigaro/ Werugha, 25/4/1988, for Native Administration; and AM, Wusi/Chawia, 28/4/1988, the pastorate. On the feminization of teaching, Mrs. GM, Shigaro/Werugha, 27/5/1988.

[70] Interviews with PM, Wundanyi/Werugha, 25/4/1988; OK, Shigaro/Werugha, 29/4/1988; BM, Wusi/Chawia, 5/5/1988; GM, Tausa/Mbololo, 31/5/1988; PM, Wundanyi/Werugha, 13/8/1988; MM, Nyolo/Bura, 15/8/1988; PM, Ilole/Bura, 16/8/1988; and WM, Choke/Mbale, 11/11/1988.

[71] Interviews with DM, Mbale/Mbale, 7/11/1988; WM, Shigaro/Werugha, 18/4/1988; GM, Kishamba/Chawia, 27/6/1988; and NK, Wumari/Chawia, 15/8/1988.

[72] All sons, not just eldest ones, could inherit a father's property. In the twentieth century, this led to a great deal of fragmentation in landholding. On inheritance, see A. Harris, "Organization," chaps. 7–8; on land fragmentation, Nazarro, "Changing Use," chap. 5.

[73] Interview with JM, Teri/Chawia, 5/8/1988.

[74] Some interviewees spoke of remitting money to their mothers (for instance, RK, Kizumanzi/ Sagalla, 9/7/1993), but when asked closely about it, most said that money, in the end, went to their fathers.

[75] "That money from [wage labor] was for father. You keep a little for food, that is all." Interview with SS, Tausa/Mbololo, 3/6/1988; virtually every interviewee asked about this in 1988 and 1993 said much the same thing.

tance networks quickly sprang up to manage the moving of money, based on lineage and neighborhood connections. When a migrant returned to the Hills, other migrants from the same neighborhood or lineage sent cash to their parents with him. People at either end relied on kinship and neighborly connections to ensure that couriers handled remitted money honestly.[76] In some neighborhoods that had many young men in Mombasa, a trusted older man traveled to the coast to gather remittances. If the older man could not count, he placed one man's earnings in the bottom of a long cloth tube, tied it off with a knot, marked the knot with a ribbon to designate the sender, and repeated the process until the cloth tube was filled.[77]

Older men's visits to the coast also let them check up on the young. Aside from such visits, though, young migrants in Mombasa lived free from the surveillance of parents and elders, and could socialize with less restraint. Some youths from the Hills merely tolerated life away from home, but many others felt some attraction to urban living. In Taita, older men still kept youths from drinking *chofi*, reserving it for their own social and ritual use. At the coast, no such norms applied, and youths had the means to purchase beer and other items. Young men's retained wages were supposed to pay for food and lodging, not alcohol, time with a prostitute, or stylish clothing.[78] Migrants commonly bought the latter items, though, and an occasional older visitor from the Hills could not stem the tide of it. Young men, while trying to honor their felt obligations to home, also began to use the fruits of their labor to indulge themselves—and once that genie slipped out of the bottle, it could never be put back. As later chapters will show, the disposal of sons' wages became more and more of a locus of cultural politics over time.

The second main obligation incumbent on Taita's early migrant laborers—also presented as an axiomatic duty—was to return home regularly.[79] Returning migrants helped with seasonal farming tasks, brought home earnings or consumer purchases for members of the lineage, made arrangements for marrying, and, thereby, ensured that all was well within their households. The visits were therefore crucial to young men's standing in local networks, and to their future as bridewealth recipients and heirs. Still, even in the first decade of the century, some young men stayed at the coast once they got there. Their break from the obligations of local community had a high social cost, defined in predominant ideology as a condition one should not fall into:

> Always I sent money home, always I went back to visit my wife and my parents, you had to do that. . . . There were a few who were just living [in Mombasa] . . . [they] were called thugs, because they never

---

[76] Such networks were described by dozens of interview informants, among them: NM, Ndome/ Mbololo, 22/6/1988; LM, Mrugua/Bura, 18/8/1988; Mrs. DM, Shigaro/Werugha, 30/5/1988; and Mrs. SM, Mwanda/Mwanda, 14/9/1988.

[77] Interview with MT, Kishamba/Chawia, 9/6/1988.

[78] Interviews with JK, Werugha/Werugha, 3/10/1988; and NK, Wumari/Chawia, 15/8/1988.

[79] Interviews with OM, Wundanyi/Werugha, 25/3/1988; MC, Ndome/Mbololo, 20/6/1988; LM, Mrugua/Bura, 18/8/1988; MN, Lushangonyi/Mwanda, 22/9/1988.

went back home to help in the fields. Those ones . . . could come back and find their fields cut for another.[80]

The existence of such outcast individuals, who began to be spoken of as "lost," underlined how older men's ideologies of control had become distinct from their ability to closely control the actions and wealth–generating activities of the young. Already, too, new strains in older men's—and older women's—authority in their small lineages were being felt within the Hills themselves.

Gender, Generation, and Work in the Hills

Migratory labor also affected patterns of work and small lineage authority in communities across the Hills. In particular, relationships and work patterns basic to production in (and reproduction of) small lineages came under new strains, stemming from the absence of so many young men. Though most men tried to get home for the main harvest season, not all could do so, which shifted more heavy work to wives and unmarried daughters. Men's absence at other times of the year transferred the burden for planting, weeding, and harvesting the second season's crop to their wives' shoulders. Young wives simultaneously had increased work obligations, less help with them, and closer supervision and increased demands on them from their parents–in–law:

> Men started going to Mombasa, so the work here got harder. . . . In the time of our fathers, [i.e., the late nineteenth century], they were only going outside to herd or to fight, . . . so they helped with farming all along. But when I married, my husband returned right away to Mombasa, and I really had to dig.[81]

At the same time, some wives felt that a share of their husbands' earning might, if given to them, put them less under the thumb of their in–laws.[82] The early years of the century, then, saw young wives try to adjust to the increased burdens and new possibilities that marriage now entailed.

Parents of a recently married couple typically added to a young wife's burdens by their handling of their sons' absence. Ideologically, they built upon the axiomatic understanding that a new wife integrated herself into her husband's small lineage. One important element of turn–of–the–century small lineage ideology involved the new wife helping with her mother–in–law's housework.

> When she married, [my] mother . . . cooked for her mother–in–law. She fed her father [–in–law] and his brothers. . . . When they finished, mother washed the plate, mother–in–law had no need of doing any-

---

[80] Having a field "cut for another" meant that a field someone expected to inherit went instead to someone else. Interview with JM, Teri/Chawia, 5/8/1988.

[81] Interview with Mrs. MM, Lushangonyi/Mwanda, 21/9/1988.

[82] Ibid.

thing. . . . Mother carried water and wood, . . . [and] brewed beer for
the men. . . . That old mother was getting her rest of old age![83]

Another was that she should labor in her in–laws' fields, and participate in her
mother–in–law's lineage or neighborhood work groups.[84] These relationships
operated in familiar social terrain: by the time of marriage, neither mothers–
in–law nor their work groups would be strangers to young wives, who came
from another branch of the same large lineage, or from the same neighborhood. Such work by the young, a backbone of how networks of mutuality and
support had long been re/constructed in local communities, was axiomatically
explained as young wives doing "the work of lineage."[85] This formulation of
group belonging was not a ruse or false consciousness, but it did express a
subtly loaded ideal of community building. The discourse explicitly encouraged young and old (but implicitly compelled the young), to fashion ties that
reproduced ongoing support structures across time, dispersing its underlying
power dynamics to the point of near invisibility:

> The mother–in–law showed her daughter the way, she went together
> with the daughter all the time, and showed her, "this is your place,"
> "these are your people." . . . If the daughter was wronged by another,
> she told her mother–in–law, and [the mother–in–law] told her husband,
> . . . and he helped her.[86]

In the long run, these networks would increasingly provide young wives
with support for their farming and household needs. Nevertheless, sanctions
loomed beneath the positive surface of small lineage solidarity. The tone and
quality of a young wife's response to her obligations affected the reputation
she carried in her lineages and neighborhood. A wife's reputation could influence a husband's ability to build social networks, his inheritance prospects,
even the inheritance prospects of the woman's sons.[87] In the short run, "good"
daughters–in–law tended to get more support when they needed it.

Work demands on young wives, already heavy in the late nineteenth century, became even more formidable with the rise of husbands' migrant labor. It
was an established practice to give newlyweds a few fields upon marriage, but
young couples still worked in the husbands' parents' fields. The young couple
also resided in the husband's parents' compound until they had a child, when

---

[83] Interview with Mrs. MO, Shigaro/Werugha, 2/8/1993. The tone of the comment left ambiguous whether the wife was offering her mother–in–law relief, or whether the mother–in–law demanded it.

[84] Interview with Mrs. SM, Ilole/Bura, 16/8/1988; and Mrs. MW, Mgange Nyika/Mwanda,
20/9/1988.

[85] Interviews with SM, Wongonyi/Mbololo, 6/7/1988; AM, Shigaro/Werugha, 2/5/1988; Mrs. RM,
Chawia/Chawia, 16/6/1988; BM, Sechu/Chawia, 11/6/1988; Mrs. PN, Mlondo/Werugha, 26/9/
1988; and DM, Teri/Sagalla, 10/7/1993.

[86] Interview with Mrs. MO, Shigaro/Werugha, 2/8/1993.

[87] On the dangers for a daughter not considered dutiful, interviews with Mrs. SM, Werugha/
Werugha, 30/9/1988; Mrs. MM, Lushangonyi/Mwanda, 21/9/1988.

they established their own compound nearby. Husbands' absences brought young wives under magnified custody and scrutiny from in–laws—especially mothers–in–law:

> *Mrs. JM:* When the husband was at Mombasa, the wife must be taken care of by his parents.
>
> *Q:* When you say "be taken care of by the parents," what did that mean?
>
> *Mrs. JM:* They were like her parents, she was just their daughter . . . She was in their door [i.e., household] like a daughter.
>
> *Q:* Was . . . [that] different from the times when her husband was home?
>
> *Mrs. JM:* Without the husband, the daughter and mother must be very close, . . . more close.[88]

Many in–laws expected young wives left in their midst to integrate themselves into the parental household all the more fully, including doing more work for the parents. This was least difficult for young women in the early stages of their marriages, when they had not yet established homesteads separate from the parents. But once a young wife began to raise children and had a conjugal homestead to maintain, matters became trickier. On the one hand, she often needed and received in–laws' help with daily tasks; on the other hand, in–laws also made demands of her that stretched her time thin, which could make it hard to keep her household and its fields in order.[89]

Around the turn of the century, young wives had little room for maneuver when it came to their seniors' expectations; unlike their absent husbands, wives' work and daily activities fell directly under the eyes of parents–in–law. Still, many young women did seek ways to limit their labor in in–laws' households and fields. Having children might ease the situation somewhat, for wives were then understood to have more responsibilities of their own. In principle, in–laws would lessen their work expectations, and even provide the wife with help from elsewhere in the small lineage; in one such case, a mother–in–law sent an unmarried daughter to help her daughter–in–law whenever the young wife's husband went away for migrant labor.[90] Too, as a young wife's children grew, she could send the children to help her in–laws with some kinds of work.[91]

Nevertheless, throughout the early decades of the century, younger women had to juggle an increasingly complex and difficult set of demands, between the needs of their husbands' households and the needs of their in–laws. Most young women went to considerable lengths to meet their in–laws' work expec-

---

[88]   Interview with Mrs. JM, Sagassa/Werugha, 7/10/1988.

[89]   Interviews with Mrs. SM, Werugha/Werugha, 30/9/1988; Mrs. MM, Lushangonyi/Mwanda, 21/9/1988.

[90]   Interview with Mrs. WM, Werugha/Werugha, 30/7/1993.

[91]   Interviews with Mrs. SM, Werugha/Werugha, 30/9/1988; and Mrs. SM, Mogho Mleche/Mbale, 4/11/1988.

tations, but tensions with them did sometimes arise. Managing those demands involved a tacit push–and–pull between the generations. In such situations, young women, like their brothers and husbands, rarely defied their seniors openly (let alone angrily), for the consequences could be severe. As one interviewee's mother was told by her aunt, "if you fight your mother–in–law you lose, but quietly–quietly, sweetly–sweetly, you win."[92]

The onset of gendered and intergenerational struggles over control of husbands' wages put further strains on the foundations of small lineage as community. From early on in the migrant labor system, some young wives wanted husbands to send wage remittances directly to them, and at least a few husbands did so. Often this meant sending a wife and parents separate packets of money; in at least one case, though, all money went to the wife, who then passed her in–laws their share.[93] Direct remittances gave the young women some new autonomy from in–laws, allowing them to lessen in–laws' powers of consent and supervision over junior households' cash spending.

Older men, who were trying to maintain control over sons' wages in the name of small lineage wealth, strongly opposed this practice. They considered it their right to control remittance money, and their responsibility to distribute it to meet small lineage needs; they did not at all like being bypassed. Parents worried, too, that remittances to daughters–in–law might weaken seniors' influence over them, and spoke of those payments as causing a "loss of respect" among young women.[94] This fear was certainly overblown—young wives were still very much embedded in and reliant on their in–laws' small lineage and networks—but some young women liked being less tightly held under their in–laws' purse–strings.[95] For a young husband, remittances could generate tensions no matter how they were routed. If he sent money to parents alone, they might not give his wife enough to satisfy her needs. But if he sent money to his wife, parents might be affronted that the young presumed to sever themselves from "lineage ways" or even control lineage resources, rather than just working for the lineage in parents' prescribed manner.[96]

Christianity, Wutasi, and Religious Challenges to Lineage and Neighborhood

The growing number of professing Christians across the Hills also stimulated intensive new cultural politicking. Colonial administration provided Christian evan-

---

[92] Interview with Mrs. SM, Mogho Mleche/Mbale, 4/11/1988.

[93] Interviews with Mrs. NM, Kizumanzi/Sagalla, 24/8/1988; Mrs. RM, Chawia/Chawia, 16/6/1988; LM, Mrugua/Bura, 18/8/1988.

[94] "My parents . . . did not like it that I sent money to my wife! 'Now we must come to our daughter to beg for money!'" Interview with LM, Mrugua/Bura, 18/8/1988; also, interview with SM, Kidaya/Chawia, 10/5/1988.

[95] Interviews with Mrs. NM, Kizumanzi/Sagalla, 24/8/1988; and Mrs. RM, Chawia/Chawia, 16/6/1988. Despite the quotation in the previous footnote, young wives usually had to request and justify access to their husbands' wages, not parents.

[96] Interview with LM, Mrugua/Bura, 18/8/1988.

gelists with the political protection Wray had considered necessary to successful evangelizing in Sagalla. Europeans' imposition of colonial rule added luster to the missionary endeavor, for some people in Taita wanted to understand and tap into the sources of power Europeans seemed to have. As a result, Christian conversions climbed steadily in the early twentieth century. No more than 1,100 people had been baptized by 1910—including roughly 950 mostly nominal Catholics[97]— but support from officials and a few prominent local figures gave the Christian bloc a weight that belied its size. Christians' outlooks and practices soon posed serious challenges to the terms of lineage and neighborhood community. Many *Wutasi* followers, seeing the challenges as fundamental, responded swiftly and sharply—this arena of early century changes probably prompted more pointed confrontations than any other. The upshot in the early 1900s was an uneasy coexistence with transformative effects: *Wutasi* followers could contain the Christian threat to a considerable degree, but not snuff it out. Christians had a corrosive effect on lineage and neighborhood as communities of belonging, while giving rise to a new set of distinctions: Christian ways and local ways. That new distinction helped catalyze a Taita identity. Christians were tolerated despite the threatening character of their beliefs, but at times had to (and, as members of their communities, at times wanted to) take part in *Wutasi* practices that violated Christian propriety.

Early Missions, Early Christians, and Their Support Structures

By 1910, the Catholic mission and two CMS stations had become nodes of proselytization in Dabida. The new colonial administration supported the missions, albeit with decided favoritism towards the Anglicans.[98] Officials in the area relied on European missionaries' local knowledge, local networks, and language skills to garner information and at times to hone and disseminate local policies. As in the 1890s, missionary involvement with officials served different immediate interests at different moments, but in the long term supported the colonial endeavor.[99] Officials returned the favor indirectly by creating a political climate that made evangelization easier, and directly by seeking to minimize local harassment of the missions and putting Christians into new positions of power and responsibility in the district administration.[100]

---

[97] CMS Correspondence, G3 A5/018, Wray's Annual Letter, 5/1/1910; Bura Mission Baptismal Records, Book I, 1893–1917.

[98] Wray's diaries, CMSA, 7–10/10/1900, 7/11/1900.

[99] As plantations sprang up in the plains around the Hills, missionaries more than once helped prevent their eating into local people's lands. See KNA, PC/Cst/1/12/31, Reddie to Sub–Commissioner 29/10/1905 and 2/11/1905. Still, mission involvement in tax collection and communal lab for tax defaulters continued into the 1910s. Maynard also brokered a land grant high in the Hills for what came to be known as Wundanyi Estate; it became very controversial in short order. Interview with OK, Shigaro/ Werugha, 6/4/1988; and *Report of the Kenya Land Commission* (London, 1934), 2755–62.

[100] The state did not, however, intervene to the full extent that missionaries had wanted, declining to ban the making of *chofi* or the performance of certain local dances (e.g., PC/Cst/1/12/28, Taita Outward, PC Tritton to DC, 25/2/1904).

The Holy Ghost Fathers' station, begun in 1892 in lower Bura, required far less strict conduct and preparation for its followers than did the CMS, and consequently performed many more baptisms early on: in 1902 alone, the Fathers baptized 225 people.[101] Through the first decade of this century, Catholicism in Bura generated little of the friction that CMS Anglicanism did in 1890s Sagalla.[102] The CMS Mbale mission, founded in 1900, also began less tensely than Sagalla. A European more diplomatic than Wray ran the mission, which enjoyed the patronage of Mghalu and took shape in the more supportive context of post–1900 colonialism. Not surprisingly, then, a core group of converts emerged more quickly than in Sagalla. By late 1904, Mbale had performed four baptisms and had thirteen catechumens. By 1909, Maynard reported Mbale's thirteen baptisms, fifteen confirmations, and fourteen new catechumens as typical, "steady progress."[103] In 1905 a third European missionary team, Vladimir Verbi and his wife, opened another CMS Dabida station, at Wusi. They saw their first candidate baptized in 1909, and that year began an industrial education program.[104] Dabida's Anglicans were sprinkled more widely across the massif than the analogous group in Sagalla, though the largest proportion lived relatively close to the missions.

Like the Holy Ghost mission at Bura, CMS missions in Dabida drew large numbers of interested people to their services: congregations of churchgoers regularly numbered in the hundreds. The Anglicans' much stricter training of candidates kept their numbers of baptized Christians down, but sought to ensure that converts would mold themselves to the missions' tight standards of Christian rectitude.[105] Early Anglican catechumens and converts in Dabida generally did take CMS standards of proper belief and conduct seriously, which made their presence far more provocative to communities in the Hills than that of the Catholics.

Underminings, Confrontations, and Rejoinders

Anglicans in Dabida soon were drawn into confrontations similar to those in Sagalla in the 1890s. CMS condemnation of *Wutasi* and its practices led to denigrating commentary on its beliefs, institutions and rituals, and pushed Christians to opt out of them. Doing so posed problems for both Christian and non-

---

[101] For Bura Church baptism rates prior to World War I, see appendix A.

[102] Interviewees around Bura unashamedly acknowledged the Catholic mission's early laxity, including Mrs. MK, Nyolo/Bura, 15/8/1988; Mrs. SM, Ilole/Bura, 16/8/1988; and LM, Mrugua/Bura, 18/8/1988.

[103] CMS Correspondence, G3 A5/017, 4/05, "Deployment of Native Christians," and G3 A5/018, Maynard's Annual Letter, 16/2/1910.

[104] CMS Correspondence, G3 A5/017, Heselwood to Maynard, 21/9/1904; Binns to Baylis, 27/3 1905; Mrs. Verbi to Baylis, 18/3/1906; Verbi's Annual Letter, 12/1909; Verbi to CMS Parent Committee, 27/12/09; and G3 A5/019, Verbi to NY Board of Missions, 6/3/1912.

[105] For example, after one catechumen's strictness wavered, Verbi delayed fifty baptisms for several months to see if any others would also "slid[e] into indifference." CMS Correspondence, G3 A5 019, Verbi's Annual Letter, 3/1912.

Christian members of local communities: non–participation threatened Christians with ostracism, and threatened *Wutasi* followers with the dissolution of the religious basis of lineage and neighborhood communities. This raised the specter of social disunity, a recipe for cosmological (and, thereafter, worldly) disaster.

Wutasi followers worried about what Christians did *not* do, as well as what they did. Some Christian prohibitions were divisive of local communities, but at least not direct spiritual affronts. Men's work groups in most of the Hills— work groups that reinforced neighborhood and lineage bonds—drank *chofi* after their labors, but in Dabida as in Sagalla, Anglicans were enjoined not to drink or serve alcohol. Strict Christians therefore could not easily hold or attend most communal work sessions.[106] Like tensions made their way into herding groups: some Christian men still did herding shifts on the plains, but would not drink beer with the others, and might use the situation to proselytize. Many *Wutasi* followers tried to avoid herding together with strict converts: "Those ones could be told, 'enough of this, you spoil the *chofi*!' . . . Those ones were called missionaries. . . . It was an insult: 'oh, sorry, you are herding with a missionary.'"[107]

These sorts of everyday tensions, even as they eroded the cohesiveness of lineage and neighborhood communities, sharpened the distinction between *Wutasi* followers and Anglicans. Christian services and beliefs still evoked curiosity from non–believers, but the prohibitive side of CMS Anglicanism made many *Wutasi* followers distance themselves socially from local Christians:

> Now they separated more and more: those who did not believe [in Christianity] a side, and those who believed a side. They did not have a good relationship because those [people] wanted their own things, and these ones are not allowed to do those things.[108]

More seriously still, Christian prohibitions sometimes threatened the spiritual basis of a community. *Wutasi*–based rituals of lineage or neighborhood well–being required group participation. Two particularly important ones were rituals for neighborhood Defense (*Fighi*) medicines and for rainmaking, but the CMS taught converts to reject these rituals as heathen falsehoods: "We had to leave those things. We could not go to rainmaking, we could not go to *Fighi*. They were just darkness."[109] But outright rejections like these could pose grave problems to *Wutasi* followers, for quarrels and anger in the hearts of members of a community might make the ritual fail, which endangered the group's well–being. Christians might then be blamed for collective misfortunes.

---

[106] Interviews with CN, Teri/Sagalla, 22/7/1993; and JM, Teri/Chawia, 5/8/1988.

[107] Interview with JM, Wundanyi/Werugha, 18/7/1988.

[108] Interview with DM, Teri/Sagalla, 10/7/1993.

[109] Interview with RN, Wumingu/Werugha, 1/10/1988; many very old Christian interviewees made like statements.

Some rejections of *Wutasi* ritual had less dire cosmological consequences for communities, but still demoralized and divided lineages and neighborhoods. When Christian parents refused to put their children through initiation, the young ones were not considered marriageable adults among *Wutasi* followers in their large lineages. Early in the century, this only marginally reduced a lineage's pool of eligible *Wutasi* followers, but the break with community standards of adulthood and marriageability caused considerable consternation:

> In those days, the ones who did not do *Mwari*, others tried to pull them back. Friends or their cousins said, "you will just stay like children, now come and be adults! How will you marry if you do not learn the secrets and become adults?" . . . Christians said no, we will not do it, we will not send children to the dances, they will not do *Mwari*.[110]

Some convert girls refused initiation despite their parents' wishes. In one case, the girl fled to a female missionary's home in Mbale. Members of her lineage surrounded the house, trying to coax or scold her out, but she repeated phrases of Christian refusal until the lineage renounced and abandoned her.[111]

Christians' disavowal of *Wutasi* also undercut aspects of lineage elders' authority. Elderhood came not only with age, wealth, and influence, but by the attainment of ritual position and abilities, as expressed in the acquisition of particular ritual shrines.[112] Rejecting the efficacy of shrines, however, became a common way for strict Christians and would–be Christians to express rectitude. In some cases, people brought low–level household shrine items to church and handed them over to the missionaries.[113] This denied a household's need (or forfeited its ability) to appeal to lineage ancestors in times of difficulty.[114] Rejection of the shrines of elderhood directly attacked the religious authority of the living. As one man explained about his father, "He said, 'what is that Stool? It is useless!'"[115] To *Wutasi* followers, such a statement smacked of apostasy: if the Stool, the second most important shrine of elderhood, commanded no respect from a strict Christian, could that Christian respect elders at all?

Converts' and missionaries' preaching at times fanned those flames of doubt. To Christians, proselytizing demonstrated their faith and helped bring

---

[110] Interview with Mrs. VM, Sagassa/Werugha, 6/10/1988.

[111] CMS Correspondence, G3 A5/019, Miss Good's Annual Letter, 22/11/1910.

[112] Interview with Mrs. NM, Kizumanzi/Sagalla, 24/8/1988; for shrine acquisition and elderhood in the early 1950s, see G. Harris, *Casting*, 34–35.

[113] CMS Correspondence, G3 A5/018, Mombasa Diocesan Magazine, 1/1909; and Verbi's Annual Letter, 12/1909.

[114] Interview with Mrs. EK, Wongonyi/Mbololo, 7/7/1988. Missionaries recognized the importance of the gesture, too: "It is a big matter to these people, because they no longer have any faith in the things they used to worship . . . yet are half afraid for a time, in case any evil should overtake them. . . . [They] have much reverence and fear for these things, except for those who now no longer believe in them." CMS Correspondence, G3 A5/018, Mombasa Diocesan Magazine, 1/1909.

[115] Interview with WM, Choke/Mbale, 11/11/1988.

others into the Church. Though the CMS employed some full time evangelists, many early Christians regarded itinerating as an integral aspect of Church membership and did it without pay.[116] Their frequent evangelical sorties did garner new potential converts, and became the main motor of CMS growth in Taita.[117] Inevitably, though, the itinerations disturbed many *Wutasi* followers, who felt that Christians' preaching disrupted the spiritual peace necessary to the well–being of their communities. Christian preaching at *Wutasi* rituals exacerbated their displeasure:

> The believers would go to funerals of *Watasi* . . . . They talked to the ones who were there about their souls, . . . and about Jesus Christ. But th[e others] did not want to hear! They were very offended. . . . The women cried louder now, louder now, so the Christians could not be heard.[118]

Missionaries, too, if they happened across a ritual, would (usually politely) express their doubts about it and briefly preach—which might, in the eyes of *Wutasi* followers, damage the efficacy of the ritual. Once, for instance, two missionaries came upon a divination rite for a sick man, commented interestedly but negatively on the proceedings, and preached briefly about the only true God. Whether and how their presence and input altered the proceedings is open to question, but the divination's prognosis for the man turned out poorly.[119]

While some people tried to accept the new beliefs of their relations and neighbors with equanimity, many *Wutasi* followers responded vigorously to the strict Anglicans' challenges to lineage and neighborhood ways. They defended *Wutasi* precepts and practices, pointedly rebuking those who left them. They also utilized the predominance of their sociocultural outlooks and their sheer numerical size to pressure Christians. They could apply massive peer pressure: by 1910 probably fewer than two hundred Anglicans had been baptized. There were perhaps an equal number of catechumens; in the unlikely event that all believed unwaveringly, they would still amount to a tiny proportion of the Hills' 1910 population of at least 24,000.[120]

Some pressures on Christians and adherents aimed to dissuade people from converting, while others were intended to make converts still conform to the

---

[116] Sagalla had one female and five male Native Agents on salary from 1900–1910; Dabida hovered around nine paid Agents before the War. See CMS Correspondence, G3 A5/017, Wray's Report of April, 1905; and G3 A5/019, Annual Letters of Verbi and Maynard, 1910–14. On unpaid evangelists, interviews with MM, Kishamba/Chawia, 8/6/1988; NK, Wumari/Chawia, 15/8/1988; and Mrs. FM, Mogho Mleche/Mbale, 2/11/1988.

[117] Interview with Peter Bostock (former CMS missionary in Taita), Oxford/England, 3/4/1989.

[118] Interview with FM, Kidaya/Chawia, 12/5/1988, (note: *Wutasi* means *Wutasi* followers).

[119] CMS Correspondence, G3 A5/019, Miss Good's Annual Letter, 22/11/1910.

[120] A lack of statistics from Mbale makes figures on CMS adherents imprecise. In 1910, Sagalla had eighty–six baptized Christians and twenty–four catechumens; Wusi had seven Christians plus sixty–four catechumens. See CMS Correspondence, G3 A5/018, Wray's Annual Letter 5/1/1910, and Verbi's Annual Letter, 12/1909. For the population figure, see PC/Cst/1/1/179, Quarterly Reports, Traill to PC, 5/1/1912; because it derives from tax–gathering data, it is likely low. The 1915 census estimated 30,260. KNA, PC/Cst/1/1/328, Censuses 1914–18.

norms and ways of their communities. Other pressures intended to punish, or to shake strict Christians out of practices and statements that *Wutasi* followers found especially damaging or odious. For instance, the grandfather of the man who scorned the Stool shrine put the young man out of his house and told others in his small lineage to shun him. Many elders in the man's large lineage did likewise, leaving him effectively cut off from the lineage. This eventually had the intended effect: after a few years the youth retreated from his strict Christian ways, began to participate in Christian–prohibited activities, and was reintegrated into his lineage's networks.[121]

In other ways, too, strict Christians were often punished for their refusals of *Wutasi*–based practices. When they attended non–Christian funerals, people might scold them and accuse them of evil doings for their non–participation in *Wutasi*:

> They could go and do nothing, they would just attend. . . . They would hear, "Now, you are the one who bewitched the dead one!" They would be told this if they were not seen to pray [in *Wutasi*–based rites] at the funeral.[122]

Non–Christians often skipped the funerals of early strict Christians, or attended but pointed out to the Christians that their God could not save their people.[123] These actions underlined the Christians' isolation from their local communities, and sometimes had the effect of pulling people back towards lineage and neighborhood ways.

Prohibitions meant to prevent people from converting also came into play. Perhaps most widespread was a gendered one: spouses often tried to block one another from converting: "a woman could not convert if the others in her family did not want it. . . . Many women wanted to convert, . . . but if the man objected, that was all. She had to wait."[124] Often this refusal was linked to the men's belief in their headship of the household; often, too, it had to do with the men's concern that a Christian wife would refuse to brew *chofi*. Some women did convert over their husbands' objections, but this could lead to beatings or the breakup of their marriage.[125] On the other hand, in polygamous households, some women tried to prevent their husbands from converting, for fear that husbands would then abandon all the wives but one. Some wives threatened to leave husbands if they became catechumens, while others tried coaxing and cajoling.[126]

Potential converts most often faced coaxing and cajoling against rejecting *Wutasi* and community ways:

---

[121] Interview with WM, Choke/Mbale, 11/11/1988.

[122] Interview with Mrs. MO, Shigaro/Werugha, 2/8/1993.

[123] Interviews with Mrs. MO, Shigaro/Werugha, 2/8/1993; MT, Kishamba/Chawia, 9/6/1988.

[124] Interview with DM, Teri/Sagalla, 3/7/1993.

[125] Interviews with DM, Teri/Sagalla, 3/7/1993; Mrs. GM, Teri/Sagalla, 24/8/1988; and Mrs. SM, Mogho Mleche/Mbale, 4/11/1988.

[126] Interviews with Mrs. DM, 30/5/1988; and Mrs. MM, Teri/Chawia, 22/7/1988. Some missionaries also noted this pattern. See CMS Correspondence, G3/A5/018, Annual Letter of Miss Barnett, 14/12/1909.

Any who are real enquirers have to endure a good deal from their heathen relatives, who persistently do all they can to cause them to return to heathen ways, and alas! in several cases they have succeeded. A young lad who was my houseboy for some time was thus led astray. . . . [He] had been pestered by his relatives and now he has gone back, entering into the worst heathen ceremonies.[127]

Sometimes, though, the efforts turned coercive. Many parents held their children out of CMS–run schools open at each mission, for fear that it would "spoil" the young.[128] Many also compelled school–going sons and daughters to undergo initiation, refusing to consider the possibility of skipping it.[129] The pressures and coercions did not slacken as Christianity consolidated its presence in the Hills over the first decade of the century; on the contrary, opposition to the CMS missions solidified, as well. At Mbale, Rev. Maynard observed in 1910 that the opposition of older people had become more pronounced over time.[130]

Under various pressures—and feeling various desires—to remain within their local communities, many potential converts in the first decades of the century drew back; too, many potentially strict Christians instead took a more flexible approach to the new faith. Their attempts to mediate the twin pulls on them played out spatially during *Wutasi* rituals: Christians often attended them, but usually hung back at the edges or the rear of the group.[131] Christian parents and children often "lapsed" when it came time for the young to undergo initiation, but reaffirmed their Christian faith in later years.[132] Some Christian men continued to serve *chofi*—and drink it—in their neighborhood and lineage, and some Christian women continued to brew it for them.[133] Some strict CMS Anglicans refused to compromise their beliefs, but other early Anglicans (a few interviewees say most of them) quietly and unobtrusively tried to mitigate the pressures on themselves in such ways.

Conclusion: New Communities, New Discourses

Though many early Christians sought to sidestep the confrontation between Christianity and *Wutasi*, the CMS religion's threat to lineage and neighborhood communities was clear. Stricter Anglicans tried to build new social and spiritual solidarity,

---

[127] CMS Correspondence, G3/A5/018, Annual Letter of Miss Barnett, 14/12/1909.

[128] This verb often described *Wutasi* followers' fears about Christianization; it meant ruination, not overindulgence. Interviews with SK, Werugha/Werugha, 29/9/1988; and JM, Wongonyi/Mbololo, 7/7/1988.

[129] Interview with Mrs. SM, Wusi/Chawia, 22/7/1993.

[130] CMS Correspondence, G3 A5/017, Maynard's Annual Letter, 16/2/1910. By then, Maynard had worked in the Hills for over a decade, and spoke Kidaßida fluently.

[131] Interviews with MW, Lushangonyi/Mwanda, 22/9/1988; JM., Teri/Sagalla, 23/7/1993; and AM, Mogho Mleche/Mbale, 4/11/1988.

[132] Interviews with Mrs. GM, Teri/Sagalla, 24/8/1988; and NM, Wundanyi/Werugha, 26/5/1988.

[133] Interviews with JM., Teri/Sagalla, 23/7/1993; and Mrs. MM, Shigaro/Werugha, 17/6/1988.

as well as deal with their semi–isolation from their prior communities, by taking steps to fashion a self–consciously Christian community in Dabida.

> Those first ones took a difficult road! . . . They really had to rely on each other, nobody would help them. They had the help of each other and the help of Jesus. . . . They could be just left alone in their *kichuku*, maybe two or three in a *kichuku*, so they . . . had to rely on other Christians very much.[134]

To some extent, this community replicated lineage and neighborhood communities: it provided a means for people to organize communal work (without beer) in their locales, networks of support in times of hardship or illness or death, a pool of young people suitable for marriage, and so on.[135] At the spiritual level, it offered a community rooted in shared belief and shared support against persecution. It also provided bases of community that had no precise parallel in local units, like the experience of shared weekly worship in congregation, or the shared daily routines and knowledge of mission schooling.

To some extent, the new CMS Christian community subdivided into clusters that fit well with the spatial (and even social) boundaries of neighborhood. In other ways, however, CMS Christian community cut across extant neighborhood boundaries and forged broader ties of shared Christian ways, beliefs, and mutual support that included all Taita's Anglicans. This broadened form of community found temporary social expression every week, in the Sunday gatherings of people, some of whom walked half a day each way to attend services. It took more lasting form in innovations like occasional marriages that transgressed local endogamy to link up Christians from different parts of the Hills, or in some Christians' departure from their own neighborhoods to settle near a mission station.[136]

Wutasi followers simultaneously began to voice their broader ties, as well. As it related to (and responded to) the CMS challenge, this often took the form of a discourse of refusal, juxtaposing Whites' ways and "our" ways:

> My grandfather said the missionaries taught people we must despise our own ways of praying . . . [and] living. . . . He did not like the missions, . . . he refused to let my father go to school. He did not want me to go to school. "It will just make you like the mission–people, like the Whites."[137]

This discourse of "our ways" expanded many people's notions of who and what fit within that "we," even as it designated a new "them." This construction of a new, broader "we" contributed to the fashioning of a new, collective Taita identity—an identity Christians would want to claim, as well. The next chapter discusses these and other aspects of the emergence of Taita identity.

[134] Interview with PN, Ngerenyi/Chawia, 9/5/1988.
[135] Interviews with BM, Sechu/Chawia, 11/6/1988; JM, Wundanyi/Werugha, 11/5/1988; Mrs. AM, Choke/Mbale, 1988; and SK, Werugha/Werugha, 29/9/1988.
[136] Interview with Mrs. SM, 23/7/1993; and PK, Kigalla/Werugha, 6/10/1988.
[137] Interview with MW, Lushangonyi/Mwanda, 23/9/1988.

5

Becoming Taita: The Coalescence and Mobilization of an Ethnic Identity, 1900–1930

> Things changed when the whites came. . . . We avoided . . .
> quarreling and making enemies. We . . . should stop treating
> each other like animals and live like one people. . . . So we
> stopped making enemies of our own brothers.[1]

Introduction

Even as lineage and neighborhood communities came under early colonial strains, another form of community, Taita ethnicity, coalesced. This verb is deliberately chosen, for Taita ethnicity did not suddenly burst onto the scene out of thin air. It took shape over the course of decades, through reworkings of prior social forms and incorporations of new ones. People mobilized the new, region–wide social identity to shape thought and action in contexts where lineage and neighborhood–based ideologies were losing salience or never had much purchase. Taita identity began to be invoked in settings from officials' utterances, to elders' gatherings, to household struggles over resources and behaviors.

As a basis of community, Taita ethnicity had two main—and contrary—aspects. Drawing as it did on lineage and neighborhood ways, Taita identity could readily and rapidly suffuse practices from the mundane to the elaborate. Its reiteration in all sorts of everyday settings eventually made it a deeply as-

---

[1] Interview with SM, Teri/Sagalla, 12/7/1993.

sumed basis of "natural" commonality: virtually a social birthmark, not unlike the ideology of lineage. Yet Taita ethnicity simultaneously bespoke a normative identity, one bound up in intense cultural politicking over how to reconstitute social relations now in flux. Competing views about what made for acceptably Taita ways informed generational and gendered struggles over authority, economic order, and religious belief, as well as struggles over formal political power in the Hills. Herein lay the central tension of Taita identity: it might be understood as a unifying claim of shared historical experience and concomitant commonality, but it was also susceptible to claims that conforming to contemporary community standards of proper belief and action validated Taitaness—and cultural politicking made those standards potentially mutable objects of dispute and negotiation.

As lineage and neighborhood communities lost some norm–setting power in the early 1900s, Taita ethnicity slowly superseded and enveloped them. This process provided a new basis for older men's assertions of power. Local communities' thick networks did not disappear, but by 1910 older men's ability to control the young through lineage and neighborhood ideologies was far less secure. Older men then tried to reassert control through a different ideology, one of proper Taita ways. Taita ethnicity did not eradicate lineage and neighborhood as social units, but it took over many of their discursive and norm–setting roles in people's struggles over the terms of social order. Taita identity emerged as a sort of super–community over ideologically weakened but still–functional local ones: struggles in lineages and neighborhoods increasingly made Taita identity their referent. Too, new intraregional interactions, the experience of labor migration, and wrangles with the colonial state helped mobilize people's sense of longstanding commonality into a more unified sense of community.

The emergence of Taita ethnicity reflected changes in the bases of cultural politicking, for axioms of propriety were shifting from justifications of what the old *could* do to the young, to insistence on what the young *should* do for their seniors. The construction of community still drew on its material base, but turn–of–the–century changes made the connection more protracted. As older men's claim of political–economic dominance shrank to a powerful but vulnerable gambit, material struggles gradually became enmeshed as much in normative propositions of propriety as in the direct power of elders over youngers. In this context, older men found that attaching claims (and sanctions) about propriety to a notion of shared Taita ways gave the claims more weight with young people and colonial officials than did claims of lineage or neighborhood. As discourses of ethnic belonging and propriety spread across neighborhoods and lineages, they recast prior community ways in a broader arena of common Taita ways. Ethnic identification also enabled the development of new networks across the Hills, based on new appreciations—and new constructions—of shared outlooks, experiences, and interests.

Older men built a key concept into their early–century assertion of Taita ethnicity: the notion of *Kidaßida*, a Taita way of doing things. *Kidaßida* mobilized long–acknowledged sociocultural similarities and commonalities across Taita into a widely agreed–upon declaration (and, later, assumption) of Taita sociocultural unity. Oral expressions of this unity bore a strong resemblance to extant neighborhood–based discourses of mutual understanding:

> What was *Kidaβida*? . . . It was our way of living! . . . When you and another Mtaita meet, then you understand each other. You know how to act with each other, there was no confusion. . . . You speak the same language, . . . you know his family. . . . If you met in Mombasa you can know each other and help each other.[2]

Kidaβida in its early–century form also provided a platform for normative assertions—claims about what sorts of outlooks and behaviors qualified as properly (or acceptably) Taita. Those normative assertions, by no means universally agreed upon, prompted struggles over what could or could not qualify as proper Taita beliefs and behaviors. Those struggles soon moved to the center of cultural politicking in the Hills, and remained there into the 1950s.

Normatively, *Kidaβida* did a new kind of boundary–setting work: with the realm of proper Taita ways came a hardened prospect of transgressing them. In terms of *Kidaβida*, rejection of (or gross failure to live up to) proper ways came to be described as "getting lost." Getting lost could occasion severe social sanctions: the lost might be ostracized, displaced from social networks, considered a source of cosmological trouble, even disinherited.[3] The language of becoming lost had no analog in prior lineage and neighborhood ideologies. In nineteenth–century Taita, because seniors had the means to control a son or daughter–in–law quite closely, people only very rarely strayed far from lineage or neighborhood ties. Young people seen as undutiful about their work obligations would be admonished, lose the benefit of networks, even be partly disinherited, but they rarely left or were severed from their lineage, and then nearly always joined another lineage elsewhere in the Hills. Parents' weaker situation in the twentieth century necessitated a stronger threat: when the young could wander far afield and diverge from parental control with relative ease, the specter of being cut off helped to hold them in check.

Older men tried to reconstruct their social predominance by eliding the normative side of *Kidaβida* into the unifying side: they linked regional historical commonality to norms of propriety. However, their conjoining of historical commonality with the contemporary naturalization of their power proved less than fully effective as the twentieth century wore on. The young sought to be

---

[2]   It was entirely possible—even probable—that two youths from Taita meeting in Mombasa would not know each other's small lineages, but they would discuss place–name geography in order to locate each other spatially, seek out mutual acquaintances, and thereby "know" each other. Interview with GM, Kishamba/Chawia, 27/6/1988.

[3]   The daily problems that could befall the "lost" included: difficulty in marrying; lack of help for household work, farming, and herding; lack of support networks in social conflicts or ecological crises, etc. Men who became "lost" by staying away from Taita for too long could find their lineages loathe to reincorporate them. For women in colonial times, just leaving Taita alone for urban work might make them considered lost. The phrase came up often in interviews, including with CM, Teri/Sagalla, 22/7/1993; SK, Wundanyi/Werugha, 15/4/1988; MM, Kidaya–Ngerenyi/Chawia, 25/4/1988; Mrs. SM, Mwanda/ Mwanda, 14/9/1988; and Mrs. JM, Sagassa/Werugha, 17/10/1988.

members of the community, yet ever more openly challenged elders' terms of Taita propriety. Norms and terms of Taita ethnicity (and even the meaning of *Kidaßida*) kept coming up for renegotiation.

Fashioning an Ethnic Consciousness

New Social Possibilities of Community, 1900–1920

Many everyday interactions reinforced the early colonial era construction of regional commonality. The disbanding of warrior groups and curtailing of intraregional raiding allowed greater freedom of movement, opening up to far larger numbers of people the medium–distance interconnections that had long required blood brotherhoods:

> Long ago, you could not just travel down to Tausa [Mbololo] and get someone who will keep your cows. No. . . . It needed special arrangements of eating blood. But my grandfather just met [X, of Tausa] at Voi. . . . "Will you keep my cattle?" "I will." Just like that. . . . They still had cattle from us when I was born, they still had cattle from us when my father died.[4]

The final deal may well have involved far more give–and–take (and far more time to finalize) than the quotation describes. Nevertheless, that an arrangement and consequent social alliance could stem from a chance meeting in town speaks volumes about the changes underway.

Similar encounters, and countless more everyday interconnections, became common by the 1910s. People often met at increasingly large and regular regional markets in the new towns of Voi and Mwatate that also had permanent shops, and at locales farther up in the Hills. Women and men from different neighborhoods frequently crossed paths to bargain, make exchanges and arrangements for future ones, and talk more generally. These everyday, commonplace interactions planted the seeds of social transformation, for networks and relationships deriving from such activities enabled the forging of ongoing ties with people from other parts of Taita, of a kind and on a scale not previously possible.[5]

On a smaller scale, mission churches performed a similar role—and not only for the dedicated believers from across the Hills who converged on the churches every Sunday, and relied increasingly on each other for support all the days in between. Though relatively few professed Christianity, mission churches on Dabida drew large crowds to Sunday services, through the 1910s.[6]

---

[4]   Interview with SM, Wongonyi/Mbololo, 6/7/1988.

[5]   "Market days were very big . . . yes, before the War of the Germans [i.e., World War I]. At Mwatate you met people from everywhere. . . . I made many friends." Interview with Mrs. RM, Chawia/Chawia, 17/6/1988.

[6]   For instance, Sunday services in Wusi were "well attended from the day we opened it," with steadily growing crowds; but adherents in 1909 numbered only sixty–four. CMS Correspondence, G3 A5/018, Verbi's Annual Letter, 12/1909.

Many people went regularly for years without converting, but wanted to perform the Sunday rituals, and hoped to gain some collateral spiritual value from them.[7] Frequent attendees mostly came from within a few hours' walk of a church, but half a dozen neighborhoods might lie inside that range. Weekly congregations did not form key social and spiritual networks for all attendees. However, the fact that such groups gathered easily and regularly helped undermine the spatial significance of neighborhood boundaries and underline the possibility of broader–based ties.

Such interactions fostered a wider sense of shared community, of a kind not felt before the 1890s. Social interconnections across the Hills became common, then embedded in routines. Soon, widely understood and agreed–upon ways of addressing strangers from elsewhere in the Hills helped people not otherwise known to each other become not–strangers. Two such people meeting in the 1910s would likely greet each other according to a now Taita–wide formula of propriety. Greeting was a powerful way of naturalizing a new level of intra–Taita recognition, for its routines quickly turned into the subconscious assuming of a "proper" form among people with underlying commonalities.[8] In a long greeting, as a prelude to a fuller conversation:

> you asked [the stranger], "where are your people from? Oh, yes, do you know So–and–So?" "No, that one is not in my lineage, do you mean [a different] So–and–So who has sugarcane at Mwatate market?" "Yes, that one." "Yes, she is my aunt." "Good, and how is she? . . . Please greet her for me."[9]

These preliminaries might well continue into a discussion about other extended kin each had, probing their networks of home, farming, wage work, trading, etc., in search of points of contact. Both the found connections and the process of seeking them placed the conversers in a mutually known, shared orbit of people and ways, effectively establishing grounds for a reconfigured version of "knowing each other."

This recitation of proper form, itself shot through with neighborhood–based ways of constructing group belonging, did two kinds of cultural work. First, it afforded a way for people to envision themselves and each other within widened webs of interrelationship. Second, it set parameters and limits of community membership by social, cultural, and linguistic forms common to (and limited to) people of the Hills. Through countless, virtually unthought reiterations like these, Taita commonality now began to supply people grounds for recognizing each other within an idiom of mutual belonging: strangers could "know"

---

[7] Mghalu numbered among these people until 1910, when he became too ill to attend. CMS Correspondence, G3 A5/019, Maynard's Annual Letter, 25/11/1912, and interview with DM, Mbale/Mbale, 11/11/1988.

[8] Discussing the Mwatate market in the 1910s, one woman explained, "people at the market just met, and greeted each other very nicely, and you knew this one is alright, she speaks to me with respect." Interview with Mrs. RM, Chawia/Chawia, 17/6/1988.

[9] Ibid.

each other, quickly "understand" each other, and thereby extend a tendril of community.

Other activities reinforced the new networks and new sense of Taita community taking shape in the Hills. Younger men, through the experience of migrant labor, built Taita–based bonds with one another; older men gathered in new, "Taita"–based fora of political and juridical power; both older men and older women tried to use the notion of Taita ways to reestablish control over the outlooks and behaviors of the young. All these activities contributed to the rapid buildup and naturalization of a discourse of shared Taita identity and proper Taita ways. In the process, they gave rise to a multiheaded discourse of Taita ethnicity; at times it was used to claim quasi–lineal descent ties to an historically–based group, but in almost the same breath it might prescribe or proscribe ways of thinking about or doing things.

Older Men and Institutional Assertions of Ethnicity

The activation of Taita identity dates to the late 1900s and early 1910s, when many older men began to invoke it as a meaningful identity for apprehending and ordering local communities. Their assertion of an ethnicized identity, though creative, did not require an improbable leap of imagination. Virtually everyone in the Hills was attuned to the region's long-standing linguistic and sociocultural similarities, and the enlarged administrative units, greater physical mobility, and broadening social networks of the era gave the similarities a new prescience. Too, some Europeans and coastal Africans had spoken of Taita's people in the collective singular since at least the mid–nineteenth century, and though the Hills' people had given little weight to that language, by the 1910s few were strangers to it.

In this context, older men concerned about the weakening of lineage and neighborhood as communities of belonging and bases of elders' authority began to pick up on the language of ethnicity, reconfigure it to their purposes, and thereby domesticate it. By 1910, older people had lived through ten years of IBEACo rule and fifteen years of colonial rule; some had long-standing experience of an administration grounded in the European assumption of the Taita as a tribe. In answering the DC's queries about local ways or presenting concerns to him, many older men were drawn into the whites' ethnicizing discourse. For instance, starting in 1909, when officials asked a few older men to explain Taita practices, they obliged with a recitation of crimes and fines. This body of material became an originary source for officials' elaboration of Taita Native Law.[10]

---

[10]   KNA, DC/TTA/3/1, Native Laws and Customs (drawn up by DC Weeks, 1909). This legal code rode roughshod over local variation. For instance, Weeks cited a much lower fine for murder than what Wray paid in 1880s' Sagalla, but a much higher one than for parts of Mwanda. Interview with MM, Mwanda/Mwanda, 12/9/1988. Assessing the gravity and appropriate punishment of a crime also depended on the mis–doer's social standing, social support, etc.

What constituted serious crime had also varied considerably. Much of central Dabida considered witchcraft a grave problem in the late nineteenth and early twentieth centuries; punishments

Officials regarded older men as the fonts of Taita law, and the old men often happily acknowledged themselves as such. The two groups formalized their collaboration on legal authority and the language of tribe through a new quasi–juridical, quasi–policy making institution, the Councils of Elders. Of the eighty–nine older men who composed the original five Councils in 1911, none had Christian names, so indigenously–oriented outlooks surely predominated on them.[11] However, the Councils were also deeply infused with the language of ethnicity:

> *JM:* My grandfather was on that Council when it started. He was really respected because he knew the Taita laws.
>
> *Q:* Taita laws? Or the laws of his lineage?
>
> *JM:* Lineage laws and Taita laws were just the same. . . . He got his respect in that Council because he was expert in Taita laws.
>
> *Q:* Could he get the same respect for being an expert on lineage laws? Or it had to be Taita laws?
>
> *JM:* Eeeh! In those Councils they did not talk about lineages.[12]

Of course, the discourse of ethnicity did not flatten out all local differences in the promulgation and interpretation of Native Law. Much to the chagrin of officials, elders in different Councils rendered judgments and fines according to local predispositions. Too, many disputes never reached the Councils, but continued to come before lineage and neighborhood elders in local settings.[13]

Still, the Councils reinforced Taitaness by invoking Taita Native Law as the basis for elders' decisions about proper ways—and "ways" were what they often rendered judgments on. They clothed themselves in the garb of Taita tradition, and applied it in a manner meant to reinvigorate their predominance. In this self–consciously Taita forum, the ways they upheld bore a remarkable similarity to older people's prior lineage and neighborhood power:

> *RM:* Those Councils, they really defended traditions! . . . I was very young when they began, I saw that they were defending *Kidaßida* [Taita ways] there.
>
> *Q:* What things of *Kidaßida*? What traditions?
>
> *RM:* Obey your parents, . . . give them respect, they are your king and queen, they know what is best. . . . Respect the old men. Respect the

---

extended to pushing a sorcerer off a cliff. Interviews with JM, Kishamba/Chawia, 12/8/1988; and MN, Lushangonyi/Mwanda, 22/9/1988. But people were less concerned about sorcery in a different part of Dabida, and punished it less harshly. Interview with SM, Wongonyi/Mbololo, 6/7/1988.

[11] By 1913, the total number of Council elders reached 630. KNA, DC/TTA/3/1, and DC/TTA/3/3, Political Record Books, Native Administration.

[12] Interview with JM, Mlondo/Werugha, 28/9/1988.

[13] Interview with GM, Kishamba/Chawia, 27/6/1988; and A. and G. Harris, "Wataita Today," 117–24.

old ones who are gone [i.e., ancestral spirits]. . . . But people left those traditions.

Q: Those were Taita traditions? Or lineage traditions?

RM: It is just the same.[14]

Older men's invocations of Taita identity in these fora reformulated their predominance along lines that would carry the force of the new Native Law. They amplified their juridical practices with comments to officials in other contexts that represented their authority as a fundamental tradition now under attack.[15] If a discourse of ethnicity helped them make the point to Europeans, they showed no qualms about slipping into it. Europeans, for their part, having long presumed African tribal societies to have strong paternal authority, considered that authority a font of rural social order. Officials therefore tended to set considerable store by elders' sentiments on the matter, and tried to support them. A 1915 government circular encouraged the Taita DC to "uphold native authority, and resist attempts by the young to subvert it."[16] Clearly, Taita ethnic discourse helped foster this elder–official alliance on the question of controlling the young.

Ethnicity and Control over Young Men

Older men also fashioned a discourse of ethnicity directly with their juniors, especially sons and daughters–in–law. Early on, they used the notion of Taita ways to claim control over young men's work.[17] Ideologies of "lineage work" were proving only partially up to this task; ethnic ideology gave older men some new leverage. Most immediately, the discourse of Taita ways carried a bite of potential sanction that lineage discourses of work had not. A lineage discourse of work might in principle have adopted tougher sanctions, but the emerging discourse of ethnicity instead displaced it. Its underlying tenets might be summarized as: sons send their earnings back to their parents and visit home regularly; it is *Kidaßida*. Sons who do not do this risk becoming lost.

---

[14]   Interview with RM, Wundanyi/Werugha, 29/7/1988.

[15]   Most commonly, this took place at group meetings with Europeans. The language shaped older men's complaints to the DC about their daughters going down to Voi. See KNA, DC/TTA/3/3/2, Political Record Book, 1913; see also their discussions about young men drinking *chofi*, PC/Cst/1/ 22/32, District Tours, 1916–20.

[16]   KNA, PC/Cst/1/1/333, PC Hobley's Circular on the Administration of Native Reserves, 1915. It vested native authority in male elders, even as colonial rule's elevation of chiefs undercut elders' authority. Also Hobley's letter to the Chief Secretary about upholding elders' authority, in PC/ Cst/1/13/72, 13/4/1915. See, too, district officials' approach to complaints about young men drinking *chofi*, PC/Cst/1/22/32, District Tours, 1916–20. The DC in 1920 described youths' drinking as a sign of weakened elders' control. PC/Cst/1/12/279, DC to PC, 10/8/1920.

[17]   The ethnicized discourse of work took shape in the era between the rise of large–scale migrant labor and the onset of World War I (i.e., between 1905 and 1914). Men who reached their teens in that era showed a far greater awareness of lineage–based notions of work than did men whose migrant work began with the War. For example, interviews with RN, Nyache/Wumingu, 1/10/ 1988; JM, Wundanyi/Werugha, 15/7/1988; and MM, Ilole/Bura, 17/7/1988.

Q: What did you do with your wages when you went to work in Mombasa [in 1919]?

SM: I sent the money to my parents here–here. . . . Nearly all of it. I kept enough for eating, but . . . nearly all of it I sent home.

Q: Why did you not keep it there with you? . . . Were you afraid it would get stolen?

SM: It was a must to send that money home. Not because of thieves, just because it is a must. All Taitas did that, except the ones who stayed [away] all the time. . . . Good sons, good Taitas, always sent the money home.

Q: What would have happened if you didn't send back money?

SM: Those ones, . . . many could not be welcomed back here [in the Hills]. . . . They were just lost.

Q: They were lost from their lineage, or they were lost from Taita?

SM: From Taita. . . . When your parents and your elders said you were lost, could you live here as a Taita? You could not![18]

One early migrant who stayed in Mombasa continuously for nine years found upon his return home that he had become "lost." Several fields he expected to inherit had gone to others; the remaining plots for him barely met his subsistence needs.[19] When another migrant failed to visit or remit money from Mombasa for several years, his lineage considered him lost and planned to obliterate his inheritance claims. His wife, however, knowing that his punishment would strike her and her children hard, persuaded his kin to let her handle it differently. She traveled to Mombasa, located the wayward husband, and removed the woman who had been "eating his wages" in his Mombasa lodgings. She then made him go back to Voi, where he worked for the railroad and spent several years living down the shame and ignominy heaped upon him.[20]

How much older men's newly ethnicized discourse of work drew upon the colonizers' ethnicizing predispositions is difficult to say. On the one hand, officials' views reinforced elders' ethnicizing discourse, even though the Europeans misperceived the situation. Officials throughout Kenya worried that young migrants loosened from elders' control would become "detribalized," dissolute, and a threat to rural and urban social order. In early colonial efforts to uphold fathers' "tribal" authority over sons, officials and older men agreed that sons should return to their homes regularly, and should remain junior members of their parents' household.

---

[18]   Interview with SM, Werugha/Werugha, 27/9/1988. Similar comments came from virtually all men interviewed on the subject, whose work careers post–dated the war.

[19]   Interview with SM, Wundanyi/Werugha, 15/4/1988.

[20]   Interview with Mrs. SM, Werugha/Werugha, 30/9/1988. Her husband's disinheritance would make her use rights to land in his lineage tenuous, and she did not want to see the lineage standing of her children lowered.

On the other hand, if colonizers' presumptions encouraged older men's ethnicization of work norms, the older men's version of doing so varied considerably from the official one. Officials cast the work/ethnicity relationship mainly in spatial–cultural (and later, in psychological) terms: work in urban areas detribalized young Africans by throwing them headlong into a modern world for which they were not ready. The (assumed) natural authority structures of tribal culture, backed up by the state, might restrain that dangerous prospect.[21] Taita's older men, however, understood that their authority could not be assumed. They knew most sons would eventually come home to find wives, land, livestock, and networks of support.[22] Their ethnicized work discourse pressured young men and women to obey parental strictures about resource control, home labor needs, and proper behavior. In these struggles, older men saw Taita ethnicity not as an old pillar to fall back on, but as a new way to make and enforce claims. They recast sons' remittances and daughters–in–law's work as ethnic ways, and tried to make them acid tests of the young's ethnic propriety.

Ethnicity and the Work of Daughters–in–Law

As the last sentence suggests, older men—and older women—in the 1900s–1910s also turned to a discourse of Taita ethnicity in struggles over work with daughters–in–law. This, too, gave lie to the European assumption of "Taita" society's extant tribal orderliness. Older people ethnicized domestic discourses not only to bind daughters–in–law to them affectively, but to reclaim control over young women's work and to preempt them from living off resources older people considered rightly theirs.

    Few women from the Hills stayed long in Mombasa in this era, with or without husbands. The city offered them few employment choices; given the high population of male migrants and a lack of wage work for women in Mombasa's early colonial economy, most unskilled migrant women probably engaged in some form of prostitution.[23] Most of Taita's men and women quickly defined it as no place for a proper woman. In instances discussed

---

[21] The "dangers of detribalization" thesis reached its apogee in the Kenya government's report on Mau Mau, which argued that the African male "is brought up in the environment of the old tribal culture, but . . . comes into contact with a different culture, which makes nonsense of many of his primitive beliefs. . . . He has lost his traditional moorings . . . the old restraints are gone. The comforting cloak of his tribalism has disappeared, and he is left to act as an individual. . . . He often becomes rudderless." Colony and Protectorate of Kenya, *The Origins and Growth of Mau Mau*, Sessional Paper No. 5 (Nairobi, 1959/60), 8–9, 263, 285.

[22] "Always I worked to come home. Always. . . . I worked for my bridewealth and I came home to marry. . . . I worked until I got enough fields to stay home and farm [i. e., after his father died]. After that, I just stayed here." Interview with FM, Kidaya/Chawia, 12/5/1988; his comments were typical of the earlier generations of migrant workers.

[23] White has written about prostitution in Nairobi, but no corresponding literature exists for Mombasa, making this assertion somewhat speculative. It does, however, accord with what many older men and women in the Hills claim. See Luise White, *The Comforts of Home: Prostitution in Colonial Nairobi* (Chicago, 1990).

with me, women who went to Mombasa and took up such work were quickly considered lost by their lineages,[24] though that didn't stop male migrants from seeking them out. Interaction with prostitutes from Taita fueled contradictory reasons for migrants to keep wives out of the city: they did not want wives on their own there during the day (potentially cheating on husbands or being harassed by other men), and many did not want wives to see how men conducted themselves there.[25] Also, parents–in–law did not want to lose the wives' labor, nor see the wives' children raised outside the local community.

So young women mostly stayed in the Hills, working under the eye (and in principal, under the control) of their in–laws. Young women generally went to great lengths to integrate themselves into their in–laws' lineage, but in trying to cope with the increased demands these changes put on them, they sometimes clashed with their in–laws' expectations:

Mrs. VM: My mother liked her mother–in–law very much.

Q: They got along well?

Mrs. VM: Yes, even when my mother was very tired, she tried hard to please her.

Q: Was she able to please her?

Mrs. VM: [laughs] That grandmother was very fierce! . . . When mother helped her, then everything was fine. But if she was doing something else, the old woman was not happy. She did not like to wait!

Q: What things did your mother do to make her wait?

Mrs. VM: . . . little things: farming, going to a shop. . . . [26]

Older men and older women responded to these tensions by linking the daughters' behavior to ethnic propriety. In the emerging language of ethnicity, "proper" Taita daughters–in–law behaved dutifully and respected their parents–in–law. More than with young men, "respect" mediated older people's expectations of young women.[27] Older people questioned the respectfulness of daughters–in–law far more often than of sons, perhaps because the young

---

[24] Though White argues that "prostitutes and respectable women are not discrete categories," (*Comforts*, 19–20, 110–16), within Taita considerable stigma was attached to becoming (or reputedly being) a prostitute. Interviews with Mrs. SM, Ilole/Bura, 16/8/1988; Mrs. MN, Teri/Sagalla, 25/8/1988; and NK, Wumari/Mwatate, 15/8/1988.

[25] In the first decades of the century, virtually no married women from Taita moved to Mombasa. Interviews with JM, Kishamba/Chawia, 24/9/1988; and Mrs. SM, Werugha/Werugha, 30/9/1988. Among the educated, this began to change in the 1930s. Interviews with JM, Shigaro/Werugha, 20/4/1988; and NK, Wumari/Chawia, 15/8/1988.

[26] Interview with Mrs. VM, Sagassa/Werugha, 6/10/1988.

[27] "You respect your parents and your husband's parents. Respect them and obey them. That is the highest thing of *Kidaβida.*" Interview with Mrs. WK, Werugha/Werugha, 30/7/1993. Fourteen female interviewees linked *Kidaβida* to the respect of one's own parents and parents–in–law. Respect featured less prominently in men's testimonies.

women came from outside the small lineages, perhaps because they faced more everyday expectations and closer scrutiny.

The positive construction of young women's respectfulness and dutiful-ness did not disappear. However, by now casting those attributes in terms of Taita ways, in–laws subtly acknowledged that their expectations and control over the young women were increasingly contested. The link between a young woman's respectfulness and ethnicity showed most starkly in negative formu-lations: young wives who crossed their in–laws' expectations of them were sometimes accused of "leaving *Kidaßida*."[28] For example, as money entered into Taita's economy, some wives became rivals of parents for a migrant worker's wages. The slight measure of economic autonomy this gave to young wives inflamed many in–laws' sensibilities:

> I am telling you, colonialism brought a big loss of respect for Taita ways! . . . Married girls did not respect their parents[–in–law], they had money from their husbands and then they lost respect for them.[29]

Older men and women tried to use ethnicity to set norms of proper behav-ior: a good Taita daughter helped her in–laws with work, whether in their fields or their compounds. Good Taita daughters–in–law did not try to take money away from the lineage, but trusted their fathers–in–law to allocate it wisely.

Changing Circumstances, Changing Consciousness, and the Construction of Ethnic Belonging

Reconfigurations of Community

The colonial era's new circumstances and struggles did not obviate people's felt need to belong to communities of mutual recognition and support. This entailed more than wanting land and security in old age; life's social and spiri-tual vagaries continued to foster commitments to groups where people felt understood, historically rooted, and accepted. Practically, lineage and neigh-borhood continued to provide much (though not all) of that support structure early in the century. However, as older men increasingly spoke of a Taita basis to society—and as colonial era experience heightened people's sense of regional commonalities—notions of community rooted in lineage and neighborhood were reinterpreted as underpinnings of Taita community.

---

[28] Interviews with LM, Mrugua/Bura, 18/8/1988; Mrs. WM, Mrugua/Bura, 19/8/1988; SM, Kidaya/ Chawia, 10/5/1988; Mrs. MO, Shigaro/Werugha, 2/8/1993; and Mrs. PN, Mwanda/ Mwanda, 3/8/1993.

[29] Interview with SM, Kidaya/Chawia, 10/5/1988; also, interview with LM, Mrugua/Bura, 18/ 8/1988.

Some of these reinterpretations gave expression to older men's claims of predominance: sons had long worked for fathers in a lineage context, so fathers' explanations in the 1910s that sons worked for them (but now as a Taita way of doing things) seemed unexceptional.[30] Much the same could be said of the new link between the propriety of daughters–in–law and proper Taita ways. Other reworkings of localized forms into Taita forms sprang from older men's attempts to strengthen shared indigenous ways against outside attacks. *Wutasi* prayers and rituals, for instance, retained a lineage and neighborhood focus, but in the 1910s, became canons of a fundamentally "Taita way of doing things." The attempt to establish *Wutasi* as a bedrock part of *Kidaßida* had more than a little to do with colonial Christian attacks on it. Christian proselytizing and condemnations of *Wutasi* spurred a widespread juxtaposition: the whites' religion and "our" religion:

> The parents of my mother refused the religion of the whites. . . . [When] my mother wanted to become a Christian, they asked her why she wanted to leave our ways to follow the whites. "You are a Taita, not a white, hold onto our religion."[31]

Dances in Dabida were similarly reconfigured. Partly this, too, reflected a regionwide juxtaposition to Christian condemnations: missionary criticisms of dances' "heathenism" prompted the defense of them as "our" traditional ways.[32] In some cases, the "Taita–fication" of dances affected their personnel: *Gonda*, for instance, opened out from its predominantly neighborhood basis on Dabida to include young adult attendees from other parts of the Hills.[33] In relatively short order *Gonda* took on a pan-Taita character, as well as a neighborhood one. By the late 1910s, some *Gondas* turned into interneighborhood competitions.[34]

The rapid reconfiguration of *Wutasi* and various dances (despite their localized orientation) into shared Taita ways indicates how some central aspects of neighborhood and lineage belonging became inscribed into Taita identity. Through these reconfigurations, people fitted long–felt local connections of belonging into their newfound Taita ethnic identity. Offering prayers to one's ancestral spirits at the lineage skull shrine still did important local work, but additionally testified to one's commitment to *Kidaßida*; in return, Taita identity embraced one's lineage ancestors.

---

[30] "Always, since very long ago, sons worked beneath their fathers. . . . Before the colonialists, it was that way. After the colonialists arrived, it was that way. It only changed recently." Interview with JM, Teri/Chawia, 5/8/1988; also, AK, Shigaro/Werugha, 25/4/1988.

[31] Interview with Mrs. NM, Kizumanzi/Sagalla, 24/8/1988. Several other interviewees raised the juxtaposition, including KM, Tausa/Mbololo, 2/6/1988; and RM, Mlondo/Werugha, 27/9/1988.

[32] Interview with Mrs. NM, Kizumanzi/Sagalla, 24/8/1988; and MC, Ndome/Mbololo, 20/6/1983.

[33] Interviews with KM, Kizumanzi/Sagalla, 14/7/1993; Mrs. CM, Shigaro/Werugha, 26/7/1993; and BM, Njawuli/Mwanda, 3/8/1993.

[34] Interview with BM, Njawuli/Mwanda, 3/8/1993.

Young Men, Labor Migration, and Wider Terms of Community

Migrant labor in the 1900s and 1910s profoundly altered interactions among Taita's young men, drawing them into a widened sense of community. The dissolution of young men's prior neighborhood associations, and the experience of leaving their locales to live amidst a large group of fellow migrants from the Hills, prompted the changes. Neighborhood warrior groups had been the main body around which young men gathered throughout the nineteenth century.[35] Though some bands occasionally acted in concert, most had been rivals that saw each other as potential enemies. Colonial rule, by ending the inter– and intraregional raiding, effectively eliminated warriors' reasons for being. Migratory labor, by removing youths from their neighborhoods, sealed the warrior bands' demise.

But migrant labor also agglomerated young men in new ways, especially in Mombasa. As they left the familiarity of home for an exciting but alien city full of coastal and upcountry Africans, Taita's migrants sought companionship with others whose language and culture they understood. Suspicions of youths from distant parts of the Hills faded, and a pan–Taita sensibility emerged:

> You heard every language in Mombasa, you wanted to spend time with people who know your language and your customs. . . . If they come from Kishamba or Mwanda [locations], it doesn't matter, you don't have to be one blood [i.e., lineage], you could just speak with each other. . . . We worked with people . . . from every place, but it was best to work with other Taitas and to stick with each other . . . we understood each other.[36]

Migrants from Taita tended to live in certain parts of Mombasa: mainly in Ziwani, then a ramshackle area at the outskirts of town, jammed with overcrowded lodgings.[37] There, people from all parts of the Hills ate, drank, socialized, and shared quarters. Narrower exclusiveness did not immediately and fully dissolve ("The house I stayed in at Mombasa . . . was . . . for those from Susu [neighborhood]. We did not want ill–feeling").[38] But most lodgings in Ziwani were not so segregated, and neither was most social and work life.[39]

Youths often found work through networks linked back to the Hills. Many such networks were rooted in neighborhood connections, but some drew on a wider base. Dairy work exemplifies the former ilk. If one man got a job with a

---

[35] They were not, however, akin to the age sets of a number of other eastern African societies.

[36] Interview with RM, Wundanyi/Werugha, 13/8/1988.

[37] Interviews with SM, Kidaya–Ngerenyi/Chawia, 25/4/1988; MM, Nyolo/Bura, 15/8/1988; and Mrs. SM, Werugha/Werugha, 30/9/1988. On housing and health conditions in Mombasa, see Karim Janmohammed, "African Labourers in Mombasa, c. 1895–1940," in *Hadith 5: Economic and Social History in East Africa*, ed. Bethwell Ogot (Nairobi, 1976), 173–74.

[38] Interview with FM, Kidaya–Ngerenyi/Chawia, 12/5/1988.

[39] Interviews with SM, Kidaya–Ngerenyi/Chawia, 25/4/1988; MM, Nyolo/Bura, 15/8/1988; and RM, Wundanyi/Werugha, 13/8/1988.

dairy owner, he helped others from his neighborhood find work there, too; and dairy owners apparently encouraged the networks.[40] Among both the educated and uneducated, however, Taita–wide networks of job finding developed. When mission–educated youths from the Hills were hired at the Mombasa post office, they helped to secure positions for schoolmates, who often came from different neighborhoods in the Hills.[41] Unskilled workers, following neighborhood–based networks, sometimes found in Mombasa that others in the Hills might help them, too:

> [X] of Mwajele, [the speaker's neighborhood, in Werugha], had gone to Mombasa before me. So I went to stay with him. . . . While we were drinking beer, [a] man from Sechu, [in Chawia location], who worked as a deputy foreman for Mombasa Municipality, came in. He asked me if I was looking for a job, and I replied yes. So I gave him my *kipande* [work identification card], and the next day I went in, and he told the clerk there he wanted a brother of his from Taita to have a job. So I started working that same day.[42]

World War I intensified migratory labor's *de facto* promotion of intra–Taita intermixing. Officials began conscripting Africans for war work that quickly earned a horrific reputation. To shield themselves from conscription drives in the reserves, young men scrambled for urban jobs and stayed at them longer.[43] As a result, ever larger numbers of men from across Taita kept each other's company in Mombasa for ever longer stretches of time. Those caught up in the maw of war work also had an increasingly intra–Taita experience of it.[44] Most did railway construction work in Kenya and (after its capture) northeastern Tanganyika.[45] In the construction camps at Mombasa, young men who twenty years earlier would have fought or avoided each other now worked, ate, and slept cheek–by–jowl, mixing together in part because they were pushed together, but also on the basis of perceived commonalities.

---

[40] Dairy workers mainly came from neighborhoods around what is now Kishamba/Chawia, and Wundanyi/Werugha. WM, Wundanyi/Werugha, 6/5/1988 made this explicit, and it subsequently became an evident pattern in the overall body of interviews. On dairy owners and labor networks, interview with SM, Kidaya–Ngerenyi/Chawia, 10/5/1988.

[41] Interview with JM, Wundanyi/Werugha, 12/8/1988.

[42] Interview with PM, Wundanyi/Werugha, 23/4/1988.

[43] The prolonged absences had an immediate cost: the combination of men's war conscription and increased migration further increased women's work burdens, and caused a precipitous fall in agricultural production. Food shortages hit in 1916, and did not end until after the war. KNA, PC/Cst/1/22/32, and PC/Cst 1/1/265, DC's Safari Reports, 1916–17.
On the war's impact on Kenya's labor patterns, see John Overton, "War and Economic Development: Settlers in Kenya, 1914–1918," *Journal of African History* 27, 1 (1986): 88. On Taita men's work patterns during the war, interview with OK, Shigaro/Werugha, 2/8/1993.

[44] Of 137 people interviewed in 1988, 128 were asked about labor in World War I. One hundred eighteen had a relative conscripted and/or were conscripted themselves.

[45] Taita's DCs largely shielded local youths from the war's notorious Carrier Corps, telling the central government that Taita youths were well–suited to railroad building, and should not be "wasted on mere load carrying." KNA, PC/Cst/1/12/132, Taita Military Porters.

In the absence of warrior bands, labor migrants' workplaces and living spaces became sites of young men's association. Personal ties formed that transcended neighborhood boundaries, and often survived the return to the Hills: "[X] lived down near Mwatate, we were friends in Mombasa during the German War. Did he leave me behind when we reached here [i.e., Taita]? No!"[46] Those ties could now be maintained at dances like the culturally broadened *Gonda*. In the longer run, the relationships helped to establish new networks across the Hills for young men, which for some became significant ties of exchange and mutuality in later years. Clearly, the experiences of labor migrancy gave Taita's young men a fuller appreciation of their commonalities, and facilitated pan–Taita connections. And though this aspect of Taita community owed little to older men's assertion of the identity, the two versions partially complemented one another.

Women's Networks and New Bonds of Ethnicity

Because most women in Taita in the early 1900s did not do migratory labor, they could not develop analogous work networks. However, through new kinds of intra–Taita interactions across neighborhood boundaries, women also began to build broader social networks and relationships. Those ties, combined with the discourse of ethnic belonging and propriety in which they participated, gave Taita identity resonance to younger and older women.

One of the main places for younger women from different neighborhoods to meet was at socially broadened dances like *Gonda*. Married women often went with their husbands or, in the husbands' absence, other members of his small lineage. Unmarried women went in groups, escorted by men from their neighborhood.[47] At the fringes of the *Gonda* dance grounds, some young men and women courted chastely (in pairs that almost invariably involved people from the same neighborhood). Virtually all other activities, including the dancing itself, were segregated by sex—even slight touches between a man and a woman daringly expressed a twosome's interest in one another.[48]

Women from different parts of Taita spent most of a *Gonda* in each other's company. They danced together, learned steps from each other, and the older ones told unmarried companions stories of married life. Married women also talked among themselves, trading stories and gossip. They were able to form ongoing connections, for they could meet again and again at dances in different neighborhoods.

> I know women from all over Chawia, . . . [and] around Wundanyi, to Kese [Werugha], and to Lushangonyi. . . . We just met at *Gonda*, "how

---

[46] Interview with DM, Mlondo/Werugha, 28/9/1988.

[47] Interviews with Mrs. GM, Shigaro/Werugha, 15/7/1988; Mrs. PN, Mlondo/Werugha, 26/9/1988; and PM, Wundanyi/Werugha, 13/8/1988.

[48] *Gonda* was danced in circles, with separate ones for men and women. Interviews with Mrs. CM, Shigaro/Werugha, 26/7/1993; DM, Teri/Sagalla, 10/7/1993; and SM, Wusi/Chawia, 29/7/1993.

are you since last time?" "how is your husband?" "you have had rain?" "I have a good story for you." Like that.[49]

Built into these encounters were important building blocks for an appreciation of shared ways: to dance together and exchange stories and knowledge helped them feel they understood one another. They could keep up relationships across time—and the relationships might prove useful in other contexts.

The development of exchange networks across neighborhood boundaries provided one such context, as well as another significant area for building up mutual understanding and interconnections. In the first decades of the century, freer movement across the Hills, combined with more hungry mouths in the area (railway staff, government staff, sisal plantation workers), spurred considerable growth in Taita's market networks. Women to a very large extent brokered the expanding local food trade.[50] This made eminent sense: women did most of the farming and food management, and so had the best knowledge of how much of a given season's crop was surplus. They were also more available for marketing; younger men often had distant wage work, and most older men gladly passed on the task—though they insisted on controlling the earnings.[51]

Women bought, sold, and exchanged food at markets established around the Hills during these decades. Typically, mature women conducted the trade, with daughters–in–law or children in tow to help carry goods. The markets fostered more than that day's trade; they became lively social centers for exchanging information, planning longer–term sales and purchases, and building up face–to–face relationships:

Mrs. RM: I got cowpeas at the market. . . . "Hee, mama [X], are your cowpeas good this year?" "Hee, there will be many."

Q: So you knew mama [X]?

Mrs. RM: Very much! We sat at the market for many years, we must know each other! . . . I saw her children grow.[52]

Women's interneighborhood connections rarely had the daily reinforcement that young men gained through migratory life in Mombasa, and did not necessarily take place in an explicit idiom of shared Taita identity or Taita ways. Nevertheless, the ties fostered an enlarged sense of interconnectedness and shared understanding across the Hills. Prior lineage and neighborhood ways had limited the breadth of women's networks to their immediate locales. Now, wider webs of relationships grew, mediated by freer movement and institutions of Taita commonality, *Gonda*, and Taita–wide involvement in markets.

[49] Interview with Mrs. MJ, Shigaro/Werugha, 26/7/1993.
[50] Interview with Mrs. RM, Chawia/Chawia, 17/6/1988.
[51] Ibid.; also, interviews with Mrs. MK, Nyolo/Bura, 15/8/1988; and NM, Wundanyi/Werugha, 28/7/1993.
[52] Interview with Mrs. RM, Chawia/Chawia, 17/6/1988.

Photo 3.   Market scene, 1920s Dabida. Margaret Murray Photo Collection, courtesy of Kenya National Archives and Documentation Service. #170/81.

When combined with reworkings of neighborhood and lineage ways into Taita ones, and with the burgeoning discourse of proper ethnic ways, these interconnections helped render Taita identity self–evidently real.

Cultural Politics and Taita Ethnicity, to the 1920s

Older men in the early twentieth century consistently emphasized *Kidaßida* over birthright in their view of Taita identity. This had a historical logic, for many outsiders had been folded into lineages and neighborhoods across the Hills in preceding centuries. Seniors' normative claims about *Kidaßida*, however self–serving, also built upon historical roots: their construals of proper Taita ways drew heavily on neighborhood and lineage ways that had naturalized their power. But *Kidaßida* had contemporary instrumental components, as well. As older men's prior predominance came in for subtle underminings and direct assaults, they crafted a discourse of proper Taita ways to try to rebuild that power—and older women and younger men sometimes allied with older men in those struggles.

The idiom of Taita identity and Taita ways increasingly mediated cultural politicking over the terms of the social order. Many of the struggles predated the rise of Taita identity, but in the 1910s and 1920s, ethnicity recast them. This cultural politicking had several arenas. In formal politics, older men, often with the support of women and younger men, tried to use "Taita" institutions and the discourse of Taita ways to rein in colonial chiefs. Within lineages, older people struggled to retain control over younger men and women. Tied into this was the related struggle over the terms of wealth, between those who argued that proper Taita wealth was livestock, and those increasingly drawn to money. Intense cultural politicking also swirled around the fundamentality of *Wutasi* to Taita identity—and, indeed, to the spiritual well–being of society. Here, *Wutasi* followers of all ages opposed Christian rejections of *Wutasi* and the religious bases of elders' predominance.

Taita Ways, "Taita" Institutions, and Colonial Chiefs

Colonial rule at once weakened the political authority of elders and afforded them ways to reclaim sway. Chiefship undercut elders' authority by giving young, often Christian men, positions of extraordinary day–to–day power, but colonial officials also respected the realm of African "traditions," and sought to uphold "traditional authority" and "traditional society." The latter stance gave older men some leverage with the state, and they tried to use state–run "traditional institutions" as a check on chiefly authority. Outside those institutions, they continued to hold that proper Taita authority was vested in age, wealth, networks, and accrued wisdom—an argument widely popular with people seeking to limit chiefs' predations and interferences in their daily lives.

The most important "traditional" Taita institution through which older men sought to check the power of chiefs was the Councils of Elders that began in 1911. In the Councils, older men easily assumed the mantle of Taita tradition that officials reflexively cloaked them in. A 1916 official may not have realized the full aptness of his comment when he wrote, "The councils are meeting with regularity, and . . . the Elders are growing to appreciate the advantages of the system."[53] These fora invented Taita traditions and codified them into Taita Native Law, by conflating lineage and neighborhood ways into Taita ways— though different lineage practices sometimes tied Councils up in long disputes over the proper Taita way to deal with a crime or dispute.[54]

Throughout the 1910s, older men tried to use the Councils to leverage some formal control over chiefs. In 1913–14, the Councils exceeded their judicial mandate to promulgate orders for tax collection and communal labor; the DC supported this, pleased to see the elders take on new administrative responsibilities.[55] The Councils did not choose their new task randomly: they were responding to

---

[53] KNA, DC/TTA/3/3, Political Record Books, Native Organization, 1916; also, PC/Cst/1/13/72, wherein the Provincial Commissioner praised the Councils in a memo to the Chief Secretary, 13/4/1915.

[54] Interviews with JM, Mlondo/Werugha, 28/9/1988; and GM, Kishamba/Chawia, 27/6/1988. The District Annual Report of 1921 described the Councils as mostly inefficient and disputatious. KNA, DC/TTA/1/1.

[55] KNA, DC/TTA/3/3, Political Record Books, Native Organization, 1916.

chiefs' notorious abuses of their powers of taxation and communal labor. Some chiefs tried to fight the Councils on the matter, but to little effect:

> When our Council of Elders started to have meetings before the German War, Mwanjila [the chief of Bura] tried to tell them . . . do this and that, and they really disliked him. . . . So they made plans behind him, and then he opposed them in the meetings. . . . When the war came to Taita, the whites removed him, they said he helped the Germans. . . . And the elders were pleased that the whites did not trust him. . . . After the war he came back again . . . but he lost his strength.[56]

Chiefs also tried a different tack, telling officials that elders bought their Council seats and abused their powers to enrich themselves—a striking redeployment of popular complaints against chiefs. Officials' investigation of the charges gave chiefs no satisfaction. The provincial commissioner convened a meeting of the Chawia Council of Elders, to probe for potential corruptions of "Taita traditions." When he asked how the Council chose its members, the recorded reply was:

> *Elders:* Clever people are selected.
>
> *PC:* Why do the Elders pay for entrance into the [Council] at Mbale and Bura, where I am told they pay, and you do not?
>
> *Elders:* [The story] is not true.
>
> *PC:* I do not desire to alter your ancient institutions.
>
> *Elders:* We select suitable persons for election.
>
> *PC:* Very well, it is your business.[57]

This, combined with the Council's denial of the corruption charge, placated the authorities. Elders' Councils scaled back to purely juridical institutions during World War I, but their ability to withstand chiefs' pressures endured: "The Elders . . . when they continued their work . . . they could not be objected to by the chief. . . . No, they would do the work [as] they liked."[58]

Older men also construed chiefs as interlopers who violated Taita ways by trying to assume authority not due to them. This argument reverberated widely among people within the Hills, finding a ready audience among people angered by chiefs' abuses:

> The chiefs started when I was already a woman. . . . People were not happy with chiefs, they asked, "why do they bring us leaders who disturb us?"[59]

---

[56] Interview with MM, Nyolo/Bura, 15/8/1988. For Mwanjila's removal and subsequent reinstatement, see KNA, DC/TTA/3/3/2, War Diary, 21/9/1914; and DC/TTA/3/3, Political Record Book, Headmen 1913–14 and Native Administration 1919–20.

[57] KNA, DC/TTA/3/1, Political Record Books, Barazas, 21/7/1913.

[58] Interview with MM, Nyolo/Bura, 15/8/1988.

[59] Interview with Mrs. FM, Lushangonyi/Mwanda, 21/9/1988.

People really feared those early chiefs a lot. If you crossed them, you could end up right in their jails, . . . they used them as personal jails of their own. You made a mistake, you were brought to jail, and you will end up working on [the first chief of Chawia's] farm for that week. Even my father sometimes dug for him that way.[60]

The lack of a prior social base for anything resembling chiefly authority exacerbated popular dissatisfaction, underlining how chiefly power was imposed from without. Powerful older men, the people least intimidated by chiefs, chastised them on those grounds. Elders, steeped in age, wealth, networks, ritual position, and hence, wisdom, sometimes treated the early chiefs as virtual children full of hubris and presumption:

My father complained often about that chief. Aii! He said, "that one is nothing, he has no knowledge of anything. He is just lost." . . . He called him Little White Man. . . . He was not afraid of him, when he passed he greeted him as a child.[61]

Younger men and women, more vulnerable to chiefs, rarely said things to chiefs that might get them clapped in jail or assigned compulsory labor tasks. But "young people agreed with what the old men said."[62]

Chiefs felt the pressures keenly. Some, like Thomas of Mbale, had the willfulness and/or prior wealth and prestige to withstand it. But the older men's accusations and contempt, and popular support for the older men's position, wore down or intimidated others. Young chiefs hoped to be elders themselves one day—even Christian chiefs hoped for influence and respect in old age. But the discourse of Taita propriety not only jeopardized that prospect, it circulated the idea that chiefs who supported colonial rules too vigorously or who over–applied or abused their authority were lost from Taita ways. This fate did befall some chiefs: Mwanjila lost most of his authority and respect within Bura, took to drinking prodigiously, was deposed by the government in 1920, and became socially isolated thereafter.[63] The first chief of Chawia location did not get drummed out of power, but failed to attain the prominence and respectability he sought after he retired.[64]

Applying ideas of Taita propriety as a check on chiefs largely proved a successful cultural political move for old men and their supporters. By the 1920s, most chiefs, not wanting to be outcasts in their local communities, treaded lightly around elders. They often conspicuously consulted and re-

---

[60] Interview with JM, Kishamba/Chawia, 24/9/1988. Dozens of other cases could be cited, for comments about chiefs' abuses ran through many interviews.

[61] Interview with GM, Kishamba/Chawia, 24/9/1988.

[62] Ibid.; also, interviews with RM, Njawuli/Mwanda, 3/8/1993, and Mrs. MM, Ilole/Bura, 16/8/1988.

[63] Interviews with NK, Wumari/Chawia, 15/8/1988; CA, Ilole/Bura, 1988; and SM, Mrugua/Bura, 19/8/1988.

[64] Interviews with JM, Wusi/Chawia, 5/4/1988 and 22/7/1993.

spected the most influential older men, saving their more heavy–handed behavior for younger men and women.[65] Most chiefs also enforced certain colonial rules—especially rules that might upset elders—more laxly than officials wanted. The chiefs of this era, when compelled to choose between Taita propriety and being seen as strong chiefs, often tilted, piecemeal and quietly, toward conforming in greater or lesser part with *Kidaßida*.

Work and Wealth: Parental Authority, *Kidaßida*, and Livestock through the 1920s

The most central *Kidaßida* axioms about parents, children, work, and wealth went as follows: proper Taita sons turned over wages to their parents; proper Taita daughters–in–law dutifully and respectfully did the work their parents–in–law expected; proper Taita sons did not pass a father's wealth in the father's lifetime; and proper Taita wealth was livestock. The leitmotif running through these axioms was the authority of the old over the young. To varying degrees, each occasioned struggles before 1930. Overall, though, parental control over adult children mostly remained firm into the early 1930s. The colonial political economy weakened older people's direct authority over the young, but discourses and sanctions of ethnic propriety provided ways to compensate for it.

Kidaßida lacked the sheer compulsory power over the young that nineteenth–century lineages exercised, but it was no mere facade. While Taita ethnicity partly bespoke an inclusive, sociohistorical identity, the prospect of being lost from *Kidaßida* raised fears of reduced rights, alienation from networks, disinheritance, and ostracism. Taita ethnicity therefore operated not only as a positive cultural identification, but as a force of control. Older men further braced *Kidaßida* by successfully reconfiguring livestock–as–wealth into proper Taita wealth. Their general control over money kept slipping throughout the 1920s, but livestock remained critical to marriage, *Wutasi* rituals, and networks of alliance and mutual support that delineated social prestige and influence in the Hills. Older men upheld their control over livestock, and could still hold livestock (and land) inheritance over sons' (and, indirectly, daughters–in–law's) heads. These resources gave parents a critical lever of power over their adult children.

The previous chapter discussed how older men established the axiom of sons turning over migrant labor wages to them, enabling older men to expand their herds throughout the 1910s and into the 1920s. In the latter decade this arrangement largely held up, but came under new strains. One strain derived from the attempts by older men to further milk the livestock economy. The early century *Kidaßida* work understanding held that fathers would provide bridewealth livestock and related goods to sons who had

---

[65] Ibid.; and interview with OK, Shigaro/Werugha, 2/8/1993.

dutifully remitted wages.[66] Bridewealth was *not*, however, to come from animals that the sons' wages purchased. Livestock that sons' wages bought was often earmarked as "for them," which the sons took to mean that the animals would accrue to them eventually, despite present placement in their fathers' herds. In this ambiguous arrangement, fathers were not supposed to exchange or use them without consulting the sons, but neither could the sons remove animals from the fathers' herds for independent use.[67]

In the 1920s, some fathers began to use livestock bought with their sons' remitted wages as bridewealth animals. It was a significant shift: in the 1900s and 1910s, sons' wage work had been rewarded with bridewealth from fathers' herds. Now, instead of having their labors acknowledged by the gift of animals, some sons worked for their bridewealth in the most direct sense.[68] A few fathers compounded this by expecting sons to meet other costs of marriage out of their wages:

> [My father] told me he would not help me with money for marrying, but he would donate goats and cows for my wedding and the money was for me [to get]. . . . So I tried and tried, and put money aside, and finally I collected [it]. . . . It was a lot. . . . My father was not poor, . . . but the money was for me [to get].[69]

To unmarried sons, these changes in bridewealth mixed the signals of migrant labor: competing with its construction as a Taita obligation to parents, an emerging view saw it as how to pay for one's marriage. In the 1920s and early 1930s, many sons made this a reason for limiting the money sent back to their fathers. If sons had to bear much of their marriage costs themselves, they would themselves save for it:

> I sent . . . money back to Taita, but I remained with some little money there [in Mombasa]. . . . I came back with it to make arrangements for getting married. . . . If you don't . . . keep money for the wedding, how will you marry?[70]

---

[66] In addition to cows and goats, bridewealth payments often included foodstuffs, *chofi*, cloth, and household goods. Interviews with SK, Chawia/Chawia, 28/5/1988; Mrs. RM, Chawia/Chawia, 16/6/1988; and Mrs. GM, Ghazi/Mbololo, 4/7/1988. Many other interviews could be cited.

[67] "[The cattle bought by a father with a son's wages] are yours, but they are his, also. . . . You get them when he dies." Interview with JM, Wundanyi/Werugha, 12/5/1988; also KM, Werugha/Werugha, 3/10/1988; and OM, Wundanyi/Werugha, 5/5/1988.

[68] Interviews with AM, Wusi/Chawia, 28/4/1988; and MW, Ghazi/Mbololo, 5/7/1988. According to JM, Wundanyi/Werugha, 17/4/1988, many fathers scrupulously used their own animals for paying bridewealth.

[69] Interview with RM, Kaya/Chawia, 4/5/1988; it took him several years to save enough money for the marriage. Also, AM, Shigaro/Werugha, 25/4/1988. Some men, like PM, Wundanyi/Werugha, 23/4/1988, arranged for fathers to put a portion of remitted money aside for wedding costs.

[70] Interview with SM, Wundanyi/Werugha, 15/4/1988.

Sons did not always scrupulously salt away the money they held back, some-times using it instead to drink and womanize in Mombasa: "I kept money [in Mombasa] for my wedding, . . . [but] it took a long time to save enough money. It was eaten by city life."[71] But regardless of how they actually spent it, unmar-ried sons now had justifications for keeping a larger share of their earnings.

A second strain on the axiom of sons giving over their wealth to their par-ents arose as young men from the Hills earned increasingly higher wages by the late 1920s, and increasingly wanted to spend money on themselves (or, if married, their households). The causal relationship between this and the changes in fathers' views on bridewealth in the 1920s is not clear from my research: fathers' bridewealth parsimony may have prompted young men to want to keep more income. Alternatively some fathers may have punished sons who reduced remittances by spending less on the sons' marriages. However it oper-ated, the two were very likely intertwined.

Taita migrants' ability to garner relatively high wages stemmed from their reputation as good workers.[72] Unskilled workers still congregated around dairies, Mombasa's Public Works Department, and casual labor at the Mombasa docks. This latter work in good months earned a young man upwards of 90/= per month, while dairy workers in the 1920s usually started at 15/=, and after a few years with the same employer rose to 30/= or more.[73] Skilled and supervisory workers often earned 80/= to 100/=, and clerical workers and teachers usually began at 30/= or more, with their salaries rising the longer they kept the same job.[74] Though paltry pay levels next to whites' salaries in Kenya, these incomes put many Taita laborers on the higher rungs of the African wage ladder.

As wages rose and fathers reduced what single sons could expect to even-tually recoup from their remittances, young men in the 1920s retained more and more of their wages. Most still sent the greater part to their fathers, but single men now "put aside" some for marrying, and spent more on the clothes, occasional luxuries, and recreation that made urban life more enjoyable or tol-

---

[71]   Interview with JM, Wundanyi/Werugha, 12/8/1988; also NK, Mwatate/Chawia, 15/8/1988.
    Officials often commented about sons dissipating their earnings. The 1924 DC noted that young men were "very fond of going to Mombasa in search of work. . . . A large number stay [there] without permanent employment, but loaf and get into bad habits." KNA, DC/TTA/1/1, Taita Dis-trict Annual Report for 1924. By 1930, complaints from chiefs and elders about "the number of young Taita men who migrated to Mombasa and were doing no good there" were filtering back to the LNC. PC/Cst/1/12/288, Local Native Council minutes, 29/10/1930.

[72]   That reputation, established in the 1910s, endured into the 1920s: the 1923 DC said that because of their good name "they have no difficulty in getting higher wages." KNA, SC/TTA/3/3, Political Record Books, Labor Supply.

[73]   On *kibarua* earnings, interview with JM, Wundanyi/Werugha, 11/5/1988. On dairy workers' earnings, interview with PM, Wundanyi/Werugha, 13/8/1988.

[74]   For skilled workers, interviews with PM, Ilole/Bura, 16/8/1988 (carpentry); and PM, Wundanyi/ Werugha, 23/4/1988 (night watchmen's foreman); for teachers, AM, Shigaro/Werugha, 2/5/1988; Mrs. GM, Shigaro/Werugha, 27/5/1988; and SM, Wusi/Chawia, 29/6/1988. For clerical workers, SM, Wusi/Chawia, 9/4/1988, WM, Shigaro/Werugha, 18/4/1988, and DM, Mbale/Mbale, 7/11/ 1988.

erable.[75] In the 1920s, too, married men increasingly sent part of their wages directly to their wives. Wives used the money to purchase clothes for themselves and their children, to buy certain household items and foodstuffs, and sometimes to pay the newly instituted school fees of their children. Many women also began to pay their household's Hut Tax themselves; in their husbands' absence, wives now sometimes acted as the effective economic head of their households.[76]

Older men and women, by no means sanguine about these changes, tried to roll back or contain them. Many older men continued to use their own animals for their sons' bridewealth, and expected sons to keep to their axiomatic role of remitting most of their wages to fathers:

> *LM:* Yes, my father provided my bridewealth.
>
> *Q:* All of it?
>
> *LM:* All of it. . . . When I began to work, he said "you will do this for us, and I will make your marriage." . . . That is how Taitas did this thing then.[77]

Through the 1920s, the preponderance of sons continued to send the bulk of their wages to parents.[78] Partly, sons still accepted the arrangement—and now respected it as a proper Taita way. Fear of being considered lost also motivated some, for older men were willing (though reluctant) to label them as such. In 1930, when the DC suggested that young men from the Hills who had settled permanently in Mombasa be repatriated, many older men coolly responded that the men could stay away forever, but should pay taxes themselves in Mombasa and no longer burden their parents.[79] Partly, too, most young men in the 1920s still considered livestock the best Taita wealth (a topic discussed just below), and expected that by handing over money now they would eventually inherit herds and networks from their fathers.

Wives who received remittances directly from their husbands usually got a much smaller share than did the men's fathers.[80] Still, tensions between a

---

[75] Interviews with JM, Wundanyi/Werugha, 12/8/1988; and JM, Teri/Sagalla, 9/7/1993; see also DC/TTA/1/1, Taita District Annual Report for 1926.

[76] Interviews with WM, Werugha/Werugha/3/10/1988; Mrs. DM, Shigaro/Werugha, 30/5/1988; KM, Werugha/Werugha, 3/10/1988; and Mrs. KM, Mogho Mleche/Mbale, 4/11/1988. In the late 1920s, primary schools initiated a fee of 3/= per term. See 1938 Annual Letter of Peter Bostock (papers privately held).

[77] Interview with LM, Mrugua/Bura, 18/8/1988.

[78] Interviews with MR, Tausa/Mbololo, 31/5/1988; JM, Teri/Chawia, 5/8/1988; and JN, Mbale/Mbale, 8/11/1988.

[79] PC/Cst/1/12/288, Local Native Council, meetings of 29/10/1930, and 22/12/1930. The Council pointedly refused to spend money for repatriating the men.

[80] "Yes, my husband sent me money . . . for sugar and tea . . . and cloth. . . . Not very much." Interview with Mrs. SM, Mogho Mleche/Mbale, 4/11/1988. She went on to describe this as typical of what women received directly in that era. Also, interviews with SM, Wusi/Chawia, 9/4/1988; and Mrs. AM, Ndome/Mbololo, 20/6/1988.

wife and her parents–in–law could arise from the mere fact of her share. Some mothers–in–law suggested that the young women were divisive, spoiled, and did not care about proper Taita ways. The tensions could be compounded if the older people felt their daughter–in–law did not work enough for them.

> It was hard to please my mother [–in–law] when I was young. A lot of work! I . . . tried to make her happy, but she said I was just spoiled . . . because I had money from my husband and I went to school. . . . [She said] I was spoiled with freedom and white ways and I could not do anything.[81]

When parents–in–law objected strenuously to the younger wives' remittances and work patterns, the young women usually thought it best to avoid direct confrontations with them, try to be as helpful as they could manage, and hope the parents would eventually recognize their efforts and the difficulties of their situation: "When they said [critical things about me], I just remained quiet. . . . I helped them and showed I was a good daughter."[82]

Almost all young wives in Taita in the 1910s–20s *did* try to keep up with obligations to their parents–in–law. Most made work in their in–laws' fields and household a high priority, along with communal labor in the work group associated with the mother–in–law.[83] If they could not help a parent–in–law with a task themselves, women with preteen or adolescent children often sent one of them to help. A few young wives even used part of their husbands' remittances to hire day laborers for the wives' fields, while the wives went themselves to help their in–laws.[84]

In the 1920s and early 1930s, young wives' juggling of cash needs and parental demands strained their in–laws' expectations, but did not lead to widespread confrontations or broad societal adjustments. Parents–in–law did often remind their daughters–in–law about Taita propriety: "[my father-in-law] said for my husband to send me money was not *Kidaßida*, and for me to have money apart from the old people was not *Kidaßida*."[85] However, I know of no case of a woman in the Hills coming to be seen as lost on these grounds. Both remittances and work would come in for extensive reworking in the later 1930s and 1940s—when the young of the early colonial period had themselves become the older generation.

The Ways of Wealth: Money and Livestock

The period of the 1900s and 1910s was the high–water mark for older men's reconstruction of the livestock economy in Taita. In that era, money became

---

[81] Interview with Mrs. FM, Lushangonyi/Mwanda, 21/9/1988. In later years, their relationship improved.

[82] Interview with Mrs. MM, Lushangonyi/Mwanda, 21/9/1988.

[83] Interviews with Mrs. FM, Lushangonyi/Mwanda, 21/9/1988; Mrs. AM, Ndome/Mbololo, 20/6/1988; and Mrs. PN, Mwanda/Mwanda, 3/8/1993.

[84] Interviews with Mrs. SM, Werugha/Werugha, 30/9/1988; Mrs. DM, Shigaro/Werugha, 30/5/1988; Mrs. PN, Mwanda/Mwanda, 3/8/1993; and Mrs. NK, Nyolo/Bura, 15/8/1988.

[85] Interview with Mrs. MM, Lushangonyi/Mwanda, 21/9/1988.

integral to livestock–as–wealth, for sons' wages provided the main means for older men to increase livestock purchases. World War I, though stressful in other ways, illuminates how the system had worked for seniors: they used sons' remitted wages from war work to buy animals seized in Tanganyika at government auctions.[86] By the mid–1920s, however, strains in the system started to show. Money circulated widely, younger men remained Taita's main generators of it, and they spent ever larger portions of it on themselves and their own households. Young men with relatively high salaries might even have more prosperous households, in terms of cash and consumer goods, than many older people.

Older men in the 1920s became increasingly concerned not only with controlling wealth, but also with controlling what counted as wealth. Some young married men in this era, continuously involved with money since childhood, were less prone than their seniors to see it mainly as a means to livestock ends:

> Our fathers understood money, yes . . . [but] we were really raised with money. We liked it better than our fathers did! We knew that money could be sweet! (laughs) . . . The fathers liked cows and goats: "a goat will give milk and it just stays, will money give milk and stay?" (laughs) "But father, I can bring more money." . . . In that way we were different.[87]

Missionaries promoted this change by encouraging the young in their orbit to partake more fully in the money economy. The mission schools taught literacy, numeracy, and crafts that would turn young men into high–wage workers and give young women skills for a monetized household economy. Parents who initially sent children to mission schools generally did so for religious reasons, but those children often emerged from school with an altered economic sensibility. There, "the Europeans made us understand about money and the good it could bring us."[88]

Older men addressed this situation with an axiom of *Kidaßida*: money was not a terrible thing, but proper Taita wealth was wealth in animals.[89] This did not simply reflect preference; older men understood the socioeconomic bases of their predominance and applied ideological and material leverage to defend it. Livestock operated as wealth to them partly through the intrinsic value of herds that could be worked for their resources. More importantly, however, older men put the animals to social uses: plentiful livestock fueled animal loans and exchanges, thereby building wider ties of patronage and mutuality. Those networks provided prestige

---

[86] Interviews with JM, Wongonyi/Mbololo, 7/7/1988; and GM, Mgange Nyika/Mwanda, 20/9/1988; see also KNA, PC/Cst/1/22/32, DC's Safari Reports from 1916.

[87] Interview with SM, Tausa/Mbololo, 3/6/1988.

[88] Though education led many WaTaita deeper into the money economy, this speaker overstated her point. Nineteenth–century traders with the coast learned of and handled money. Later, taxation, labor migration, and commodity inflow drew many into some engagement with money and capitalism well before the spread of mission education. Interview with Mrs. SM, Mogho Mleche/Mbale, 4/11/1988.

[89] This axiom was mentioned in scores of interviews, among both men and women.

and support in various public and private settings; they were vehicles for becoming well respected, well connected, and, ultimately, an elder.[90]

Young men's increasing respect for money posed a problem, for their potential opting out of livestock–as–wealth threatened the older men's system of predominance. Older men stepped in to try to prevent this from happening, and to shore up the supporting values they thought most critical:

> To have standing and respect . . . you needed cows. . . . No, money could not do it. [Would] people trust you because you had money? No! Money, that is a European thing, for Taita elders money had no respect. . . . If you have cows, . . . [then] you have age, . . . [and] surely you know many things. . . . When you have cows, . . . [you and other people] know each other.[91]

They associated livestock–as–wealth with social elements crucial to being Taita: knowledge (i.e., knowledge of *Kidaßida*), and knowing one another—a key basis of Taita community.

Older men enforced their association of livestock–as–wealth with *Kidaßida* in several ways. They highlighted the historical weight behind the construction: livestock–as–wealth had operated within the Hills' lineages for over a century. Networks of alliance and patronage had developed and endured around livestock, passed along (with inevitable modifications) through multiple generations. Settling long–term debts implied dismantling one's social networks, an isolating act that would certainly translate to lost prestige and lost support in political or jural encounters, in times of famine, illness, or other hardship.

The association of animals with wealth in the Hills lost its deeply naturalized quality by the 1920s; still, though demoted to ideology by becoming explicit, it remained widely agreed–upon, with many reinforcing cultural trappings drawn from lineage discourses and practices. Fathers also had material levers for ensuring continued acceptance of livestock–as–wealth. Inheritance counted heavily here: sons who drifted too far from the livestock economy might not be considered lost, but almost certainly reduced their inheritance prospects.[92] Reduced inheritance applied not only to a father's livestock, but, more importantly for many sons, to land. Some cash sales of land took place within a lineage or neighborhood, but most men received much of their land through inheritance.[93] Reduced inheritance also carried with it a measure of social stigma.[94] Under these circumstances, the views of older men carried the day. Livestock was acknowledged as the most Taita, most respectable form of wealth.

---

[90]   Interviews with OK, Shigaro/Werugha, 2/8/1993; and LM, Kizumanzi/Sagalla, 21/7/1993. Many others agreed.

[91]   Interview with MM, Ilole/Bura, 17/8/1988.

[92]   Interviews with GM, Kishamba/Chawia, 12/8/1988, and DM, Werugha/Werugha, 29/9/1988.

[93]   The importance of inheritance for receiving land was commonplace among men interviewed, including SK, Chawia/Chawia, 28/5/1988; SM, Wusi/Chawia, 29/6/1988; and LM, Teri/Sagalla, 27/6/1988.

[94]   "When a man lost his inheritance, people knew about it. . . . They spoke [badly] about him." Interview with Mrs. MM, Lushangonyi/Mwanda, 21/9/1988.

Christian Evangelism, Wutasi, and *Kidaßida*

Christianity slowly but steadily gained adherents in the 1910s and 1920s in Taita. By 1920, Christians numbered 1,367 (4.5 percent of a population estimated at 30,000): a tiny minority, but a growing one.[95] As Christianity spread, it established itself as a competitor for people's spiritual and ritual loyalties. Especially in Anglican circles, Christianity's claim to exclusive divine truth compelled more and more people to contemplate rejecting *Wutasi* beliefs and practices. Some did, using metaphors that suggest acceptance of mission ideology:

> The changes really reached here when people started to know about Christianity. . . . [in English] "Now we are people of light, that darkness we don't like." . . . [back to KiSwahili] To fight the darkness we started to learn. We learned to leave behind bad things and immoral things.[96]

Wutasi–following adults of both sexes opposed this, seeing it as socially–divisive and fearing its potential cosmological consequences. As a result, when some older men tried to contain Christian expansion and limit the behavior of Christians through a discourse of proper Taita ways, they received considerable social support.

A combination of institutional weight, evangelical itinerations, mission control over the educational system, and state support aided Christianity's growth. Catholic missionaries in Taita concentrated more on a strong base than on outreach. Bura, their sole mission station, owned 1,000 acres of freehold territory in prime valley bottomland, and the staff used its locale as their main evangelical tool. They sought converts by attracting them to their land and facilities, and did little itinerating.[97] In 1900, an informal division of evangelical territory between the CMS and the Holy Ghost Fathers allotted the Catholics a rather small part of Taita, within which they deemed itineration unnecessary.[98] Bura's impressive church sat within relatively easy reach of almost all the Catholic "sphere," and sizable crowds already came to services.[99]

The CMS made itineration the centerpiece of the Church's growth. Europeans coordinated the evangelizing and sometimes still undertook it. By

---

[95] KNA, DC/TTA/1/1, District Annual Report, 1920. A 1913 report had put the number of Christians at 280. See DC/TTA/3/3/2, Political Record Books.

[96] Interview with BN, Wusi/Chawia, 5/5/1988.

[97] For the Holy Ghost Fathers' general mission strategy, see J. A. Kieran, "Holy Ghost Fathers in East Africa, 1863–1914" (Ph.D. diss., University of London, 1966). Also, interview with MM, Nyolo/Bura.

[98] The French missionaries disliked this border, which they felt shortchanged them. The CMS Bishop of East Africa appears to have thought it up, and it gained official sanction when the EAP's Taita official at that time, Mr. Hope, agreed with it. See Wray's Diaries, CMSA, 30/8 to 8/9/1900, and 7–9/10/1900.

[99] Holy Ghost Fathers, *Bulletins de la Congregation*, Tomes 1–11, describe little itinerating from Bura. Bura's church had great drawing power. It would not have excited attention in a European village, but as Taita's first large European–style structure it made a powerful enough impression that people came from all over the Hills to see it. Interview with PM, Ilole/Bura, 18/8/1988. Bura remained the biggest and most dramatically set church in Taita for decades.

Photo 4. Jonathan Kituri, Werugha, early 1920s. Margaret Murray Photo Collection, courtesy of Kenya National Archives and Documentation Service. #55/81.

the late 1910s, however, CMS itinerations in Taita had assumed a different character: African preachers and teachers carried most of the load of spreading the Anglican gospel to far–flung corners of the Hills. Increasing numbers of a new kind of evangelizer now supplemented the handful of full–time Native Agents: "local people who had discovered something that really was important to them—so important that they had to share it."[100] European tasks shifted toward management of the mission stations.

Paid Native Agents and educated, devout Africans (who often worked for the missions in other capacities) were the evangelical elite, immediately recognizable by their sober, heavy clothes. Western–style dress was common in mid–1920s Taita, but strict Anglicans added a formality and fastidiousness that set them apart. One such person was Jonathan Kituri, born in Werugha/Dabida in the late 1880s and taken to the coast during the famine of the late 1890s. There, in the custody of a CMS mission station, he began schooling and converted to Christianity. Around 1900 he returned as far as Mbale mission, where he continued his education and itinerated.[101] In the late 1900s, he went to the coast for further religious education, coming back to Taita in 1912 as a full–time evangelist, what one missionary referred to as a "quasi–pastor."[102] By the mid–1920s, he was an ordained minister. At that juncture, he returned to his lineage's neighborhood in Werugha, to set up a church and school, and evangelize that part of the Hills.[103]

Most evangelists in the 1920s, though, were unpaid laypeople. These men and women lived some distance from a mission station and had little formal training, but as they came to heartfelt belief in Christianity, they sought to spread the faith in their home communities. In these cases, an evangelist might build up a Christian following and then reach out to a mission, rather than vice versa.

> One of the best places [for conversions], one of the most lively places, was in Mbololo at Ndile.[104] . . . The man there, Albert Mwangeka, had . . . perhaps three years of schooling, at the most. He was probably 45–50 at that time, he could just read, not very easily. . . . But that place flourished because there was real life in him which was not dependent on . . . learning, [but] . . . on spiritual experience. . . . This whole community, the church community, was growing on its own, with its own impetus, with its own initiatives.[105]

---

[100] Interview with Peter Bostock, Oxford, England, 3/4/1989.

[101] Interview with PK, Kigala/Werugha, 6/10/1987.

[102] Ibid., for the biographical information. For the missionary assessment of his standing, Margaret Murray photograph collection, Kenya National Archives, caption of photograph no. 55/81.

[103] Interview with PK, Kigala/Werugha, 6/10/1987. Also CMS Correspondence, G3 A5/L15, Baylis to Wray, 8/3/1901; and Baylis to Wray, 4/4/1902.

[104] Ndile is on the plains at the eastern edge of the Hills. The walk from there to the nearest large mission, Mbale, takes a full, strenuous day.

[105] Interview with Peter Bostock, Oxford, England, 3/4/1989.

Photo 5. Female students, late 1920s. Margaret Murray Photo Collection, courtesy of Kenya National Archives and Documentation Service. #287/81.

An Anglican community arose similarly in Wongonyi, Mbololo in the early 1930s.[106] The first few converts in Wongonyi traveled off the plateau–top locale to Mbale mission (nearly a day's walk), or to small outstation churches at Ghazi or Ndile (closer, but still involving several hours of descent and climb) during the 1920s.[107] In 1933, four Anglican households asked that the CMS establish a church there. CMS missionaries went for several days, built facilities, then left the new operation in the care of two local men. Each had a slight education, and both received minimal stipends for their considerable efforts over the next years.[108] They itinerated extensively around Wongonyi, preaching and teaching a straightforward message about the importance of Christian faith, winning over a good many converts.[109]

---

[106] Wongonyi sub-location sits atop the northeastern–most ridge of Dabida, and has very difficult access.

[107] Interviews with Mrs. EK, Wongonyi/Mbololo, 7/7/1988, and SM, Wongonyi/Mbololo, 6/7/1988.

[108] The main evangelist received 8/= a month, less than a sisal cutter's wages. The second man evangelized and taught without pay until 1935, when he was granted 4/= a month. Interview with DM, Wongonyi/Mbololo, 6/7/1988.

[109] Interviews with Mrs. EK, Wongonyi/Mbololo, 7/7/1988; and JM, Wongonyi/Mbololo, 7/7/1988.

Factors other than faith also supported Christianity's spread in Taita. The material benefits of education also played a part. The CMS's elite converts exemplified what many later converts sought from the missions: well educated in the colonial idiom, their skills and acculturation helped them find good paying jobs in the colonial economy. By the 1920s, some saw Christianity as part of a package that included Western–style education and subsequent economic opportunities. Education was gaining popularity among non–Christians, but available only at mission schools. As a result, an expanding pool of girls and boys was evangelized and converted to Christianity.[110] Few parents or young converts took an unabashedly opportunistic view of Christianity, but many did consider mission education and Christianity part of a milieu that brought with it worldly benefits.[111] Some, initially enamored by Christianity's educational and economic prospects, eventually became profound believers.[112]

Farming out the educational system to the missions was the state's single most important gesture of support for Christianity in Taita, but it helped in other ways, as well. Early in the century, officials had regarded powerful elders like Mghalu as important political figures, and courted older men as significant public and political figures. By the 1920s, however, officials switched their favor to the Christian elite. The re–narrowing of Councils of Elders' duties to jural matters reflected this, as did the 1925 establishment of a Taita Local Native Council (hereafter LNC). The LNC initially included chiefs, the DC, and several men appointed by him to represent native opinion, with a total African membership of ten. A majority of those appointees were Christians, as were the majority of the (also appointed) chiefs.[113]

The supplanting of older men and Elders' Councils by the Christian elite and the LNC indicated that Christian influence was growing at *Wutasi* followers' expense. So, too, did the spread of Christianity to far–flung corners of the Hills. Still, though older *Wutasi* followers were losing political influence with the state by the 1920s, their social influence remained strong. They responded to Christianity by insisting that *Wutasi* and its practices were fundamental aspects of *Kidaßida*—a construction that persisted into the 1950s.[114] Early in the

---

[110] In 1923, Wusi and its satellite schools averaged eighty–six students, Mbale and its satellite schools averaged 208, and Bura and its satellite schools averaged 150. By 1930, the numbers rose to 604 at Mbale schools, and 806 at Bura schools (no overall figures for Wusi were reported). See KNA, DC/TTA/1/1, District Annual Reports of 1923, 1930.

[111] Though this line of argument does not foreclose the former possibility, and some people may have been cynically instrumental about Christianity, nobody I interviewed gave that impression, or spoke of anyone else in those terms.

[112] Typical of these people is one woman sent to school by parents who thought European education good for the skills it taught girls, from literacy to agriculture, and because an educated girl brought parents a better bride–price when she got married. Interview with Mrs. VM, Sagassa/Werugha, 7/10/1988.

Too, a Wongonyi man sent his sons to school because without mission education and Christianity they would end up "down at the [plantations], cutting sisal." Interview with JM, Wongonyi/Mbololo, 9/7/1988.

[113] KNA, DC/TTA/1/1, 1925 Taita District Annual Report.

[114] See G. Harris, *Casting*, Introduction.

century, to not take part in *Wutasi* rituals meant risking being considered lost. In a few parts of Taita, that opprobrium applied:

> The Christian girls did not go there to do *Mwari* [female initiation], no. How could they be adult women without *Mwari*? They could not! . . . The Christians here could only marry each other. Here in Mwanda, who would marry a girl who did not do *Mwari* in those days? Only another Christian. To the others they . . . were not proper Taita women, they were lost. They just had to stay apart, nobody would help them. . . . Those Christian girls were just lost.[115]

By the 1920s, Christians were rarely called lost solely because of religion, but many *Wutasi* followers did use the idea of *Kidaßida* to limit Christian interference in (and compel much Christian accommodation to) *Wutasi* rituals and outlooks. Discursively, people invoked *Kidaßida* to defend *Wutasi* as "our" beliefs against the onslaught of "outside" rejectionism. In everyday actions, this involved spurning the preachings of Christians, resisting the conversions of spouses and children, continuing *Wutasi* rituals, and preventing Christian interruption of them. For a long time, too, it involved pressuring Christians to take part in important rituals of group well–being; here, again, people used the notion of Taita ways to defend the cohesiveness and spiritual health of more local groups.

Most immediately, many people attempted to prevent others from converting. Sometimes one spouse converted because of another, but often, too, one spouse blocked another. A spouse's conversion had implications for her or his partner—all of them, from a *Wutasi* follower's vantage point, adverse. Each spouse had responsibilities in household *Wutasi* practice, and the conversion of one spouse would leave some responsibilities unmet.[116] Social isolation of a Christian spouse would likely affect the partner's life, as well. Usually, then, if one member of a *Wutasi*–following couple became interested in Christianity, either both people converted or, after confrontation or discussion, neither did.[117] Most confrontations involved husbands blocking their wives' conversions. The husband might simply try to refuse to allow it, then turn to physical force or leave the wife.[118]

Many parents also blocked children's conversions. Some parents feared that once they died no one would properly attend to ancestral deities, bringing

---

[115] Interview with Mrs. SM, Mwanda/Mwanda, 14/9/1988.

[116] Grace Harris delineates male and female spheres of religious responsibility throughout *Casting*. In a household with a Christian wife and a polygamous husband, the husband could to some degree get around this problem, because other wives could attend to women's ritual and medicinal responsibilities.

[117] "After I married, my wife and I began to go to religion classes . . . and I got a Christian name. . . . But I made another woman pregnant . . . and agreed to marry her [also]. . . . So we all remained outside." Interview with SM, Tausa/Mbololo, 3/6/1988.

[118] Of thirteen cases in my research where a spouse prevented the other from converting, eleven involved husbands blocking wives. Two such cases were Mrs. FM, Tausa/Mbololo, 21/9/1988, and MM, Nyolo/Bura, 15/8/1988.

misfortune to the lineage. Some, too, worried that children who did not respect *Wutasi* would lose respect for them.[119] In opposing children's conversions, parents resorted to several possible measures. Some were material, such as not dispersing use–rights in property to a child, cutting a child out of mutual and kin support networks, or threatening a son's inheritance. Emotional or psychological expressions of disapproval also had strong effects in Taita's close–knit lineages.[120] The discourse of Taita ways lent itself well to such disapproval:

> I went to school, and my parents did not mind. But when I decided to become a Christian, my father said [that] I must not be defeated by the whites' things, it is better to hold onto Taita ways. "Hold onto those things and you cannot be lost."[121]

If a male parent felt strongly enough on the matter, he might resort to violence:

> After initiation, . . . my daughter . . . wanted to become a Christian. . . . I did not mind, . . . I wanted to go also, I wanted Christianity. . . . Then we were stopped by my husband and his brother near the shops, and they caned her. . . . Then my husband told the sons if they try to get Christianity he will hit them, too. . . . So we all stayed outside Christianity until he died.[122]

Nor did parents necessarily go easier on adult children who had established their own households:

> [My husband's] parents and my parents were very angry at us. So my mother and mother–in–law . . . said to each other they would not help with [care of] my baby. "She cannot leave the baby, so . . . she will stop going to Mbale [mission], . . . she will be overcome." But I went on, just carrying my child with me.[123]

Many parents in the 1920s felt that the best way to prevent younger children from converting was to keep them out of the mission schools. [124] Despite the growing popularity of schools with non–Christians, most children in Taita

---

[119] On the importance of attending to ancestral deities, see G. Harris, *Casting*, 82–85. On parents' concerns about children losing respect for them, interview with NM, Wundanyi/Werugha, 26/5/1988.

[120] "I told my father that I wanted to go to classes . . . and get Christianity, but he was very angry. . . . He said why should I leave our ways to take up the whites' religion. . . . I did not want him to be angry . . . I waited until he died, then I got religion." Interview with JM, Wundanyi/Werugha, 18/7/1988.

[121] Interview with EK, Ndome/Mbololo, 22/6/1988.

[122] Interview with Mrs. FM, Lushangonyi/Mwanda, 21/9/1988.

[123] Interview with Mrs. EK, Wongonyi/Mbololo, 7/7/1988. The walk from Wongonyi to Mbale took half a day. This testifies both to parental pressure and to the daughter's determination. Some parents allowed children to "defect" and choose their own religion once they had their own household. Interview with RM, Wundanyi/Werugha, 29/7/1993.

[124] This was commonplace in interviews, e.g., MT, Kishamba/Chawia, 9/6/1988; and Mrs. HM, Ndome/Mbololo, 22/6/1988. Some young people went anyway, but had to guard their books and papers, to prevent family members from destroying them. Interview with OK, Shigaro/Werugha, 2/8/1993.

did not yet attend one. Many *Wutasi*–following parents and elders had serious misgivings about education. Some parents, and many a grandparent, thought it would "spoil" them, making them lose their understanding of *Kidaßida*:

> In schools . . . the missionaries taught that all [*Wutasi*] things . . . festivals, dances, ceremonies, games, and so on, all those were things of Satan. They said all the old ways were sinful, . . . even when you used knowledge of roots to cure diarrhea, because that was *Kidaßida* knowledge they called it sinful. So that brought . . . problems between . . . education and *Wutasi*.[125]

A young husband's migrant labor could exacerbate tensions between a wife and her in–laws over education, for in his absence his parents might try to override the young couple's decision to school their children.[126]

Apart from the schools, *Wutasi* followers sometimes responded to Christian evangelizing with strong words or deeds. When the above–mentioned Jonathan Kituri returned to his natal neighborhood in the 1920s, people twice pulled down his house.

> Sometimes people chased him away for preaching, they said they didn't want the religion of whites. . . . They used to refuse him, he got problems, and it really took time. When he came here to start teaching they used to just chase him away.[127]

However, when the state enforced the physical toleration of Christians in their midst,[128] *Wutasi* followers turned to preventing disruption of and disrespect for *Wutasi* practices and beliefs, and to preserving the spiritual peace (*sere*) of the lineage and/or neighborhood. In the former area, they sometimes defended their prerogatives with words:

> When the old men [performed ritual beer libations at a ritual] and a Christian came to tell them about God, he would be told, "Go away, you idiot!" and he would say thank you, and go away as ordered.[129]

Sometimes, as at important rituals like funerals, they threatened force:

> Those [*Wutasi* followers] became wild with madness. . . . They shouted, "Go away, you people, . . . go away!" And the Christians were chased

---

[125] Interview with GM, Kishamba/Chawia, 24/9/1988. Another reason, discussed below, was that school made boys unavailable for the four–day cycles of herding cattle, and hurt girls' ability to help with farming and household work.

[126] In one case, this entailed direct and open opposition; in another, the in–laws kept asking that their granddaughter help with tasks, causing her to miss many days of classes. Interviews with Mrs. FM, Lushangonyi/Mwanda, 21/9/1988; and Mrs. VM, Sagassa/Werugha, 6/10/1988.

[127] Interview with PK, Kigala/Werugha, 6/10/1988.

[128] In Werugha, for instance, several people were thrown in jail for having pulled down Kituri's house. Interview with SM, Werugha/Werugha, 27/9/1988.

[129] Interview with JM, Josa/Chawia, 9/4/1988.

away. . . . When they saw Christians coming, some came out with sticks, saying, "Beat these people, what are they coming to do here?"[130]

Beneath those confrontations ran the implication that overly zealous Christians risked losing inheritance and standing in their lineages. Faced with this sort of pressure, most Christians tried not to stir up trouble with others in their lineage or neighborhood.[131] They left aggressive evangelization to paid Agents and the handfuls of devout, strongly motivated Christians.

Many *Wutasi* followers also tried to draw Christians in their lineage into some *Wutasi* rituals. Because non–participation by Christians in important rites could threaten group spiritual well–being, *Wutasi* followers often pressured them to take part. Most Christians did not want the social stigma of being blamed for a failed ritual; nor did they want to lose out on inheritance, or damage other material and emotional ties to kin and neighbors. Little documentary evidence on this subject exists, but the oral evidence is interestingly contradictory: most Anglicans interviewed claimed they did not participate in *Wutasi* rituals after converting; a few old Anglicans, however, say that not only did they themselves participate in *Wutasi* rituals after converting, so did many others:

> *OK:* They were there! . . . They just stood quietly in the back.
> *Q:* Did they come to preach Christianity?
> *OK:* No! [snorts] Some might say so now, but they were there for the rain[making].[132]

These incidents of small–scale backsliding were apparently common. It happened in other contexts, as well—often around alcohol, which the CMS considered sinful in itself, and which furthermore had a place in many *Wutasi* rituals. Many Anglican men continued to drink *chofi*, seeing it as an important vehicle for continued social interaction, and also because they liked it.[133] Many Christians also quietly attended dances, again mostly hovering at the edges and watching.[134]

Nevertheless, both Christians and *Wutasi* followers describe the era as one of separation. Christians trying to minimize their backsliding avoided compromising situations by spending their time with other Christians. *Wutasi* followers also often avoided the company of Christians, to minimize tensions and unwanted preachings.[135] Even children and teens often split into separate groups:

---

[130] Interview with SM, Wundanyi/Werugha, 22/4/1988.

[131] Interviews with KM, Kizumanzi/Sagalla, 14/7/1993; Mrs. SM, Mogho Mleche/Mbale, 4/11/1988.

[132] Interview with OK, Shigaro/Werugha, 2/8/1993.

[133] Interviews with OK, Shigaro/Werugha, 29/4/1988; KM, Tausa/Mbololo, 2/6/1988.

[134] Interviews with CM, Teri/Sagalla, 22/7/1993; Mrs. MM, Teri/Chawia, 22/7/1988; Mrs. PN, Mlondo/Werugha, 26/9/1988; and AM, Mogho Mleche/Mbale, 4/11/1988.

[135] Interviews with GM, Kishamba/Chawia, 12/8/1988; PK, Kigalla/Werugha, 6/10/1988.

> You didn't stay together [with non–Christians], you stayed separate, your education made it difficult to stay with them, and they also didn't want to stay with you. They don't want you to tell them . . . to let go of their things. . . . They didn't have any fear of us, they were just sarcastic. . . . So we stayed apart from each other.[136]

The combination of conflict and separation tested the cohesiveness of lineages and neighborhoods that had both Christians and *Wutasi* followers—which by the late 1920s meant nearly all of them.

However, by that juncture, terms of coexistence were also taking shape. Among *Wutasi* followers, Christians were not exactly considered lost, but seen as severely diminished:

> For a [*Wutasi* follower], . . . your child being a Christian had a meaning like he had run away from you. . . . Many commitments continued, he will still help you [with money], give you clothes or anything, . . . you still leave him cows and fields when you are old and when you die. . . . But in rituals and in . . . [social situations] he did not follow you. That is like your hand has been cut off.[137]

By the late 1920s, *Wutasi* followers felt that Christians did not really understand *Kidaßida*, but did not try to cast them out from Taita identity. This accommodation, in *Wutasi* followers' minds, placed Christians within but at the bottom of a Taita hierarchy, below people who did or eventually would "understand Taita ways."[138] At the summit of the hierarchy stood male lineage elders, with their specialized knowledge, animal wealth and networks, ritual position, and so on. Just beneath them came older men not yet elders. Below the older men, but well above all Christians, were women and younger men who continued in *Wutasi* and took part in indigenous rituals and practices. This hierarchy of *Kidaßida* had considerable hegemonic authority even among Christians.

Placing Christians at the bottom of a Taita hierarchy had at least one salutary effect: it prevented local communities from dissolving in disarray. The arrangement nonetheless saddened *Wutasi*–following older people, and indicated how much the terms of religious order in Taita had changed by the 1920s:

> If a person . . . joined [Christianity], your parents saw that they were left alone. That is, they thought they will not be represented in traditional matters. . . . "That child has left me, he has left *Kidaßida*. He will take things, but he has not inherited me in full. . . . He has taken the things of foreigners, he has left the things of his own."[139]

---

[136] Interview with Mrs. DM, Shigaro/Werugha, 30/5/1988.

[137] Interview with JM, Kishamba/Chawia, 24/9/1988.

[138] "Of course they were Taitas, the Christians. . . . But they did not really understand Taita customs. . . . They did not have the knowledge of the [*Wutasi* followers]." Interview with AM, Sagassa/Werugha, 4/10/1988.

[139] Interview with NM, Njawuli/Mwanda, 3/8/1993.

From Cultural Politics to Formal Politics: Some Early
Limits of Ethnic Mobilization

Land and Lineage, Land and Ethnicity

Two related arguments about the ethnicization of societies have linked the process to colonialism or the emergence of the modern nation–state. One holds that colonial states for all practical purposes imposed ethnic divides upon Africans, encouraging rivalries between them to prevent Africans from forming a common front against colonialism.[140] The other claims that ethnicization was in large part a regional response to the emergence of modern, centralized states: ethnicized blocs arose as a way for groups to defend their perceived common interests within the new, large scale polity.[141]

Both views contain important insights—the former into the structuring and consciousness–shaping power of states, the latter into the compatibility of modernity and ethnicity. Still, the rise of Taita ethnicity did not conform neatly to either. It emerged first and foremost as a response to local concerns: how older people could maintain authority over their youngers, how to keep communities together, how to defend social and cultural institutions that were eroding. To be sure, those concerns were not innocent of colonial state influence. Colonially–promoted changes catalyzed much of the cultural politics that gave rise to Taita ethnicity. Europeans' assumptions of Africans' inherently tribal character encouraged the people's embrace of the wider identity, and objections to European ways solidified an outside "them" against which to hone an "us." Still, ethnicity was not imposed on Taita from without, but seized upon from within. Furthermore, Taita's cultural politics before the 1930s did not by and large make the state their referent, but the terms of Taita identity—what counted as proper Taita ways.

To the limited extent that people mobilized Taita ethnicity into a tool for its most pressing state–level political issue before the mid–1930s, it proved largely ineffective. In the contentious politics of land, the colonial state's assumption of Taita ethnicity and Africans' presentation of a shared ethnic agenda in fact militated against local interests. Two difficulties explained this: first, colonial land issues went to the heart of lineage and neighborhood property rights; there was no such thing as Taita ethnic property. Second, those at the forefront of Taita ethnicity in this era, older men, were neither inclined nor well–suited to mobilize Taita identity into a formal political bloc. It would take a group of younger men allied to elders, starting in the late 1930s, to effectively mobilize Taita ethnicity as a political force.

Three kinds of alienations excised large blocks of land from local usage in Taita: the takeover of plains land for sisal plantations, the granting of a large block of prime lowland to a mission, and the development of a coffee plantation in the upper zone. The alienations for sisal proceeded from an early cen-

---

[140] The best known such study is Vail, *Creation of Tribalism.*

[141] Geertz, "Primordial Sentiments."

tury colonial assessment of the plains as open land. They had provided prime pasturage and seasonal agricultural fields in the mid–nineteenth century, but the droughts and famines of the 1880s–1890s parched the terrain and killed off a large proportion of local people.[142] By the turn of the century, the plains had fallen into scattered, irregular use. Colonial officials considered the land available for other endeavors, and so leased out large blocks of it to European enterprises.

European sisal cultivation began in the plains in 1906, with a host of companies granted concessions in the next several years.[143] Until World War I, most of the companies existed only on paper, and the war, which spilled into the district, shut the working ones down for two years.[144] People from the Hills meanwhile used the undeveloped claims seasonally, in patterns shaped by prior local land rights. Many neighborhoods had rights to particular parts of the lowland immediately around the Hills; within a neighborhood block, lineages held rights to individual fields. As Taita's population climbed out of the trough of the 1890s, much of the European–claimed but undeveloped plains came back into regular local use.[145]

Once the War left Taita in 1916, a land crisis ensued. Sisal had become a highly profitable wartime crop, and Taita's haphazard patchwork of unworked concessions now quickly consolidated into three well–capitalized concerns totaling nearly 185,000 acres.[146] The inevitable result was a land squeeze. As plantations went into production, they evicted people who had farmed or herded on that land. Also, people could not open new lowland fields if their neighborhood lands fell within

---

[142] There are no estimates for death rates in Taita, but for the same period and like conditions, Muriuki posits a 50–95 percent death rate in Kikuyuland. See Godfrey Muriuki, *A History of the Kikuyu, 1500–1900* (Nairobi, 1974). Since at least some people from Taita found refuge at the coast, the death rate in Taita was probably lower.

For the impact of the drought and famine on Ukambani in these decades, see Ambler, *Kenyan Communities*, chaps. 5, 6; for the coast above Mombasa, see Cynthia Brantley, *The Giriama and Colonial Resistance in Kenya, 1800–1920* (Berkeley, 1981), 31, 34–36.

[143] These included the Deutsche Ost Afrika Kompagnie (85 square miles), the London and South Africa Co. (200 square miles), the Afro–American Trading and Navigation Co. (200 square miles), and Jolly Biggs and Co. (25 square miles). See PRO, CO/533/11/67 (8/2/1906); CO/533/28/225 (10/6/1907); CO/533/76 (12/9/1910).

[144] In 1917, the governor of Kenya reported one plantation operating: the DOAK Estate, confiscated from its German owners and given to the British East Africa Co. Kedai Estate, also seized from German owners, reopened later that year. PRO, CO/533/191 (4/1/1917).

[145] DC Reddie recognized local land–use practices early on, and wrote to the colony's Land Inquiry Committee, "It is the case that although certain areas about a native settlement may present the appearance of not having been cultivated for years, . . . this land may in all justice be considered the property of the tribe." KNA, PC/Cst/1/12/51 (14/11/1904). His opinion was disregarded.

[146] As sisal prices rose and sisal–processing technology improved, it became a major cash crop, accounting for 22 percent of Kenya's exports in 1916–17. Profitable when sold at £25 per ton, during the war its price went as high as £75. After the war the price fell some, but averaged £40 per ton in 1923–29. PRO, CO/533/197 (1916–17 Annual Report); and Guillebaud, *Economic Survey*, 9.

The acreage was divided between Voi Estate (100,000), Taita Concessions, Ltd. (72,000, near Mwatate and Bura), and Kedai Estate (10,000, on the plain north of Dabida). They amounted to 290 square miles; the Hills totaled 500 square miles. The plantations were not excised from Taita; I juxtapose the figures only for a sense of scale.

a plantation's boundaries. The land squeeze therefore hit Taita unevenly: some neighborhoods lost no land to plantations, while others lost a great deal.

From the outset, however, colonial land policies did not account for the neighborhood basis of landholding. Since officials assumed all land to be Taita land, they considered any open–looking piece as available to a Taita farmer as any other:

> The [several hundred] natives [farming in an area that a company wanted to claim] refused to part with their land at any price, . . . stating that they had cultivated these [farms] for generations. They persisted in their refusal even when I pointed out an equally good tract available to them [a few miles away]. . . . I am of the opinion that there is no valid reason for the natives thus obstinately refusing to cultivate [that] area . . . in exchange for reasonable compensation.[147]

Though this opinion dates to 1906, the Kenya Land Commission (KLC) of 1932 would make similar assumptions in its attempt to deal with land loss around Taita. Local societies found the approach untenable: people could not simply accept a colonial grant of different land in territory other than their own, for other lineages in other neighborhoods had rights there. The alienations hit neighborhoods in the locations of Chawia, Bura, and Mbololo particularly hard.

Two regions within the Hills had problems over land alienations, as well. In Bura, the Holy Ghost Fathers' mission gained a freehold to 1,000 acres of prime valley bottomland.[148] Local cultivators could use some of this land—*if* they brought their children in for Catholic baptism.[149] As Bura's population rebounded over the first quarter of the century, tensions over land rights occasionally arose between local people and the mission, for its holdings cut heavily into the land rights of several Bura lineages. People summarized their view of the relationship in their nickname for the Father–in–Charge of the mission: *Mwapea* (someone who gets things from others).[150]

Another 1,288 acres of alienated land lay in a highland valley of Mbale location.[151] In the 1900s, the CMS missionary at Mbale, Maynard, received a freehold for the land, intending to start an industrial mission farm to improve local agriculture.[152] But the mission farm never got off the ground, and after

---

[147] PC/Cst/1/1/115, Skene Inward, 13/8/1906.

[148] KNA, DC/TTA/3/8/97. Actual freehold title to the land was granted in 1906. See Les Spiritains, *Bulletin de la Congregation, Tome Onzième, 1905–07.*

[149] Many people in Bura willingly had infants baptized for the sake of land access (and probably for other reasons, as well). Soon after the mission set its condition, the vast preponderance of those baptized became infants. For Baptismal Records, Bura Mission, see appendix B.

Interviewees state that this semi–compelled baptism of infants spawned little resentment, for the Fathers left the matter there: once baptized, the infant might never again set foot inside the mission church. Interviews with CA, Ilole/Bura, 17/8/1988; and Mrs. WM, Ilole/Bura, 19/8/1988.

[150] Interview with PN, Ngerenyi/Chawia, 9/5/1988.

[151] Administrative boundaries have since shifted; the area now falls within the Werugha location.

[152] Maynard said, "We did not want to displace people, we wanted to help them, and we were only going to use those parts of the land that were not being used by the people." KNA, *Kenya Land Commission,* 2756–60.

being resold several times, a 1916 group incorporated it as Wundanyi Ltd.[153] In this guise, the plantation shed its initial mission of improving local farming, and instead uprooted whatever fields on the freehold stood in the way of its expanding coffee operation. In 1920, Major Dru Drury took over management of the plantation: "[Drury] said that the mission brought him there, because the mission was . . . the ones who got that land. . . . But he was really just a settler and a businessman."[154] And, indeed, Drury set about his business with vigor:

> When Mr. Drury came he uprooted growing crops from the people's [fields]: banana trees, crops, and maduma. . . . We were very upset over this, and we came before Mr. Platts [the DC]. Mr. Platts and Mr. Drury came up, and Mr. Platts pointed out that Mr. Drury could culti-vate in such and such a place, but not on the other side of the Wundanyi stream. We saw afterwards that Mr. Drury was increasing his cultiva-tion, and was planting coffee and uprooting crops that were in the [field]. . . . Every [DC] . . . has heard our complaint, [but] . . . we have had no help in this matter.[155]

In a densely populated neighborhood with limited land, the erstwhile mission farm left the lasting impression that it forcibly deprived lineages of some of their best land.

Responses to land alienations in and around the Hills were highly frag-mented in the first three decades of the century. In the early 1930s, when the KLC held hearings all across the colony, some local people did testify before it in the name of the Taita as a whole. As a strategic identification on behalf of local interests, however, Taita ethnicity had no formal political value. Older men, at the vanguard of asserting Taita identity and the terms of *Kidaßida*, played a conspicuously small role in political struggles with the state over land.[156] The notion of *Kidaßida* afforded little help in dealing with officials. Some older men explained that there were "traditional" Taita claims on the land, but that led to official responses that "the Taita" could be given other land, thus missing the lineage and neighborhood limitations on such a solution.

---

[153] According to Nazarro, "Changing Use" (pp. 86–87, 93), the 1916 owners re–formed themselves as Wundanyi, Ltd., to distance themselves from the missionary endeavor. See also testimony by Maynard in *Kenya Land Commission*, 2756–57.

[154] Interview with OK, Shigaro/Werugha, 29/4/1988. He also said Maynard initially supported Drury at Wundanyi, which cost Maynard some goodwill among the area's inhabitants. Maynard clearly distanced himself from Drury between 1920 and his 1933 testimony to the KLC, *Kenya Land Commission*, 2755–62.

[155] Testimony of Daniel Peter, *Kenya Land Commission*, 2747–48. He is remembered in Taita as the major local opponent to Drury. Interview with NM, Wundanyi/Werugha, 26/5/1988; similarly, interviews with JM, Wundanyi/Werugha, 17/4/1988; MT, Kishamba/Chawia, 9/6/1988; and Mrs. GM, Shigaro/Werugha, 15/7/1988.

[156] Older men were virtually absent from colonial records of discussions and negotiations over land. Officials mostly dealt, according to all written records, with chiefs, squatters, some educated young people, and missionaries.

The situation put them in a bind, for their main political fora, the Elders' Councils, were in no position to address large scale land issues. Nor did elders pronounce on the issue in public fora, for that ran counter to their notions about their dignity and proper conduct. They discussed the situation with officials one–on–one, emphasizing lineage and neighborhood land rights to particular pieces of land, and other people also discussed localized claims with the KLC. However, while some district officers sought solutions at local levels of society, other district officers and virtually all officials with a larger–than–district perspective did not, insisting on trying to find tribe–wide solutions.[157] To the extent that Taita Africans couched land appeals in the discourse of tribe, they reinforced official tendencies to gloss over the crucial intricacies of local land claims. Consider the testimony of Chief Thomas Mghalu to the Commission:

> What I wish to talk about is increasing the size of our country, because our country is small . . . and there is no room in it. The population is increasing these days. . . . The land is insufficient for us and our property, because the country is small. . . . For these reasons we complain to the Government that they should increase our land, that we may get sufficient room for anything that may happen.[158]

By these terms, any land added could be considered a "tribal" solution—and the KLC eventually *did* add "tribal" land to the Taita reserve, which in practice benefited a few neighborhoods only.

A more direct form of land politics by those most in need worked more effectively. It made no reference to Taita identity and was not aimed, in the first instance, at the state. Quite simply, if people whose land had been alienated to the sisal plantations, Bura mission, or Wundanyi, could find an undeveloped piece of land in those properties that fell within the purview of their lineage lands, they squatted on it and stolidly stayed put.[159] Local officials, sympathetic to local African land needs, actually became allies in this. First, they turned a blind eye to local squatting on the Taita Concessions, Ltd. plantation (hereafter, TCL). Then they advised the owner that throwing the squatters off might endanger his labor situation. In the late 1920s they stipulated that no squatter could be thrown off land kept in continuous cultivation.[160] Finally, the DC suggested to the plantation manager that circumstances and the company's

---

[157] For a local official's awareness of the local basis of land rights, see *Kenya Land Commission, Evidence and Memoranda*, memo from former DC Marchant, p. 2732; for non–consideration of it, and the adoption of an ethnic perspective, former DC Slade–Hawkins, pp. 2792–95. For final reliance on an ethnic–based solution to land problems in Taita, *Kenya Land Commission*, Summary and Conclusions. Only one Taita elder, Maganga wa Kifu, testified to the Commission.

[158] Ibid., Evidence and Memoranda, 2745–46.

[159] Interviews with MT, Kishamba/Chawia, 9/6/1988; and GM, Kishamba/Chawia, 12/8/1988 and 24/9/1988. Also, see PRO, CO 533/325 letters of 21/7/1924 and 14/11/1924.

[160] See in particular PRO, CO 533/385/3, letter of 16/5/1929, in which the owner of Taita Concessions, Ltd. protested that state of affairs to the Colonial Office.

own practices made encroachments on TCL land all but inevitable, and offered no hope of ceasing them in the near future.[161]

This form of politics created a conflict that compelled the state to make hard choices—and when squatters realized that officials actually respected their primacy of place, they considered it a good solution. The KLC settlement in fact worsened squatters' lot, for the land they occupied was exchanged for another block elsewhere: a block where other neighborhoods had rights.[162] In the late 1930s, however, a new coalition linked Taita ethnicity to land issues and became a formidable political force: a group of young, politicized men harnessed grass roots land concerns to ethnic identification, wrapping both around symbols that appealed to older men's and *Wutasi* followers' sensibilities. That coalition took aim at the colonial state and Taita's progressive, Christian elite.

---

[161] "I would . . . point out that [the encroached–upon] plots are unoccupied and undeveloped by [TCL] and . . . are neither fenced nor demarcated by visible and unmistakable boundaries. . . . As these are either all surrounded by Native Reserve or partially so, any expectation that these areas will remain absolutely inviolate is contrary to general experience. . . . I appreciate that [TCL] ha[s] a clear title to the land. I only mention these facts to illustrate the difficulties with which we are faced." KNA, DC/TTA/3/8/45, Taita Concessions Ltd., DC to TCL manager, 23/3/1933.

[162] *Kenya Land Commission*, Summary and Conclusions, Taita.

6

Being Taita, I: Progressivism, Education, and Changing Terms of Kidaßida, *1930–1950*

The problem . . . remains . . . a search for the best method of impinging modern progress onto the primitive organization of tribal society.

DC, Taita, 1948[1]

Introduction

By the early 1930s, Taita ethnicity was a widely agreed–upon social identity across the Hills. The days when lineage and neighborhood ties made people regard other parts of the region with hostility had receded into memory. Now men and women, Christians and *Wutasi* followers, the young and their seniors all still maintained local affiliations, but also acknowledged themselves to be Taita. Taita identity did not refer to the bald fact of local residence, or to a simple recognition of linguistic and cultural similarities. It bespoke a belief that a shared perspective on the world bound Taita's people together: they formed a community of people who "understood" one another—a vast, vague, but effective extension of the discourse of neighborhood ties. People sometimes mobilized Taita community into networks of mutual support, or, less demandingly, made it a vehicle for sociality or on-going interaction across prior localized social boundaries. Most broadly, Taita

---

[1]   KNA, DAO/TTA/1/1/164, Taita District Annual Report, 1950.

identity defined an "us," as against other groups and the state—even though that "us" did not hold together easily. Struggles over proper Taita ways revealed tensions of generation and gender, of Christianity and *Wutasi*, of colonialism's supporters and its questioners. The tensions led some people to situate themselves as defenders of Taita interests and ways, opposing what they saw as the ways of outsiders.

Despite general agreement on the fact of a Taita identity, then, just what constituted Taita identity was very much contested. Did Taita identity turn primarily on historical and ancestral ties, or on its normative aspects, i.e., on notions of proper Taita beliefs and ways—and what might those norms be? The binding together of identity and norms was not inevitable, but *Wutasi*–following older men and their supporters often tried to make it seem so. Through their use of *Kidaßida*, they sought to associate Taita identity with behaviors and beliefs that one had to follow or, at a minimum, respect.

Of course, the older men of the 1930s did not understand *Kidaßida* in quite the same way as older men of the 1910s; the former, after all, had been the *younger* men of the 1900s–1910s who had begun to unsettle prior ways. For that matter, *Wutasi*–following older men in the late 1940s understood *Kidaßida* differently than did older men in the early 1930s; and by the late 1940s, a sizable number of old men did not even follow *Wutasi*. The remainder of this study tracks the continually changing character of *Kidaßida*; nevertheless, the concept itself remained embedded in the discourse of Taita identity that succeeding generations deployed from the 1910s to the 1950s.

As the century wore on, more and more people challenged received terms of Taita ways. The vast majority of challengers, however, saw themselves *as* Taita, and had deep psychological, emotional, and practical investments in the identity. Even as they struggled to reshape norms of proper behavior, the challengers saw Taita identity as defining a community to which they fundamentally belonged, where their ties of historical rootedness, mutuality, and social support lay. They therefore sought to alter beliefs and practices without themselves being considered lost. Most challengers tried to manage this in the first instance by treating Taita identity as a kind of birthright: a quasi–lineal, historical identity demarcated by linguistic similarities and shared cultural background.[2] Second, they increasingly tempered their reworkings with attempts to placate *Wutasi* followers. They showed respect and sought compromises of practice and outlook that would help minimize norm–based qualms about their Taita identity.

Wutasi–following older men and their supporters had never fully made *Kidaßida* conflate identity with proper ways, and the strategy lost effectiveness over time. Older men still had key elements of influence: control over lineage lands and livestock, position in networks of support and mutuality, and the respect and authority that lineage ideology bestowed to them with age. But as

---

[2] By then, shared cultural background mattered as a historical marker, not as a guide to contemporary norms.

they lost their stranglehold over material wealth, their control over the terms of Taita propriety weakened, as well: it became harder to construct community and their domination over its terms as virtually one and the same thing. Certainly, as the next chapters show, *Wutasi*–following older men did not lose all authority and influence by the early 1950s. However, younger men and women, and Christians of all ages altered many local practices and beliefs in the 1930s and 1940s. In so doing, they compelled a reworking of the terms of Taita identity and began to metamorphose *Kidaßida* from a set of normative strictures into a claim of cultural heritage.

This chapter examines the ideology from which many challenges to *Kidaßida* sprang: a nexus of interlocking beliefs and practices that by the late 1920s were glossed as progressivism. It discusses what composed progressivism, the circles of people associated with it, and the role of colonial education and economic change in spreading it across the Hills. The next chapter turns to how progressivism and cumulative colonial economic changes in Taita catalyzed tremendous socioeconomic flux in the 1930s–1940s. I analyze how those changes fueled struggles in the Hills that affected lineages, neighborhoods and households, profoundly reshaping notions of proper Taita behavior and proper Taita wealth.

Taita Progressivism

Progressive Ideology

By the 1930s, progressivism was an umbrella term for a tremendous range of ideas and practices in Taita. It originated in the missions' vision for the modernization of Africans, and it influenced some people in the Hills from the first decades of the 1900s. As it became widely understood and practiced from the late 1920s on, progressivism embraced European–introduced notions of "improvement" in moral, social, cultural, and material realms of African life:

> The Europeans really wanted us to progress, to push ahead. . . . Doing those things we learned from them . . . we made life in this place better than it had been for our elders. . . . We made ourselves better, and we made this place better.[3]

Progressivism in Taita (as elsewhere in colonial Kenya), had several main assumptions. First, it accepted colonialism as a positive, educative experience for Africans. Virtually all the progressives of the 1920s–30s were believing and practicing Christians, and recognized that the missions' social ideology reinforced governmental "improvement" policies. Progressivism thus elaborated upon the Europeans' view of colonialism as a civilizing mission. Progressives

---

[3] Interview with RM, Nyache/Wumingu, 1/10/1988.

Photo 6. A Christian progressive couple, early 1930s. Margaret Murray Photo Collection, courtesy of Kenya National Archives and Documentation Service. #316/81.

often expressed this through mission–learned metaphors of lowliness and enlightenment:

> The changes really reached here when people started to know about Christianity. . . . [in English] "Now we are people of light, that darkness we don't like." . . . [back to KiSwahili] To fight the darkness we started to learn. . . . I went to mission school and learned there. . . . I became shamba–boy [i.e., field hand] at Wusi [mission], then the missionaries gave me tools and I learned carpentry . . . and I made good money, [30/= per month in 1925], and defeated darkness.[4]

Progressives who matured in the later 1930s and 1940s often emphasized Christianity less, and did not so easily abandon locally rooted religious and social practices. Though at least nominally Christian, many later progressives took it more as a socioeconomic stance.

The above quotation illustrates another assumption of progressives in the 1930s, that "improvements" mutually interlocked—especially in the realms of religion, education, and economics. Colonial education initially drew mainly from among the small circles of Christian believers, but that changed as people saw how literacy, numeracy, and/or craft skills garnered graduates better–paying jobs in the labor market.[5] In addition, the schools' horticultural classes introduced crops and techniques that spawned a group of successful Taita market gardeners selling vegetables in Mombasa. These economic benefits made interest in education snowball far beyond its original religiously–minded constituency, until, by the late 1930s, a popular clamor for schooling ran through Taita.[6] Though an instrumental desire for many, the champions of Taita progressivism in the 1930s considered education for socioeconomic "improvement" and Christian mores two sides of the same coin.[7]

Progressives of the 1930s often expressed the link between Christianity and monetized, capitalist economics less obliquely than through metaphors of dark-

---

[4] Interview with BN, Wusi/Chawia, 5/5/1988.

[5] Interviews with MM, Lushangonyi/Mwanda, 22/9/1988; AM, Shigaro/Werugha, 2/5/1988; and JN, Mbale/Mbale, 8/11/1988. Until the 1920s, Catholic education was only in local vernacular, making it less popular than CMS education that additionally taught students KiSwahili and English. Interviews with NK, Mwatate/Chawia, 15/8/1988, and PM, Ilole/Bura, 16/8/1988.

[6] In 1928 there were 653 students on the rolls at mission schools in Taita. By 1930 enrollment jumped to 1,410. In 1935 the number approached 2,900, and in 1943 hit nearly 4,000. After World War II, officials and missionaries scrambled for funds to keep pace with demand. KNA, DC/TTA/1/1 and DC/TTA/1/2, District Annual Reports for 1928, 1930, 1935, 1943. Also see the local government estimates 1938–45 in PC/Coast/2/3/106, wherein education absorbed over half its expenditures. For postwar discussions of the ensuing fiscal crisis, see DAO/TTA/1/1/86.

[7] See, for example, Allen Madoka, *Taita na Kanisa la Kristo katika Miaka Hamsini, 1900–1950*, [*Taita and the Christian Church over Fifty Years, 1900–1950*] (Nairobi, 1950), 13–16. Missionaries in Taita were also explicit about the linkage: "We had a very close association between the Church and education . . . and the welfare, as we understood it, of the whole tribe." Interview with Peter Bostock, Oxford, England, 3/4/1989.

ness versus light. Some spoke of "the virtue of thrift [as] a Christian virtue,"[8] while others referred to how "the Europeans made us understand about money and the good it could bring us."[9] Many religious progressives of the 1930s associated Christianity with the willingness to work hard, and thought *Wutasi* a source of laziness:

> Those elders who were *Watasi*, they spent a lot of time making prayers with beer. . . . I do not say they were just drunks, it was that drinking was a part of praying, . . . [so] when they met in the afternoon to pray, . . . they were finished for the day, and that was that. But their wives were still working, their children remained in the fields. . . . Christians left that—Christian men worked more than *Watasi*.[10]

In the 1940s, the religiosity of progressivism declined (for reasons discussed below), and secular improvement stepped to the fore. "Progressive farming" oriented agriculture more to the money economy, and embraced techniques (e.g., new forms of soil conservation or intercropping) based on colonially introduced ideas about resource management. But while many progressive farmers distanced themselves from the Christian side of progressivism in the 1940s, others still connected agricultural improvement to Christian–inspired moral stances. Some WaTaita promoted progressive farming *as* moral advancement. One man proposed to start a 4–H Club to stem the backwardness of:

> OLD MEN: who mostly stick to their old fashioned superstitions . . . YOUNG MEN: [who] usually lead modern lives in the wrong ways . . . which in the reserve makes for wild habits of humanity such as overcoming drunkenness, smoking, . . . and shameful social enjoyments. . . . Both [young and old] hat[e] hard work on their gardens and stock keeping. [They maintain] loose design of their homes and of their country as a whole. Both grow lazy. . . . [Most local people and

---

[8]   The word translated as "virtue" was "*uzuri*." It literally means "goodness," but in this context I believe "virtue" best expresses the speaker's intent. Interview with DM, Wongonyi/Mbololo, 6/7/1988.

   The ideas here invite parallels with Weber's *Protestant Ethic and the Spirit of Capitalism*, but the parallels soon break down. Puritan sects morally sanctioned material success, but aescetically decried self–indulgent uses of wealth. Missionized Anglicans and Catholics in Taita, however, deliberately consumed conspicuously, to demonstrate the "better" ways they lived, from housing to clothing. Missionaries and colonial officials usually encouraged them in this, seeing the progressives' material culture as signs of advancement.

   Taita here more tellingly parallels David Parkin's study of how Islam figured in some men's attempts to break with a local redistribution network and embrace individual accumulation. *Palms, Wine, and Witnesses: Public Spirit and Private Gain in an African Farming Community* (San Francisco, 1972).

[9]   Interview with Mrs. SM, Mogho Mleche/Mbale, 4/11/1988; though education deepened people's involvement with money and colonial capitalism, she overstated her point. Traders from the Hills had long understood and handled money. Too, taxation, labor migration, and the growing inflow of commodities by the 1910s drew nearly everyone in Taita into money–consciousness before the wide diffusion of mission education.

[10]   Interview with JM, Kishamba/Chawia, 12/8/1988.

their leaders] do not attain real appreciation as to the meaning of scientific methods of agriculture and its aim as the only central powerful
force of advance in Economic, Political, and Social bases.[11]

Implicit in the above quotations, and following closely from the other assumptions, came a third: that colonial rulers had a benevolent vision of the
future for Africans and their societies. It was a socioeconomic benevolence,
encouraging Africans to advance themselves and their groups, which usually
meant their tribes. A formulation laced with paternalism, it justified colonial
rule by further assuming that Europeans were best suited to set the terms of
advancement, then guide and judge the Africans' progress. Not surprisingly,
European benevolence did not extend to an acceptance of political debate.[12]
Many progressively minded WaTaita accepted this political limitation; sometimes out of conviction, sometimes as an implicit accommodation of state power,
they steered clear of disagreement with colonial authorities about politically
charged issues.

But not all were reticent. In the mid–1930s, some educated WaTaita raised
voices of dissent about particular policies and over the state's attempt to
maintain a choke-hold over colonial African politics, and many others in
Taita quietly supported the dissenters. The challengers were mainly younger
adults, mostly male, and sometimes Christian. But, as will be seen below,
even the Christians among them rejected progressive views of colonialism
as an unproblematic, purely benevolent system with which they should
gratefully and unquestioningly cooperate. That rejection opened a channel
of Taita oppositional politics that continued until Mau Mau broke out in
1952.

A relatively small core group, the dissenters focused on conflicts over land
rights and land usage, which at once broadened their local following and an-
tagonized Taita officialdom. They also crafted a language of dissent that explicitly linked up with the older men's terms of *Kidaβida*—a political positioning that gained them the support of many *Wutasi* followers, and quiet backing
from less strict Christians, as well. Arrayed against the dissenting coalition were
chiefs, the Christian elite and devout, and the more devoted progressives. In
the cultural politics of this conflict, the latter group was vulnerable to having
its Taitaness questioned.

---

[11] KNA, DAO/TTA/1/1/86, letter from Alexander Nina to Assistant Agricultural Officer, 19/8/
1949.

[12] A few district officials allowed, in retrospect, that opposition politicians might have had altru-
istic intentions and good cause, but still thought opposition an unreasonable stance—a view stiff-
ened by the dubious tactics and arguments that their opponents sometimes utilized. Interviews
with Peter Walters, Surrey/England, 25/2/1989; and Michael Power, Surrey/England, 24/2/1989.
Some officials tried to co–opt local opponents, with mixed success. Interview with Kenneth Cowley,
Surrey/England, 23/2/1989.

    In the 1930s–1940s, most officials treated oppositional politics with unvarnished hostility. See KNA,
DC/TTA/3/1/71 (Native Associations and Agitators, 1945–51); DC/TTA/3/1/72 (Taita Fighi Union,
1949–52); ARC/MAA/2/3/19 (Coast Province Intelligence Reports, 1940); PC/Coast/1/11/40 (Taita
Land Claims and the Taita Hills Association, 1942–44); CNC/10/101 (Taita Land Claims, 1943).

Progressivism and Taita Identity

A further progressive assumption by the 1930s drew upon both European assumptions about Africans and local reformulations of social identity. Taita
progressives, like everyone else in Taita, held that historical ties of language,
culture, and descent contributed to a common Taita identity. Unlike most older
men, however, progressives did not consider contemporary adherence to norms
of *Kidaßida* crucial to Taita identity. Progressives instead paralleled official and
missionary assumptions, emphasizing that historical ties sufficed to bestow a
common identity and a collective character. Ancestry made ethnicity a "natural" social category of broad inclusion:

> *Q:* Did some people say, "ah! those ones are not Taita, they just follow
> the whites?"
> *DM:* Those things were said, but we knew it was not true. Our fathers
> were of this place [Sw: *wenyeji*], our mothers were of this place, all our
> ancestors were of this place. . . . We had the blood of Taita, so we did
> not believe those things.[13]

DM exaggerates slightly: many progressives (like many other WaTaita) had relatively shallow kinship histories in the Hills, and, as will be seen, many *did*
worry about others' views of their Taitaness. Still, the statement shows how
belief in their historical Taita roots undergirded progressives' sense of Taita
identity.

The progressives' view of ethnicity shared colonial ideology's belief that
tribes had collective characters; and just as an individual's character could
"improve" over time, so, too, might the character of a tribe. Much discussion among Europeans (and between progressive WaTaita and Europeans)
either took up or assumed this point, often in assessments of the Taita tribal
character and how to improve it. It was a staple topic of district Annual
Reports:

> [1931] [The WaTaita are] placid, good–tempered, tractable and pleas-
> ant people. It must at the same time be admitted that they are in many
> directions extremely self–satisfied, conservative, and lacking in any
> great desire to progress. Though careful and grasping . . . they are, at
> the same time, intensely honest, . . . straightforward, open and frank.

> [1934] The Taita, with their readiness to become self–sufficient, are be-
> ginning to appreciate [progressive agricultural methods]: this connotes
> advance.

> [1936] [WaTaita have a] somewhat sordid cupidity, coupled with an
> inherent conviction of their own superiority which facts do not alto-
> gether justify. Nevertheless this peculiarity, making the introduction
> of novelties difficult, often results in genuine efforts to improve condi-

---

13   Interview with DM, Mlondo/Werugha, 28/9/1988.

tions once it is realized that new methods advocated should bring an increased . . . return to the cultivator.[14]

Progressives used a similar language:

> We were trying to push the tribe ahead, you understand? Long ago the Taita were a very backward people. . . . Our grandfathers were very superstitious. . . . We pushed, pushed to bring progress to our little country.[15]

As against efforts to link Taita identity to *Kidaßida*, progressives portrayed Taita ethnicity as a given (i.e., their natural historical identity). From that perspective, advocating individual or group "improvements" did not make a person or group any less Taita. Still, the changes they advocated often led to conflicts with *Wutasi*–following older people and their supporters. In that cultural politics, the progressives' opponents often emphasized the importance of *Kidaßida* and ethnic propriety, rebuffing progressives' terms of Taita identity.

Progressivism and *Kidaßida*–based notions of Taita identity each had bases of social power. Progressivism drew upon an alliance between its adherents and the state. Its most substantial state support came from the progressives' control over education, but also from colonial laws, administrative personnel choices, and official predispositions—though, because of the state's simultaneous and contradictory support for "traditional" authority, officials did not back progressivism unequivocally.[16] Still, colonial rule and missionary influence gave progressivism social power that transcended the relatively small number of its wholehearted adherents. As promoted by schools, progressive chiefs, committed Christians, and the Local Native Councils, progressivism became an agenda–setting ideology in colonial Taita. Beyond its core believers, however, many felt ambivalent towards it. Particular innovations, such as cash cropping, book education, or certain kinds of colonially introduced soil conservation typically gained wider acceptance than did progressivism as an ideological whole.

Terms of society rooted in *Kidaßida* drew continuing authority from prior social and cultural forms and mores that had been reworked and naturalized as proper Taita ways. *Kidaßida*'s specifics changed over time, but remained based in older men's attempts to retain social predominance. In the early 1930s, older men still controlled many material underpinnings of local societies, which buttressed their efforts to conjoin their notions of proper Taita ways to the popular

---

[14] KNA, DC/TTA/1/1, Taita District Annual Reports.

[15] Interview with RK, Kizumanzi/Sagalla, 18/7/1993.

[16] For instance, in 1938, Chief Thomas tried to require all households in Taita to have pit latrines with two stalls, but colonial officials objected, considering it intrusive and inflammatory as well as impractical. See KNA, PC/Cst/2/3/106, Taita LNC Minutes and Estimates. Also, when Mbololo's chief opened a 1946 meeting on soil conservation with Christian prayers and hymn singing, the DC wrote, "I do not like this—it does not suit the pagan Elders who I am most concerned to enlist as aids to administration." DC/TTA/3/1/12, Mbololo Location, 26/5/1946.

embrace of Taita identity as a community of belonging. Too, the vast majority of WaTaita remained *Wutasi* followers into the early 1950s. *Wutasi*'s cosmology, rituals, and influence over social relations (as a system of explanation and intercession in daily life) continued to have wide currency in the Hills, even among some Christians.[17]

Well into the 1940s, insistence on *Wutasi*–based perspectives or *Kidaßida* might restrain or redirect progressive–minded changes. Older people who felt their authority or influence over the young declining might call upon respect for Taita ways—and threaten sanctions rooted in them. A *Wutasi* diviner, for instance, might name a Christian youth as the cause of anger in a parent's heart and therefore the source of a particular misfortune. If s/he did not ritually appease the parent, others in the lineage might suffer the consequences. Anyone who refused such an act of amelioration might then be blamed for letting ancestral anger become a more far–reaching curse.[18] The person's standing, prospects, and networks within local society would likely dwindle. This sort of potential approbation often pressured Christians into participation in *Wutasi* rites of group well–being.

As ideologies of the 1920s–30s, then, progressivism and *Kidaßida*–based terms of society were opposed ideal–types in a struggle over the terms of Taita's social order, each championing a competing vision of Taita identity. Neither entirely dominated the other before the early 1950s, nor did most individuals fall entirely into one or the other camp. As people negotiated particular situations, principle and circumstance informed one another: should a well–paid, educated migrant worker remit his earnings to his parents? His wife? Both? In what proportion? Should he retain some? How much? Should he purchase livestock, or would that be presumptuous for a younger man? Or was livestock an old–fashioned waste of money? If his wife moved to Mombasa with him, would they be considered lost and be penalized at home? Should a Christian girl not undergo initiation and raise questions about her standing as an adult Taita woman? Should devout Christians avoid all association with *Wutasi* and risk having their standing as Taita denigrated? Most people's answers usually turned not just on precept, but on an interplay of belief and circumstance.

Sometimes neither progressivism nor indigenously rooted terms of society offered good options. Women straining under heavy workloads, politically minded men who questioned colonial assumptions, migrant laborers facing multiple demands on their earnings: each might chafe against aspects of both ideologies. Ultimately, though, most people searched for ways to meet their needs and beliefs that could pass muster as acceptable "Taita" behavior—but

---

[17] Some European sources and interviewees spoke of *Wutasi*'s influence over Christians into the 1950s, though most Christians I interviewed denied it. Christian nominalism in Taita greatly concerned missionaries in the early 1940s. See Peter Bostock's 1941 Annual Letter to CMS, CMSA. Also G. Harris, *Casting*, 27. On the side of Taita evangelized by the Holy Ghost Fathers, interviewees spoke freely of religious straddling, for it carried less stigma. Interviews with Ms SM, Ilole/Bura, 16/8/1988, and FW, Mgange Nyika/Mwanda, 20/9/1988.

[18] G. Harris, *Casting*, 80–81, 109–12. She adds that some young men in the 1950s thought such accusations a parental ploy for keeping sons under control.

many also worked to stretch the boundaries of acceptability. In the 1930s and 1940s, the wife of a migrant worker might renegotiate labor expectations that her in–laws had for her. While setting aside other tasks to work for them, she might also politely insist on being less available than they wished. She might time work for her in–laws to fit her needs, even if less convenient for them; or ask her husband to hire his parents a laborer.[19] In such ways, people sought to accommodate norms of appropriate Taita behavior, even as, piecemeal, they tried to alter them.

Education and the Spread of Progressivism

In the 1930s and 1940s, demand for Western education burgeoned in Taita, largely because non–Christians sent their children to school for the economic and social advantages it offered. School attendance, minuscule in the 1910s, shot up to 43 percent of Taita's children by 1944.[20] In 1948, over 50 percent of Taita's total population had at least some education, a remarkable figure for colonial Kenya.[21] Half that group was non–Christian, for Christians comprised roughly 25 percent of Taita's population by 1950.[22] To try to keep pace with demand, the CMS and Holy Ghost Fathers expanded their school systems rapidly during the 1930s and 1940s. Aside from theology, the two systems taught much the same curriculum. Personnel at the main mission schools included some European staff, but depended mostly on African teachers. The more re-mote out–schools managed with untrained teachers providing a grade or two of rudimentary education. Students then switched to a school with trained staff and a full curriculum.[23] An Education Board composed of African teachers and officials, European missionaries, and district administrators oversaw the sys-tem.[24]

Education grew so quickly because of its economic advantages to children and parents. Mission education allowed sons to secure better (and better–pay-ing) jobs, jobs often juxtaposed against the Taita benchmark of undesirable work:

---

[19]   Interviews with Mrs. HM, Ndome/Mbololo, 21/6/1988; and Mrs. JM, Werugha/Werugha, 30/9/1988.

[20]   Annual Letter of Peter Bostock, CMSA, 1944.

[21]   KNA, ARC(MAA)–2/3/39iv, Coast Province Annual for 1948. In 1949, Taita's primary educa-tion met colonywide enrollment targets for 1956. Its thirty–one schools were "full to overflowing and [had] to run double streams." Taita demand had no equal in Coast Province. See same file, Coast Province Annual for 1949. In 1948, the Taita LNC's grant for education became the highest percentage education allocation of any LNC in the Colony, reaching 66 percent of the total budget in 1951. KNA, DAO/TTA/1/1/86, Education.

[22]   Interview with Peter Bostock, Oxford, England, 3/4/1989; and Power, "Local Government," 29.

[23]   Interview with DM, Wongonyi/Mbololo, 5/7/1988. By 1946, the system expanded to twelve main schools staffed by fifty–nine trained African teachers, plus a dozen or so remote out–schools with untrained teachers. KNA, DAO/TTA/1/1/86, Schools African Teachers' List, 1946, appended to Education Board meeting, 1/3/1946.

[24]   Taita's District Education Board was founded in 1936. See KNA, DAO/TTA/1/1/86, Education; and DC/TTA/1/1, 1936 Annual Report. There were also two CMS school supervisors, usually teachers of long–standing promoted into the job. Interview with AM, Shigaro/Werugha, 2/5/1988.

Photo 7. An out-school at Mwakinyungu, Taita, in the early 1930s. Margaret Murray Photo Collection, courtesy of Kenya National Archives and Documentation Service. #261/81.

field labor on a sisal plantation.[25] Sons' higher wages promised greater remittances to parents, making sons' education an investment in later parental well–being. Schooling girls had economic value to parents, as well: by the 1930s, educated daughters commanded larger bridewealth payments than uneducated ones.[26] Still, female education rates lagged behind: some parents thought it unnecessary or even undesirable for a girl, saying it compromised their daughters' morality or made them haughty;[27] some parents thought it a net loss to educate daughters, since school reduced a child's household work and daughters later married out of the small lineage.[28] School fees sometimes compelled parents to choose which children they could afford to educate, and sons' education was thought a far better investment.[29] Education of daughters depended more on households that aimed to educate all their children.

---

[25] Among many possible citations here are interviews with MM, Kishamba/Chawia, 8/6/1988 (whose father observed during World War I that when educated men were conscripted, they were assigned clerical or skilled work, not the Carrier Corps); PM, Ilole/Bura, 16/8/1988; and RM, Mgange Nyika/Mwanda, 19/9/1988.

[26] Interviews with Mrs. VM, Sagassa/Werugha, 7/10/1988; and Mrs. CM, Shigaro/Werugha, 26/7/1993.

[27] Interviews with Mrs. FM, Lushangonyi/Mwanda, 21/9/1988; and Mrs. EK, Wongonyi/Mbololo, 7/7/1988.

[28] Interviews with Mrs. GM, Shigaro/Werugha, 27/5/1988; and Mrs. CM, Shigaro/Werugha, 26/7/1993.

[29] Interview with Mrs. GM, Shigaro/Werugha, 27/5/1988.

Mission education imparted virtually every aspect of progressivism. Most broadly, students began to learn how Europeans understood and manipulated the world. This had contradictory effects: it demystified writing, reading, and Western bodies of knowledge and material technologies, moving them from the magical to the realm of learned skills and techniques. This did not eliminate all the distance that educated WaTaita felt between themselves and Europeans, but did diminish it considerably:

> Education helped us understand the whites, . . . to understand their ways. . . . You know, our parents and grandparents thought the whites had great medicines that made them strong, . . . but we learned . . . [that] it was not a matter of medicines . . . or witchcraft. . . . In school we learned things that our grandparents thought were the whites' secrets. And we went home and told them, it is this and this.[30]

On the other hand, schools held up the West's belief systems and material achievements as a higher standard, the ways of a better society that the young should strive to absorb. European missionaries and African teachers imparted far more than academic subjects: they sought to inculcate progressive outlooks, values, and habits in the daily routines of students, a process Jean and John Comaroff have called the colonization of African consciousness.[31]

Officials and missionaries in the 1930s openly hoped that education would "help the children to become Christian citizens"—a concise gloss of their vision of progressivism at that time, tidily linking literacy, numeracy, and material skills with the Europeans' religious and moral structures.[32] As one student put it:

> School did not separate teachings of life from teachings of religion. . . . We learned that a Christian who loves God must learn many other things, for God gives us the ability to know those things, compared to those who don't know God.[33]

Education's progressive impact on local consciousness reached into the particulars of everyday life. For many, *Wutasi*'s cosmological explanations of illness were displaced by Western medical explanations of equally invisible forces; however, the Europeans' greater ability to cure many diseases gave Western science a legitimacy corrosive of *Wutasi* ("we learned that diseases came from germs, not from witchcraft").[34] Western time–consciousness, important to much of colonial labor and production, began for most with mission education ("they

---

[30] Interview with SM, Tausa/Mbololo, 3/6/1988.

[31] Comaroff and Comaroff, "Colonization"; see also their *Of Revelation*, 4–6, and chaps. 6, 7.

[32] The official position was that without Christian training, the education Africans received could put them "in danger"; of what is not specified. District Annual Report for 1937, KNA, DC/TTA/1/1.

[33] Interview with JM, Shigaro/Werugha, 20/4/1988; also, interview with Peter Bostock, Oxford, England, 3/4/1989.

[34] Interview with JM, Shigaro/Werugha, 20/4/1988.

Photo 8. Mbale School students, late 1920s. Margaret Murray Photo Collection, courtesy of Kenya National Archives and Documentation Service. #262/81.

taught us about punctuality, how to really keep time").[35] Schools required students to take up European standards of dress and hygiene through uniforms, dress codes, and inspections. Besides considering the clothing and cleanliness regimes practical and healthful, their champions thought them exemplary outward manifestations of internal moral rectitude ("we learned that a Christian in her life had to be clean, so that she was like a light to the others").[36]

By the 1940s, the embrace of progressivism often had sweeping cumulative effects on students that stirred up conflicts between the educated and the uneducated:

> When I came home from [Wusi boarding] school for vacation, . . . I didn't want a dirty friend from before staying together with me. . . . We even started to be hated by our brothers, the ones we left at home, . . . when we saw that they were dirty.[37]

Nevertheless, many uneducated parents in the 1940s went along with education for their children, not only for its economic benefits, but because many in

---

[35] Interview with AK, Shigaro/Werugha, 25/4/1988; see also Timothy Mitchell's discussion of inculcating Western time–consciousness through education, in *Colonising Egypt* (Cambridge, 1988), chap. 3.

[36] Interview with Mrs. MM, Teri/Chawia, 22/7/1988.

[37] Interview with JK, Kidaya/Chawia, 3/5/1988.

Photo 9.   Mbale School show, 1928. Margaret Murray Photo Collection, courtesy of Kenya National Archives and Documentation Service. #272/81.

that generation of young parents thought education a positive good in itself. Gradually, these parents, together with older people who accepted education, achieved a critical mass:

> My parents had to struggle to get their education [in the 1920s], but for the ones who came later [in the 1940s] it was not a problem. . . . Everybody was getting educated then. . . . The grandparents just . . . [shrugs his shoulders]. What could they do? Nothing! Everyone was . . . getting education. For the ones of before it was a problem, but for the ones who came later, no. . . . You don't make trouble for the grandparents, . . . you respect them, and they don't give you trouble about school.[38]

In part, too, tensions over education eased after World War II as progressivism's meaning shifted in ways that decreased the significance of Christianity. Wartime and the postwar years ushered in "native development," as part of a technical and political–economic "second colonial occupation."[39] This revised progressivism's shape in education and, thereafter, everyday life.

---

[38]   Interview with JM, Kishamba/Chawia, 12/8/1988.

[39]   The shift to development consciousness in British policy dates to the 1940 and 1944 Colonial Development and Welfare Acts. See R. D. Pearce, *The Turning Point in Africa: British Colonial Policy 1938–48* (London, 1982), and David Goldsworthy, *Colonial Issues in British Politics, 1945–1961* (Oxford, 1971). For its application in East Africa, Low and Smith, eds., *East Africa*, vol. 3, chaps. 5–7.

Still, school curricula had several constants in the 1930s and 1940s. New students first learned reading, writing, and Christianity. Non-Christians in the Catholic schools were likely offered baptism early on, while in the CMS schools the first opportunity usually came after a year or two.[40] Days were tightly time–ordered by period, beginning with parade, then religion class, then other subjects for the remainder of the day. Studies emphasized literacy, numeracy, and agriculture. From the 1930s on, the latter subject included soil conservation techniques, more intensive methods of raising crops, and the introduction of new crops—some of them meant for sale.[41] Part of the day also had gender–specific classes: boys learned craft skills and could take more advanced math, while girls were taught progressive homemaking skills.[42] In the mid–to–late 1940s, technical education began to displace Christianity in the classroom.[43] Though most students still became Christians in the 1940s, missionaries, officials, and other Africans all noted a large rise in Christian nominalism: the schools' rapid expansion and changing curriculum watered down their ability to promote thorough–going Christianity.[44]

Kidaβida and Progressive Ideology

Constraining Progressives in the 1930s and 1940s

Wutasi followers did not simply concede the terms of Taita society to progressivism. On the contrary, many older *Wutasi* followers and their supporters compelled significant compromises from progressives, even as progressives did the same of them. *Kidaβida* provided the main ideological counterweight to progressivism. *Kidaβida* was used as a rejoinder to attacks on *Wutasi* from the educational system and Christianity in general. Older men also used it to rein in the socioeconomic changes that progressives (and the young in general) supported in Taita. Most crucially here, *Kidaβida* up-

[40] Interviews with Mrs. WM, Mrugua/Bura 19/8/1988; PM, Ilole/Bura, 15/8/1988; and RM, Wundanyi/ Werugha, 29/7/1993.

[41] Interviews with JK, Kaya/Chawia, 3/5/1988; and MN, Lushangonyi/Mwanda, 22/9/1988.

[42] Interviews with Mrs. GM, Shigaro/Werugha, 27/5/1988; Mrs. WM, Werugha/Werugha, 30/7/1993; and Mrs. PM, Mwanda/Mwanda, 3/8/1993.

[43] Interviews with Peter Bostock, Oxford, England, 3/4/1989; and AM, Shigaro/Werugha, 26/3/1988. World War II brought a European agricultural officer to Taita, and led to an enormous expansion of the African agricultural staff. Both put a great deal of time into school programs. See KNA, DAO/TTA/1/1/222, Agricultural Safari Diaries 1940–50; and DAO/TTA/1/1/27, Taita District Agricultural Annual Reports, 1939–50.

[44] Education's increasing secularization also stemmed from the colonial Education Department's standardization of the curriculum. Some felt it effected "too great a divorce between the Pastoral and Educational sides of the work." Annual Letter of Rev. Bostock, 1941.

Christian nominalism in 1940s Taita greatly worried missionaries. See Bostock's Annual Letters of 1938, 1941, and 1944. Devout Christian WaTaita also decried increased nominalism in education and Christian society during the late 1930s and 1940s. Interview with AM, Shigaro/Werugha, 2/9/1988.

held Taita (i.e., livestock) wealth, as against money wealth in the colonial capitalist order.

Still, *Kidaßida* did not prevent all (or even most) progressive beliefs and practices from gaining some sort of purchase. Christianity and education became commonplace in the Hills, and unquestionably were reworking consciousness, social and cultural forms, and everyday life in the Hills. The next chapter shows how progressive forces and colonial capitalism spurred tremendous changes in the socioeconomic order. *Kidaßida*'s coercive social power, then, was waning. By the late 1940s, the very concept of *Kidaßida* was growing vulnerable to progressives' treatment of it as nostalgia: as a sign of common Taita cultural heritage increasingly divorced from Taita identity's contemporary content. However, *Kidaßida* as an ideology of propriety was far from finished. It had a tremendous constraining and shaping influence on the changes of the 1930s and 1940s.

Education and *Kidaßida*

Many *Wutasi* followers rejected the progressive Christian ethic that "improvement" was perfectly compatible with a historical Taita ethnicity. Their reservations about mission education summarized the disagreement: they felt that education made a person lose touch with beliefs, practices, and everyday ways they considered essential parts of Taita identity. Education's emphasis on Christianity and social and moral "improvement" in the 1930s stoked the *Wutasi* followers' misgivings, and carried forward long–standing concerns among *Wutasi* followers:

> I entered school in 1933, but my grandfather grabbed me out of there! The old men refused to have this thing. . . . They said it will ruin us, it will fill us with foreign things and make us lose respect for Taita ways, we will be lost to them. . . . So [PN's grandfather] sent an old warrior, Nyambu, from our lineage. He came to Bura [school] with a sword and grabbed us out of there.[45]

The quotation succinctly summarizes many *Wutasi* followers' concerns. They felt, often rightly, that the educated lost respect for uneducated youths and older people. Interviewees on both sides of this cultural divide confirmed such tensions. Some educated children, many of their teachers, and some of their Christian parents, felt that they shouldn't mix with the "dirty" and "ignorant" uneducated young people who would just try to "drag us back" or "confuse us with their dark ways."[46] *Wutasi*–following young people, for their part, often harassed or mocked the educated—sometimes out of disdain for them, and sometimes from resentment:

---

[45] Interview with PN, Ngerenyi/Chawia, 9/5/1988.

[46] Interviews with MW, Lushangonyi/Mwanda, 22/9/1988; DM, Teri/Sagalla, 10/7/1993; and Mrs. PM, Mwanda/Mwanda, 3/8/1993. Many others could be cited.

SM: In those days, we followed the Christians home from school and called them names, or we hid in the trees and threw [pebbles] at them.
Q: Why?
SM: They thought they were better than us. . . . They said bad things about us.[47]

Many *Wutasi* followers worried that the tensions generated a great deal of anger among people, potentially stirring up cosmological difficulty and worldly misfortune. They blamed the conflicts on education and Christianity, for "[the schools] taught young people to despise Taita ways and to leave *Kidaβida* behind. This brought many troubles."[48]

Older *Wutasi* followers and their supporters took a number of steps to preserve Taita ways against what they saw as education's attacks on *Kidaβida*. First, as in previous decades, many prevented children from attending school. Now, however, it was increasingly grandparents who tried to hold the children out of school, which put children's parents on the spot. Several interviewees who wanted to go to school in the 1930s said that their parents were willing, but grandparents or other older relatives objected.[49] One interviewee wanted to send his sons to school in the late 1930s but "was forbidden by my father. . . . He said I am letting the boy leave the life of *Kidaβida* and become lost from us. So my children could not go to school until the old man died."[50] As educating the young became the rule rather than the exception in the 1940s, older men defending *Kidaβida* resorted to strong pressure to hold the eldest son of a household out of school, so that he could move into *Wutasi*–based elderhood later in life.[51]

As parental support for schooling consolidated in the 1940s, *Wutasi* followers encouraged the students to acquire secular skills and knowledge, but to shun the religious side of education. Older men might compliment students for their abilities, yet admonish them to stick to *Wutasi*:

My uncles and aunts and grandfathers were very pleased that I could read and write. . . . They brought me pieces of paper . . . [that] they found here or there, . . . a newspaper or a piece of paper with numbers. . . . I said, "I will read the Bible to you." "No. The Bible says Taita ways are bad, doesn't it? Do not read us that book. . . . Do not listen to the Christians."[52]

Sometimes a sharper tone prevailed:

47 Interview with SM, Mwanda/Mwanda, 15/9/1988.
48 Interview with OK, Shigaro/Werugha, 2/8/1993.
49 In addition to PN, Ngerenyi/Chawia, 9/5/1988, interviews with AK, Shigaro/Werugha, 25/4/1988; SM, Teri/Sagalla, 12/7/1993; and Mrs. MM,Werugha/Werugha, 30/7/1993.
50 Interview with GN, Mgange Nyika/Mwanda, 20/9/1988.
51 G. Harris, *Casting*, 58.
52 Interview with KM, Werugha/Werugha, 3/10/1988.

When I came home from school, I could find my grandmother waiting for me. . . . She did not like education. . . . "The priest said that I am a 'heathen,' didn't he? He said our customs and traditions are 'superstition.' . . . They pull you . . . with money, but they pull you from your people." [53]

The situation slowly became less fraught, for the *Wutasi* followers' stance in the late 1940s dovetailed well with the changing ideology of progressivism. As education became more secularized, the older *Wutasi* followers were more easily reconciled to it. The newly educated often knew little of what elders considered *Kidaßida*, but became less likely, even if baptized, to condemn non–Christian proceedings and disrupt rituals: "The old men did not complain about school. . . . We greeted them nicely . . . and they greeted us very nicely. . . . They had meetings with their beer and we just stayed away." [54] Devout Christians now tended to ignore devout *Wutasi* followers, sensing that their time was passing. Too, as the decades diminished the ranks of *Wutasi* followers, succeeding generations of *Wutasi* followers adopted more flexible attitudes to the Christian influx—a transition discussed just below. These shifts, combined with growing Christian nominalism, allowed people on both sides of the religious divide to agree upon education as a source of economic opportunity.

Misgivings about the Christian character of education did not entirely disappear. This was most apparent in Taita's independent schools movement, which ran from 1943 to 1946. Officials and missionaries thought it both a sign that the mission system lagged behind demand, and a tentacle of the colony's most activist African political association, Central Province's Kenya African Union. [55] Also important, however, was local dissatisfaction with the Christian nature of mission education, and a desire for schools that did not attack *Wutasi* and its social and cultural values. This aspect of support for the independent schools was explicitly described by some of those involved as an attempt to defend Taita ways. [56]

Wutasi, Christianity, and *Kidaßida*

Nevertheless, tensions over education generally eased by the late 1940s, reflecting a wider, if uneasy, truce between most *Wutasi* followers and most Christians over Taita identity. The antagonisms of the 1920s and 1930s over conversion and *Kidaßida* settled down into a (sometimes strained) live–and–let–live atmosphere. As one interviewee put it, *Wutasi* followers agreed to live–and–

[53] The words heathen and superstition were said in English. Interview with RM, Wundanyi/Werugha, 29/7/1993.

[54] Interview with SM, Teri/Sagalla, 12/7/1993.

[55] KNA, DAO/TTA/1/1/130, Handing Over Report, DC Leslie to Dowson, 1946, and DAO/TTA/1/1/164, and DC/TTA/1/2, District Annual Reports, 1945–46. Also, Annual Letters of Rev. Peter Bostock, 1943, 1945.

[56] Interviews with CA, Ilole/Bura, 17/8/1988, and MM, Mwanda/Mwanda, 15/9/1988; also A. Harris and G. Harris, "WaTaita Today," chap. 5.

let–live, and Christians intervened less in *Wutasi* followers' activities.[57] Older *Wutasi* followers still maintained that Christians lacked real knowledge of *Kidaßida*, but as long as Christians behaved civilly and respectfully, and—in a new twist—as long as their small lineages were *represented* at rituals, they were deemed to not pose an ongoing threat to the social order.[58]

The spread of religious nominalism and a resurgence of religious mixing contributed to the rapprochement of the 1940s, despite a steady stream of admonitions against both by firm Anglicans and CMS missionaries.[59] More Christians were willing to take part in *Wutasi* rituals, and fewer Christians obstructed or demeaned them. Both trends mitigated the impact of Christians' conversion on non–Christian kin and neighbors. Many Christians also took part in more minor events that fell within older people's rubric of Taita ways, which kept them thoroughly enmeshed in the networks of their local communities:

> For these Christians, the dances . . . like *Kinyandi* and *Kishawi* were not allowed. . . . The missionaries told them the dances are very bad. . . . But at night these Christians saw the fire [at the dance site], they stole away and went to dance, and went home again before the morning.
>
> My wife was a Christian, we went to the dances together. Her parents were Christians, they knew she was at the dances, . . . they were very annoyed. . . . But when I gave bridewealth, her father took my *chofi* [sugar cane beer], he didn't mind.[60]

Simultaneously, *Wutasi* was becoming increasingly subject to nominalism. This, too, had a generational aspect: many of the young who became educated but did not convert to Christianity nonetheless had less faith or interest in *Wutasi*. Some among the younger generations did not maintain household or lineage shrines or take much active part in rituals:

> JM: According to the customs my fathers and grandfathers followed, a few months after someone dies you remove the skull [from the person's grave] and put it in a special cave . . . with others from your lineage, so the ancestor can be worshipped there. . . . By the time I was getting mature, [the 1940s] sometimes my age mates did that with their ancestors, and sometimes they did not.
>
> Q: Your age mates were Christian?
>
> JM: I am talking now of *Watasi* [i.e., *Wutasi* followers]! . . . Some would not take the skulls to the caves, . . . or they would not maintain the caves as they were taught.[61]

---

57 Interview with PM, Ilole/Bura, 16/8/1988.

58 Ibid. "Some person from the Christian houses always came. . . . It was enough."

59 In the words of one informant, "the first Christians were very strict, but many [of those] who followed were more half–half." Interview with JM, Shigaro/Werugha, 20/4/1988.

60 Interview with MM, Nyolo/Bura, 15/8/1988. MM was a *Wutasi* follower, but his wife was a Christian even before they married in 1939, indicating further the extent to which mixing might go on by then.

61 Interview with JM, Kishamba/Chawia, 24/9/1988.

Some officials and missionaries noted this falling–off of belief in *Wutasi*, as well.[62] Nominal *Wutasi* followers increasingly appreciated not Christianity itself, but how Christians lived. By the 1940s, after decades spent on the job market and living among Christians, nearly all *Wutasi* followers had long since taken up Western–style dress. Now, as education spread widely among non–Christians, the younger among them began to follow school–taught routines of hygiene, house construction, farming, and the like, indicating a slow dissemination of Christian–rooted, progressive ideas into Taita society.

As the above indicates, even as the line between Christians and *Wutasi* followers was blurring in the 1940s, it was crosscut by a generation gap. As one official put it:

> There is a sharp and ever widening conflict of view, between the older people and the rising generation; the latter show extreme intolerance to established and long–standing custom. This attitude brings the youth of the tribe into direct opposition to the tribal elders on all major issues.[63]

The divide drew younger, more nominal Christians and younger, more nominal *Wutasi* followers together, through various shared experiences: for men, migratory labor and life experiences outside Taita; for women, farming without husbands in subordination to the husbands' parents; for both men and women, the strains of parental controls over them in a changing political–economic context. However, differences of outlook prevented older Christians and *Wutasi* followers from forming a countervailing alliance.

Christians also realized that generational turnover was working against *Wutasi* followers: the latter were aging in aggregate, for fewer young people stepped into their dying elders' shoes. In this context, Christians in the 1940s tended to preach less to *Wutasi* followers than in earlier decades.[64] Succeeding generations of elders retained a commitment to the idea of proper Taita knowledge and ways, but most of the newer generations of elders took less offense at the Christians. By the 1940s, most elders accepted Christianity and some progressive "improvement" as compatible with Taita identity.

Meanwhile, as the terms of *Kidaßida* grew more flexible in the 1940s, most Christians sought acceptance in Taita's social order, even if it was still influenced by *Wutasi*. Christians did not claim allegiance to *Kidaßida*, but most continued to insist on their Taita identity and their definite place in Taita society.

PK: We were true Taitas, yes!

Q: Even without following *Wutasi*?

PK: Those were the things of our grandfathers, we did not need them. . . . That life of *Kidaßida* was long ago.[65]

---

62 District Commissioners made note of it in 1948, 1949, and 1950. KNA, DAO/TTA/1/1/164, District Annual Reports. Also, Peter Bostock's Annual Letter of 1944, and interview, 3/4/1989.

63 KNA, DAO/TTA/1/1/164, District Annual Report for 1948.

64 "Those elders kept drinking their *chofi* . . . [and] doing their dances. . . . The old ones, we left them alone." Interview with PM, Wundanyi/Werugha, 13/8/1988.

65 Interview with PK, Werugha/Werugha, 6/10/1988.

Most Christians stayed in lineage and neighborhood networks, and pursued social advance through those networks in ways similar to *Wutasi* followers. Older Christian men tried to command the respect of elderhood, despite their lack of ritual position and knowledge of *Wutasi*. Christians might accept such men as legitimate elders, as did state institutions for elders like native courts,[66] but non–Christians and many Christian elders themselves understood it as a highly attenuated elderhood:

> The Christians who called themselves elders, they thought . . . age is what gives them the respect of elderhood. . . . Yes, age brings respect, they had that respect of age, . . . but they knew nothing. . . . elders with real knowledge could not respect them, the Christians could not get their respect.[67]

Nevertheless, being a Christian in the late 1940s no longer put one at the fringes of Taita identity, even in the eyes of *Wutasi* followers. Rather, it put Christians in the middling position observed by Alfred and Grace Harris from 1950 to 1952: most *Wutasi* followers and most Christians saw themselves as parts of a loose cultural whole, albeit one marked by some tensions and divisions.[68]

One group stood as a caveat to the above discussion: some firm Christians in the 1930s and 1940s made themselves a quasi–autonomous community in Taita, relocating spatially to corners of various lineage holdings where they could live near one another.

> If a goat was slaughtered in the neighborhood [for *Wutasi* divination of a problem or an illness], and a Christian refused to [take part], it was difficult to live together. . . . When my father became a Christian he really grabbed the religion, . . . so it became difficult to live together with non–Christians. He built [a new house] down over that way, where the Christians stayed together.[69]

In such Christian enclaves, networks of Christian community provided mutual support, both social and spiritual, making the Christians less dependent on daily ties with *Wutasi* followers. Firm Christians living this way usually were not considered lost, but "many difficulties, many incidents" ran through their relations with surrounding communities. They were often shunned by neighbors and other members of their lineages.[70]

---

[66] For Christians treating older, respected Christian men as elders, interview with BM, Wusi/Chawia, 5/5/1988. On older Christian men taking on the airs of elders, A. Harris and G. Harris, "WaTaita Today," 141. On Christians' presence as elders in Native Tribunals, see KNA, DC/TTA/3/3/4, List of Tribunal Members for 1947.

[67] Interview with CA, Ilole/Bura, 17/8/1988.

[68] A. Harris and G. Harris, "WaTaita Today," 219–25.

[69] Interview with AK, Shigaro/Werugha, 25/4/1988.

[70] Ibid.; and interview with GM, Kishamba/Chawia, 24/9/1988. Also, Comaroff and Comaroff, *Of Revelation*, 204.

Spiritually, firm Christians responded to the secularization of the 1940s by turning to revivalism. Coming in three waves between 1939 and 1950, revivalism aimed to replace the formality and rule–boundedness of prior Taita Christianity with an emphasis on emotional and spiritual experience.[71] This spiritual purification extended the distance between them and *Wutasi* followers, and led to further incidents between the groups.[72] However, it did not worsen relations significantly, for revivalism, as an inwardly turned movement, aimed mainly to reawaken the already converted. The revivalists concentrated on testifying to other Christians, strengthening the spirituality at the core of their constituency. By and large, they left *Wutasi* followers alone, and most *Wutasi* followers responded in kind.

---

[71] Interviews with BM, Wusi/Chawia, 5/5/1988, and Mrs. GM, Shigaro/Werugha, 27/5/1988. The CMS supported this by initiating an annual "Week of Witness" in 1943; Annual Letter of Peter Bostock, 1943.

[72] In 1951, revivalists took up the old practice of disrupting *Wutasi* rituals, to give testimony to how they came to convert. Revivalists also preached in the African District Council, the successor body to the LNC. KNA, DAO/TTA/1/1/141, Intelligence Reports, 8/7/1951; and interview with BM, Wusi/Chawia, 5/5/1988.

7

Being Taita, II: The Cultural Politics of Socioeconomic Change, 1930–1950

> White people and Indians came and said, "if you grow this
> crop and this crop we will pay you this and that for them."
> That is when the men started growing vegetables . . . and,
> later, peppers. . . . Those are the crops of business.
> —NM, Wundanyi/Werugha[1]

Introduction

The maturation of labor migrancy and the rise of cash crop agriculture in 1930s Taita drove multifaceted socioeconomic changes that in turn extended several kinds of intergenerational struggles. By the late 1940s, much of what older men championed as *Kidaßida* in the 1910s and 1920s was falling by the wayside: for many practical purposes, money supplanted livestock as the main form of wealth; sons often had more material wealth than parents; young married women gained more independence from their parents–in–law, and often had better access to their husbands' wealth than the men's parents; and lineage herds started to shrink, sometimes dramatically. Progressive ideas about work, wealth, and social progress encouraged and underscored the changes.

All this profoundly affected the terms of Taita society. Older men's claims over the wealth of adult sons lost footing in the 1930s, as younger men effectively compelled a reformulation of the *Kidaßida* axioms of parental wealth control. Young women also managed to revise axioms about how dutiful Taita

---

[1]   Interview with NM, Wundanyi/Werugha, 26/5/1988.

daughters–in–law behaved. However, while less dependent on parents–in–law and more influential in the running of their own households, young wives now struggled to prevent migrant–laboring, cash–cropping husbands from overworking them on subsistence fields. As money became the main daily medium of wealth and herd sizes fell, older men also faced another crisis in their terms of *Kidaßida*: the dwindling herds under their control lost significance as the axiom of livestock as proper Taita wealth came under siege.

Despite these changes, older non–progressives in the 1930s and 1940s still had levers of power over the terms of Taita society. For older men, the most critical and effective one remained control of land. As Taita's population rose during the century, land in the Hills became increasingly scarce. Older men tightly restricted the development of a monetized land market through the 1940s, rarely selling parcels of land, and then only to others in their lineage or neighborhood.[2] Most men still received most of their land through inheritance, and their seniors utilized that dependence. Older men and women also continued to dominate important networks of social support, alliance, patronage and clientship, and mutuality, a dominance that gave them real sway over sons and daughters.

Overall, though, older people in this era used their power to influence the terms of socioeconomic change, not obstruct it. The highly controlling terms of *Kidaßida* that older men asserted in the 1910s became less tenable as time passed, and were gradually altered and relaxed. Circumstances and younger people pushed for those changes, but generational turnover played a part, too. Most older men and women of the 1940s had matured during colonialism. Their own experiences helped them appreciate the perspectives and desires of their adult children, as well as the competing demands on the young. Older men and women sought to protect their influence, and pressured the young to support them and respect their ways and values, but most fashioned more flexible expectations of the young. And as older people let go of earlier *Kidaßida* axioms, *Kidaßida* itself began to assume a different meaning.

Economic Change and the Cultural
Politics of Households and Wealth, 1930–1950

Migratory Labor, Remittances, and Households, 1930–1950

Migratory labor continued to play a critical part in Taita's economy. Parents still sent single sons out of the Hills to earn money, and continued to expect those sons to remit the bulk of their wages. Young, single sons mostly continued to do so, although many now kept more for themselves in the name of marriage expenses. Gross remittances also dipped in the early 1930s, when the world depression hit the migrant labor system, cutting into African wages across

---

[2]   Interviews with SK, Chawia/Chawia, 28/5/1988; SM, Wusi/Chawia, 29/6/1988; and LM, Teri/ Sagalla, 27/6/1988.

the board. *Kibarua* dock labor in Mombasa plummeted in pay and availability. Other kinds of unskilled work in Mombasa also became harder to get and less remunerative. Many young men from Taita had to seek work in the nearby (and dreaded) sisal plantations.[3] Some Taita plantations had a nearly 70 percent local labor force in the early 1930s. By 1936, however, the worst of the crisis had passed, and both the young men's labor and the plantations' hiring reverted to predepression patterns.[4] The depression hit educated labor migrants less hard. Highly skilled and literate African labor remained rare enough that Taita's educated workers by and large found steady work, though many saw their wages dip.[5] Still, by the late 1930s Taita's young men again had good labor market prospects: demand and wage levels recovered, and since a relatively large proportion of WaTaita in the work force was educated, many secured high–wage work.

Labor still flowed out from the Hills and remittances still flowed back, but a late 1930s revision in remittance patterns took shape. Far more than previously, marriage marked a critical turning point in remittances. Despite parental objections, husbands now commonly sent portions of their wages to wives as well as to parents:

> *JM:* I split that [remitted] money between them: tea for my wife, tea for [my] parents.
>
> *Q:* Did you send the money together, or separately?
>
> *JM:* I just carried it myself. Each one, here is yours, here is yours. Each one privately.
>
> *Q:* Did your wife get a bigger portion? Or the parents? Or they were the same?
>
> *JM:* One time my father wins, maybe the next time my wife.[6]

As this suggests, at least some wives received portions comparable to those given to parents, though most interviewees say wives received less.[7] A few even went the other way: one man, earning 90/= per month as a carpenter in the 1930s, gave roughly 20/= to 40/= a month to his father and 30/= to 50/= to his wife.[8] The former amount was quite a tidy sum, since older men mostly used their sons' remitted wages to pay Hut Tax (now 12/= annually), meet a

---

[3]   KNA, DC/TTA/1/1, Taita District Annual Reports/Labor, 1931–1934; many interviews provided corroboration.

[4]   KNA, DC/TTA/1/1, Taita District Annual Reports, 1931–36; the 70 percent figure dates to 1934. The 1936 report begins with a statement of Taita's return to prosperity.

[5]   Interviews with SM, Wusi/Chawia, 9/4/1988; JM, Wundanyi/Werugha, 12/8/1988; and LM, Teri/Sagalla, 23/8/1988.

[6]   Interview with JM, Teri/Sagalla, 9/7/1993; "tea" is slang for money. Many other interviews could be cited.

[7]   Interviews with Mrs. MM, Lushangonyi/Mwanda, 21/9/1988; KM, Werugha/Werugha, 3/10/1988; and Mrs. FM, Mogho Mleche/Mbale, 3/11/1988.

[8]   Interview with JK, Kaya/Chawia, 3/5/1988; he also kept about 15/= to 20/= per month with him in Mombasa.

few material wants, and buy livestock. Though most migrant workers made less than the carpenter, even a monthly remittance of 5/= in the 1930s could meet seniors' cash needs and still leave enough to buy a few animals.[9]

Wives had a number of uses for the money given them. Early in the century, the senior household of a small lineage paid the Hut Tax of junior households, but by the 1930s each household usually paid its own tax. With husbands often away during tax collection season, wives typically put aside tax money and paid it. School fees, instituted for all grades by the mid–1930s, became a second major expense as demand for education expanded. Older people sometimes obstructed children's education by withholding school fee money from children's mothers; to skirt this, young husbands often included that money in remittances to their wives.[10] In addition, most wives now took responsibility for buying household items for themselves and their children. Progressive households also purchased a range of other items that denoted "improved" and "civilized" ways of living.[11]

As husbands' remittances to wives became common, young married women depended less on their in–laws while husbands were away. This did not dissolve the relationship between senior and junior households, for many important ties between young wives and their in–laws remained in place: young women's marriage into their husbands' lineage still enmeshed the women and their in–laws in multifaceted networks of support, obligation, and mutuality. Those networks still provided social sustenance and an immediate community—albeit one in which a young wife's sense of belonging was sometimes ambiguous.

Too, senior households still had some material power over junior ones. Most significantly, young wives and husbands worked land "cut" for their households from the husbands' parents' fields, but did not inherit significant holdings of their own until the husbands' fathers died. That power over land encouraged married sons and daughters–in–law to be dutiful and respectful, and to provide their elders with money and labor. Nevertheless, wage remittances gave most young wives in Taita a new measure of socioeconomic autonomy from their in–laws.

Q: So, then, who made decisions about money in your household?

Mrs. SM: Me, when my husband was . . . in Mombasa.

Q: And his parents, did they have that power . . . over your money, too?

---

9   Interview with MT, Kishamba/Chawia, 9/6/1988.

10   "[My husband's father] did not pay our tax. . . . He did not pay school fees for the children. He did not pay for our clothes. I paid for those things. The money came from my husband." Interview with Mrs. MM, Lushangonyi/Mwanda, 21/9/1988; also, interviews with Mrs. CM, Shigaro/Werugha, 26/7/1993; and Mrs. MM, Werugha/Werugha, 30/7/1993.

11   Stores near the mission stations stocked items desired by stricter Christians and more dedicated progressives: kerosene, plows, bicycles, condensed milk, tea, needles and thread, better–quality cloth, and some ready–made clothing. KNA, PC/Cst/1/19/82, and interview with AM, Shigaro/Werugha, 2/5/1988.

Mrs. SM: No, . . . they must let me run my household. It was not their money, not theirs.[12]

In place of the *Kidaßida* axiom that young men turned over wages to parents (who looked after their long–term interests) stood a new level of financial commitment between labor migrants and their wives, and a new degree of distinction between junior and senior households. In the new order, junior households staked out some independence in economic decision making. Many women also *needed* the latitude that the new arrangement gave them in intergenerational relations, for, as will be seen below, their husbands increased work burdens on them in the 1930s and 1940s. In the ensuing labor crunch on young wives, work for in–laws was among the first areas to suffer.

These changes in men's remittances to parents, and in daughters–in–law's work for them, caused less of an intergenerational crisis than it might have. Of course, this is not to say that confrontations simply ended:

Q: Were there [arguments] about helping your parents?

JM: I did not like to argue with them.

Q: Did you argue with them?

JM: [laughing] Very much! Very much!

Q: [laughing] But you did not like it?

JM: I was . . . very serious then.

Q: What did you argue about?

JM: Money! . . . My father said I was starving them! . . . Some months they had 15/= [from me], it was a lot of money then.[13]

But several factors usually tempered the conflicts, so that they rarely descended into threats of declaring sons and daughters lost. First, sons did continue to remit money, often sizable sums, to their parents. The sons saw this remittance as a reciprocal obligation and an indicator of respect:

I always gave my father shillings. It was necessary to do that. They worked and worked, now they can rest a little. . . . Now you must help them, . . . you must [show] thanks for their work. . . . You must give them their respect.[14]

As a growing proportion of Taita's work force became educated, young men in skilled jobs could send parents the equivalent of an unskilled worker's entire wage, yet still keep most of their earnings in their own household. For instance, a tractor driver/mechanic in the mid–1940s gave his parents 30/= a month

---

12   Interview with Mrs. SM, Werugha/Werugha, 30/9/1988. This was the baldest statement of new financial autonomy I heard, but several others resembled it in effect if not in tone.

13   Interview with JM, Teri/Sagalla, 9/7/1993.

14   Interview with AM, Shigaro/Werugha, 1/8/1993.

(more than sisal cutters earned) from a take–home wage of 100/=.[15] As parents lost strength in old age, sons across the Hills felt it their duty to keep them well fed and comfortable.[16]

Second, and similarly, young wives maintained the discourse of dutifulness to their in–laws even as they loosened those ties somewhat. They still backed up the discourse with work—though increasingly according to their own sense of what they could manage, which remained a sore point with mothers–in–law expecting work relief as they aged.[17] Young wives still took part in lineage networks of work exchange: in fact, those networks grew in importance for young women. They continued to look to their husbands' lineages for ties of reciprocity and support; and for the sake of those claims, too, it was important to do some farming and household labor for parents–in–law.[18] They still hired day labor to work on their own fields, so they could go themselves to their in–laws. In all, even as they cut back on some actual work for in–laws, they still subscribed to the ideology of that work, (and of respect for in–laws), as Taita cultural ideals. They deferred to their in–laws' authority by seeking to minimize overt disagreements with them, maintaining the manner of dutiful daughters despite their growing economic autonomy.

Older men and women, for their part, relaxed some of the expectations about sons and daughters that had been pillars of *Kidaßida* in the 1910s and 1920s. To some extent this was foisted on them, but by the 1930s and 1940s, most older men had once done migrant labor, and most older women understood first–hand some of the pressures confronting migrant laborers' wives. Many older people rued their lost primacy of place, commonly complaining, for instance, that young women were losing respect for their in–laws.[19] But the complaint now carried little leverage or threat: by the 1930s and 1940s, older people no longer considered it a pillar of *Kidaßida* that senior women should closely control the labor of junior women in the lineage, nor that the former should have much say in the running of the latters' households.

During these decades another early axiom of *Kidaßida* fell by the wayside: parents made their peace with migrant laboring (and cash–crop farming) sons surpassing them in money wealth:

> That custom started changing . . . when children got themselves into money more. . . . They continued caring for their fathers, but they kept

---

[15] Interview with JN, Mbale/Mbale, 8/11/1988.

[16] Interviews with JM, Wusi/Chawia, 5/4/1988; AK, Shigaro/Werugha, 25/4/1988; and MM Mwanda/Mwanda, 12/9/1988.

[17] Interviews with Mrs. MM, Lushangonyi/Mwanda, 21/9/1988; Mrs. WM, Werugha/Werugha, 30/7/1993; and Mrs. PN, Mwanda/Mwanda, 3/8/1993.

[18] Interviews with Mrs. MM, Shigaro/Werugha, 17/6/1988; Mrs. EK, Wongonyi/Mbololo, 7/7/1988; and Mrs. GM, Teri/Sagalla, 24/8/1988.

[19] Some of this allowed parents to avoid criticizing sons: "My in–laws always found fault with me . . . [because] they did not like to say bad things about my husband. . . . We all knew." Interview with Mrs. GM, Shigaro/Werugha, 15/7/1988.

money for themselves. . . . I passed my father in money, . . . [and] many, many others [did], too.[20]

But while the older men's control over lineage wealth declined as a *Kidaßida* axiom, another axiom—a compromise one—replaced it: the Taita young should see to the needs and wants of their elders, especially as they became physically limited by old age. Proper Taita sons did this by supplying enough money to keep parents comfortable, a rather more elastic notion than the one it superseded. Proper Taita daughters did their part by relieving their seniors of work burdens. But now daughters claimed more say in the process, and, because of other needs, were inclined to consider less work sufficient. Older households now managed wealth and labor far less closely than before: lineage as a basis of resource control lost much of its bite.

These changes in socioeconomic relationships and everyday practices flew in the face of earlier terms of *Kidaßida*. Yet so long as the young abided by the looser terms they had worked out (however tentatively and tensely) with their seniors, they were not deemed lost. Speaking of one's children as lost did not come easily, either materially—for the children's contributions to their seniors' well–being would end—or affectively. The new terms of acceptable behavior, then, significantly shifted the terms of Taita identity. Other socioeconomic aspects of Taita ethnicity were being renegotiated in the 1930s–40s, as well.

Cash Cropping, the Decline of
Livestock–as–Wealth, and Taita Identity

Cash cropping became the other major source of socioeconomic change in Taita from the 1930s onward. Officials briefly thought that cash–crop farming might remake Taita's economy and society, largely replacing subsistence farming, commoditizing most of Taita's agriculture, and vastly extending the commodification of its labor. This capitalist transformation would push "excess" people permanently out of the Hills, and feed into another mid–century colonial aspiration: the creation of a permanent, stable working class in Mombasa.[21] In the event, Taita cash cropping did not nearly fulfill officials' grand ambitions, but its incorporation into the agricultural economy did have dramatic effects. It reoriented land–use patterns and practices in the Hills, altered relations of agricultural production, and to some extent *did* further the commodification of agriculture and labor within Taita.

Increased commodification accelerated a devaluing of indigenous terms of economic order among many younger people: cash cropping figured prominently in the decline of livestock–as–wealth, a pillar of *Kidaßida*. Commodification also spurred a greater gendering of agricultural labor, which

---

[20]   Interview with AM, Shigaro/Werugha, 2/5/1988.

[21]   KNA, DAO/TTA/1/1/30, Vegetable Trade, and ARC(MAA)–2/3/39iv, Coast Province Annual Report, 1948. On hopes for creating a settled African working class, see Cooper, *Waterfront*, chap. 4.

in turn made wives further rework their relations with their in–laws. By the early 1950s, these struggles settled into a series of uneasy compromises. All in Taita declared livestock the most "Taita" form of wealth, and most men continued to take part in livestock–based social networks, though on a slightly different and much reduced scale. However, most people also acknowledged their increasing *de facto* orientation towards money, and many began treating livestock as a commodity. Men claimed control over cash–crop production and long–distance marketing. Women, relegated to a yet greater share of subsistence farming, remade female work groups into networks of subsistence labor aid, and further reduced the amount of work they did for parents–in–law.

The Political Economy of Cash Cropping:
An Aerial View, 1918–1950

The exporting of food from Taita has a long precolonial history, but cash crops (i.e., crops raised to sell) were a colonial phenomenon. The main cash crops raised, garden vegetables, were high–value items from the 1910s through World War II.[22] Though they required considerable labor and careful handling, they usually provided a good return for the effort, and sometimes an excellent one.[23] By 1948, cash crops accounted for 18 percent of the total African income in Taita.[24]

The first recorded instance of cash cropping dates to 1918, but at that juncture European officials doubted its economic value relative to migrant labor.[25] In the 1920s, a few individuals, all Christian, educated men, raised and sold vegetables. Some learned about the crops at schools, where missionaries espoused both economic farming and local vegetable consump-

---

[22] Local people developed a taste for some of them, but most were grown strictly for sale. By 1951, the list of items sent from Taita to Mombasa included cabbage, carrots, beets, leeks, green onions, radish, parsnip, parsley, tomatoes, celery, lettuce, cauliflower, Brussel sprouts, cucumbers, English peas, onions, spinach, turnips, zucchini, pumpkins, eggplants, chilies, and bell peppers. A wide variety of fruits was sold as well. KNA, DAO/TTA/1/1/152, Taita Vegetable Returns, 1951.
Chilies, an unusual crop in this group, tolerated hotter, drier conditions than other vegetables, and so could be raised in the low zone. Their main boom period came later than other produce, after World War II: in 1951 and 1953, chilies surpassed the income earned from all other vegetables. But prices fell briefly in 1952, then lastingly in 1955, and production waned accordingly. DAO/TTA/1/1/27, Taita Agricultural Annual Reports, 1946–58.

[23] Vegetables usually paid far higher prices than cereals. In 1940, the leading vegetable farmer made 280/= on his crop; not a lot compared to the wages of a skilled migrant worker, but an excellent return for part time work while living at home; KNA, DAO/TTA/1/1/27, Taita District Agricultural Annual Report, 1940. Figures on personal income later in the war are not available, but several interviewees described vegetable farming as considerably more profitable by 1945; interviews with OM, Wundanyi/Werugha, 5/5/1988; DM, Werugha/Werugha, 29/9/1988; and JK, Werugha/Werugha, 3/10/1988.

[24] Marketed produce earned £15,800, as opposed to £73,080 in wages. See A. Harris and G. Harris, "WaTaita Today," 86.

[25] In 1918, two Christians began raising cabbages, potatoes, and onions to sell at Voi and Mombasa. KNA, DC/TTA/1/19/84, Taita Produce, 16/6/1918 and 22/8/1918.

[26] Interviews with JM, Wusi/Chawia, 5/4/1988; and AM, Shigaro/Werugha, 26/3/1988; also, KNA, DC/TTA/1/1, Taita District Annual Report for 1927.

tion.[26] Others were introduced to them by the European manager of the Wundanyi coffee plantation.[27] Still others decided to try raising them after seeing them on sale in Mombasa.[28] A trickle of state support came from Taita's progressive–dominated LNC, which in 1926 voted funds for vegetable seed production and distribution. Until the 1930s, European officials' involvement was virtually nil.[29] Meanwhile difficulties in marketing produce deterred most farmers from considering cash–crop agriculture.

In the early 1930s, however, colonial administrators started to encourage Taita cash cropping. Their newfound interest was part of a colonial policy shift across Kenya, in response to the world depression. Briefly, the depression shattered settler farming, so the state encouraged African agricultural expansion as a way to keep the railway and port active, and keep Africans on the tax rolls. The state also used revenues from African agricultural production to maintain itself financially and bail out settler farmers.[30] The policy, as elucidated in the 1932 Native Affairs Annual Report, aimed to foster new African cash crops and organize their marketing.[31] In 1933, an agricultural assessment of Coast Province singled out Taita vegetable production as a target for growth.[32] An Agriculture Department circular in 1934 then instructed district officials to encourage farmers to set aside land for cash crops, then use "all permissible means and unremitting propaganda," including pressure from chiefs, to raise production levels.[33] Policy directives now backed Taita cash cropping—and prodded it in the back.

The 1934 Taita DC saw that cash cropping had a ready and expandable constituency if infrastructural problems could be overcome.

> The Taita . . . fully appreciate the value of economic crops but satisfactory marketing arrangements are wanting. . . . Even now some of the more progressive natives market their produce in Mombasa, but this only emphasizes future possibilities.[34]

---

[27] Interviews with WM, Shigaro/Werugha, 18/4/1988; and OM, Wundanyi/Werugha, 5/5/1988. The plantation manager gave the vegetable farmers horticultural advice and dispensed seeds cheaply.

[28] Interviews with JK, Ngerenyi/Chawia, 11/5/1988; and JM, Wundanyi/Werugha, 11/5/1988.

[29] For the LNC vote, see KNA, DC/TTA/1/1, District Annual Report, 1925; for limited official reporting, District Annuals of 1925 and 1932 (same file); and PC/Cst/1/12/288, Local Native Council, 27/5/1930.

[30] The 1931 Kenya Native Affairs Department Annual Report (pp. 4–5) stated, "The difficulties of the year have focused attention on the imperative necessity of developing to their utmost capacity the resources of the Native Reserves." For a fuller discussion of Kenya's colonywide agricultural policy in the 1930s, see Bill Bravman, "Towards a Political Economy of Upper Nyanza Agriculture During the Depression," (Ms., 1986).

[31] Kenya Native Affairs Department Annual Report, 1932, 94.

[32] KNA, PC/Cst/2/4/16, Report on Coast Province Agricultural Development, 5/4/1933, Appendix A.

[33] KNA, AGR/1/1244, Native Areas Agriculture.

[34] KNA, PC/Cst/2/4/16, Report on Coast Province Agricultural Development, 5/4/1933, Appendix A.

Local officials turned the general directive into two subsequent initiatives: first, they encouraged vegetable farming through propaganda and instruction at schools and in extension work. Second, they worked on marketing infrastructure. In 1935 a European agricultural officer joined the district staff, doubling its European administration. The next year the officers set up a cooperative society for Taita's vegetable growers, to collect their harvests, bulk produce to Mombasa, and coordinate its sale there.[35] The LNC provided free vegetable seeds to all who wanted them until 1939, when it established nominal fees. By that year, Taita's agricultural staff, in addition to the European officer, had swelled to seven African instructors, six assistants, and a clerk for the cooperative.[36]

These arrangements spurred immediate and rapid growth in vegetable farming. The DC stated in 1936 that nearly 3,800 farmers intended to use the cooperative's facilities. Even allowing for overestimation, this was a huge jump. The number of farmers that used the cooperative is not known, but by 1939 a core group of sixty–one members ran it.[37] In 1937, the cooperative handled 84,000 pounds of vegetables in nine months. In 1938, this rose to 182,000; in 1939 it swelled to 487,810. The vegetable tonnage exported from the district did not nearly meet the demand in Mombasa; standing orders for produce far outstripped the supply.[38] Small, independent marketing companies sprang up to try to fill the gap.

Then came World War II, which lashed vegetable production to the war effort. Cash–crop farming and marketing went on wartime footing, with heavy state involvement at every level; Taita farmers growing vegetables were exempted from conscription for other war work.[39] Produce from Taita largely went to Mombasa's ships' chandlers for Indian Ocean marine traffic.[40] In 1941, the LNC acquired a truck to bulk vegetables to Taita's railheads, then a second truck the following year. In 1944, the cooperative added two trucks of its own. The European agricultural officer made the spread of vegetable farming his main work, and African agricultural staffing grew throughout the war, raising the number of instructors from seven in 1938 to eleven in 1946.[41]

With all this encouragement, the number of farmers growing vegetables and the amount of vegetables produced mushroomed. The base level and impressive growth of the late 1930s were dwarfed by wartime expansion (see Table 1).

After the war, officials developed still more grandiose plans for Taita cash cropping: it would be the centerpiece of a social engineering policy. Some offi-

---

[35] KNA, PC/Cst/2/4/29, Marketing Fruits and Vegetables, 1936–39; and DC/TTA/1/1, District Annual Report, 1935.

[36] KNA, DAO/TTA/1/1/45, Vegetable Seeds, 4/10/1939; for agricultural staff, see DAO/TTA/1/1/27, District Agricultural Annual Report, 1939.

[37] KNA, PC/Cst,/2/4/29, Marketing Fruits and Vegetables, 28/2/1936, and 11/2/1941.

[38] Ibid., 11/2/1941.

[39] Interview with JM, Wundanyi/Werugha, 11/5/1988.

[40] KNA, PC/Cst,/2/4/29, Marketing Fruits and Vegetables, 8/5/1942.

[41] KNA, DAO/TTA/1/1/27, District Agricultural Annual Reports, 1941–46.

TABLE 1. Produce Shipped to Mombasa by the Government–Run Cooperative (excluding potatoes and fruits)

Year	Weight (lbs)
1937 (9 mos.)	84,000
1938	182,000
1939	487,810
1940	665,570
1941	1,060,903
1942	1,716,840
1943	3,040,636
1944	3,075,157
1945	1,988,052[42]

cials thought Taita on the verge of a long–term carrying–capacity crisis, for it had a large and growing population in a small territory, very limited land (and that highly fragmented by landholding patterns), declining cereal production, and areas of severe soil erosion. Officials argued that only the replacement of subsistence farming with cash cropping would cure these ills. As the Deputy PC of Coast Province put it in 1946:

> The salvation of the Taita Hills depends very largely on the substitu-tion of suitable cash crops, (of which vegetables are the most obvious), for cereal planting, which must inevitably lead to over–cultivation and the ruin of the land.[43]

Officials felt cash cropping had several advantages over subsistence farming. Taita needed to conserve soil better, and virtually all of its vegetables grew on bench terraces.[44] Cash crops had higher economic yields per acre than cereals, and while officials were trying to close badly eroded parts of Taita to farming, "at the same time the reduced areas of cultivation . . . must . . . be made to yield a greater return."[45] Reducing the acreage being farmed would mean that:

---

[42] KNA, PC/Cst,/2/4/29, Marketing Fruits and Vegetables, 11/2/1941, and DAO/TTA/1/1/27, District Agricultural Annual Reports, 1940–46. Potatoes peaked at 131,000 lbs (1942); fruits totaled as much as 108,040 lbs.
      A severe drought hurt production in 1945. Postwar demand and prices in Mombasa dropped from wartime levels, which adjusted Taita supply downward from the 1943–44 peak. Between 1946 and 1951, exports of vegetables fluctuated between roughly 1,100,000 and 1,862,000 lbs. KNA, DAO/TTA/1/1/27, District Agricultural Annual Reports, 1946–51.

[43] KNA, DAO/TTA/1/1/30, Vegetable Trade, 24/10/1946; see also DC/TTA/3/1/17, District Development Team, memo of 7/11/1950: "For some considerable number of years now, depart-mental officers have advocated the substitution of high–priced cash crops in Taita for staple food crops, . . . until now Government policy states that the true agricultural economy of Taita IS as stated above."

[44] KNA, DAO/TTA/1/1/185, Soil Conservation, 5/1/1943.

[45] KNA, ARC(MAA)–2/3/39iv, Coast Province Annual Report for 1948.

[m]any Africans have got to be divorced from the soil and depend on employment for their livelihood. . . . The extent to which the Taita men are already off the land is indicated by the fact that . . . no less than 4,600 [of roughly 13,000 adult Taita males] are out at work. Their dependents, however, continue to till the soil, and the men . . . return . . . when too old to earn their living elsewhere.[46]

The officials concluded that along with promoting cash cropping as the basic, high–value agriculture of Taita, male workers should be encouraged to take their families out of the Hills with them, and resettle in towns.[47]

This did not come to pass; by 1950 the plan was ruled unworkable and dramatically scaled back. The policy failure stemmed in part from people in Taita refusing to abandon subsistence networks and their land, a topic discussed below. The vagaries of markets also contributed to its demise, for Taita vegetable farmers were sensitive to the costs of cash–crop agriculture. A thorough switch-over would have required them to buy their cereals in markets, a very unattractive prospect after the war. Furthermore, vegetables, labor–intensive to grow, went through a substantial price drop in the postwar years.[48] At the same time, the colony's weak marketing infrastructure, combined with semidrought conditions across Kenya, made Taita's staple food, maize, at once much in demand and prohibitively expensive. As one official noted, "when the Taita grower has to . . . market at least three pounds of European vegetables to obtain the price of his "daily bread," it is not surprising that more and more maize is planted on land which should be reserved for more valuable crops."[49] Many farmers in Taita agreed.[50] By the early 1950s, cash crops had a place in many households' agricultural regimes, but always in combination with subsistence farming.

The Socio-Economics of Cash Cropping: Gender and Generation in the Hills

Cash cropping gave rise to socioeconomic changes and social tensions that reverberated throughout Taita. Raising vegetables for sale was not in itself controversial; though older generations did less of it than younger ones, all appreciated its profitability. Too, everyone wanted to have sons and husbands spend

---

[46] Ibid. This mirrored a 1945 statement by the doyen of Kenya soil conservation, Colin Maher. He argued that families must be resettled outside the present reserves, where "surplus adults" would need to be trained and incorporated into industrial work. Remaining agriculture then could be "capitalized more highly and put into the higher gear of more scientific farming." KNA, AGR/1/1065, Soil Erosion in Native Areas, 30/1/1945.

[47] KNA, ARC(MAA)–2/3/39iv.

[48] KNA, DAO/TTA/1/1/30, Vegetable Trade, 1945–50; and DAO/TTA/1/1/91, Vegetable Marketing, 1945–50; for implications of falling prices on agricultural policy, DC/TTA/3/2/46, Agricultural Development Policy, 1949–50.

[49] KNA/DAO/TTA/1/1/164, Taita District Annual Report for 1948.

[50] Interviews with JM, Shigaro/Werugha, 20/4/1988, and BM, Sechu/Chawia, 11/6/1988.

more time at home, and vegetable farming facilitated that.[51] But cash cropping altered household relations of production in ways that set off new social conflicts in Taita and exacerbated some existing ones. It sharpened the gender division of labor, further reordered intergenerational and intralineage work responsibilities, boosted the cultural significance of money wealth, and correspondingly attenuated the value of animals as wealth. Those changes, in turn, altered received terms of Taita identity.

Cash cropping prompted multifaceted changes in household relations of production in the 1930s and 1940s. As discussed earlier, farming in Taita before the era of labor migration had only minimal gender differentiation. Men had tended to do less farming, and some agricultural task differentiation operated (men did more of the heaviest clearing work, while women did more sowing and weeding), but by and large men and women had toiled side by side on most farming tasks. Labor migration altered this by making young men less available for agricultural work, which increased the farming burden on women.

Cash cropping reconfigured work relationships still more. From the outset, men claimed cash crops as "theirs" to raise and sell, and were able to make the claim stick.[52] How men seized control of European vegetable farming is not entirely clear from people's testimonies, but interviewees offered pieces of an explanation. First, men had long since established themselves as controllers of wealth: older men controlled lineage resources, and younger men gradually came to control much of their wages. By the 1930s, many younger women managed household money, but in principle did so in lieu of absent husbands.[53] Some men held that because cash cropping generated wealth, it was, like migrant labor or herding, their preserve: in Taita, one interviewee said, making wealth is man's work.[54]

Secondly, local agricultural instructors—all men—concentrated their cash–cropping instruction on men, both in schools and in extension work. Too, male laborers were more likely to be exposed to it in the 1920s and 1930s by seeing vegetables on sale in Mombasa.[55] Finally and conversely, some women described it as their responsibility to ensure that their families were fed, which required their greater involvement in subsistence agriculture.

---

[51] Interviews with GM, Kishamba/Chawia, 12/8/1988; and SK, Werugha/Werugha, 29/9/1988; also A. Harris and G. Harris, "WaTaita Today," 77–78, 102.

[52] Interviews with SM, Kidaya–Ngerenyi/Chawia, 25/4/1988, JM, Wundanyi/Werugha, 12/5/1988, Mrs. GM, Shigaro/Werugha, 27/5/1988, and Mrs. JM, Sagassa/Werugha, 7/10/1988. In a handful of households, both women and men raised vegetables. Interviews with JM, Wundanyi/Werugha, 17/4/1988, and Mrs. SM, Werugha/Werugha, 30/9/1988. But over 90 percent of interviewees that grew European vegetables in the 1930s and 1940s took the former course.

[53] Interviews with Mrs. MK, Nyolo/Bura, 15/8/1988; and Mrs. WM, Werugha/Werugha, 30/7/1993. The latter continued to manage household finances even when her husband was back, for she had more continuous knowledge.

[54] Only five men made some version of this argument, not quite a reliable number: SM, Wundanyi/Werugha, 15/4/1988; MM, Kishamba/Chawia, 8/6/1988; MW, Lushangonyi/Mwanda, 23/9/1988; NM, Wundanyi/Werugha, 28/7/1993; and OK, Shigaro/Werugha, 2/8/1993; the last one is quoted.

[55] For agricultural instruction, interview with Mrs. DM, Shigaro/Werugha, 30/5/1988; for seeing it elsewhere, DM, Werugha/Werugha, 29/9/1988.

Who will bring food into the house for eating? It was the wife, that was her duty. We grew that food. . . . Men went off to Mombasa . . . and . . . sent money, . . . or they grew vegetables for the [cooperative] society. . . . But at night they must eat, that was the work of women.[56]

Husbands' further absence from subsistence fields because of vegetable farming required women to spend ever larger amounts of time on subsistence agriculture. It amounted to a sizable increase in the women's work burden.[57]

Cash cropping also altered land–use patterns within lineages. Vegetables would not grow anywhere in the Hills; they needed cooler, moister conditions than prevailed in the low zone, and benefited greatly from rich soils. The best cash crop fields were prime valley bottom land in the middle zone, and better–watered fields in the upper zone. Many such fields occupied fairly steep slopes, and colonial officials, the LNC, and chiefs required that sloped vegetable fields be bench–terraced to conserve soil.[58] Once that labor went into a field, it remained a vegetable field for years to come.[59] Those fields—among the most productive in Taita—were thus removed from subsistence agriculture.

Because cash cropping required prime fields, single or newly–married young men hardly participated in it; they would not get much access to such fields at a young age. Cash changed this little, for older men would not likely sell or rent prime fields to a very young man, even one from the same lineage.[60] As young men matured, and if they worked at building social networks in the neighborhood, they might secure loans of suitable fields from older men; they also gradually came into better portions of their lineage's lands. But they expanded their cash cropping most when fathers died and land was redistributed.[61]

---

[56] Interview with Mrs. MM, Teri/Chawia, 22/7/1988; also, Mrs. JM, Sagassa/Werugha, 7/10/1988.

[57] All these explanations beg some questions: men's historical dominance of wealth had not previously prevented jointly–performed labor. Why draw a gender line in labor tasks now? Men's initial exposure to vegetables by seeing them raised and sold elsewhere afforded no basis for changing the division of labor, either. It also seems unlikely that most women accepted husbands' increasing of their work burdens with the equanimity that the above comments imply. However, my interviews yielded no further insights into the topic (perhaps because few interviewees willingly told me about conflicts with their spouses), and colonial sources skip over the gender dynamics of cash cropping altogether. In short, a fuller explanation will require further research.

[58] In the upper zone, the average slope of vegetable fields was estimated at 24 percent. See KNA, DAO/TTA/1/1/27, Taita Agricultural Annual Report, 1946. For pressure to do bench terracing, PC/Cst/2/4/16, Coast Province Agricultural Development Report, 1933, Appendix A; PC/Cst/1/12/290, LNC Resolutions, 16/4/1940; DAO/TTA/1/1/27, Taita Agricultural Annual Report, 1940; and AGR/5/5/7, Coast Province Agricultural Annual Report, 1940.

[59] "When the terraces were built, that's it, it was a vegetable field." Interview with MM, Wundanyi/Werugha, 21/7/1993; also, DM, Werugha/Werugha, 28/9/1988; and KM, Werugha/Werugha, 3/10/1988.

[60] It was a commonplace that colonial–era older men were loath to accept cash for land from young men or outsiders; among the many who mentioned this were AT, Sagassa/Werugha, 4/10/1988; and JL, Mogho Mleche/Mbale, 3/11/1988. For a fuller discussion of land sales and loans in lineages and neighborhoods, see A. Harris, "Organization," 278–317.

[61] Interviews with AT, Sagassa/Werugha, 4/10/1988; and JL, Mogho Mleche/Mbale, 3/11/1988.

The altered land–use patterns and new gender division of labor from vegetable production hurt subsistence farming. Women put in longer hours and assumed heavier tasks on subsistence fields, but could not fully replace the cumulative loss of male labor to vegetable farming and labor migration. This had deleterious effects on land conditions and food output. Women often had to clear fallowed subsistence fields by the early 1940s, and, finding this work time consuming and onerous, they tended to use cleared fields longer. This depleted soils and caused steep declines in subsistence yields per acre. By 1950, subsistence production was dropping sharply in neighborhoods with heavy concentrations of cash cropping—the parts of the Hills with the richest farmland.[62]

Women responded to their increased subsistence burdens by partially reorganizing their work methods, and by reducing some extra–household labor obligations. Both changes affected local understandings of Taita ways. Young women reorganized their work by making new use of women's lineage–based work groups (ngua); labor migration and cash cropping all but ended the men's ngua.[63] In the women's ngua, older women—usually wives of senior men who controlled the small lineage's lands—presided over a group, and tilted the group's efforts towards senior men's fields.[64] In the later 1930s and 1940s, however, younger women began to turn ngua to a different purpose: helping each other with the increased burden of subsistence:

That began at the time of the war of the Italians [i.e., World War II]. . . . We sisters helped each other with farming. . . . What would we do? Men were just gone from the farms. They sold vegetables and went to Mombasa or . . . to the war. . . . So we helped our sisters, here a little a little, tomorrow [points] there a little a little.[65]

This new use of ngua reduced the senior women's control over it. Some women said their in–laws understood the need for this ("it was a very difficult time, . . . they did not want their grandchildren to starve"), but acknowledge that many mothers–in–law did not like the reduction in their position and authority.[66] Compounding it, many daughters–in–law further reduced the amount of direct labor they provided to their parents–in–law.[67] These changes entailed certain social risks and sometimes engendered conflicts, for they collided pointedly with axioms of female propriety:

---

[62] A. Harris and G. Harris, "WaTaita Today," 79–81, 103–104.

[63] Men's involvement in work groups, though much reduced, did not entirely cease. Interview with Mrs. FM, Lushangonyi/Mwanda, 21/9/1988.

[64] Interviews with Mrs. DM, Shigaro/Werugha, 30/5/1988; Mrs. MM, Shigaro/Werugha, 20/6/1988; and Mrs. WM, Werugha/Werugha, 30/7/1993.

[65] Interview with Mrs. WM, Werugha/Werugha, 30/7/1993.

[66] Ibid., for the quote. Also, Mrs. PN, Mwanda/Mwanda, 3/8/1993; Mrs. SM, Mwanda/Mwanda, 14/9/1988; and Mrs. SM, Werugha/Werugha, 30/9/1988.

[67] Interviews with Mrs. MM, Ilole/Bura, 17/8/1988; Mrs. SM, Mwanda/Mwanda, 14/9/1988; and Mrs. VM, Sagassa/Werugha, 7/10/1988; several others could be cited.

Mrs. MM: My husband's mother said I must be very lazy. I told her I am working very hard. "I never see you working here, what work are you doing?" "I am feeding the children." . . . "You have no time for your elders? . . . Maybe you are lazy, or maybe you do not work well."

Q: So you did not get along well?

Mrs. MM: I loved her and she loved me, . . . but sometimes I could not please her.[68]

Such confrontations could make relations between younger women and their in–laws tense. Older people often complained about a decline in Taita women's character, and might shuffle inheritance to favor households with more helpful daughters–in–law.[69] Amidst these tensions, younger women continued to consider work for their in–laws important, and provided it to the degree that they could, using a combination of themselves, their children, and hired hands. As noted earlier, too, they continued to show respect for in–laws in other ways, such as taking part in *Wutasi* rituals, even if they were Christian. Still, their relations with parents–in–law were often difficult. Many younger women of the 1930s and 1940s endured slights about the declining character of Taita women, until they became senior women of subsequent generations.

Constraints on Cash Cropping, and the Persistence of Subsistence

For all the damage that cash cropping did to subsistence farming, and for all the European hopes pinned on Taita's vegetable crops after World War II, it had sharp limits as a potential replacement for subsistence farming. The role of Kenya's weak market infrastructure in this has already been discussed; on social grounds, too, a thorough substitution of cash crops for subsistence farming never had a chance. The amount of land suitable for growing cash crops in Taita was quite limited, and almost entirely in the higher, wetter parts of the Hills.[70] Since any one farmer had fields scattered across differing climates and differing access to water, vegetable fields could only be part—often only a small part—of the farmer's holdings.[71] Most of a farmer's remaining fields were more suitable to staple crops.

To cease subsistence farming would also have withdrawn men and women from networks of land loans, work groups, and exchange, greatly attenuating their ties with kin and neighbors. It would have been seen as extinguishing

---

[68]   Interview with Mrs. MM, Werugha/Werugha, 30/7/1993.

[69]   Interviews with SM, Kidaya/Chawia, 10/5/1988; Mrs. MM, Lushangonyi/Mwanda, 21/9/1988; and NM, Wundanyi/Werugha, 28/7/1993.

[70]   The main vegetable growing regions of Taita were upper Mbale, upper Chawia, Werugha, parts of Bura and Mwanda, and the upper reaches of Sagalla.

[71]   A. Harris, "Organization," chap. 8; and A. Harris and G. Harris, personal communication, 7/1987.

long–time relationships of mutuality and social support that were structured around subsistence. People in Taita would not likely give up on these bonds for the sake of an unreliable market economy. Too, despite officials' wishes for a settled urban working class, virtually no Taita man or woman willingly gave up land rights in the Hills. Labor migrants would not do so after years of re-mitting wages to fathers, visiting regularly, accumulating livestock within their fathers' herds, and developing local social networks. Women would not aban-don their land–based networks of social support, nor their subsistence rights. Their access to land was the only surety of subsistence for them and their chil-dren. Finally, land in the Hills denoted home in a very deep sense: through land men and women had a basis for belonging in Taita. Without land, they risked alienation from the historical and contemporary communities with which they identified. And without participating in subsistence farming, long–term access to Taita's land was very vulnerable.[72]

What Is Taita Wealth?:
Money and Livestock in the 1930s–1940s

Cash cropping drew Taita's inhabitants ever further into the money economy and money consciousness. In so doing, it escalated conflicts over the *Kidaβida* axiom that livestock was proper Taita wealth. Cash cropping brought elements of capitalist farming to Taita, partly through its effect on relations of produc-tion, and more so in leading people to see some crops as commodities. In the words of one farmer, "people found out that agriculture is money."[73] Money went to a widening number of capitalization and consumer uses, and became the main *de facto* form of wealth in everyday life.[74] Many in Taita retrospec-tively describe themselves as becoming "[people] of money" in the 1930s and 1940s, as opposed to their parents, who were "people of cattle."[75]

The juxtaposition between money and livestock generated intense cultural politics. Though young men and women increasingly jockeyed with their se-niors over wage remittances, until the 1930s all had accepted that livestock was the wealth that mattered in Taita. Indeed, older men had used sons' remit-tances to augment their herds in the early decades of the century. However, herd sizes, the infrastructure for maintaining herds, and the social value at-tached to them all declined in the 1930s and 1940s. One reason for the decline was that from the late 1920s on, sons gave over a declining percentage of their wages, which reduced their fathers' resources for buying animals:

---

[72] The Shimba Hills resettlement scheme at the coast, initiated in 1948, failed in part because it was not considered a place of Taita belonging: it lacked Taita's social networks and its social and historical rootedness. For a trenchant critique of the scheme, see PRO, CO 533/569/10, letter by A. Harris and G. Harris, 25/3/1951.

[73] Interview with OM, Wundanyi/Werugha, 5/5/1988; see also the epigram of this chapter.

[74] Interviews with WM, Shigaro/Werugha, 18/4/1988, SK, Chawia/Chawia, 28/5/1988, and Mrs. EK, Wongonyi/Mbololo, 7/7/1988.

[75] Interviews with WM, Shigaro/Werugha, 18/4/1988, GM, Kishamba/Chawia, 6/6/1988, RM, Wundanyi/Werugha, 13/8/1988, and GN, Mgange Nyika/Mwanda, 20/9/1988.

My father did not have a large herd like his father's herd. . . . You could not just raid Pare for them, you had to buy them with money. . . . Cows were not cheap, they were expensive, every year more expensive, and my father . . . did not have much money. . . . I helped him with money, . . . [but] he could only buy them one, one, one.[76]

The curtailing of wage remittances mattered little in the 1920s, when herds were large and natural increase kept them growing steadily, but droughts in the 1930s and 1940s drove herd sizes down faster than purchased animals could rebuild them. In the early 1930s, sons' falling wages made it harder still for their fathers to buy animals quickly enough to replenish herds. By the late 1930s, sons' remittances more than recovered, but did not keep pace with climbing livestock prices.[77] Many older men simply could not replace animals as quickly as inclement conditions claimed them.

Another reason for shrinking herd size was the shortening supply of labor to maintain them. Sons doing migrant work might send parents some money to buy cattle, but their absence made them unavailable to herd it.

[My father] started reducing the herd . . . [because] there was nobody to herd. . . . He was getting too old and weak . . . [and] I had my work. . . . He did not have enough strength. I told him not to bother with that herding and getting problems, he should just rest.[78]

Colonial education in Taita also ate into pastoral labor. Sons regularly in school often could not take off for four–day herding shifts—another reason why grandfathers so often tried to pull sons out of classes. Many young men received only a brief education and did shifts of herding when home from migrant labor, but others—and more every year—remained in school for five or more years, then entered white collar or clerical professions. The well–educated men not only missed herding time while in school, but often became poorly disposed to it afterwards.[79]

Too, in the 1930s and 1940s, some sons began to view livestock differently than did their fathers. Older men in these decades now saw livestock–as–wealth (a pillar of their authority) come in for fundamental challenge. They had some experience of their sons' circumstances, for they, too, had done labor migration in earlier decades. But in the 1900s to 1920s, they had not questioned the transformation of their wages into livestock for use within Taita's networks of exchange and power. In short, they had been less enmeshed in the money economy

---

[76] Interview with SM, Ndome/Mbololo, 28/6/1988.

[77] Interviews with SM, Tausa/Mbololo, 3/6/1988; KM, Kizumanzi/Sagalla, 14/7/1993; and MM, Wundanyi/Werugha, 21/7/1993. Several other older men described this remittance/price squeeze. Official records of livestock prices would give this more specificity, but there are none; the general point, however, has a consensus in people's memories, and is consistent with other findings.

[78] Interview with AM, Shigaro/Werugha, 2/5/1988.

[79] Interviews with JM, Wongonyi/Mbololo, 7/7/1988, NK, Mwatate/Chawia, 15/8/1988, and JM, Teri/Sagalla, 23/8/1988.

and commoditized thinking than their sons were now. Older men in the 1930s and 1940s still wanted to use livestock for networks of patronage, clientship, and alliance, as well as for ritual purposes and for their milk and meat. To them, a Taita man's networks of livestock loans assured him respect and standing.[80] Some sons, however, imbued with a consciousness shaped by progressivism and colonial capitalism, began to think of animals in other terms: as a commodity.

> My father used to have many cows, but they had no importance, they were just grazed. Nobody bought the meat, they knew no business, they didn't sell to get money. . . . [The fathers] were just careless. Those who kept cows later . . . came to realize that meat is money. Milk also has money.[81]

In the later 1930s, adult sons who bought cattle often purchased "improved" or "grade" cattle rather than local cattle. Grade cattle needed closer care, but had more monetary value if sold. Meanwhile, it gave more milk, the surplus of which could also be sold.[82]

In sum, by the late 1930s, older men faced a decline in resources for replenishing herds, a shortage of labor to tend them, and a generation of adult children whose sense of wealth was increasingly monetized and commoditized. By 1950, Alfred Harris, an anthropologist in Taita, would observe that very few men owned large herds.[83] As herd sizes declined, less livestock was available for local network building. Young adults increasingly enmeshed themselves in market–based networks—like milk, meat and produce cooperatives, in which money measured and mediated wealth, and in which Taita's historical livestock–as–wealth system played no part. Not only did this still further threaten fathers' control over their sons, it cut to the core of received terms of Taita identity.

Yet livestock–as–wealth did not entirely, or even nearly, disappear by 1950. Though the animal wealth system was attenuated by then, older men prevented its total demise. They clung to their claim that animal wealth was the most respectable wealth for a proper Taita man, and made the axiom stick: the notion remained a discursive staple of Taita propriety to the end of the colonial period.[84] It was a crucial issue for older men, for the end of livestock–as–wealth could damage their authority irreparably. And so, as the conflict over livestock–as–wealth crystallized, they applied those levers they still had to compel acceptance of it. First, they continued to insist that high standing in Taita's sociopolitical order could only come through animal–based networks:

---

[80] Interview with AM, Shigaro/Werugha, 2/5/1988.

[81] Interview with SM, Wundanyi/Werugha, 22/4/1988.

[82] Ibid.

[83] A. Harris, "Organization," chap. 7.

[84] Virtually all informants asked about the subject agreed that cattle was the respectable form of wealth in Taita through the 1940s. For example, NM, Ndome/Mbololo, 22/6/1988, CA, Ilole/Bura, 17/8/1988, AT, Sagassa/Werugha, 4/10/1988, and AM, Mogho Mleche/Mbale, 4/11/1988; also A. Harris, "Organization," chap. 7.

Cows were the key! If you had large herds, . . . if you had loans with this one and that one, if you gave that one goats as a gift, you could be climbing, climbing. . . . Money was not the same. Money is gone, ffffft! [throws open his right hand]. . . . These days money brings power, yes. But not [in] those days.[85]

Elders in the 1940s still commanded considerable influence through cattle–based networks, and remained leaders and senior authorities in Taita society. Popular ambivalence about chiefs' power made elders' livestock–based networks of influence and authority look all the more respectable and populist by comparison. Elders' influence operated alongside and below the channels of official governance; they often attended to issues and concerns before the matters reached official ears.

Building livestock networks also remained a viable way to build up pre-eminently respectable, properly Taita power. In a long–standing cyclical process, livestock wealth helped to make elders, who in turn reiterated and reproduced the importance of livestock networks as a basis of authority. Those networks continued to do important social work, providing mutual aid during crises, support in social disputes, and ties that helped ensure people's material and spiritual well–being. Wealthier elders atop those networks garnered widespread respect and prestige that men more enmeshed in money and state power could not. By the 1930s and 1940s, no older men were strangers to money, and most used it on a regular basis, but they upheld livestock wealth networks as the basis of their political power.[86] In so doing, they helped ensure that livestock wealth would remain the most "Taita" form of wealth.

Older men had other ways to compel continued acceptance of livestock–as–wealth. The most substantial material one was inheritance. Sons who skimped too much on helping their fathers with money or provided no herding help (either themselves or with hired herders) ran the risk of reduced inheritance when the fathers died.[87] Reduced inheritance applied not only to a father's livestock holdings, but, more importantly for many sons, to land. Too, through the 1940s, sons' inheritance included networks of crosscutting loans, exchange, and alliance. Some livestock debts and credits were settled when older men died, but most rolled over into networks for sons, maintaining the relationships that fathers had established or inherited.[88] To settle one's livestock debts once and for all implied dismantling one's social networks, an act that could cost support in political or jural encounters, in times of famine, spiri-

---

[85] Interview with JM, Teri/Sagalla, 23/7/1993.

[86] "Money was for helping. . . . Our fathers understood money, . . . they used it. Money did not have respect to them, but it had use." Interview with SM, Tausa/Mbololo, 3/6/1988. In 1950, Alfred Harris found livestock herds still indispensable for political standing as an elder; "Organization," chap. 7.

[87] Interviews with GM, Kishamba/Chawia, 12/8/1988, and DM, Werugha/Werugha, 29/9/1988.

[88] Interviews with KM, Tausa/Mbololo, 2/6/1988, GM, Kishamba/Chawia, 12/8/1988, MN, Lushangonyi/Mwanda, 22/9/1988, and MM, Ilole/Bura, 17/8/1988; also A. Harris, "Organization," chap. 7.

tual difficulty, illness, or other hardship. It could also make daily social interactions more strained. If younger men meant to maintain inherited social networks—and virtually all did in the 1930s and 1940s—they had to keep up some
investment in livestock, and in "Taita" (as opposed to market–based) valuations of livestock–as–wealth.

Despite the growing importance of money, then, sons in the 1930s and 1940s
had good reasons to keep believing in Taita terms of livestock–as–wealth. Pro-
saic, pragmatic reasons played a part, too. Animals provided milk and meat,
and, as long as they weren't killed by drought, disease, or wildlife, they multi-
plied; a frequently recurring phrase in interviews for this study was that animals make a good bank.[89] It entailed more risk than having money in a savings
account, and the 1930s and 1940s were difficult environmental decades, but it
remained common knowledge that herds offered a greater potential rate of return than money in the bank.[90] Men could then use the additional animals as
commodities, as "Taita wealth," or (as many did) as both.[91] By keeping at least
some cattle and operating to at least some degree within cattle–based networks,
sons maintained standing as properly respectful and respectable Taita men.

The continuation of livestock–as–wealth (and older men's continued sway
over it) showed a way through extant struggles over another *Kidaßida* axiom:
that sons should not pass their fathers' wealth in the fathers' lifetimes. By emphasizing animals as proper Taita wealth, older men could discount the significance of sons having more money than they did. By the late 1940s, the revised axiom held that sons should not surpass their fathers in *proper* Taita wealth:

> *SM:* Yes, I had more money than [my father]. [His sons] all did. . . . He
> did not mind. He did not want money, that was for Europeanized
> people! [laughs]. . . . His respect was in cows, cows and goats.
>
> *Q:* Did you have more cows than him?
>
> *SM:* Oh, no! We could not do that. It was a must that father had more
> cows.[92]

Up to the 1950s, older men controlled lineage herds as long as they had
the vigor to do so. Sons contributed money to buy animals, and to hire herding
labor, as well.[93] Sons also agreed ideologically that money was less respectable
than animal wealth. They willingly acknowledged their fathers' predominance
in animal wealth and the social networks based on it. Though the livestock

---

[89] For example, interviews with RM, Kaya/Chawia, 4/5/1988, SS, Tausa/Mbololo, 3/6/1988, MN,
Ghazi/Mbololo, 4/7/1988, and LM, Mrugua/Bura, 18/8/1988.

[90] Based on research in the early 1950s, a time of fairly good rains and no unusual animal epidemics, Alfred Harris estimated that herds in Taita could grow at up to 10–15 percent annually; A.
Harris, "Organization," chap. 7.

[91] Interview with SM, Wundanyi/Werugha, 22/4/1988.

[92] Interview with SM, Tausa/Mbololo, 3/6/1988; it was a typical explanation for young adult
men in the 1940s–50s.

[93] Interview with DM, Werugha/Werugha, 29/9/1988.

base shrank and money mediated everyday material life, animal wealth retained social and cultural cachet. Even many Christian, progressive cash–crop farmers gave it primacy of respectability:

> [Between cows and goats and money], without a doubt cows and goats had more respect. . . . Cows and goats were the wealth of our fathers, . . . they were the strength [i.e., socio–economic power base] of the lineage. . . . I was a person of money, more than my father, but I also got cows and goats . . . for respect, . . . [and] lent some of them.[94]

Most men whose fathers died in the 1930s and 1940s continued to keep some livestock. If they often took a more commoditized view of animals, they still used some to build or lubricate social networks.[95] Sons who inherited little livestock could more easily take on a money orientation, but they might seek to acquire animals, hoping to improve their standing within livestock–based social networks.[96] For sons with animals, treating them as respectable Taita wealth remained an important way to maintain local standing. Involvement in animal networks also allowed them to retain firm social footing as Taita, despite their more monetized social outlook.

Revamping *Kidaßida*

By the late 1940s, the notion of *Kidaßida* had changed dramatically from its 1910s version, and even from what it might have meant in the early 1930s. Crucial to those changes were social struggles that gradually altered proper Taita ways, proper Taita beliefs, even proper Taita wealth. Through *Kidaßida*, older men had tried to build a discursive link between people's belief that they belonged to a common sociohistorical community and the older men's efforts to set community norms. By the late 1940s, social struggles had altered so many of those norms that the very notion of *Kidaßida* began to shift under the impact of contemporary cultural politicking. *Kidaßida* by no means disappeared as an ideological construct: it was (and remains) the touchstone of Taita identity. But by the 1940s its meaning started to inch away from being a set of admonitions, and towards being a claim of common heritage.

The changes in *Kidaßida*'s meaning summed up the broader social changes of the first half of the century. Succeeding generations each had a hand in it: the older men who first crafted the notion of *Kidaßida* in the 1910s (together with their many supporters) drew upon the example of the relationships they once had with their own parents in the late nineteenth century. By the 1920s, some younger men and women at both ends of the colonial migrant labor sys-

---

94 Interview with WM, Lushangonyi/Mwanda, 23/9/1988.

95 Interviews with SM, Tausa/Mbololo, 3/6/1988, and WM, Choke/Mbale, 10/11/1988.

96 On the former possibility, interview with SM, Wundanyi/Werugha, 22/4/1988; for the latter, interview with NM, Ndome/Mbololo, 22/6/1988.

tem challenged those terms. By the 1930s, many older people had been the youths of early colonialism, and had perhaps struggled with *their* parents over money, work, and religion. By the late 1940s, most older women had experienced the youthful absence of migrant husbands, and understood better than their predecessors the pressures under which young women labored. At that juncture, too, many older people appreciated why young parents wanted their children educated, and more people tolerated a spreading Christianity that was itself less confrontational.

The 1940s did not ring in perfect social harmony, but for the most part, intergenerational tensions lessened as young and old, Christians and *Wutasi* followers showed greater flexibility towards each other. The older generation conceded much of the socioeconomic ground that the young claimed, while the young continued to respect and support their elders, if not to the degree nor in the ways that preceding generations of the young had. All involved were able to reconfigure loose terms of propriety that they agreed upon as acceptable behavior.

In effect, by the late 1940s *Kidaßida* began to shed its skin as a narrow set of strictures about Taita propriety. There were still limits, of course: a labor migrant who consistently failed to return or send money surely was considered lost, as were single women moving to Mombasa alone. Short of severe transgressions, however, young men, women, and Christians gained a great deal of latitude vis–a–vis parents and *Wutasi* followers. Some elders were still acknowledged to have deep knowledge of Taita ways, but *Kidaßida* now began to be used as a claim to a shared historical and cultural heritage based on descent, without reference to a person's current practices:

> *GM:* What was *Kidaßida*? It was all the things we shared here, each person. . . . It was our ancestry, language, the traditions of our elders.
>
> *Q:* Did you follow those traditions?
>
> *GM:* No, but my grandfathers did.
>
> *Q:* Was that enough . . . for you to be Taita?
>
> *GM:* My ancestors did those things, . . . so I must be Taita, isn't it?[97]

---

[97]   Interview with GM, Kishamba/Chawia, 12/8/1988.

8

Formal Power, Political Mobilization, and Struggles over Taita Identity, 1930–1952

If you are lost, . . . then where will you go? Where is your home? Those people just died alone in Mombasa, or went to Shimba to die with [ex–chief] Nimrod.[1]

Introduction

Tensions around political authority generated especially intense cultural politicking in Taita during the 1930s and 1940s. As cultural politics, these conflicts were at once more explicit and more murky than the kinds of cultural politics previously discussed. Arguments and actions pertaining to landholding and land use—and to who did (and should) have decision–making power over those matters—became the grist of open confrontations in public settings. Discursively, this soon worked its way into familiar cultural–political terrain, for the arguments quickly became intertwined with opinions about how to act (or not act) as a good Taita. Claims of Taitaness—and accusations about someone's lack of it—therefore became far more visible than ever before. The clashes were not instigated by elders, but did reinforce elders' ongoing efforts to rein in the young chiefs.

---

[1] Interview with NM, Ndome/Mbololo, 22/6/1988. Nimrod, chief of Mbololo from the late 1930s to 1951, moved to a government sponsored resettlement scheme in the Shimba Hills, at the coast, shortly after he retired.

229

Yet two factors muddied up this cultural politics relative to other social realms: first, it turned on formal political commitments, not on received norms of Taita propriety. The challengers of governmental power over land denigrated the Taitaness of their opponents, the progressive Christian elites who supported colonial authority. Yet many challengers had progressive tendencies themselves, and their associations backed progressive causes like education and soil conservation.[2] In this context, a second factor came into play: the public character of this attempt to delimit Taita identity, combined with its tenuous connection to prior, normatively–based delimitations, often blurred the distinction between cultural political concerns and formal political rhetoric.

Two sets of conflicts, both enmeshed in struggles over Taita propriety and identity, overlapped in this arena. First, chiefs and elders continued their struggles over formal authority. Colonial laws, rules, police, and imprimatur in principle allowed the chiefs to command compliance and a respect borne of fear.[3] Elders, on the other hand, could call upon prestige and stature gained through long–standing—but now eminently Taita—accruals of age, networks, and influence. Here, older men turned *Kidaßida* into a sharp tool for cultural politicking: by its lights, young, Christian chiefs inherently lacked the knowledge, experience, and wisdom conveyed by rightful authority. This construction of political propriety sat well with many women and younger men across the Hills, who juxtaposed it to what they considered the chiefs' meddlesome and coercive impulses. Chiefs' responsibility to uphold unpopular land laws reinforced the intergenerational alliance against them.

In this struggle, older men and their supporters largely succeeded at upholding a restrictive notion of proper Taita ways. With broad popular backing, older men defended the political prestige and power of elderhood, compelling most chiefs to recognize that *Kidaßida*–based authority carried far more respectability and standing in local communities than chiefly authority—and that both as young men and older retirees, chiefs had to live within those communities. This placed strong limits on the effective power of most chiefs.

The other major political struggle of this era began in 1939, and fueled social conflicts in Taita for a dozen years thereafter. This set of conflicts turned on the emergence and aims of Taita political associations. Like other groups in Kenya and Africa, relatively young men, many of them with at least some education, organized Taita's political associations.[4] Similarly, too, Taita's main association took a critical view of many colonial policies, spoke to popular concerns, sought popular backing for its agenda, and built ties

---

[2] The associations did not back all soil conservation schemes, which sometimes became political hot potatoes, but did support many. This is discussed more below.

[3] As one official told a gathering of Taita's chiefs, they were responsible for the advancement of their locations, and their duties made them like location DCs. See KNA, DC/TTA/3/1/25, Chiefs and DC's Meetings, 11/11/1948.

[4] For associations elsewhere in Kenya, see J. F. Munro, *Colonial Rule and the Kamba: Social Change in the Kenya Highlands, 1889–1939* (Oxford, 1975); R. L. Tignor, *The Colonial Transformation of Kenya: The Kamba, the Kikuyu, and the Maasai from 1900 to 1939* (Princeton, 1976); and Carl Rosberg and John Nottingham, *The Myth of Mau Mau: Nationalism in Kenya* (Stanford, 1966), chap. 5.

with like–minded groups across the colony. Finally, like other Kenyan associations, its politics were mostly local. Taita's associations built their popular base around the Hills' most pressing, impassioned issues: conflicts over land rights and land use.

By the mid–1940s, Taita's main political association also invoked a nostalgic form of *Kidaßida*, identifying itself as properly Taita by appropriating terms and symbols laden with *Wutasi*–following sensibility. This strategy meant little to colonial officials, but resonated deeply in the cultural politics of formal authority among WaTaita. The association's version of nostalgic *Kidaßida* posited an intergenerational alliance of opponents to the state's handling of land issues, consolidated it around culturally resonant symbols of Taita commonality, and isolated the state's local supporters. This nostalgic *Kidaßida* put chiefs and Christian progressives very much on the defensive, portraying them as unmindful of proper Taita interests.

In both sets of struggles, *Wutasi*–following older men and young association activists heightened an insider/outsider dichotomy in Taita ethnic consciousness. The dichotomy did not target genuine outsiders so much as local people who drew power from or supported colonial rule, casting a shadow over progressives' and chiefs' Taitaness. Typically, that shadow acted as a brake on the chiefs' behavior, contributing to the cautious, looking–over–the–shoulder approach many chiefs adopted towards colonial and progressive agendas. It also dampened the procolonial zeal of all but the most committed progressives. In a few cases, this cultural politics ran to its logical conclusion: some aggressively progressive chiefs ended up lost.

Chiefs, *Kidaßida*, and the Limits of State–Based Power, 1930–1950

Chiefly Power in Principle

At the center of the chiefs' position in Taita in the 1930s and 1940s lay a paradox: they had great power, and yet they didn't. European officials granted them wide–ranging executive and policing powers over people's labor, agriculture, drinking habits, and public conduct.[5] Chiefs also carried their power symbolically, in their uniforms and accouterments of office—symbols that the chiefs took very seriously, for they augmented the chiefs' air of authority, and represented their right and ability to control their locations. Chiefs wanted items to command people's attention from afar (whistles), items that carried European–like authority and a subtle threat of violence up close (swagger sticks), and items that represented their position with maximal flourish (elaborate badges of office).[6]

---

[5] A. Harris and G. Harris, "WaTaita Today," 110.

[6] For example, KNA, DC/TTA/3/1/25, Chiefs' and DCs' Meetings: 3/1947, 9/5/1949 and 31/12/1951.

Photo 10. Taita's Chiefs at a public meeting, 1933. Margaret Murray Photo Collection, courtesy of Kenya National Archives and Documentation Service. #190/81.

European officials expected chiefs to carry out orders passed down the line to them, and to see that people obeyed rules and laws.[7] Administrators felt

---

[7] Taita DCs instructed their successors to "[r]egard the chiefs as junior administrative officers, not as representatives of their locations but as the servants of administrators." KNA, DAO/TTA/ 1/1/130, Taita Handing Over Reports, DC Leslie to Dowson, 1946. DCs made the same point to chiefs, telling them that, like DCs, chiefs "were appointed government servants, and accordingly must carry out the orders received from the government to the best of their ability." DC/TTA/3/ 1/25, Chiefs' and DCs' Meetings, 11/11/1948.

that state backing gave the chiefs sufficient authority to perform those functions; beyond that, chiefs were to maintain (colonially defined) order within
their locations. Their charge, at once broad and far–reaching, assumed the nor-
mality of extensive state control over mundane routines of everyday life: matters like where and how people could or couldn't farm, where and how they
could or couldn't sell goods, what communal work people must do, even how
disputes could or couldn't be settled.

In the 1930s and 1940s, some chiefs did try to exert the authority that European administrators envisioned, and a few pulled it off. Thomas, son of
Mghalu, was Taita's archtypical "strong" chief from the early 1910s to 1937,
effectively combining old, inherited connections with new outlooks. Mghalu's
death shortly after Thomas took office gave Thomas a measure of seniority
and network–based influence that helped him with other elders early in his
career.[8] Yet the Christian Thomas quickly became a leading progressive and
supporter of the state even as he maintained (and indeed expanded) his inherited social networks. By taking care not to offend the religious sensibilities of
Wutasi–following older men and adroitly handling authority issues with them,
Thomas upheld his social standing and exercised strong leadership throughout his career and into his retirement.[9]

Richard Mwangeka, one of Thomas's assistants, succeeded him as chief of
Mbale in 1937. Richard also came from an influential lineage, and, like Thomas, had a forceful personality and a strong progressive bent.[10] Mbale location
was by now singularly receptive to this sort of chief. Twenty–five years under
Thomas acculturated Mbale's people to that style and outlook, and Mbale then
had the highest concentration of Christians in Taita (for it hosted the oldest
and largest CMS mission in Dabida). Finally, when Richard came into office,
Mbale was also the location most influenced by and accustomed to colonial
officialdom. A European–staffed hospital was built there in 1929, a European
agricultural officer was based there in the mid–1930s, and a model farm and
government offices took over the site of the old Wundanyi coffee plantation,
which the government purchased and converted in 1935.[11] These facilities and
influences afforded a progressive like Richard an unusual degree of local and
European support. He oversaw the location closely, and firmly upheld state
policies without damaging his long–term reputation and social standing.

Other chiefs certainly had domains of power, as well. By the 1930s and
1940s, virtually all commanded enough authority to enforce many colonial regulations—most easily, ones that did not offend or greatly inconvenience older
men or the preponderance of a community.[12] In addition, mandated practices

---

8   Interview with DM, Mbale/Mbale, 7/11/1988.

9   Ibid.

10   Interviews with AM, Mogho Mleche/Mbale, 4/11/1988; and WM, Choke/Mbale, 11/11/1988.

11   The KLC found that local people had an "excellent claim" on plantation land. See its Summary
and Conclusions. The British government thereafter paid £5,500 for the property. See PRO, CO
533/449/5; and CO 533/453/1.

12   Interviews with PN, Ngerenyi/Chawia, 9/5/1988; and GM, Mgange Nyika/Mwanda, 20/9/1988.

that demonstrably yielded good returns for reasonable effort could generally be enforced; rules about basic soil conservation techniques, for example, fit this category.[13] In general, too, chiefs could more easily impose regulations and demands on younger men and women, and on members of their locations' less prominent and influential lineages. This showed in relatively strict enforcement of rules about public drunkenness among the young, or in uneven patterns of chiefly recruiting for mandatory communal labor or porterage duty:

> When the chief needed . . . porters for the DC, his police did not go to the houses of the important families, no. . . . He did not send them to . . . the houses of the Christians! . . . They came to the house of the poor man, they came in like bulls: "You! You must carry [loads] for the DC!"[14]

Nevertheless, the power of chiefs like Richard and Thomas was exceptional. Chiefs in Taita's seven other administrative locations usually lacked such support, and could not bring like networks of influence and respectability to the position. Most chiefs who tried to enforce unpopular laws or impose progressive innovations despite popular disaffection risked denouncements or intrigues against them by influential people; their reputations might decline in their communities, or worse. Most did not have the social wherewithal to long endure such local resistances and pressures. Chiefs' effective power, then, typically proved vulnerable to disapproval from prominent older men or their locations' wider populace.

Chiefly Power, Elders' Power, and the Power of Community Disapproval

Through the 1940s, elders (and many others) maintained a different view of Taita chiefs' proper role from the European one. They still saw chiefs as useful intermediaries with officials, but chiefs' pretensions to high authority remained an affront to older men:

> The chiefs of [colonial] time[s] had force, . . . and some [chiefs] thought their force gave them the right to tell people, 'do this, do that, or you will be grabbed and sent to Voi' [i.e., to jail, or to the DC]. . . . They were not big men, but they thought their force made them big.[15]

---

[13] As early as 1940, the Coast Province Agricultural Officer considered the Taita very mindful of and receptive to soil conservation efforts. See KNA, AGR/5/5/42, Handing Over Report, 3/1940. Even the oppositional Taita Hills Association strongly supported soil conservation that involved reasonable efforts and were seen to work; see their flyer urging soil conservation in AGR/5/5/33, Quarterly Agricultural Reports, Provincial Agricultural Officer to Director of Agriculture, 18/5/1940. A perusal of AGR/5/1/305, Soil Conservation Reports, 1947–52, makes clear that people in Taita voluntarily did the most widespread and advanced conservation work in Coast Province.

[14] Interview with AM, Mogho Mleche/Mbale, 4/11/1988.

[15] Interview with DM, Mlondo/Werugha, 28/9/1988.

Europeans' predisposition for vigorous, active chiefs led them to appoint men in their thirties and forties to the position—an inherently problematic choice to many older people, including many older Christians. The young men likely still had living parents, and thus no experience heading a small lineage or social networks of their own. In short, as junior members of their lineages, they had no experience, wealth, respect, knowledge, influence, or standing. Too, these young men, now invariably Christians, knew nothing of *Wutasi*. In short, they lacked credibility among older people.

> When I became a chief, I was at that time . . . just 32 years old. And at that time, beginning with my own father, he thought I was too young. . . . If I went to a [meeting], . . . all people would stand up, but my father feels that this child is too young. . . . He will not stand up for me. . . . It was the tradition that a man of authority must be an old man. . . . But . . . people saw that I was wearing the government uniform . . . and carrying all the badges of office. They had no choice but to stand, . . . whether they like it or not.[16]

This man typified the chiefly conundrum. He was well educated, taught school for twelve years, and had a solid reputation with missionaries and officials. He considered himself knowledgeable about local customs, but was Christian and a junior member of his lineage. Had he followed *Wutasi*, he would still have been too young for the sort of position that denoted real knowledge. In older people's eyes, he may have held a government office and worn all its symbols, but that did not give him proper authority.[17]

In most circumstances, people in Taita obeyed chiefs' orders and respected the office to the extent necessary. More progressive Christians often went beyond that, enthusiastically supporting energetic chiefs. Most of the more vigorous chiefs, though, mainly garnered a respect inspired by acknowledgment of colonial force—for chiefs might fine or jail the blatantly disrespectful. Beyond that modicum of respect lay a substantial gray zone that became apparent when people objected to particular rules or directives: as often as not (and then usually without sharp confrontation), they ignored or quietly disobeyed them. European officials had a general sense of this attitude, and considered it part of the Taita tribal character: "The WaTaita . . . are receptive to [governmental] advice . . . provided its logic is clearly explained, but compulsion is anathema to them."[18]

Many examples supported this observation. In a typical instance, in March 1945, the chief of Mwanda organized a mass meeting where the (European) agricultural officer would explain new soil conservation measures to which people objected. Nobody attended, and people who lived nearby made it clear to the official that the chief's order "carried no weight in this matter at all."

---

[16] Interview with JM, Wusi/Chawia, 5/4/1988.

[17] Ibid. See also A. Harris and G. Harris, "WaTaita Today," 137–39.

[18] KNA, DAO/TTA/1/1/130, Handing Over Report, Bradford to Strange, 29/6/1942.

When the officer then discussed the new rules with several people, he came across "resistance of the wordy type": elders and other influential people agreed on the rules' value, but then detailed why they were impossible to follow. The European reported skeptically that the chief promised a collective punishment for non–attendance of the meeting; the officer asked for no assurances, and received no subsequent word about it.[19]

Typically, too, people flaunted rules about how to farm on steep slopes, farming near water sources, closure of eroded lands, and disposal of agricultural waste, often in close proximity to chiefs' homes and offices; this last point especially vexed European officials. When chiefs tried to enforce unpopular rules on a particular plot, they were often taken to the older men of the lineage that controlled the lands. At times subtly and other times pointedly, the older men made excuses to the chiefs, or reprimanded them for trying to tell their elders what to do. They made it clear that they did not consider themselves beholden to the chiefs' rules:

> Oh! Sometimes my grandfather was rude to the chief, today you cannot act like that, [or] . . . say things like he said to him, even if you are an old man. . . . He called him "my child," . . . and he scolded him like a father scolds a child who behaves badly. . . . Really, there was no respect there.[20]

Non–elders, as the most likely objects of chiefs' unwanted demands, often supported elders' depiction of vigorous chiefs as disrespectful, callow youths lacking proper authority.[21] The elders' juxtaposition of chiefly authority with their own became an important source of older men's standing and power in the 1930s and 1940s, as their economic and religious leverage eroded.

Chiefs, meanwhile, walked a tightrope. It was no small matter to prosecute influential older men for breaking rules, or to incur their anger for prosecuting their children. Doing so could bring community approbation down on a chief, hurting his standing within his neighborhood and lineage. This might have short–run consequences like intrigues against him, or personal slights indicating lack of respect for him, and disapproval of him by his community: "[Chief] Nimrod, ahh! . . . Some people left the path to miss greeting him!"[22] In the long run, it ensured a chief low regard in his community upon his retirement. Chiefly attempts at vigorous enforcement of unpopular rules might also push a community into a widespread disregard for even innocuous rules or orders.[23]

Chiefs, painfully aware of the social weakness of their authority, responded to such situations in three main ways.[24] Some chiefs pursued the

---

[19] This example is taken from KNA, DAO/TTA/1/1/183, Soil Conservation Safaris, 3/4/1945.

[20] Interview with SM, Mrugua/Bura, 19/8/1988.

[21] For the popularity of this perspective among non–elders, see A. Harris and G. Harris, "WaTaita Today," 137–40, 142.

[22] Interview with NM, Ndome/Mbololo, 22/6/1988; also MN, Ghazi/Mbololo, 4/7/1988.

[23] A. Harris and G. Harris, "WaTaita Today," 137–40.

[24] "They could not get respect from [their standing with] Europeans." Interview with MN, Ghazi/Mbololo, 4/7/1988.

Mbale model, hoping to bend people to their way and will; they tried to bulldoze through elders' and communities' resistance. Nimrod of Mbololo chose this route when he became chief in 1938, and paid dearly for it.[25] Mbololo's most progressive Christians supported him, but after World War II, he faced a growing wall of hostility that overwhelmed his allies and drove him from office. He became the object of intrigues designed to obstruct him, embarrass him before colonial officials, and decimate his social standing in Mbololo.[26] Though he did not relent in attitude, the strain took a great toll on his health and the social ferment in the location rendered him ineffective. In 1951, the DC discreetly concluded that Nimrod's infirmity "and other factors" had caused development in the location to slip, and retired him. Nimrod shortly thereafter left Taita for good, moving to the highly unpopular Shimba Hills resettlement scheme at the coast;[27] his dogged vigorousness rendered him well and truly lost.

Some chiefs tried to find a middle way. They had progressive outlooks and looked to enforce key rules, but were selective and careful not to antagonize important older people in their locations. These men tried to ingratiate themselves with elders, and to build networks of wealth, exchange, and influence along typical community lines. This strategy looked to duplicate the networks and relationships of Thomas and Richard in Mbale; one chief of Chawia notably pursued it in the 1930s and 1940s. He hoped to retain a good reputation and gradually acquire standing in the community despite his youth, Christianity, and enthusiastic progressivism.[28] His case illustrates the perils of the approach: elders largely rebuffed his efforts at network building. He faced continuous animosity, and became a target for acts of revenge when he retired.[29] At that juncture, as a (perhaps desperate) gesture of his desire to gain the respect of proper Taita elderhood, he married a second wife. This got him thrown out of the Anglican church, but did not improve his social standing or credibility among the elders of his community.[30]

Most chiefs in Taita took a third path. Recognizing the severe limits their society placed on them, they became circumspect about enforcing rules and promoting change. They made a point of treating elders respectfully, and did

---

[25] For Nimrod's appointment as chief, see KNA, DC/TTA/1/2, Taita District Annual Report, 1938.

[26] Interviews with JM, Wongonyi/Mbololo, 7/7/1988; NM, Ndome/Mbololo, 22/6/1988; and MN, Ghazi/Mbololo, 4/7/1988.

[27] On Nimrod's forced retirement, see KNA, DAO/TTA/1/1/141, Monthly Intelligence Report, 7/4/1951. The unpopularity of the Shimba Hills scheme (begun in 1948) is a staple in Taita remembrances; for written confirmation and a scathing assessment of the scheme by A. Harris and G. Harris, see PRO, CO/533/569/10 (1951).

[28] Interviews with GM, Kishamba/Chawia, 9/6/1988 and 27/6/1988.

[29] Interview with JM, Wusi/Chawia, 5/4/1988; also, A. Harris and G. Harris, "WaTaita Today," 145.

[30] Interview with JM, Wusi/Chawia, 5/4/1988; the ex–chief nevertheless was given a Christian burial when he died.

not press enforcement of policies they knew to be controversial in their communities.[31] They often turned a blind eye to infractions of unpopular rules; after making a show of rigor for officials, they tested their communities' responses to measures:

> SM: Chief [X] was very good! . . . He knew how to impress the whites.
> Q: Was he a progressive?
> SM: A little, a little. He went to the elders and asked, "Old man, what do you say about this thing and this thing? . . . Can we try these things here?" . . . If they said no, they are not good, he left those things.[32]

This approach kept their community reputations relatively intact and did little or no damage to their respectability—ground they could reasonably hope to make up later as older men.

The last approach did not, however, render chiefs effective in European terms; it exasperated colonial officials through the early 1950s. The 1933 DC considered none of Taita's chiefs "outstanding," and warned that "constant urging . . . is necessary to keep them up to the mark."[33] In 1946, the departing DC pointedly chided the chiefs for what he saw as their habitual laziness, and warned his successor, "not one of them understands the meaning of systematic and conscientious work."[34] A European official in Taita from 1950 to 1952 felt that the problem lay in who was recruited:

> A lot of the best talent in the district went into education rather than into administration. . . . In spite of having some very well educated schoolmasters, . . . nearly all our chiefs were, well some of them were barely literate. . . . [Being a chief] wasn't a very popular job. It tended to go to successful tribal policemen. . . . They were pretty ineffective.[35]

Though most of Taita's well educated young men *did* prefer other work, chiefs' main problem was not a lack of innate ability. Some surely were ineffectual, but the overall limits on chiefs had less to do with talent than with the strong social constraints operating on them. To get along well as junior members of their communities and have decent prospects for their old age, most chiefs had to accommodate the elders' Kidaßida–based standards of suitable behavior for a young Taita man. This might not make chiefs effective in the Europeans' eyes, but Europeans did not live in the Hills for a lifetime, nor depend on Taita as a place of community belonging.

[31] Interviews with SM, Teri/Sagalla, 24/8/1988; and JM, Kishamba/Chawia, 24/9/1988.
[32] Interview with SM, Teri/Sagalla, 24/8/1988.
[33] KNA, DC/TTA/1/1, Taita District Annual Reports for 1931, 1933.
[34] KNA, DC/TTA/3/1/14, DC Circular to Chiefs, 22/3/1946; and DAO/TTA/1/1/130, Handing Over Report, 1946.
[35] Interview with M. G. Power, Surrey, England, 24/2/1989.

Progressives, Associational Politics,
and Taita Identity, 1938–1952

Local Politics, Larger Contexts

The emergence of associational, populist politics in the late 1930s catalyzed heated cultural politicking over formal authority and Taita identity. Issues of land access and land use, which dogged Taita's people and officials throughout the colonial period, spurred the rise of the associations. Land politics in colonial Taita had their origins in the British government's alienations of lowland tracts around the Hills for European–owned sisal plantations, and of large Hills plots for Bura mission and the Wundanyi coffee plantation. Among the lowland alienations, the most politically divisive plantation proved to be the one abutting the southeastern edge of the Hills, adjacent to Chawia location and near the town of Mwatate. By the mid–1920s, it would be known as Taita Concessions, Limited (hereafter TCL).

The TCL plantation acquired successive plots of land through the 1910s,[36] when the area's population was still at a low ebb from prior droughts and famines, and conditions kept most remaining people on higher ground. But the population began to rebound rapidly in the 1910s,[37] pushing people back into plains farming by the 1920s. Many from Chawia returned to fields in a plains locale called Mwatunge—a tract now leased to TCL, but not yet planted with sisal.[38] When the Kenya Land Commission of 1932–1933 tried to resolve the rival claims by returning a *different* portion of TCL to the reserve, it succeeded only in granting land access to a different set of lineages: the people who claimed rights in Mwatunge had none in the newly designated area.[39]

The situation was further complicated by the temporary presence of Kasigau's population in Mwatunge.[40] Kasigau's people had been exiled to the coast during World War I, then sent to Mwatunge in 1920, where they cultivated side by side with lineages from Chawia. When the WaKasigau were allowed back into their own corner of Taita in 1937, all land rights in Mwatunge reverted to TCL, much to the dismay of the Chawia farmers on it.[41] Though many Taita officials by now agreed on the validity of the Chawia farmers' historical claims and present need for Mwatunge fields, duty required them to

---

[36] For the original grants of land to private concerns, see PRO, CO 533/11/67 and CO 533/28/225, both 1907. Later additions took place in 1910 (CO 533/32/443). Boundary adjustments in the 1910s and 1920s gave the plantation better water access. These changes slightly increased the size of the TCL plantation, and gave it rights in a block called Mwatunge. See CO 533/325, 330, 333, 343–44; plus CO 533/378/2, and CO 533/385/3.

[37] By 1932, it was growing at an estimated 3.5–4.5 percent rate. See KLC, Evidence and Memoranda, 2720, 2733.

[38] PRO, CO 533/325, 21/7/1924; and interview with RM, Kaya/Chawia, 4/5/1988.

[39] KLC, Summary and Conclusions, Taita.

[40] Kasigau, it will be remembered, is the smallest of the Taita Hills, and the furthest one from Dabida.

[41] KNA, PC/Cst/1/11/40, Taita Land Claims, 23/5/1942.

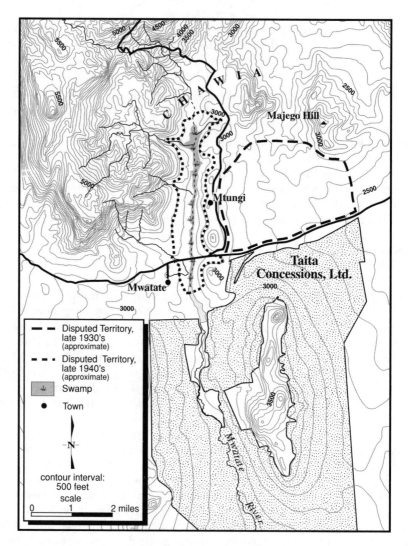

Map 3. Chawia location and Taita Concessions, Ltd. Produced by UMBC Cartographic Laboratory.

enforce the plantation's boundary rights.[42] This engendered considerable distrust of officials among people who lost land rights to the plantation, and among others who feared for the future of their extant lowland holdings.

These concerns crystallized after the departure of the WaKasigau in 1937, and became the main mobilizing issue for a new African political association soon there-

---

[42] Kenya Land Commission, Evidence and Memoranda, 2729–2738, 2770–95; also KNA, PC/Cst/ 1/11/40, Taita Land Claims, 23/5/1942, and CNC/10/101, Taita Land Claims, 1943.

after. That body, the Taita Hills Association (THA), was also a product of wider political trends in Kenya: African political protest–and–advancement activism had animated the founding of similar associations across Kenya since the 1920s. The Taita group formed in 1939, under the leadership of Woresha Mengo and Jimmy Mwambichi, two educated men interested in colonywide African politics.[43] The THA's links to wider political currents ran through its early history: it began as a branch of the Kikuyu Central Association (KCA). Though re-formed as the THA in March 1940, it remained in regular contact with the KCA.[44]

The THA followed the pattern of several of its contemporary African associations in colonial Kenya, combining broader colonial awareness with a localized identity and agenda. In working to gain popular support in the Hills, the THA placed far more emphasis on local issues than on colonywide ones. By changing the name of the group from KCA–Taita Branch to Taita Hills Association, the association's leaders declared it a body primarily for Taita's people who, by implication, had common concerns. In a letter to the governor of Kenya listing the THA's objectives, Mengo took the assumption of commonality a step further:

> [Among the Taita Hills Association's objectives are] to help the Taita community in social and economic progress; and [to] protect and safeguard the rights and privileges and interests of the Taita community in every possible way.[45]

The THA thus explicitly held that the Taita formed a large–scale community, a coherent whole with common interests and common concerns. The THA declared itself champion of that larger community's interests. This claim did not go unchallenged, for some progressive, Christian WaTaita disagreed with the THA's agenda and methods. Nevertheless, by its existence and tactics the THA set the terms of popular mobilization in a way that heightened struggles over Taita identity: it ethnicized Taita's colonial–era popular politics from the outset—a maneuver that subtly elided the old norm–driven version of Taita ethnicity into a *de facto* claim that Taitaness turned on one's political commitments.

This gave the activists a leg up over their political opponents. The firmly progressive elite assumed the existence of a Taita community with common Taita interests, but saw the main common interest as "progress"—a platform that offered little hope of alleviating widespread distress at the Europeans' positions on land issues. Because of the THA's adroit positioning, political conflicts between it and Taita's progressive elite were played out as a struggle over which group (or which perspective on colonialism) best represented Taita interests. Thus, when an organization of progressive leaders formed to oppose the THA, it listed as its foremost

---

[43] Nathan Mnjama has done the most thorough study of the THA. For sketches of Mengo and Mwambichi, see his "The Taita Hills Association" (Ms., 1991; Revision of B. A. Thesis, 1987, U. of Nairobi), 5–7.

[44] Ibid., 7–11, 24, 32. The THA maintained a courier and coordinator of activities between the two groups.

[45] KNA, PC/Cst/2/3/115, Taita Hills Association, Mengo to Governor, 1/4/1940; also, Mnjama, "Taita Hills Association," 34–36.

goal "the development of the Taita people."[46] Given the political flatness of this claim when set against the young activists' promise to defend Taita against outsiders' depredations, it comes as no surprise that the progressive body received virtually no popular support.

The Political Associations of Taita

The KCA–linked forerunner of the Taita Hills Association first held open meetings to raise funds and disseminate its views in 1939.[47] Direct confrontations with colonial authorities began early the following year, when the government, with vocal support from Taita's progressive elite, prohibited the association from collecting membership dues.[48] This prompted Mwambichi to call a four-day sit–down strike at the DC's office in Voi, an action that involved roughly two hundred people. The strike, coinciding with trials of accused trespassers on the Mwatunge block of TCL, was forcefully broken up and its leaders arrested.[49] The confrontation in Voi spurred further disturbances and acts of trespass around Mwatunge; officials put them down by a combination of negotiation and force, culminating in the removal of local farmers from Mwatunge. The KCA in Central Province had a representative at both actions, Jessie Kariuki, who addressed the participants at Voi and Mwatunge, and took part in the negotiations.[50]

Two months later, Mengo announced the group's re-forming as the Taita Hills Association; he claimed a dues–paying membership of four thousand people, and presented Kenya's governor with a list of two hundred "leaders" of the body.[51] The membership figure, though likely exaggerated, may well have reflected—even undercounted—the number of non–members sympathetic to the THA.[52] Even with some massaging of the figures, the THA was notable as the area's first political association with a large membership and wide popular appeal, and as the first body organized on the basis of Taita ethnicity. The THA's wide popularity also points up the shortsightedness of the DC's view of it in

---

[46]   KNA, DC/TTA/3/1/71, Native Associations and Agitators, Richard Mwangeka to DC, 11/9/1947.

[47]   KNA, DC/TTA/1/2, Taita District Annual Report, 1939, Political and General.

[48]   The government's prohibition of KCA–Taita branch dues was in principle based on a measure passed by Taita's LNC. See KNA, DC/TTA/1/1, Taita District Annual Report, 1939.

[49]   KNA, ARC/MAA/2/3/19, Coast Intelligence Reports, 20/2/1940; the cases against the strikers were subsequently dismissed on grounds of insufficient evidence. On those trials, see ARC(MAA)/7/306, entries for 2/1940.

[50]   Mnjama, "Taita Hills Association," 9–11, argues that Kariuki was a calming influence on Taita's more hot–headed, inexperienced leaders. The 1940 DC speculated that the KCA masterminded the disturbances, but even the evidence in the official records suggests that direct KCA involvement followed on the heels of local activism. The KCA had earlier tried to arouse fears of a Ukamba–style de–stocking drive in Taita (ibid., 3–5), but this had not captured popular attention.

[51]   KNA, PC/Cst/2/3/115, Taita Hills Association, Mengo to Governor, 1/4/1940.

[52]   Though retrospect has surely raised the number of people claiming sympathy with the THA, many interviewees said that they supported the THA secretly, but did not join; for instance, interviews with AK, Shigaro/Werugha, 25/4/1988, RM, Kaya/Chawia, 4/5/1988, and NM, Wundanyi/Werugha, 26/5/1988.

1940 as the handiwork of outside agitators. The KCA lent its name to the initial Taita movement and gave it tactical advice in its first months, but outsiders could not conjure up the extensive support and participation that the THA rapidly generated over land issues.

Colonial officials found the THA's emergence particularly ill–timed. Hostile to African associational politics at the calmest of moments,[53] officials now trying to marshal the colony's resources for World War II had less patience still. They feared the associations would undermine the mobilization, and so took a hard–line approach to them. In June of 1940, the colony banned the THA, KCA, and Ukamba Members Association, and deported Mengo and Mwambichi from the Hills.[54] However, Taita–based officials soon acknowledged that the THA's influence did not cease with its proscription. Land–based political agitation continued in Taita, and the THA's lower–level leaders remained active even with their association officially defunct.[55]

Trespassing and agitation continued at Mwatunge: African farmers swept out of Mwatunge in early 1940 soon re–encroached. In 1942, prompted by local officials, the state reopened the question of what to do about the encroachments. A new report concluded that the squatters *did* have just claims, but that "political agitators had spoilt any case the tribe might have had . . . by misstatement and illegal action." Officials now hoped that defusing the main land question would end the shadow THA's *raison d'être*.[56] Acting on the new report, the colony gave temporary recognition to local claims on Mwatunge in 1943, and began negotiating with TCL to reacquire the land. Mwambichi and Mengo were then allowed back into the district.[57]

Official hopes that resolving Mwatunge would lower the curtain on associational politics proved ill–founded. Former THA members, prominent among the squatters who had reoccupied Mwatunge after 1940, with some justice declared the 1943 settlement a triumph for Taita political mobilization.[58] They led a movement to reject temporary permits for the Mwatunge land, and when legal delays held up its final transfer for several years, local suspicions of governmental intentions flared up again.[59] The old THA leaders also kept up ties

---

[53] Bruce Berman, "Bureaucracy and Incumbent Violence: Colonial Administration with the Origins of the 'Mau Mau' Emergency," in Berman and Lonsdale, *Unhappy Valley*, vol. 2, 239–42.

[54] On the state's opposition to and banning of the THA, see PRO, CO 533/523/6 (1940), and CO 533/529/8 (1941); KNA, ARC/MAA/2/3/19, Coast Intelligence Reports, 1940, and PC/Cst/2/3/115, Taita Hills Association, 1940.

[55] KNA, PC/Cst/1/11/40, Taita Land Claims and the Taita Hills Association, DC to PC, 16/2/1942, 7/5/1942 and 23/5/1942; also Bull to DC, 28/5/1942 (same file).

[56] The quote is from KNA, CNC/10/101, Taita Land Claims, 7/9/1943. See also, PC/Cst/1/1/40, Taita Land Claims and the Taita Hills Association, Bull to DC, 28/5/40.

[57] KNA, PC/Cst/1/11/40, Taita Land Claims and the Taita Hills Association, Report on Chawia location agriculture, 8/1942; and DC to PC 6/9/1942, 31/1/1943, and 19/2/1943.

[58] KNA, TTA/3/1/71, Native Associations and Agitators, 9/3/1945.

[59] KNA, ARC(MAA)–2/3/39iii, Coast Province Annual Report, 1946. The government *was* serious about securing the land from TCL, even threatening to invoke a fifty–year–old compulsory purchase act originally applied to Indians. The owner disliked the state–proposed price, which led to protracted negotiation. See PRO, CO 533/556/4, 1945–47.

in colonywide politics, organizing a branch of the Kenya African Study Union (KASU) in 1945, which became part of the Kenya African Union (KAU) in 1947.[60] Finally, in 1949, the activists founded a successor group to the THA in personnel, in focus on local issues, and in claiming to representing the Taita and their interests: the Taita Fighi Union. These organizations were not paper tigers; a postwar DC observed that the former THA leaders brought "a considerable following" with them to the new bodies.[61]

New land disputes kept the shadow THA active and popular in Taita. TCL again figured in the proceedings, building a dam in late 1948 that local officials termed a "flagrant" violation of Kenyan law. The dam flooded over 35 acres of prime farmland in the Ngulu section of Chawia location—the same location that had been embroiled in the Mwatunge dispute. The dam inflamed local distrust of the government all across the Hills; it is no coincidence that the Taita Fighi Union formed soon after it was built. The dam also put the administration over a barrel, for district officials, too, were horrified by its construction, but were overruled on its legality by Nairobi.[62]

The administration compounded local distrust in 1950, when it set up strict rules for farming near Ngulu's swamplands. Though the DC saw the dam and the farming rules as separate matters, Taita's inhabitants linked them closely.[63] The dam remained a source of political mobilization for the THA and a thorn in the government's side until mid–1952, when those who had lost farmland agreed to monetary compensation from TCL.[64] The effectiveness of the farming rules depended on enforcement by the Chawia chief, and in this highly charged environment, he chose discretion over vigor; the rules were only sporadically followed.[65]

The district administration also hoped to quell the THA by co–opting its leaders into local administrative institutions. This policy, initiated after the war, led to Mengo gaining a seat on the Local Native Council in 1946, and

---

[60] Mengo headed the KAU–Taita Branch, and announced its formation in a flyer that invited others to join. See KNA, DC/TTA/3/1/71, memo of 2/9/1947. See also the same file, letter of 9/3/1945, on the opening of a KASU branch.

[61] KNA, DC/TTA/1/2, Taita District Annual Report for 1946.

[62] KNA, DAO/TTA/1/1/164, Taita District Annual Report for 1949. The dam was approved after the fact by Kenya's Director of Agriculture, Cavendish–Bentick (the first settler given a senior post in the Kenya administration), over the DC's strenuous objections.

[63] KNA, DC/TTA/3/2/47, Safari Reports of 25/7/1950, 28/8/1950, and 31/8/1950; also, interview with JK, Kaya/Chawia, 3/5/1988. Later, the DC indicated that he understood the farmers' position. DC/TTA/3/12/32, Ngulu Swamp, DC to PC, 4/6/1951.

[64] KNA, DAO/TTA/1/1/159, AAO Safari Diary 2/12/1951, and DO to DC, 11/1/1952; also DC/TTA/3/12/32, Ngulu Swamp 1950–51; on the settlement of the dispute, DAO/TTA/1/1/156, Monthly Intelligence Report, 4/10/1952; and DC/TTA/3/8/45, Taita Concessions Limited, 1952–53.

[65] On the ineffectiveness of the rules, see KNA, DC/TTA/3/12/32, Ngulu Swamp 1950–51. On the Chawia chief's low profile around this crisis, interviews with BM, Sechu/Chawia, 11/6/1988, and JM, Teri/Chawia, 5/8/1988; also, DAO/TTA/1/1/222, Agricultural Safari Diaries, AAO to DC on two trips to Chawia, 7/1950.

Mwambichi being appointed a Native Court Elder in 1948.[66] Official standing did not prevent them from continuing their involvement with African oppositional politics in Taita. Mengo helped organize Taita's KASU and KAU branches, and is remembered by colonial officers as an adversary through the early 1950s.[67] The co–optation policy may have had some effect, however. When the State of Emergency was declared in 1952, former THA activists distanced themselves from Mau Mau, and Taita oppositional politics went very quiet.

Formal Politics, Cultural Politics, and Taita Identity

Associational politics in Taita did not only target "outsiders" like colonial officials and TCL. The Taita associations' members and supporters also had concerns that drew them into cultural politicking over Taita identity. They hoped to forge a broad social bloc behind their vision of Taita commonality and Taita interests, but almost as soon as the KCA–Taita Branch started in 1939, some in Taita rejected their agenda and methods. The association's supporters thereafter set out to bolster their local credibility, and to isolate and neutralize their Christian progressive opponents. The association did both by wrapping their broader politics in *Kidaßida*–based language and symbolism. This nostalgic evocation and appropriation of *Kidaßida* appealed to the *Wutasi*–practicing majority, particularly to elders and their supporters.

The move also cast Christian progressive opponents of the association as people estranged from true Taita values, proper Taita ways, and real Taita interests. The tactic effectively put the association's opponents on the defensive in the 1940s and early 1950s, forcing them to retreat into avowals that the progressive Christian vision was consonant with Taita identity and Taita interests. Missionaries and the state backed the progressives' claim, but attempts to build an association around their vision of Taita identity drew no popular following. Less strict Christians, less committed progressives, and everyone else in Taita responded better to the formal politics of Taita interests versus outsiders' interests, and to the cultural politics of nostalgic *Kidaßida*.

The composition of the Taita Hills Association offers clues to how the supporters of associational politics forged a coalition around their vision of Taita identity. Of the 199 THA leaders listed by Mengo in 1940, sixty-one had Christian names.[68] Nearly a third of the activists, then, were at least nominally Christian, and the popularity of education in Taita implies that another (uncountable) proportion, like Mengo, had some schooling but did not convert. Probably the largest portion was composed of Wutasi follow-

---

[66] KNA, DC/TTA/1/1, District Annual Report, 1946. By 1948 the DC claimed with undue optimism that Mengo and Mwambichi "have been effectively absorbed." See ARC(MAA) 2/3/39iv, Coast Province Annual Report, 1948.

[67] KNA, TTA/3/1/71, Native Associations and Agitators, 9/3/1945, and 2/9/1947, and interviews with Michael Power, Surrey/England, 24/2/1989, and Peter Walters, Surrey/England, 25/2/1989.

[68] KNA, PC/Cst/2/3/115, Taita Hills Association, Mengo to Governor, 1/4/1940.

ers with little or no education. This proportioning reflected the simultaneous appeals that the THA mustered.

One appeal was to educated young men. Like their counterparts elsewhere in Kenya, they paid increasing attention to politics and wanted a say in local issues. Many such men were teachers or clerks; some even worked in administration:

> Some educated people followed [the THA], . . . they saw that [Mengo] was talking the truth about our country. . . . We went to those meetings of the association, . . . we had them in secret, because the Government did not want them. . . . Many of the teachers followed the THA, but . . . secretly because of the government and the missionaries.[69]

> My father helped [the THA] and supported them, even though he was an Assistant Chief. Without a doubt, he could not join them openly.[70]

A second appeal that spoke across the region was the THA's focus on land rights in Taita, a concern that united many against a common outside threat. It touched not only those who had lost land, but young men who wanted to uphold local rights in the farms they expected to inherit. The THA helped steer these concerns towards a language of an ethnic whole: "We didn't want Taita, our country, to go to the Europeans. . . . Even if [my land] was not taken, I would defend my brothers'."[71] It spoke to young women, too: "If we were pushed away from [Mwatunge], my family would go hungry, how will I feed them? . . . Therefore I prayed that the Association will win."[72] Finally, land greatly concerned older people as their source of wealth and of daily welfare.

Third, the THA worked hard to foster support among elders and *Wutasi* followers. At the heart of this appeal lay the association's deliberate referral to long–standing, *Wutasi*–based notions of community defense, especially defending land against spiritual evil and plunder by outsiders. The THA's frequent invoking of defense in its brief above–ground life therein carried strongly *Wutasi*–centric connotations.[73] The emphasis struck a chord among elders and *Wutasi* followers, and became a staple of how people remembered the group: "They were defending our land from the Europeans, that is why elders agreed with them, to defend the land. . . . They were . . . the young educated ones, . . . but they defended the land."[74] Before colonial rule, the land to be defended

---

[69] Interview with AM, Shigaro/Werugha, 2/5/1988; AM was a prominent teacher in the CMS system at the time. Others expressed similar sentiments, including GM, Kishamba/Chawia, 6/6/1988, and JM, Teri/Chawia, 5/8/1988.

[70] Interview with WM, Shigaro/Werugha, 18/4/1988.

[71] Interview with AM, Shigaro/Werugha, 2/5/1988.

[72] Interview with Mrs. RM, Chawia/Chawia, 16/6/1988.

[73] "What did they say? They said that they were defending us! . . . The whites would not defend our farms, . . . they helped their white brothers. The Association was for defending *us*." Interview with MM, Kishamba/Chawia, 8/6/1988. Also, SN, Wumari/Chawia, 5/6/1988; and Mrs. MM, Teri/Chawia, 22/7/1988. Many others could be cited.

[74] Interview with SM, Kidaya–Ngerenyi/Chawia, 25/4/1988.

had been lineage land; in the 1940s, the THA redefined "the land" as Taita land, and the change was readily accepted. The THA and its successor groups thus appropriated and reinvigorated a central tenet of *Kidaßida*: that Taita identity was rooted in *Wutasi*–based knowledge and practices.

This deployment of nostalgic *Kidaßida* for formal and cultural politics reached its apogee in 1949, as the Ngulu controversy neared its peak: Mengo and others from the old THA announced the formation of the Taita Fighi Union.[75] *Fighi* was a *Wutasi*–based medicine of community well–being known as the Defender. *Fighi* protected a neighborhood against outside enemies, ensuring the physical and spiritual peace of the community.[76] Mengo used *Fighi* in a more expansive way, listing as the Union's first aim the uniting of all the lineages of the Taita tribe.[77] When speaking at a Fighi Union meeting, his deployment of *Fighi* as a basis of pan–Taita unity, if not historically accurate, was shrewd cultural politicking. He invoked the Defender as a source of long–standing Taita commonality, and then turned it into an assertion of common Taita cause:

> *Fighi* reigned over all the people of Taita and the country of Taita before the rule of the Europeans arrived. When the Europeans arrived, they were received and welcomed by the *Fighi* elders with affection and friendship. . . . If we want to uphold the respect of our heritage, it behooves us to join together through [the Taita Fighi Union]. . . . The meaning of our coming together is to search for the new means of defense, such as education and similar useful things.[78]

Some officials observed Mengo's speech that day, and the recorded text of it generally complimented the government. Even in so polite an oration, however, Mengo's historical sketch and call to action had ambiguous implications: while we welcomed Europeans in good faith, Taita now required defending, for only we can "uphold the respect of our heritage." Taita, he suggested, must be defended by a united, vigilant people who could apply Western–acquired skills to the task, but who also honored and drew upon Taita ways. For anyone versed in *Wutasi*, this call for defense carried the clear implication that forces were upsetting a community's peace and well–being; it was a veiled shot across the bow of the government and its elite progressive allies. Mengo made the same point less ambiguously in a letter to the DC when the Fighi Union was founded: while embracing many material aspects of progressive change, the Union would resist interferences "from within and without" in Taita's well–being.[79]

---

75 KNA, DC/TTA/3/1/72, Taita Fighi Union, 1949–52.

76 For more on the role and meaning of *Fighi* in the late 1940s, see G. Harris, *Casting*, 14–15, 22, 33, 125–27, 134.

77 KNA, DC/TTA/3/1/72, Taita Fighi Union, Mengo to DC, 28/6/1949.

78 KNA, DC/TTA/3/1/72, Minute za kwanza za mkutano wa chama cha Taita Fighi Union [First minutes of meeting of the Taita Fighi Union society], 11/11/1950.

79 Ibid., Mengo to DC, 28/6/1949.

Taita's oppositional associations greatly profited by this approach. As a movement-building strategy, it helped them assemble a broad, deep coalition. Colonial officials acknowledged the associations' wide support among younger people who were not strict Christians. Many older *Wutasi* followers thought well of them, too. Even though the association's young activists embraced elements of the progressive agenda, their affirmation of *Wutasi* and a *Kidaßida*–derived notion of defense gave them credibility with elders:

> Some of those [THA] leaders, who I call politicians, . . . they were modern, they dressed smartly. They were true leaders, but many were not . . . Christians. Even some were baptized, but were not true Christians. . . . Mengo was a true leader, but he was not a Christian. He was in the traditional religion. . . . He was not very old, but he was *Mtasi* [i.e., a *Wutasi* follower], and the elders knew he was faithful [to them].[80]

This cultural politics of Taita identity also helped isolate and sully their opponents. The most obvious opponents, colonial officialdom, acted against Taita interests in giving away their land to their fellow whites. Officials appear to have been oblivious to that cultural politicking. In their eyes, the Taita associations mainly spun demagoguery and grandiose or petty lies, which could be countered with facts, a stern, steady hand, and a degree of co-optation.[81] Officials also did not have to live with the long–term consequences of the cultural politics; they were just passing through. Missionaries, who often saw themselves as defenders of African interests, were more stung by the cultural politics that accounted them enemies of Taita ways.[82] But, missionaries, too, would ultimately return to their distant homes.

Though activists' verbal attacks did not lastingly score the Europeans, such public confrontations reminded the audience who would defend Taita and who posed threats. Still, the most immediate and vulnerable targets of this cultural politics were not Europeans, but people who sprang from and would remain in the Hills: WaTaita who supported the state, especially the tight social nexus of vigorous chiefs, strong progressives, and strict Christians. In the hands of the associations, nostalgic *Kidaßida* became a sturdy stick with which to strike them.

The overt confrontations contained a powerful cultural political subtext that rocked the Christian progressive elite back on its heels. When chiefs tried

---

[80] Interview with AK, Shigaro/Werugha, 25/4/1988. Despite the absolutism in this quote, the elders' trust had limits. Many, for instance, were suspicious of the leaders' ties to Kikuyu politicians. Interviews with NM, Wundanyi/Werugha, 26/5/1988; and NK, Mwatate/Chawia, 15/8/1988.

[81] Interviews with Peter Walters (former DC Taita) 25/2/1989, and Michael Power (former DO Taita) 24/2/1989. Walters, however, also described Mengo as having a quick mind and often–friendly manner that he found disarming. Michael Cowley (former DC Taita), interviewed 23/2/1989, who initiated the policy of trying to co–opt him, felt similarly.

[82] This feeling was evident in Nathan Mnjama's interview with Rev. Peter Bostock, Oxford/England, 19/7/1980; I am grateful to Mr. Mnjama for providing me a copy of the transcript.

to enforce land use rules or prevent trespassing, they nearly always faced harassment from association members and supporters. If they spoke at public fora on land or land use issues, activists often heckled them in terms that cast them as less–than–fully–Taita:

> *GM:* When [Chief] Solomon tried to tell people not to farm at [Ngulu] swamp, people criticized him. Some called him names to his face!
>
> *Q:* Who did that?
>
> *GM:* The people of the Fighi society. . . . "You are just here for the white man! You are not here for the people of the country, . . . maybe you like the whites better!"[83]

As early as 1940, the provincial commissioner of the Coast noted that the THA had seriously hurt the authority of chiefs and the LNC. By the late 1940s, this cultural politics so weakened chiefs that district officials finally began to acknowledge their bind; said one former official, "they were the ham in the sandwich."[84] Chiefs in Taita did indeed face a no–win situation: some in fact sympathized with the associations but could not say so publicly, and so remained vulnerable to opprobrium. Others really opposed the associations' aims and tactics, and resented the way they further crippled chiefs' standing in their communities. However, in order not to compound the strains in their locations and further weaken their own positions, hostile chiefs often turned a blind eye to association activities and land–related lawbreaking.[85]

Christians of all stripes also came under heavy pressure from this cultural politics. Strict Christians were sometimes insulted with turn–of–the–century vehemence, accused of preferring whites' ways and the whites' God to proper Taita ways:

> We were called every kind of name by the [Taita Hills] Association people, by the [Taita] Fighi [Union] people. . . . They said we were traitors . . . to our people. They said that because we loved Christianity we helped the whites grab our country. Ah! They said very scurrilous things about us, . . . [and] too many people believed them.[86]

For less strict Christians, the situation created a polarization that forced many to choose between the church and the associations. Through most of the 1940s, the associations got the better of the showdown, and the ranks of devout Christians sank noticeably:

---

[83] Interview with GM, Kishamba/Chawia, 27/6/1988; and AK, Shigaro/Werugha, 25/4/1988; for other examples, KNA, PC/Cst/1/11/40, Taita Land Claims, DC to PC, 6/9/1942 and 30/12/1942; along with DC/TTA/3/12/32, Ngulu Swamp, 31/8/1950, 17/1/1951, and 22/11/1951.

[84] Interview with Michael Power, 24/2/1989.

[85] Interviews with WM, Shigaro/Werugha, 20/4/1988, AK, Shigaro/Werugha, 25/4/1988, and RM, Kaya/Chawia, 4/5/1988.

[86] Interview with AM, Shigaro/Werugha, 2/5/1988.

A major onslaught on the authority of the church developed. . . .
Some of the strongest centers of church life were attacked, . . . and
for the next few years the church survived in these areas only because of a handful of people who held out against the popular dissatisfaction. . . . It was not so much punishment as social ostracism,
and the whole district turned away from these people. The local
community turned away from the church. . . . [The] one or two
people who held firm lost their following entirely to Mwambichi
and Mengo.[87]

In the face of the decline, leaders of the Christian, progressive nexus attempted a counterattack. In 1947, they started a rival association, the Taita–
Taveta Union (TTU), headed by four Taita Anglican ministers, four Christian
chiefs, and four prominent teachers from CMS schools; the European CMS dean
of the Coast, a former missionary in Taita, held an advisory role.[88] In laying out
the group's vision, they proclaimed their main mission to be advancing the
"progress of Taita."[89] In a subsequent letter to the Kenya African Union, the
TTU leaders spelled out the progressive line in this struggle more fully:

We are striving for the progress of religion [i.e., Christianity] and the
country [i.e., Taita] and the tribe, for we know that our true progress
requires us to hold together firmly [as a tribe], and follow the direction of God.[90]

Within the formulation lay the familiar progressive case for Taita identity: it
was inherent as a birthright and consonant with the progressive agenda.
Through true religion and progressive attention to the needs of the tribe, all
the Taita could advance.

The Taita Taveta Union leaders also declared the postwar Taita branch of
the KAU a front for the interests of (Kikuyu) outsiders, while the TTU had its
interest mainly in the tribe.[91] This rhetoric, an attempt to enter into ethnicizing
discourse by emphasizing intergroup difference, only underlined how small a
base (and unpopular a case) the TTU had. When it came to public advocacy of
Taita interests, Mengo, Mwambichi, and their version of Taita identity had much
more credibility than the Christian progressive elite—even among most Chris-

---

[87] Interview with Peter Bostock by Nathan Mnjama, Oxford/England, 19/6/1980. Bostock, citing his
1943 Annual Letter, admitted that the mission, despite misgivings about injustices being done to the
Taita, drew fire upon itself by taking sides on the Mwatunge land dispute and other issues: "It seemed
clear that the Christian part was to stick by the Christian DC, . . . and at the same time . . . help the
Africans to see the wisdom of sacrificing their [short-term] interests for the lasting benefits that would
[eventually] accrue [through cooperation with the government]." He acknowledged that the stance
devastated the church in Taita, and during the interview second–guessed the decision.

[88] KNA, DC/TTA/3/1/71, Native Associations and Agitators, Richard Mwangeka to DC, 11/9/
1947; and Coast Rural Dean to Mengo, 17/10/1947.

[89] Ibid., Richard Mwangeka to DC, 11/9/1947.

[90] Ibid., Taita Taveta Union to KAU–Nairobi, 17/2/1948.

[91] Ibid., Coast Rural Dean to Mengo, 17/10/1947.

tians.[92] Partly because it lacked credibility, partly because it championed no popular issues, and partly because it had no knack (or taste) for mass mobilization or populist cultural politicking, the Taita Taveta Union sank without a trace in late 1948 or early 1949.

The Mau Mau and early independence years saw the progressive Christian vision of Taita identity regain (and surpass) its lost ground, but while Taita cleavages in formal and cultural politics changed in that era, they were not resolved. Yet again, disputes with TCL fed into those politics.[93] Post–1952 conflicts lie beyond the scope of this study, but in overview the 1950s and 1960s saw the final decline of early–century elders' view of Taita ethnicity as a norm–driven identity defined by (their terms of) *Kidaßida*. In the context of Taita's strong loyalism during Mau Mau and the crowning of progressive moderates as independent Kenya's leaders, nostalgic *Kidaßida* also lost its 1940s role of cultural–political polarization. In the 1960s, as Christians became a majority, progressive and nostalgic versions of Taita identity merged: birthright became the core of Taita identity, not norms. But even for strict Christians, birthright included a sentimental—and unifying—acknowledgment that all Taita ancestors had been *Wutasi* followers. When *Wutasi*–following ancestors could be recalled with indulgent pride, the transformation of *Kidaßida* from an active body of norms, outlooks and sanctions into a common cultural heritage was complete. Local social struggles and conflicts did not thereby end, but came to be expressed in different terms, ones now outside the language of Taita ethnicity.

---

[92] Interviews with AK, Shigaro/Werugha, 25/4/1988, AM, Shigaro/Werugha, 2/5/1988, SM, Kidaya/Chawia, 10/5/1988, and GM, Kaya/Chawia, 12/8/1988.

[93] For an analysis of Taita land politics in the independence era, see Tom Wolf, "Leadership, Resources, and Locality–Center Relations in Taita, a Political Subsystem of Kenya's Coast Province: 1960–1975" (Ph.D. diss., University of Sussex, 1985).

CONCLUSION

All through the period under study, people in Taita looked to foster collective relationships and to do well for themselves within those circles. That truism, however, needs historicizing in order to help us understand the dynamics of social processes, for a wide variety of interactions gradually altered the character of communities in the area. If the terms of community in Taita were always at risk in principle, the years following the 1880s in practice put them far more dramatically up for grabs. Available evidence suggests that male elders in the early nineteenth century's lineage and neighborhood communities had greatly constricted the scope of cultural politics. Older men had gained tremendous effective control over material and cultural resources, a leverage that allowed them to present their terms of social order not as debatable or even conceivably opposable claims, but as axiomatic social truths. Challenges to that hegemony from women and younger men were relatively rare and necessarily subtle.

The broad changes of political–economy and sociopolitical context that followed European intrusion into the region opened up new possibilities for altering terms of community. Not only did the character of community begin to fluctuate in ways that threatened senior men's predominance, people also fashioned and negotiated a wholly new level of community, Taita ethnicity, that added extra layers and possibilities to claims they made about themselves and upon one another. Taita ethnicity initially created a widened social terrain upon which older men tried to reconfigure their predominance. In their minds, the new identity preserved localized relationships but endowed them with new, supportive meanings: seniors subordinated their lineal youngers not just as a fact of kinship and functional power, but also as a matter of Taita ways.

Their vision did not entirely prevail, and lost much of its force over time, for two main reasons: older men were losing their stranglehold over material wealth, and Taita ethnicity's social potential proved far more multivalent than they anticipated. As the second part of the book has shown, Taita identity did not reproduce the close control that senior men had held in the mid–nineteenth century over interlocked social, economic, political, and cultural changes. The terms of Taita community slowly (and unevenly) slipped out of the grasp of older men, older women, and *Wutasi* followers.

Within the ethnic rubric, too, people established new relationships that did not directly undermine seniors, but diluted their effective influence by weakening the social authority of local communities. Marriage patterns give one indication of how deeply that change eventually cut. Localized endogamy had long reinforced the social density—and social centrality—of lineage and neighborhood networks. When some people began to use Taita identity as a basis for marrying outside neighborhood and lineage lines in the 1930s, marriage–related ties correspondingly started to become more spatially diffused, socially "thinner," and more unwieldy for seniors to operate:

> *Mrs. AM:* I came [to Shigaro] from Mbale when I was married. . . . My in–laws did not know [my parents] very well. The old women had not dug together.
> *BB:* Did they start to dig together after you married?
> *Mrs. AM:* No, my parents had their neighborhood; now me, I had a new neighborhood, new lineage.
> *BB:* Did your parents and your in–laws start to cooperate on other things together?
> *Mrs. AM:* A little, a little. Not very much.[1]

Firm Christians first used claims of Taita commonality to break with local endogamy, because it provided that small, scattered group a way to marry one another. By the 1950s, the practice had become widespread among Christians, and even *Wutasi* followers could contemplate the prospect.[2]

There was a definite overall arc to the changes in the terms of Taita identity over the first half of the twentieth century. Older men initially asserted it as a community of affective belonging that simultaneously pressured lineage members to adhere to a body of "proper" beliefs and behaviors; failure to do so could curtail one's connection to the community, potentially culminating in the miscreant's becoming "lost" from Taita. Nevertheless, many young men and daughters–in–law, and some Christians of both sexes, challenged the older men's terms of Taita identity from the outset; in fact, their behaviors and beliefs had to no small extent inspired the senior men's claims.

In the ensuing decades, the challengers slowly undermined much of what the elders of the 1910s declared to be proper Taita ways. This overturning did not replace one carefully delimited body of norms and terms with another narrowly specified set. Instead, it bit by bit displaced the norm–driven version of Taita identity with one that put primary emphasis on birthright. Some of those who took up new outlooks and beliefs still wanted to

---

[1] Interview with Mrs. AM, Shigaro/Werugha, 2/5/1988.
[2] Interviews with: PM, Wundanyi/Chawia, 13/8/1988; SM, Mrugua/Bura, 19/8/1988; Mrs. AM, Choke/Mbale, 10/11/1988; Mrs. SM, Wusi/Chawia, 22/7/1993; and Mrs. MM, Werugha/Werugha, 30/7/1993.

pass normative muster as acceptably Taita. Others, the firm progressives, argued that ways hardly mattered; descent, they held, sufficed to establish their credentials *for* belonging, and gave them their sense *of* belonging. The former, who maneuvered quietly and with outward respect against the old version of Taita ethnicity, in time weakened its normative character. The latter, eventually, made their descent–oriented claim about Taita ethnicity its new basis.

Opponents of the progressives' baldly descent–based Taita ethnicity briefly rallied in the 1940s. Politically minded young men during that decade forged an alliance with *Wutasi*–following older men, as well as with a wider Taita populace aggrieved over land issues. The Taita identity promoted by the associations, however, turned more on political commitments than on social norms. The activists treated *Kidaßida* as a symbolic touchstone that resonated positively across the different sectors of their coalition and rankled the sensibilities of their adversaries. Though the THA and Taita Fighi Union invoked the medicines of their grandfathers, they did not promote the grandfathers' vision of proper ways. The most steadfast progressives, the object of the activists' politics, saw their standing briefly diminished and had to endure denigrations of their Taitaness during the late 1940s. But wider Taita misgivings over the Mau Mau quieted activist politics in the early 1950s, severed the link between oppositional politics and Taita identity, and allowed the progressives to reclaim political and social stature.

In the long run, several factors contributed to the ascension of the progressive version of Taita ethnicity. When the wage–labor economy put money in young men's hands, it gave them new leverage in their longer–term efforts to gain some control over a lineage's economic resources. As the older men's economic grip over their sons weakened, seniors' overall control over the conduct of junior households began to slowly slide away. Young wives, increasingly able to obtain economic resources without needing recourse to parents–in–law, could parlay their husbands' wage remittances into more say over the amount, character, and timing of their contributions to lineage life. Parents' desire to educate children as a means of boosting their wage–earning potential helped spread progressives' beliefs and attitudes ever more widely among the young.

Generational turnover reinforced the change in attitudes and actions that undermined the normative version of *Kidaßida*. Young adults who challenged the ways of their seniors in the 1910s and 1920s became the seniors of the 1930s and 1940s. By the latter decades, many older people had themselves been young adults in the era of wage labor, and understood the experiences, concerns, and outlooks of their children far better than *their* parents could have. Indeed, many among the emerging generation of seniors shared some of the same values as their adult children, and joined them in working to undermine earlier versions of proper Taita ways. By the late 1940s, the senior ranks of firm *Wutasi* followers had thinned considerably, and a fair number of equally venerable old people tolerated or even embraced much of the progressive world view. The adult generation just behind them tilted far more decidedly towards the world of money–wealth, western education, and Christianity.

Kidaßida as a body of ways did not ring hollow to that younger generation by the late 1940s, for at a minimum it evoked a shared ancestry, a shared historical culture that helped people feel bound together. But *Kidaßida* no longer worked well on that generation in the ways it had a few decades earlier: as the discursive linchpin of a system that disciplined the beliefs and behaviors of subordinate group members, even as it beckoned them into a community of deeply–felt belonging. Successive generations had displaced elders' attempts in the 1910s to naturalize a norm–driven version of Taita ethnicity that embraced *Wutasi*, animals as wealth, and a lineage–based system of older men's predominance. Now, whether Christians claimed it as a non–normative, all–embracing marker of broadly shared heritage, or political activists used it as a pointed tool to distinguish supporters from opponents, the discursive focus of *Kidaßida* shifted elsewhere: towards nostalgia for a world substantively left behind.

APPENDICES

Appendix A:
Bura Church Baptism Rates Prior to World War I.

The year 1902 was a peak year, but until World War I, every year's figures still ran near or ahead of the total CMS pace:

1903:	56
1904:	43
1905:	63
1906:	45
1907:	47
1908:	23
1909:	102
1910:	136
1911:	71
1912:	80
1913:	102

Source: Bura Church Baptismal Records, Book I.

Appendix B:
Baptismal Records, Bura Mission, 1893–1917.

Year	Total Baptisms	Baptized as Infant/Older
1893	2	0/2
1897	17	9/8
1898	52	22/30 *2nd half of yr. mostly infants
1899	53	39/14
1903	56	47/9
1909	102	75/27
1910	136	108/28
1913	102	85/17
1917	35	33/2

Source: Baptismal Records, Book I, Bura Mission, Taita.

BIBLIOGRAPHY

Interviews in Taita

All interviews in Taita were conducted between 26/3/1988 and 12/11/1988, or between 5/7/1993 and 6/8/1993. Below is an alphabetized list of persons interviewed, followed by a list of the number of interviews held in different administrative locations of Taita. Because anonymity was guaranteed to speakers in order to encourage them to speak freely on sensitive subjects, first names, sex, dates, and locations of individual interviews in Taita are not indicated. A number in parentheses after a name indicates multiple interviews with that person; a repeated surname and first initial indicates different people.

Azae, C.
Chola, J.
Chonga, M.
Isangaiwishi, H.
Kalela, S.
Kalendo, J.
Kamarza, M.
Kilangi, S.
Kilinda, J.
Kimbichi, M.
Kimbio, R.
Kimega, E.
Kimore, N.
Kiringo, S.
Kishaga, J.
Kishago, E.
Kituri, P.
Kole, J.
Konde, O. (3)
Kubo, A.
Longosi, J.
Lukindo, J.
Machaku, N.
Madoka, A.
Maganga, M.
Maganga, S.
Marura, M.

Mataka, G.
Mbasho, S. (2)
Mbogho, M.
Mbogho, M.
Mboti, C.
Mcharo, L.
Mdawida, J. (2)
Mganga, G.
Mghalu, D.
Mghalu, D.
Mikawasi, S.
Mjomba, G. (4)
Mjomba, H.
Mjomba, S.
Mjombo, C.
Mkaiwawi, J.
Mkamburi, V.
Mkangangwa, M.
Mlango, S.
Mlongo, S.
Mnjala, S.
Mnjama, G.
Mnyanya, W.
Mnyika, M.
Msabaa, M.
Mshimba, M.
Mshimba, R.

Msigo, J.
Msinga, N.
Mswahili, J.
Mughambi, R.
Mugho, W.
Musa, P.
Mvoi, S.
Mwabiri, S.
Mwachanga, F.
Mwachofi, N. (2)
Mwachofi, R.
Mwachofi, R.
Mwachoo, L.
Mwachuga, K.
Mwadime, M.
Mwadime, R.
Mwadime, S.
Mwaghali, B.
Mwagunde, K.
Mwailinda, M.
Mwairo, S.
Mwaita, G.
Mwaita, J.
Mwaka, H.
Mwakale, G.
Mwakamba, J.
Mwakatini, M.
Mwakibola, N. (2)
Mwakimori, J.
Mwakina, L.
Mwakio, D.
Mwakio, M.
Mwakisha, S.
Mwakughu, J. (2)
Mwakuli, V.
Mwalekwa, M.
Mwalufu, D.
Mwambada, A. (2)
Mwambingu, E.
Mwambingu, F.
Mwambingu, M.
Mwamburi, A.
Mwamburi, F.
Mwamburi, P.
Mwamburi, W.
Mwamrizi, M.
Mwanake, W.
Mwangala, S.
Mwanganyi, S.
Mwangeka, R.

Mwangombe, A.
Mwangombe, J.
Mwanjala, S.
Mwanjama, K.
Mwanyama, D.
Mwanyumba, B.
Mwanyumba, S.
Mwarimbo, J. (2)
Mwasaru, S.
Mwashigadi, B.
Mwashigadi, S. (2)
Mwashimba, J.
Mwasi, A.
Mwasi, G.
Mwasi, S.
Mwasi, W.
Mwasigwa, M.
Mwasindo, W.
Mwatati, J.
Mwatoa, J.
Mwawasi, D.
Mwazige, J.
Mwazurumbi, M.
Mwikamba, E.
Mwisanga, S.
Mzae, J.
Mzae, O. (2)
Mzuga, P.
Ng'ara, M.
Ngeti, G.
Ngima, P.
Ngoo, R.
Nyambo, M.
Nyambu, P.
Nyange, S.
Nyata, J.
Nzano, J.
Nzano, M.
Osmond, J.
Ragasi, M.
Shala, P.
Shungula, S.
Tangai, F.
Tole, A.
Tole, M.
Tufwa, M.
Wachenje, F.
Wanje, M.
Wanjio, M.
Wanyika, M.

Total Number of Taita Interviews: 168
Interviews with Men 112
Interviews with Women 56

Administrative Locations of Taita Interviews

Location	# of Interviews
Bura	11
Chawia	30
Mbale	12
Mbololo	20
Mwanda	17
Sagalla	17
Werugha	57
Wumingu	3

Interviews in England

Mr. Kenneth Cowley, (former DC, Taita)	23/2/1989
Mr. Michael Power, (former DO, Taita)	24/2/1989
Mr. Peter Walters, (former DC, Taita)	25/2/1989
Rev. Peter Bostock, (former missionary, Taita)	3/4/1989
Rev. Peter Bostock, (by Nathan Mnjama)	19/6/1980

Documentary Sources

Kenya National Archives

Coast Province Files

PC/CST/1/1/21b	1898	Mombasa Outward
PC/CST/1/1/45	1899	Ukamba Inward
PC/CST/1/1/97	1903	Mwatate Inward
PC/CST/1/1/109	1904–05	Mombasa Outward
PC/CST/1/1/115	1906	Taita Inward
PC/CST/1/1/128	1907	Mombasa Outward
PC/CST/1/1/179	1911	Quarterly Reports
PC/CST/1/1/265	1917–18	District Annual Reports
PC/CST/1/1/267	1918–23	Censuses
PC/CST/1/1/287	1912	Inspection Visit
PC/CST/1/1/295	1912	Quarterly Reports
PC/CST/1/1/326	1915–18	Inspection Visits to Voi
PC/CST/1/1/327	1914–18	Censuses
PC/CST/1/1/333	1915–26	Administration of Native Reserves
PC/CST/1/2/42	1913	Economic Crops
PC/CST/1/2/85	1916–19	Native Crops and Food Shortages
PC/CST/1/2/86	1917–19	Native Crops and Food Shortages
PC/CST/1/2/92	1915–25	Maize Crops
PC/CST/1/2/105	1919	Native Crops and Famine

PC/CST/1/9/2	1908–09	Labour Supply/Recruiting
PC/CST/1/9/13	1912–13	Labour, Taita District
PC/CST/1/9/25	1914–17	Taita Labourers
PC/CST/1/11/40	1942–44	Taita Land Claims and T.H.A.
PC/CST/1/11/51	1929–30	Land Concessions
PC/CST/1/11/101	1913–14	Native Reserve Boundaries
PC/CST/1/11/269	1918	Land in Voi District
PC/CST/1/11/270	1915–26	Land and Habib Nanji
PC/CST/1/12/28	1904	Mombasa Outward
PC/CST/1/12/31	1905	Taita Inward
PC/CST/1/12/36	1906	Outward Mwatate
PC/CST/1/12/40	1907	Taita Inward
PC/CST/1/12/51	1904, 1909	Taita Inward
PC/CST/1/12/249	1917–18	Voi District Markets
PC/CST/1/12/269	1917–19	Handing–over Reports
PC/CST/1/12/279	1919–20	Native Affairs Reports
PC/CST/1/12/288	1929–30	Local Native Council
PC/CST/1/12/290	1936–44	LNC Resolutions
PC/CST/1/13/72	1915	Native Tribunals
PC/CST/1/13/132	1917	Taita Military Porters
PC/CST/1/19/66	1911–12	Blue Books
PC/CST/1/19/82	1917–18	Taita Shops
PC/CST/1/19/84	1918	Taita Produce
PC/CST/1/19/115	1915–27	Trading Centers
PC/CST/1/22/32	1916–20	District Tours
PC/CST/2/3/75	1931–36	LNC Estimates
PC/CST/2/3/106	1938–45	LNC Minutes and Estimates
PC/CST/2/3/115	1940	Taita Hills Association
PC/CST/2/4/16	1930–37	Agricultural Development
PC/CST/2/4/29	1936–43	Marketing Fruits and Vegetables
PC/CST/2/5/34	1934–47	Agricultural, Medical and Sanitation Reports
PC/CST/2/8/10	1929–40	Water Supplies
PC/CST/2/11/49	1931–33	Land Alienations
PC/CST/2/11/64	1931–38	Grazing Land, Voi
PC/CST/2/11/65	1931–38	Native Reserve Boundaries
PC/CST/2/11/66	1931–40	Natives on Crown Land: Kasigau
PC/CST/2/11/72	1933–35	Alienated Crown Land: Wundanyi Estate
PC/CST/2/16/5	1932	Unemployed Native Artisans, Taita
PC/CST/2/16/6	1935–38	Labour Conditions, TCLtd.
PC/CST/2/16/7	1935–37	Labour Returns, Administration
PC/CST/2/16/11	1929–44	Labour Conscription, Taita
PC/CST/2/18/8	1933–41	Taita Trading Centers
PC/CST/2/27/99	1938	Staff Expenditures and Estimates

District Commissioner—Taita

DC/TTA/1/1	1919–37	Annual Reports
DC/TTA/1/2	1938–48	Annual Reports
DC/TTA/3/1	1910–12	Political Record Books
DC/TTA/3/1/5	1945–51	Slum Clearance, WaTaita outside NLU

DC/TTA/3/1/6	1950	Ndara Location
DC/TTA/3/1/8	1946–56	Bura Location
DC/TTA/3/1/10	1946–48	Kasigau Chiefs
DC/TTA/3/1/12	1946–54	Mbololo Location
DC/TTA/3/1/14	1945–52	Native Authority Correspondence
DC/TTA/3/1/17	1950–57	District Development Team
DC/TTA/3/1/18	1952–54	District Team Meeting Minutes
DC/TTA/3/1/25	1947–52	Chiefs' and DCs' Meetings
DC/TTA/3/1/57	1941–54	Visits by Governor
DC/TTA/3/1/59	1938–53	PCs' Tours
DC/TTA/3/1/61	1949–54	Administrative Tours and Safaris
DC/TTA/3/1/66	1951–56	Tribal Laws and Customs
DC/TTA/3/1/71	1945–52	Associations and Agitators
DC/TTA/3/1/72	1951–52	Taita Fighi Union
DC/TTA/3/1/80	1946–57	Native Affairs Correspondence; Insurance
DC/TTA/3/2/2	1951–53	Crop Production and Marketing
DC/TTA/3/2/46	1947–55	Agricultural Policy
DC/TTA/3/2/47	1947–52	Safari Reports
DC/TTA/3/3	1914–34	Political Record Books
DC/TTA/3/3/2	1913–21	Political Record Books/War Diary
DC/TTA/3/4/4	1931–47	Visitors, LNC and Tribunal Members
DC/TTA/3/6/7	1932–52	Communal Labour
DC/TTA/3/8/14	1936–52	Roman Catholic Plots
DC/TTA/3/8/45	1929–52	TCLtd., Land Exchanges
DC/TTA/3/8/97	1932–51	General Land Surveys and Maps
DC/TTA/3/12/32	1950–52	Ngulu Swamp
DC/TTA/3/16/29	1947–57	Handing–over Reports
DC/TTA/3/19/5	1948–50	Control of Imports, Local Manufactures, Rice and Wheat
DC/TTA/3/19/7	1949–53	Maize Control
DC/TTA/3/22/3	1949–54	Cooperatives—Voi Dairymen's
DC/TTA/3/22/4	1938–53	Trade and Trade Licenses
DC/TTA/3/22/5	1949	Traders: Mwanake Kala
DC/TTA/3/22/6	1952–53	Loan to TVCS Ltd.
DC/TTA/3/22/7	1948–54	Pepper Growers' Cooperatives and Others
DC/TTA/3/28/15	1949–50	Bakeries
DC/TTA/4	1951	"WaTaita Today," by Alfred and Grace Harris
DC/TTA/8/1	1925–32	Native Coffee Growing

District Agricultural Files

DAO/TTA/1/1/17	1947–50	Cowpeas, Green Grams
DAO/TTA/1/1/27	1939–58	Agricultural Annual Reports
DAO/TTA/1/1/29	1946–49	Cooperatives
DAO/TTA/1/1/30	1930–53	Vegetable Trade
DAO/TTA/1/1/45	1939–50	Vegetables
DAO/TTA/1/1/86	1946–53	Agricultural Education
Ibid.	1950–51	Mombasa Retail Vegetable Prices
DAO/TTA/1/1/91	1942–52	Vegetable Marketing
DAO/TTA/1/1/101	1941	Maize and Wheat

DAO/TTA/1/1/130	1941–52	Agricultural Handing–over Reports
DAO/TTA/1/1/141	1939–50	Crop Reports, Intelligence Reports
DAO/TTA/1/1/148	1952–56	Monthly Crop Reports
DAO/TTA/1/1/152	1951–52	TVCS Produce Bulking Records
DAO/TTA/1/1/156	1952–56	Monthly Intelligence Reports, DO Wundanyi
DAO/TTA/1/1/159	1951–53	Agricultural Safari Diaries
DAO/TTA/1/1/162	1941–49	Mbololo Agricultural Instructors' Reports
DAO/TTA/1/1/163	1948–52	Taita Betterment Scheme: Quarterly Reports
DAO/TTA/1/1/164	1945–50	Annual Reports, Non–agricultural
DAO/TTA/1/1/183	1946–52	Soil Conservation
DAO/TTA/1/1/185	1938–43	Soil Conservation
DAO/TTA/1/1/222	1940–50	Agricultural Safaris
DAO/TTA/1/1/229	1948	Agricultural Notes
DAO/TTA/1/1/265	1950–52	Minutes of Public Meetings

Ministry of African Affairs/Chief Native Commissioner

CNC/10/101	1943	Taita Land Claims
CNC/10/125	1937–38	Soil Erosion Policy
ARC/MAA/2/3/12ii	1940–44	Native Affairs Annuals, Coast
ARC/MAA/2/3/19	1940	Monthly Intelligence Reports, Coast
ARC/MAA/2/3/39iii	1945–46	Annual Reports, Coast
ARC/MAA/2/3/39iv	1947–48	Annual Reports, Coast

Agricultural Department

AGR/1/1065	1943–46	Native Areas Soil Erosion
AGR/1/1079	1946–54	Native Areas Soil Conservation
AGR/1/1244	1934–51	Native Areas Agriculture
AGR/5/1/304	1942–50	Soil Conservation Reports
AGR/5/1/305	1947–49	Soil Conservation Reports, Coast
AGR/5/5/7	1940	Coast Agricultural Annual Report
AGR/5/5/33	1939–47	Coast Agricultural Monthly and Quarterly Reports
AGR/5/5/42	1940–43	Coast Province Agriculture Handing–Over Reports
AGR/5/22/3	1948–49	Market Organization, Fruits and Vegetables
AGR/5/27/1	1934–38	Agricultural Shows

District Officer—Taveta

DO/TAV/1/1/41	1940–51	Chiefs' and DOs' Meetings
DO/TAV/1/3/11	1952	Loans to Africans

Other Official Sources

United Kingdom. Parliament. *Report of the Kenya Land Commission.* 1934. Cmnd. 4556. Her Majesty's Stationary Office.
Colony and Protectorate of Kenya. *The Origins and Growth of Mau Mau.* Nairobi: Sessional Paper No. 5 of 1959/60.

Other Sources

Margaret Murray Photograph Collection, Kenya National Archives

Public Records Office, London

Colonial Office
CO/533/

1–5	1905	Despatches
9, 10	1905	Individuals
11–19	1906	Despatches
23, 24	1906	War, Miscellaneous
25, 26	1906	Individuals
27–33	1907	Despatches
38–40	1907	Individuals
41–48	1908	Despatches
53–56	1908	Individuals
57–64	1909	Despatches
69–70	1909	Individuals
71–78	1910	Despatches
83–84	1910	Individuals
85–93	1911	Despatches
98–100	1911	Individuals
101–109	1912	Despatches
114–115	1912	Individuals
116–125	1913	Despatches
130–131	1913	Individuals
132–143	1914	Despatches
147–148	1914	War, Miscellaneous
149–150	1914	Individuals
151–157	1915	Despatches
160–162	1915	War
164–165	1915	Individuals
166–172	1916	Despatches
174–175	1916	War
177	1916	Individuals
178–186	1917	Despatches
189	1917	War
191–192	1917	Individuals
193–199	1918	Despatches
202	1918	War
204–205	1918	Individuals
206–216	1919	Despatches
225–228	1919	Individuals
229–238	1920	Despatches
250–254	1920	Individuals
255–265	1921	Despatches
273–274	1921	Individuals
275–284	1922	Despatches

291	1922	Individuals
292–299	1923	Despatches
306–307	1923	Individuals
308–315	1924	Despatches
325–327	1924	Individuals
328–334	1925	Despatches
343–344	1925	Individuals
345–348	1926	Despatches
355	1926	Individuals
636	1925–26	Alienation of Land to Missions
652	1926–27	1925 Medical Annual Report
667	1926	1925 Annual Report
371/3	1927–29	Annual Confidential Reports
371/10	1927	1926 Annual Report
378/2	1928–29	Mwatate/Voi Concession: Goldman
378/5	1927–29	1927 Annual Report
379/4	1927–28	African Agricultural Education
382/13	1928–29	1927 NAD Annual Report
384/2	1929	Famine Relief, Natives
384/9	1929–30	Kenyatta's Visit to UK
385/3	1929	Voi–Mwatate Concession: Goldman
388/15	1929–30	Female Labour on Farms
391/6	1929–30	1928 Annual Report
401/5	1930–31	Sisal Industry Bill
401/12	1930–31	1929 Agricultural Annual Report, Comments & Suggestions
411/5	1930–31	1930 Agricultural Projects Summary
411/11	1931	Extension of Sagalla Mission Lease
416/7	1931–32	1930 Agricultural Annual Report: Comments
419/6	1931–32	Sisal Machinery: Colonial Development Fund Assistance
422/5	1931–32	Proposal: Sisal Bag Industry
422/6	1932–33	Sisal Industry Development Scheme
423/7	1932	1930 NAD Annual Report: Governor's Comments
423/8	1932–33	1930 NAD Annual Report: Publication
425/23	1931–33	Economic Development of Reserves: Recommendations
436/4	1933	Sisal Industry Development Scheme of Mr. Hogg
437/17	1933–34	Voi/Mwatate Concession: Request to Return Land to Reserve
439/5	1933–34	Sisal Industry: Machinery Experiments
439/16	1933–34	Sisal Industry: Lower Electricity Rates Request
440/11	1933–34	Ibid.
443/2	1934–35	Agricultural Advances
445/9	1934	Sisal: Proposed Loan for Machinery Development
449/5	1934–35	Wundanyi Estate: Proposed Purchase
450/13	1934	Voi/Mwatate Concession: Proposed Water Supply
451/3	1934–35	1933 Education Department Annual Report: Comments
453/1	1935	Wundanyi Estate Purchase
454/11	1935–36	Sisal Industry: New Machinery Tests
457/8	1935	1933 NAD Annual Report
458/17	1935	1933 Agricultural Annual Report: Governor's Comments
459/8	1935	WaKasigau: Delay in Removal from TCL
461/3	1935–36	1934 Education Department Annual Report

462/1	1936	Wundanyi Estate: Valuation of Furniture by Drury
464/2	1936–37	Sisal Machinery Failure, Loans made, Grants
468/5	1936	Voi/Mwatate: Settlement of WaKasigau
475/9	1936	Grogan's Application for Taveta Land
476/1	1936–37	Wundanyi Estate: Claim vs. Drury Waived
479/9	1937–39	1936 NAD Annual Report
482/3–5	1937	Sisal Experiments: Payment of Loan
483/6	1937	Soil Erosion: Proposed Campaign
486/3	1937	Taita LNC Funds: Irregularities
491/5	1937–38	1937 NAD Annual Report
496/1	1938–40	Anti–Soil Erosion: CDF grant
507/7	1939–41	1938 Agricultural Annual Report
508/7	1939	Voi/Mwatate Concession
517/17	1938–40	1938 NAD Annual Report
518/12	1940–41	1939 Agricultural Annual Report
518/13	1939–40	Agricultural Policy, Wartime
519/9	1939–40	Voi/Mwatate Concessions
523/6	1940–41	Native Political Associations
526/6	1940–42	Agricultural Policy in Wartime
527/15	1941	1940 Education Department Annual Report
529/8	1941–44	Native Political Associations: KCA, UKA, THA
535/4	1944	Ibid.
553/3	1948	Reconditioning of Land in Native Areas
556/4	1945–47	Acquisition of Land for Public Purposes: TCL
560/2	1949	Memo, Bostock: Cost of Living in Reserves
569/10	1951	Taita Hills Scheme

Supplementary
CO 537/

26	1914	Despatches: EAP
28	1914	Officers and Individuals

Foreign Office
FO 84/2552 195   Despatches

Parliamentary Papers
United Kingdom. Parliament. *Report by Sir A Hardinge on the Condition and Progress of the East Africa Protectorate from Its Establishment to the 20th July 1897.* 1897 Command 8683.

Church Missionary Society Archives, Birmingham, England

Correspondence Files
G3 A5/01–19   East Africa Mission to London, 1882–1914
G3 A5/L3–L10   London to East Africa Mission, 1883–1913

Precis Books
Group III, East Africa Mission, 1880–1910

Personal Collections
Diaries of J. Alfred Wray, 10 volumes, 1893–1912
Edith Baring Gould Collection (photographs), 1891–1939

Rhodes House Library, Oxford

Collections
Coryndon Papers
Heubner Papers
Hobley Papers
Hollis Papers
Perry Papers
Stephens Papers
Swynnerton Papers

Archive of La Congregation du St. Esprit, Paris
Bulletins de la Congregation, Tomes 3–11, 1891–1908

Other Primary Sources
Annual Letters of Rev. Peter Bostock, 1938–46, held by himself.
Baptismal Record of Bura Mission, Taita, Books I–V, 1893–1942, Bura Church, Taita,
Kenya.

Secondary Sources

Adam, Heribert. 1995. "The Politics of Ethnic Identity: Comparing South Africa."
    Ethnic and Racial Studies 18, 3.
Alpers, E. A. 1975. *Ivory and Slaves in East Central Africa*. London: Heinemann.
Ambler, Charles. 1988. *Kenyan Communities in the Age of Imperialism: The Central
    Region in the Late Nineteenth Century*. New Haven: Yale University Press.
Anderson, Benedict. 1983. *Imagined Communities: Reflections on the Origin and Spread
    of Nationalism*. London: Verso.
Anderson, David, and David Throup. 1985. "Africans and Agricultural Production
    in Colonial Kenya: The Myth of the War as a Watershed." *Journal of African
    History* 26,3.
Anderson, W. 1973. "A History of the Church in Kenya, 1844 to Now." Occasional
    Research Papers: Christianity in Contemporary Africa, vol. 10, 2. Kampala,
    Uganda: Makerere University.
———. 1977. *The Church in East Africa*. Dodoma, Tanzania: Central Tanganyika Press.
Anonymous, "Ethnicity and Pseudo–Ethnicity in the Ciskei." In *The Creation of
    Tribalism in Southern Africa*, edited by Leroy Vail. Berkeley and Los Angeles:
    University of California Press.
Appiah, Kwame Anthony. 1992. *In My Father's House: Africa in the Philosophy of
    Culture*. New York: Oxford University Press.
Atkinson, Ronald. 1989. "The Evolution of Ethnicity among the Acholi of Uganda:
    The Precolonial Phase." *Ethnohistory* 36,1.
———. 1992. *The Roots of Ethnicity: The Origins of the Acholi of Uganda before 1800*.
    Philadelphia: University of Pennsylvania Press.
Barker, S. G. 1933. *Sisal: A Note on the Attributes of the Fibre and Their Industrial
    Significance*. London: Her Majesty's Stationary Office, for the Empire Mar-
    keting Board.
Barth, Frederik, ed. 1969. *Ethnic Groups and Boundaries*. Boston: Little, Brown.

Baxter, P. T. W., Jan Hultin, and Alessandro Triulzi, eds. 1996. *Being and Becoming Oromo: Historical and Anthropological Inquiries.* Lawrenceville, N.J.: Red Sea Press.

Beidelman, T. O. 1982. *Colonial Evangelism: A Social Historical Study of an East African Mission at the Grassroots.* Bloomington: Indiana University Press.

Beinart, William, and Colin Bundy. 1987. *Hidden Struggles in Rural South Africa: Politics and Popular Movements in the Transkei and Eastern Cape 1890–1930.* London: James Currey.

Berg, F. J. 1974. "The Coast from the Portuguese Invasion to the Rise of the Zanzibar Sultanate." In *Zamani: A Survey of East African History*, 2d ed., edited by B. A. Ogot. Nairobi: East Africa Publishing House.

Berman, Bruce. 1990. *Control and Crisis in the Colonial State: The Dialectic of Conflict.* Athens: Ohio University Press.

Berman, Bruce. 1992. "Bureaucracy and Incumbent Violence: Colonial Administration and the Origins of the 'Mau Mau' Emergency." In Bruce Berman and John Lonsdale, *Unhappy Valley: Conflict in Kenya and Africa, Book Two: Violence and Ethnicity.* Athens: Ohio University Press.

Berman, Bruce, and John Lonsdale. 1980. "Crises of Accumulation, Coercion, and the Colonial State: The Development of the Labor Control System in Kenya, 1919–1929." *Canadian Journal of African Studies* 14, 1.

Berry, Sara. 1989. "Social Institutions and Access to Resources." *Africa* 59, 1.

Bickford–Smith, Vivian. 1995. "Black Ethnicities, Communities, and Political Expression in Late Victorian Capetown." *Journal of African History* 36, 3.

Bikales, Thomas. 1989–90. "Bricoleurs and Boundaries: Ethnicity and Social Change on the Swahili Coast." *Journal of the Seward Anthropological Society* 19, 1–2.

Booth, Newell, Jr. 1977. "An Approach to African Religion." In *African Religions: A Symposium*, edited by Newell Booth Jr. New York: NOK Publishers.

Bostock, Peter. 1950. *The Peoples of Kenya: The Taita.* London: Macmillan.

Bourdieu, Pierre. 1977. *Outline of a Theory of Practice.* Cambridge: Cambridge University Press.

———. 1979. "Symbolic Power." *Critique of Anthropology* 4, 13–14.

Bozzoli, Belinda. 1983. Introduction to *Town and Countryside in the Transvaal*, edited by Belinda Bozzoli. Johannesburg: Ravan Press.

———. 1987. "Class Community and Ideology in the Evolution of South African Society." In *Class, Community, and Conflict: South African Perspectives*, edited by Belinda Bozzoli. Johannesburg: Ravan Press.

Brantley, Cynthia. 1981. *The Giriama and Colonial Resistance in Kenya, 1800–1920.* Los Angeles and Berkeley: University of California Press.

Bravman, Bill. 1986. "Towards a Political Economy of Upper Nyanza Agriculture during the Depression." Ms., Stanford University.

———. 1990. "Using Old Photographs in Interviews: Some Cautionary Notes about Silences in Fieldwork." *History in Africa* 17.

———. 1992. "Becoming a Taita: A Social History, 1850–1950." Ph.D. diss., Stanford University.

———. 1994. "The Politics of Meaning in Taita, Kenya: Local Societies in the Nineteenth Century." Paper presented to the African Studies Association annual conference, Toronto, Canada.

———. 1996. "Practices and Discourses of Work, and Struggles over Ethnic Community in Taita, Kenya." Paper presented to Seminar on Improvisation and the Practice of Everyday Life, Institute of Advanced Study in the African Humanities, Northwestern University, Evanston, Ill.

———. 1996. "Disrupted Imaginations: Visions of Community and the Other in Sagalla, Kenya, 1880–1900." Paper presented to the Society for the Sociology of Religion annual conference, New York.

———. 1996. "Rethinking Resistance: Africans, Europeans, Confrontation, and Interaction in Nineteenth–Century Taita, Kenya." Paper presented to the African Studies Association annual conference, San Francisco.

———. 1998. "Teaching Students about Ethnicity in Africa." In *Teaching Africa*, edited by Misty Bastian and Jane Parpart. New York: Greenwood Press.

Brett, E. A. 1973. *Colonialism and Underdevelopment in East Africa*. London: Heinemann.

Brown, Michael. 1996. "On Resisting Resistance." *American Anthropologist* 98, 4.

Bruck, W. F. 1913. *Die Sisalkultur in Deutsch–Ostafrika*. Berlin: Arbeiten der Deutschen Landwirtschaft–Gesellschaft.

Butler, Judith. 1993. *Bodies that Matter: On the Discursive Limits of "Sex."* New York: Routledge.

Calhoun, Craig. 1993. "Nationalism and Ethnicity." *Annual Review of Sociology* 19.

Chanock, Martin. 1985. *Law, Custom, and Social Order: The Colonial Experience in Zambia and Malawi*. Cambridge: Cambridge University Press.

Chappell, David. 1993. "Ethnogenesis and Frontiers." *Journal of World History* 4, 2.

Chittick, Neville. 1974. "The Coast before the Arrival of the Portuguese." In *Zamani: A Survey of East African History*, 2d ed., edited by B. A. Ogot. Nairobi: East Africa Publishing House.

Clayton, Anthony, and D. Savage. 1974. *Government and Labour in Kenya, 1895–1963*. London: Frank Cass.

Cohen, Abner. 1971. "Cultural Strategies in the Organization of Trading Diasporas." In *The Development of Indigenous Trade and Markets in West Africa*, edited by C. Meillassoux. London: Oxford University Press.

Cohen, David. 1994. *The Combing of History*. Chicago: University of Chicago Press.

Collier, Jane, and Sylvia Yanagisako, eds. 1987. *Gender and Kinship: Essays Toward a Unified Analysis*. Stanford: Stanford University Press.

Comaroff, Jean. 1985. *Body of Power, Spirit of Resistance: The Culture and History of a South African People*. Chicago: University of Chicago Press.

Comaroff, Jean and John Comaroff. 1988. "Through the Looking Glass: Colonial Encounters of the First Kind." *Journal of Historical Sociology* 1, 1.

———. 1989. "The Colonization of Consciousness in South Africa." *Economy and Society* 18, 2.

———. 1991. *Of Revelation and Revolution: Christianity, Colonialism, and Consciousness in South Africa*. Vol. 1. Chicago: University of Chicago Press.

———. 1992. "Of Totemism and Ethnicity." In *Ethnography and the Historical Imagination*. Boulder: Westview Press.

Cooper, Frederick. 1980. *From Slaves to Squatters: Plantation Labor and Agriculture in Zanzibar and Coastal Kenya, 1890–1925*. New Haven: Yale University Press.

———. 1987. *On the African Waterfront: Urban Disorder and the Transformation of Work in Colonial Mombasa*. New Haven: Yale University Press.

———. 1994. "Conflict and Connection: Rethinking Colonial African History." *African Historical Review* 99, 5.

Cowen, Michael. 1972. "Differentiation in a Kenyan Location." Ms., University of Nairobi.

———. 1975. "Wattle Production in the Central Province: Capital and Household Commodity Production 1903–64." Ms., University of Nairobi.

Darnovsky, Mary, Barbara Epstein, and Richard Flacks, eds. 1995. *Cultural Politics and Social Movements*. Philadelphia: Temple University Press.

De Vos, George. 1995. "Introduction: Ethnic Pluralism: Conflict and Accommodation." In *Ethnic Identity: Creation, Conflict, and Accommodation*, 3d ed., edited by George De Vos and Lola Romanucci–Ross. Walnut Creek, Calif.: AltaMira Press.

Dundas, Charles. [1924] 1968. *Kilimanjaro and Its People*. Reprint, London: Frank Cass.

Eliot, Sir Charles. 1905–06. "Progress and Problems of the East African Protectorate." *Proceedings of the Royal Colonial Institute*.

Eller, Jack David, and Reed Coughlan. 1993. "The Poverty of Primordialism: Demystification of Ethnic Attachments." *Ethnic and Racial Studies* 16, 2.

Farrant, Leda. 1975. *Tippu Tip and the East African Slave Trade*. New York: St. Martin's Press.

Feierman, Steven. 1974. *The Shambaa Kingdom*. Madison: University of Wisconsin Press.

———. 1990. *Peasant Intellectuals: Anthropology and History in Tanzania*. Madison: University of Wisconsin Press.

Fischer, H. J. 1973. "Conversion Reconsidered: Some Historical Aspects of Religious Conversion in Black Africa." *Africa*. 43, 1.

Fisher, Jeanne. 1954. *The Anatomy of Kikuyu Domesticity and Husbandry*. Nairobi: Department of Technical Cooperation.

Fleuret, Patrick. 1985. "The Social Organization of Water Control in the Taita Hills, Kenya." *American Ethnologist*. 12, 1.

Foster–Carter, Aiden. 1978. "The Modes of Production Controversy." *New Left Review* 107.

Frontera, Ann. 1978. *Persistence and Change: A History of Taveta*. Waltham, Mass.: Crossroads Press.

Gann, L. H., and Peter Duignan. 1967. *Burden of Empire*. London: Pall Mall.

———. 1978. *The Rulers of British Africa*. Stanford: Stanford University Press.

Geertz, Clifford. 1973. *The Interpretation of Cultures*. New York: Basic Books.

Gissing, C. E. 1884. "A Journey from Mombasa to Mounts Ndara and Kasigau." *Proceedings of the Royal Geographical Society* 6, 10.

Glassman, Jonathon. 1995. *Feasts and Riot: Revelry, Rebellion, and Popular Consciousness on the Swahili Coast, 1856–1888*. Portsmouth, N.H.: Heinemann.

Goldsworthy, David. 1971. *Colonial Issues in British Politics, 1945–1961*. Oxford: Clarendon Press.

Gramsci, Antonio. 1971. *Selections from the Prison Notebooks*. New York: International Publishers.

Greene, Sandra. 1996. *Gender, Ethnicity, and Social Change on the Upper Slave Coast: A History of the Anlo–Ewe*. Portsmouth, N.H.: Heinemann.

Groves, C. P. 1954. *The Planting of Christianity in Africa*. 2 vols. London: Lutterworth Press.

Guillebaud, C. 1958. *An Economic Survey of the Sisal Industry of Tanganyika*. Welwyn, England: James Nisbet.

Guyer, Jane. 1981. "Household and Community in African Studies." *African Studies Review* 24, 2–3.

———. 1996. "Diversity at Different Levels: Farm and Community in Western Nigeria." *Africa* 66, 1.

Gwassa, G. 1969. "German Intervention and African Resistance in Tanzania." In *A History of Tanzania*, edited by I. N. Kimambo and A. J. Temu. Nairobi: East

Africa Publishing House.

Halévy, Elie. 1961. *A History of the English People in the Nineteenth Century*. London: Ernest Benn.

Hall, Stuart. 1989. "Ethnicity: Identity and Difference." *Radical America* 23, 4.

Hamilton, Carolyn, and John Wright, 1990. "The Making of *AmaLala*: Ethnicity, Ideology, and Relations of Subordination in a Precolonial Context." *Southern African Historical Journal* 22.

Harries, Patrick. 1987. "'A Forgotten Corner of the Transvaal': Reconstructing the History of a Relocated Community through Oral Testimony and Song." In *Class, Community and Conflict: South African Perspectives*, edited by Belinda Bozzoli. Johannesburg: Ravan Press.

Harris, Alfred. 1958. "The Social Organization of the WaTaita." Ph.D. diss., Cambridge University.

Harris, Alfred, and Grace Harris. 1955. "WaTaita Today." Ms., Kenya National Archives.

Harris, Grace. *Casting Out Anger: Religion among the Taita of Kenya*. Cambridge: Cambridge University Press.

Harris, Joseph. 1987. *Repatriates and Refugees in a Colonial Society: The Case of Kenya*. Washington: Howard University Press.

Hay, Margaret Jean. 1972. "Economic Change in Luoland: Kowe 1890–1945." Ph.D. diss., University of Wisconsin.

Henige, David. 1974. *The Chronology of Oral Tradition: Quest for a Chimera*. Oxford: Clarendon Press.

Heussler, R. 1963. *Yesterday's Rulers: The Making of the British Colonial Service*. Syracuse: Syracuse University Press.

Hindorf, R. 1925. *Der Sisalbau in Deutsch Ostafrika*. Berlin: D. Reimer.

Hobbes, Thomas. 1962. *Leviathan*. London: Collier Macmillan.

Hobley, C. W. 1895. "Upon a Visit to Tsavo and the Taita Highlands." *Geographical Journal*. vol 5.

———. [1929] 1970. *Kenya from Chartered Company to Crown Colony*. 2d ed. Reprint, London: Frank Cass. (Original edition, 1929).

Hodge, Alison. 1971. "The Training of Missionaries for Africa: The Church Missionary Society's Training College at Islington, 1900–1915." *Journal of Religion in Africa*.

Hollis, A. G. 1900. "The Origins of the People of Taveta." *The Taveta Chronicle*.

Horowitz, Donald. 1985. *Ethnic Groups in Conflict*. Berkeley and Los Angeles: University of California Press.

Horton, Robin. 1971. "African Conversion." *Africa* 41.

———. 1975. "On the Rationality of Conversion." *Africa* 45.

Humphrey, Norman. 1947. *The Liguru and the Land: Sociological Aspects of Some Agricultural Problems of North Kavirondo*. Nairobi: The Government Printer.

Iliffe, John. 1972. "The Organization of the Maji Maji Rebellion." In *Perspectives on the African Past*, edited by M. Klein and G. Johnson. Boston: Little, Brown.

———. 1979. *A Modern History of Tanganyika*. Cambridge: Cambridge University Press.

Isaacman, Allen, and Barbara Isaacman. 1976. *The Tradition of Resistance in Mozambique: The Zambesi Valley, 1850–1921*. London: Heinemann.

Jackson, Kennell. 1976. "Dimensions of Kamba Pre–Colonial History." In *Kenya Before 1900*, edited by B. A. Ogot. Nairobi: East Africa Publishing House.

Janmohammed, Karim. 1976. "African Labourers in Mombasa, c. 1895–1940." In *Hadith 5: Economic and Social History in East Africa*, edited by B. A. Ogot. Nairobi: Kenya Literature Board.

Jenkins, Richard. 1994. "Rethinking Ethnicity: Identity, Categorization, and Power." *Ethnic and Racial Studies* 17, 2.

Jordan, Glenn, and Chris Weedon. 1995. *Cultural Politics: Class, Gender, and Race in the Postmodern World*. Cambridge, Mass.: Blackwell.

Kanogo, Tabitha. 1987. *Squatters and the Roots of Mau Mau, 1905–1963*. Nairobi: Heinemann Kenya.

Kieran, J. A. 1966. "The Holy Ghost Fathers in East Africa, 1863 to 1914." Ph.D. diss., University of London.

Kimambo, I. N. 1969. *Political History of the Pare of Tanzania*. Nairobi: East Africa Publishing House.

———. 1991. *Penetration and Protest in Tanzania: The Impact of the World Economy on the Pare, 1860–1960*. Athens: Ohio University Press.

Kimambo, I. N., and C. K. Omari. 1971. "The Development of Religious Thought and Centers among the Pare." In *The Historical Study of African Religion*, edited by T. O. Ranger and I. N. Kimambo. London: Heinemann.

Kirby, Jon. 1994. "Cultural Change and Religious Conversion in West Africa." In *Religion in Africa: Experience and Expression*, edited by Thomas Blakely, Walter van Beek, and Dennis Thomson. Portsmouth, N.H.: Heinemann.

Kitcher, Philip. 1985. *Vaulting Ambition: Sociobiology and the Quest for Human Nature*. Cambridge, Mass.: MIT Press.

Kitching, Gavin. 1980. *Class and Economic Change in Kenya: The Making of an African Petite Bourgeoisie, 1905–1970*. New Haven: Yale University Press.

Kiwanuka, M. 1973. *From Colonialism to Independence*. Nairobi: East Africa Literature Bureau.

Krapf, J. L. [1860]. 1968. *Travels, Researches, and Missionary Labours during an Eighteen Years' Residence in Eastern Africa*. London: Trübner; Reprint, New York: Johnson Reprint.

Kratz, Corrine. 1981. "Are the Okiek Really Maasai? Or Kikuyu? Or Kipsigis?" *Cahiers d'Etudes Africaines*. 79, xx-3.

———. 1988. "Emotional Power and Significant Movement: Womanly Transformation in Okiek Initiation." Ph.D. diss., University of Texas.

———. 1997. "Conversations and Lives." Paper presented at a conference on "Words and Voices: Critical Practices of Orality in Africa and in African Studies," Bellagio, Italy.

Krut, Riva. 1987. "The Making of a South African Jewish Community in Johannesburg, 1886–1914." In *Class Community and Conflict: South African Perspectives*, edited by Belinda Bozzoli. Johannesburg: Ravan Press.

Kurien, Prema. 1994. "Colonialism and Ethnogenesis: A Study of Kerala, India." *Theory and Society* 23.

Landau, Paul. 1993. "When Rain Falls: Rainmaking and Community in a Tswana Village, c.1870 to Recent Times." *International Journal of African Historical Studies* 26, 1.

———. 1995. *The Realm of the Word: Language, Gender, and Christianity in a Southern African Kingdom*. Portsmouth, N.H.: Heinemann.

Larson, Pier. 1994. "Desperately Seeking 'the Merina': Reading Ethnonyms and Their Semantic Fields in African Identity Histories." Paper presented to the African Studies Association annual conference, Toronto, Canada.

Lentz, Carola. 1994. "'They Must Be Dagaba First and Any Other Thing Second': The Colonial and Post–Colonial Creation of Ethnic Identities in North–western Ghana." *African Studies* 53, 2.

Lewontin, R. C. 1984. *Not in Our Genes.* New York: Pantheon.

Lindblom, Gerhard. 1920. *The Akamba in British East Africa.* Uppsala: Appelberg.

Livingstone, David. 1857. *Missionary Travels and Researches in South Africa.* London: Murray.

Lonsdale, John. 1986. "The Depression and the Second World War in the Transformation of Kenya." In *Africa and the Second World War*, edited by D. Killingray and R. Rathbone. New York: St. Martin's Press.

———. 1992. "The Moral Economy of Mau Mau: Wealth, Poverty and Civic Virtue in Kikuyu Political Thought." In Bruce Berman and John Lonsdale, *Unhappy Valley: Conflict in Kenya and Africa, Book Two: Violence and Ethnicity*, Athens: Ohio University Press.

Lonsdale, John, and Bruce Berman. 1979. "Coping with the Contradictions: The Development of the Colonial State in Kenya, 1895–1914." *Journal of African History.*

Low, D. A., and John Lonsdale. 1976. "Introduction" in *History of East Africa*, vol. 3, edited by D. A. Low and A. Smith. Oxford: Clarendon Press.

Low, D. A. and A. Smith, eds. 1976. *History of East Africa*. Vol. 3. Oxford: Clarendon Press

Madoka, Allen. 1950. *Taita na Kanisa la Kristo katika Miaka Hamsini, 1900–1950.* Nairobi: W. Boyd, for Taita Rural Deanery.

Magubane, Bernard. 1976. "The Evolution of Class Structure in Africa." In *The Political Economy of Contemporary Africa*, edited by P. Gutkind and E. Wallerstein. Beverley Hills: Sage.

Mahmood, Cynthia, and Sharon Armstrong. 1992. "Do Ethnic Groups Exist?: A Cognitive Perspective on the Concept of Cultures." *Ethnology* 31, 1.

Mandala, Elias. 1990. *Work and Control in a Peasant Economy: A History of the Lower Tchiri Valley in Malawi, 1859–1960.* Madison: University of Wisconsin Press.

Marks, Shula. 1986. *The Ambiguities of Dependence in South Africa: Class, Nationalism and the State in Twentieth–Century Natal.* Baltimore: Johns Hopkins University Press.

Mbiti, John. 1969. *African Religions and Philosophy.* Nairobi: Heinemann Kenya.

McDermott, P. L. 1893. *British East Africa or IBEA: A History of the Formation and Work of the Imperial British East Africa Company.* London: Chapman and Hall.

Meinertzhagen, R. 1957. *Kenya Diary: 1902–1906.* London: Oliver and Boyd.

Merritt, E. Hollis. 1975. "A History of the Taita of Kenya to 1900." Ph.D. diss., Indiana University.

Mills, Megan. 1991. "The Integration of Ethnicity: Notes on a Social Scientific Opportunity for Religious Studies." *Method and Theory in the Study of Religion* 3, 1.

Mitchell, Timothy. 1988. *Colonising Egypt.* Cambridge: Cambridge University Press.

Mnjama, Nathan. [1987]. 1991. "The Taita Hills Association." Ms., revised BA thesis, University of Nairobi.

Moore, S. F. 1986. *Social Facts and Fabrications: "Customary" Law on Kilimanjaro.* Cambridge: Cambridge University Press.

Mungeam, G. H. 1966. *British Rule in Kenya, 1895–1912.* Oxford: Clarendon Press.

———, ed. 1978. *Kenya: Select Historical Documents 1884–1923.* Nairobi: East Africa Publishing House.

Munro, J. F. 1975. *Colonial Rule and the Kamba: Social Change in the Kenya Highlands, 1889–1939*. Oxford: Oxford University Press.

Muriuki, Godfrey. 1974. *A History of the Kikuyu, 1500–1900*. Nairobi: Oxford University Press.

Mwakio, James. 1978. "The Origins of the Wataita, Their Culture, and Their Political Evolution between the Early Sixteenth Century and 1963." Master's thesis, University of Nairobi.

Mwaniki, H. S. K. 1973. *The Living History of Embu and Mbeere to 1906*. Nairobi: Kenya Literature Bureau.

Mwanzi, H. A. 1985. "African Initiatives and Resistance in East Africa, 1880–1914." In *Africa Under Colonial Domination 1880–1935*, edited by A. A. Boahen. Vol. 7 of UNESCO *General History of Africa*. Berkeley and Los Angeles: University of California Press.

Nazarro, Andrew. 1974. "Changing Use of the Resource Base among the Taita of Kenya." Ph.D. diss., Michigan State University.

Neuenfeldt, Karl. 1995. "The Kyana Corroboree: Cultural Production of Indigenous Ethnogenesis." *Sociological Inquiry* 65, 1.

New, Charles. 1971. *Life, Wanderings, and Labours in Eastern Africa*. 3d ed. London: Frank Cass.

Nixon, Rob. 1993. "Of Balkans and Bantustans." *Transition* 60.

Ngugi wa Thiong'o. 1967. *A Grain of Wheat*. Nairobi: Heinemann.

Nurse, Derek. 1978. "The Taita–Chaga Connection: Linguistic Evidence." Ms., Institute of African Studies, Nairobi.

Ochieng', William. 1972. "Colonial African Chiefs—Were They Primarily Self–Seeking Scoundrels?" In *Politics and Nationalism in Colonial Kenya: Hadith 4*, edited by B. Ogot. Nairobi: East Africa Publishing House.

———. 1975. *Pre–Colonial History of the Gusii of Western Kenya, 1500–1914*. Nairobi: East Africa Literature Bureau.

———. 1977. *The Second Word*. Nairobi: East Africa Literature Bureau.

Ogot, Bethwell. 1974. "Kenya Under the British, 1895–1963." In *Zamani: A Survey of East African History*, 2d ed., edited by B. A. Ogot. Nairobi: East Africa Publishing House.

Okoth–Ogondo, H. W. O. 1989. "Some Issues in the Study of Tenure Relations in African Agriculture." *Africa* 59, 1.

Oliver, Roland. 1964. *The Missionary Factor in East Africa*. 2d ed. London: Longman.

Ortner, Sherry. 1995. "Resistance and the Problem of Ethnographic Refusal." *Comparative Studies in Society and History* 37, 1.

Overton, John. 1986. "War and Economic Development: Settlers in Kenya, 1914–1918." *Journal of African History*.

Papstein, Robert. "From Ethnic Identity to Tribalism: The Upper Zambezi Region in Zambia, 1830–1981." In *Creation*; edited by Vail.

Parkin, David. 1972. *Palms, Wine, and Witnesses: Public Spirit and Private Gain in an African Farming Community*. London: Intertext Books.

p'Bitek, Okot. 1971. *African Religions in Western Scholarship*. Nairobi: East Africa Literature Bureau.

Pearce, R. D. 1982. *The Turning Point in Africa: British Colonial Policy 1938–48*. London: Frank Cass.

Pearson, David. 1988. "From Communality to Ethnicity: Some Theoretical Considerations on the Maori Ethnic Revival." *Ethnic and Racial Studies* 11, 2.

Peel, J. 1977. "Conversion and Tradition in Two African Societies: Ijebu and Buganda." *Past and Present* 77, 1.

Power, M. G. 1954. "English Local Government in Taita District, Kenya." *Journal of African Administration*.

Prins, A. H. J. 1950. "An Outline of the Descent System of the Teita, a Northeastern Bantu Tribe." *Africa* 20.

———. 1952. *The Coastal Tribes of the Northeastern Bantu.* London: International Africa Institute.

Ranger, Terence. 1972. "Connections between 'Primary Resistance' Movements and Modern Mass Nationalism in East and Central Africa." In *Perspectives on the African Past*, edited by M. Klein and G. Johnson. Boston: Little, Brown.

———. 1979. "European Attitudes and African Realities: The Rise and Fall of the Matola Chiefs of South–East Tanzania." *Journal of African History.* 20, 1.

———. 1983. "The Invention of Tradition in Colonial Africa." In *The Invention of Tradition*, edited by E. Hobsbawm and T. O. Ranger. Cambridge: Cambridge University Press.

———. 1985. *Peasant Consciousness and Guerilla War in Zimbabwe.* London: James Currey.

Roberts, Richard. 1987. *Warriors, Merchants, and Slaves: The State and the Economy in the Middle Niger Valley, 1700–1914.* Stanford: Stanford University Press.

———. 1990. "Reversible Social Processes, Historical Memory, and the Production of History." *History in Africa.*

Rosberg, Carl, and John Nottingham. 1966. *The Myth of Mau Mau: Nationalism in Kenya.* Stanford: The Hoover Institution.

Sahlins, Marshall. 1976. *The Use and Abuse of Biology.* Ann Arbor: University of Michigan Press.

———. 1981. *Historical Metaphors and Mythical Realities: Structure in the Early History of the Sandwich Islands.* Ann Arbor: University of Michigan Press.

———. 1985. *Islands of History.* Chicago: University of Chicago Press.

Scott, James. 1985. *Weapons of the Weak: Everyday Forms of Peasant Resistance.* New Haven: Yale University Press.

———. 1990. *Domination and the Arts of Resistance: Hidden Transcripts.* New Haven: Yale University Press.

Sheriff, Abdul. 1987. *Slaves, Spices and Ivory in Zanzibar.* London and Dar Es Salaam: James Currey and Tanzania Publishing House.

Sinfield, Alan. 1994. *Cultural Politics—Queer Reading.* Philadelphia: University of Pennsylvania Press.

Smith, A. D. 1990. "The Supersession of Nationalism?" *International Journal of Comparative Sociology* 31, 1–2.

Somers, Margaret. 1994. "The Narrative Constitution of Identity: A Relational and Network Approach." *Theory and Society* 23.

Soper, Robert, ed. 1986. *Taita–Taveta District Socio–Cultural Profile.* Government of Kenya and Institute of African Studies/University of Nairobi.

Sorrenson, M. P. K. 1968. *Origins of European Settlement in Kenya.* Nairobi: Oxford University Press.

Spear, Tom. 1981. *Kenya's Past: An Introduction to Historical Method in Africa.* Harlow, England: Longman.

———. 1993. Introduction to *Being Maasai: Ethnicity and Identity in East Africa*, edited by Spear and Richard Waller. Athens: Ohio University Press.

Stahl, Ann. 1991. "Ethnic Style and Ethnic Boundaries: A Diachronic Case Study from West–Central Ghana." *Ethnohistory* 38, 3.

Stahl, Kathleen. 1964. *History of the Chagga People of Kilimanjaro.* The Hague: Mouton.

Starr, Jerold, ed. 1985. *Cultural Politics: Radical Movements in Modern History.* New York: Praeger.

Stedman Jones, Gareth. 1983. *Languages of Class: Studies in English Working Class History, 1832–1982.* Cambridge: Cambridge University Press.

Stichter, Sharon. 1982. *Migrant Labour in Kenya: Capitalism and African Response, 1895–1975.* Harlow: Longman.

Stock, Eugene. 1899. *History of the Church Missionary Society.* 3 vols. London: Church Missionary Society.

Strayer, Robert. 1978. *The Making of Mission Communities in East Africa: Anglicans and Africans in Colonial Kenya, 1875–1935.* Albany: State University of New York Press.

Sutton, John. 1990. *A Thousand Years of East Africa.* Nairobi: British Institute in East Africa.

Temu, A. J. 1972. *British Protestant Missions.* London: Longman.

Thompson, Richard. 1990. *Theories of Ethnicity: A Critical Appraisal.* New York: Greenwood Press.

Thomson, Joseph. 1883. "Mr Thomson's Report on the Progress of the Society's Expedition to Victoria Nyanza." *Proceedings of the Royal Geographic Society.*

———. 1884. "Through Masai Country to Victoria Nyanza." *Proceedings of the Royal Geographic Society.*

———. 1968. *Through Masai–land.* 3d ed. London: Frank Cass.

Thornton, Richard. 1865. "Notes on a Journey to Kilima–ndjaro, Made in the Company of Baron Von Der Decken." *Journal of the Royal Geographical Society.*

Tignor, R. L. 1976. *The Colonial Transformation of Kenya: The Kamba, the Kikuyu, and the Maasai from 1900 to 1939.* Princeton: Princeton University Press.

Tonkin, Elizabeth. 1992. *Narrating Our Pasts: The Social Construction of Oral History.* Cambridge: Cambridge University Press.

Vail, Leroy, ed. 1991. *The Creation of Tribalism in Southern Africa.* Berkeley and Los Angeles: University of California Press.

van Beek, Walter, and Thomas Blakely. 1994. Introduction to *Religion in Africa: Experience and Expression,* edited by Thomas Blakely, Walter van Beek, and Dennis Thomson. Portsmouth, N.H.: Heinemann.

van Binsbergen, Wim. 1994. "The Kazanga Festival: Ethnicity as Cultural Mediation and Transformation in Central Western Zambia." *African Studies* 53, 2.

van den Berghe, Pierre. 1981. *The Ethnic Phenomenon.* New York and Oxford: Elsevier.

van Zwanenberg, R. M. A. 1972. "The Agricultural History of Kenya to 1939." *Historical Association of Kenya Papers,* no. 1. Nairobi.

———. 1975. *Colonial Capitalism in Kenya, 1919–1939.* Nairobi: East Africa Literature Bureau.

Vansina, Jan. 1965. *Oral Tradition: A Study in Historical Methodology.* Chicago: Aldine Publishing.

———. 1985. *Oral Tradition as History.* London: James Currey.

Wagner, Roy. 1991. "Dif/ference and Its Disguises." In *On the Other: Dialogue and/or Dialectics: Mark Taylor's Paralectics,* edited by R. Scharlemann. Lanham, Md.: University Press of America.

Warren, Max. 1967. *Social History and Christian Mission.* London: SCM Press.

Weber, Max. 1958. *The Protestant Ethic and the Spirit of Capitalism*. New York: Charles Scribner's Sons.

Were, Gideon. 1967. *A History of the Abaluyia of Western Kenya c.1500–1930*. Nairobi: East African Publishing House.

White, Luise. 1990. *The Comforts of Home: Prostitution in Colonial Nairobi*. Chicago: University of Chicago Press.

———. 1994. "Between Gluckman and Foucault: Historicizing Rumor and Gossip." *Social Dynamics* 20, 1.

Willis, Justin. 1992. "The Makings of a Tribe: Bondei Identities and Histories." *Journal of African History* 33.

———. 1993. "The Nature of a Mission Community: The Universities' Mission to Central Africa in Bonde." *Past and Present*, 140.

———. 1995. "'Men on the Spot' and Labor Policy in British East Africa: The Mombasa Water Supply, 1911–1917." *International Journal of African Historical Studies* 28, 1 (1995).

———. 1995. "History, Identity, and Ritual in Bonde: The Making of Community in North–Eastern Tanzania, 1850–1916." Ms., British Institute in East Africa, Nairobi.

Wilmsen, Edwin, with Saul Dubow and John Sharp. 1994. "Introduction: Ethnicity, Identity, and Nationalism in Southern Africa." *Journal of Southern African Studies* 20, 3.

Wilmsen, Edwin, and Patrick McAllister, eds. 1996. *The Politics of Difference: Ethnic Premises in a World of Power*. Chicago: University of Chicago Press.

Wolf, Tom. 1985. "Leadership, Resources, and Locality–Center Relations in Taita, a Political Subsystem of Kenya's Coast Province: 1960–1975." Ph.D. diss., University of Sussex.

Wolff, R. D. 1974. *The Economics of Colonialism*. New Haven: Yale University Press.

Woodward, H. W. 1913–1914. "Kitaita or Kisighau as Spoken on the Shambala Hills above Bwiti." *Zeitschrift fur Kolonial Sprachen* 4, 2.

Worby, Eric. 1994. "Maps, Names, and Ethnic Games: The Epistemology and Iconography of Colonial Power in Northern Zimbabwe." *Journal of Southern African Studies* 20, 3.

Wray, J. Alfred. 1894. *An Elementary Introduction to the Taita Language, Eastern Equatorial Africa*. London: Society for the Promotion of Christian Knowledge.

———. 1913. *Kenya, Our Newest Colony: Reminiscences, 1882–1912*. London and Edinburgh: Marshall Brothers.

Wright, John. 1992. "Notes on the Politics of Being Zulu, 1820–1920." Paper given at "Conference on "Ethnicity, Society, and Conflict in Natal," University of Natal/Pietermaritzburg.

Wright, John, and Carolyn Hamilton. 1996. "Ethnicity and Political Change before 1840." In *Political Economy and Identities in Zwazulu–Natal: Historical and Sociological Perspectives*, edited by Robert Morrell. Durban: Indicator Press.

Zuesse, Evan. 1979. *Ritual Cosmos: The Sanctification of Life in African Religions*. Athens: Ohio University Press.

INDEX

Agricultural policy, 214, 216–17
Anglicanism, 1, 3–4, 132, 169–70; Anglicans and *Watasi*, 132–37, 167, 171–76; indigenous enframings of, 91; and nominalism, 202; official support of, 131; revivalism, 205; similarity to Wutasi, 93–94; vs. Wutasi, 90. *See also* Evangelism
Animals as wealth, 44–45, 55–56, 118, 255; challenging the idea of, 165–66; compromise over, 226–27; conflicts over the idea of, 222–26; converting money into, 120–21, 164–65; generational conflict over animals, 45–46, 48
Axioms, 45–46, 117, 119–21, 123, 126–28, 160, 165, 220–22, 224, 252; erosions of, 160–63, 207, 210–11; new axioms, 212, 226; reduced to gambits, 140

Bantu-language speakers, 29
Binns, Harry, 64, 66–67
Blood brotherhood, 34, 59–60, 104; obsolescence of, 142; and trade, 59; and wider identities, 50–51, 74
Bridewealth, 31, 37, 45–46, 119–20; attenuation of, 160–62; education and, 194
Bura: location, 106, 116, 158–59, 179; valley, 23, 25, 47, 65–66, 81–82, 85–86. *See also* Mbogholi; Mwanjila
Bura mission, 105, 132, 167, 181. *See also* Holy Ghost Fathers

Captives, 30–31, 55, 70, 74; for slave trade, 59
Cash-cropping, 206–7, 212–13, 222; and agricultural policy, 213–17; and gendered work, 217–21; limits of, 221–22; and progressivism, 191
Cash remittances, 120–22, 125–26, 147–48, 192, 194, 222–23, 254; bridewealth and, 160–62; gender, generation and, 130, 163–64; revised patterns of, 207–12
Casual labor. *See Kibarua* labor
Catholicism, 105, 131–32, 179. *See also* Holy Ghost Fathers
Chawia location, 111, 114, 159, 179, 237, 239, 244; Ngulu, 244
Chiefs. *See* Cultural politics; Mghalu, Thomas; Mwandango, Johana; Mwanjila; Native Authority; Nimrod
Chofi, 34, 100, 101, 105, 126, 133, 136–37, 175, 202
Church Missionary Society (CMS), 62, 68, 89, 104, 135, 167, 193. *See also* Anglicanism; Wray, J. Alfred
Climatic zones, 25–27, 32, 177; and cash-cropping, 219
Commodification of animals, 224. *See also* Animals as wealth
Community: Christian, 80, 89–90, 97, 105, 204–5; Christian and local, 103, 137–38; as concept, 4–7, 15–17, 41–44; ethnic, 139–40, 142–46, 152–56, 183–84, 252–53; local, 42, 48–54, 60, 107–8, 109–10, 119, 131, 133; Sagalla,

279

61–62, 77, 79; Sagalla community, 73; and THA, 241. *See also Kidaßida*
Conversions to Christianity, 96–97
Councils of Elders, 145–46, 171, 181; and chiefs, 157–58; decline of, 171
Cultural politics, 48, 89–90, 140, 156–57, 177, 191, 252; and Christianity, 103, 105, 130–31; as concept, 4, 8–9, 43–44, 140; of *Kidaßida*, 227–28; of political authority, 160, 229–30, 247–49; of wealth, 117, 222–27

Dairy work, 123, 152–53, 162
Dance. *See Gonda; Kinyandi; Kishawi; Mwari*
Defender. *See Fighi*
"Dorobo," 28
Drought, 25, 27, 30, 32, 39, 48, 51, 55, 60–61, 68, 71–72, 75–76, 94, 96, 102, 178, 217, 223, 226
Drury, Major Dru, 180
Duruma, 57

Education, 193–98; struggles over, 199–201
Elderhood, 36–41
Elders and juniors. *See* Animals as wealth; Community; Cultural politics; Money as wealth
Ethnicity, concept of, 7, 9–15, 48–49
Evangelism, 69, 89, 92, 99, 167–70, 175; Africanization of, 167–70; Anglican, 99; Catholic, 85, 167; and education, 171; state support for, 130–31

Famine, 18, 25, 27, 30–31, 40, 55, 61, 94, 104, 169; and blood brotherhood, 51; *Njala ya WaSagha*, 58, 72–75; and wider networks, 48–49
Fighi, 40, 55, 103, 133, 247, 249, 254
Frere Town, 64

Giriama, 24, 57, 75; ties with Sagalla, 31, 49, 53, 74
Gonda, 51–52, 54, 151, 154–55

Hegemony, 5–6, 8, 12, 14–15, 62, 117, 176, 252
Holy Ghost Fathers, 86, 105, 132, 167, 179, 193

IBEACo/EAP soldiers, 66, 78, 81–88
Imperial British East Africa Company (IBEACo), 64–66, 69, 77–79, 81–83, 86, 108, 144
Inheritance, 31, 36, 38, 43, 45, 125, 128, 147, 160, 166, 173, 175, 207, 221, 225
Initiation, 1–3, 18, 38, 51–52, 54, 90–91, 103, 107, 134, 137, 172–73, 192

Kamba, 24, 55, 58
Kariuki, Jesse, 242
Kasigau, 23, 31, 59, 62, 64, 92, 95, 99, 239–40
Kenya African Study Union (KASU), 244–45
Kenya African Union (KAU), 201, 244–45, 250
Kenya Land Commission, 179–82, 239
Kenya–Uganda Railway, 122
Kibarua labor, 124
Kichuku. See Lineage
Kidaßida, 2–4, 7–9, 145–46, 150, 156–57, 160–61, 164, 166, 171–72, 174, 176, 211–12, 226, 230, 247–48, 251, 254–55; changing terms of, 184, 206–7, 227–28; emergence of, 140–42; nostalgic, 231, 245, 254; and progressivism, 191–92, 198–203
Kikuyu Central Association (KCA), 241–43; Taita Branch, 241, 245
Kilimanjaro, 24, 30–31, 52, 56–58, 74
Kilindini harbor, 124
Kinyandi, 202
Kirindi, 38–39. *See also* Initiation
Kishawi, 202
Kishingila (Vishingila), 47–48, 52, 54, 59, 60, 79, 81, 83, 86, 104, 110, 112
Kituri, Jonathan, 169, 174
Krapf, Johannes, 62, 64, 70

Labor migration, 111, 119–27, 152–54, 161–62, 208, 223, 254; visiting home, 126–27, 147

Land: colonial conflicts over, 177–82, 229, 239–44, 246–49; gender, generation and, 37–38, 207, 209, 220; and identity, 222; and inheritance, 160, 166, 225; landholding patterns, 32–36, 55, 60, 219–21; maintaining rights to, 222; officials' concern about overcrowding, 216–17

Lineage: large and small, 35–36; resources, 32–35. *See also* Community; Cultural politics; Elderhood

Livestock. *See* Animals as wealth

Local Native Council (LNC), 171, 191, 214–15, 244

Lost: being considered, 141, 146–47, 149, 159–60, 163–64, 171–72, 192, 200, 212, 229, 231, 253; Nimrod, 237

Maasai, 12, 57–58; impersonation of, 81

Mashika, 82

Mau Mau, 189, 245, 251, 254

Maynard, John, 104, 132, 137, 179

Mbale, 29, 48–49, 57, 58; Mbale location, 105, 179, 233; cooperation with IBEACo, 85–86

Mbale mission, 104–5, 132, 169, 170

Mbogholi, 65, 86, 88–89, 105, 115–16

Mbololo, 30; location, 169, 179, 237

Medicine of defense. *See Fighi*

Medicine of warfare, 54, 56, 58

Mengo, Woresha, 241–48, 250

Mgange, 29–30, 67, 84

Mghalu, 115. *See also* Mbale

Mghalu, Thomas, 105–6, 116, 159, 181, 233–34, 237

Missionaries. *See* Church Missionary Society; Holy Ghost Fathers; Maynard, John; Wray, J. Alfred

Mlaghuli, 40

Mlungu, 39, 73

Mombasa, 59, 62; colonial labor policy and, 212; migrant workers' life in, 123, 126, 162; and Taita identity, 152; Taita's women and, 148–49; vegetable exports to, 215. *See also* Labor migration

Money as wealth, 117–19, 206–7; and decline of animals as wealth, 222–24; limits on, 224–27; revised axioms of, 211–12; wives' management of, 209–10

Mtero. See Blood brotherhood

Munya, 29

Mwakichucho, 67–69, 74, 79, 86

Mwambichi, Jimmy, 241–43, 245, 250

Mwanda, 29, 47–48, 59, 81–82, 84–85, 89, 112; location, 172, 235–36

Mwanda (early migrant to Taita), 29

Mwandango, Johana, 114–15

Mwangeka, 47–48, 59, 81–82, 85. *See also Kishingila*

Mwangeka, Albert, 169

Mwangeka, Richard, 233–34, 237

Mwanjila, 106, 116, 158–59

Mwari. See Initiation

Mwatate, 110, 125, 142–43, 154, 239; as district headquarters, 108

Mwatunge, 239, 242–44, 246

Native Authority: implementation of, 111; officials' expectations of, 111–12, 231–33

Ndii, 66, 83–84, 86, 88, 108

Ndile, 169

Neighborhood: as community of belonging, 41–42; social/geographical basis, 32–34

Networks, resource and relationship, 21, 25, 34–38, 41–42, 44, 46–49, 62, 68, 72–73, 102, 104, 115–16, 126, 128, 138, 140, 143–44, 152, 154–56, 166, 183, 202, 204, 207, 209, 211, 221, 224–25, 234, 253

Ngasu, 29

Ngua. See Work groups

Nimrod, 229, 236–37

Pare, 23, 30–32, 51–52, 54, 55–58, 69, 74, 223
Postal work, 125
Progressivism, 185–89; and education, 193–98; power bases, 191; and Taita identity, 190. *See also* Kidaßida
Propriety, 45, 140, 143, 148–49, 151, 159–60, 164, 185, 191, 199, 220, 224, 228, 230. *See also* Axioms; *Kidaßida*
Prostitution, 126, 148–49
Public Works Department (PWD), 123

Raiding, 45; decline of, 110, 152; intra-Hills, 30, 49, 58; long distance, 30, 55–56; of passing caravans, 66, 69, 81–82
Railway labor, 123
Rain, 25, 27, 32, 73–75; as greeting topic, 155. *See also* Drought
Rainmaking, 40–41, 73, 133; Christian, 94–96; Christians at *Wutasi*, 175
Rebmann, John, 62–64, 70
Remembrances, 28

Sagalla mission: aggrandizement and fall, 1880s, 75–79; famine and the two hundred Friendlies, 74–75; founding of, 66–68; reestablishment of, 86–87. *See also* Church Missionary Society; Wray, J. Alfred
Sere, 72–73, 87, 174. *See also* Wutasi
Shambaa, 32, 54; warriors from Taita in, 56–57
Shungwaya, 29
Sisal: plantation labor, 111, 121–22; plantations, 179, 239–40
Slave trading, 59, 70, 73, 104. *See also* Captives

ßaramu, 39

Taita Concessions, Ltd. (TCL), 181, 239–40, 244. *See also* Sisal, plantations
Taita Fighi Union, 244, 247, 254

Taita Hills Association (THA), 240–48. *See also* Cultural politics; Mengo, Woresha; Mwambichi, Jimmy; Taita Fighi Union
Taita Native Law, 111, 144–46, 157
Taita-Taveta Union, 250
Taxation, 88, 107, 112, 117–18, 120, 163, 208–9, 214; chief/elder struggles over, 157–58; and gender, 163, 209
Teaching profession, 99, 193; and gender, 125; status and salary of, 124
Teri, 67, 70, 73–78, 99
Trade, 23; colonial, 120–21, 142; colonial, women in, 155; marketing vegetables, 213–17; precolonial, 47, 50, 52–53, 55, 58–60, 66, 81–82, 117

Ukambani, 29–30, 51, 57–58, 66
Usambara, 23, 30–32, 52, 56, 69, 74. *See also* Shambaa

Vegetable farming, 187, 206, 213–17, 221; and the gender division of labor, 219–20. *See also* Cash cropping
Voi, 84, 109, 122, 142, 242

Wanya. *See* Munya
Wongonyi, 170
Work groups, 91, 100, 128, 133, 164, 213, 220–21
World War I, 153, 158; and chief/elder conflicts, 158; sisal plantations and land during, 178–79
World War II: and cash-crop production, 215–16; and gendered farming, 220; and Taita politics, 243
Wray, J. Alfred, 64, 66–79, 87–89, 92–93, 97. *See also* Rainmaking, Christian
Wundanyi, 181, 233
Wundanyi Ltd, 180
Wusi mission, 132. *See also* Anglicanism; Evangelism; Mbale mission; Wray, J. Alfred

Wutasi: and ascriptivism, 71, 92–93; attenuation of, 201–2, 254–55; as belief system, 38–40, 72; and felt community, 42; as nostalgia, 251; and older men's authority, 37, 41, 192; as "Taita" norm, 151, 171–72, 200–201; and the THA, 246–47. *See also* Anglicanism; Cultural politics; *Fighi*; Rainmaking

Zanzibar, Sultan of, 64
Ziwani, 152

About the Author

BILL BRAVMAN is Assistant Professor of History at the University of Maryland, College Park.